TRANSFORMERS
LOST LIGHT

VOLUME 4

Facebook: **facebook.com/idwpublishing**
Twitter: **@idwpublishing**
YouTube: **youtube.com/idwpublishing**
Tumblr: **tumblr.idwpublishing.com**
Instagram: **instagram.com/idwpublishing**

COVER ART BY
NICK ROCHE

COVER COLORS BY
JOSH BURCHAM

COLLECTION EDITS BY
JUSTIN EISINGER
AND ALONZO SIMON

COLLECTION DESIGN BY
CHRISTA MIESNER

PUBLISHER
GREG GOLDSTEIN

ISBN: 978-1-68405-410-7   22 21 20 19   1 2 3 4

Originally published as THE TRANSFORMERS: LOST LIGHT issues #19–25.

Greg Goldstein, President and Publisher
John Barber, Editor-In-Chief
Robbie Robbins, EVP/Sr. Art Director
Cara Morrison, Chief Financial Officer
Matt Ruzicka, Chief Accounting Officer
Anita Frazier, SVP of Sales and Marketing
David Hedgecock, Associate Publisher
Jerry Bennington, VP of New Product Development
Lorelei Bunjes, VP of Digital Services
Justin Eisinger, Editorial Director, Graphic Novels & Collections
Eric Moss, Senior Director, Licensing and Business Development

Ted Adams, IDW Founder

Special thanks to Ben Montano, Josh Feldman, Ed Lane, Beth Artale,
and Michael Kelly for their invaluable assistance. Thanks to William for
"Afterspark." Thanks to Kit for "Vaporex." And thanks to all the *More
Than Meets The Eye* and *Lost Light* readers over the years.

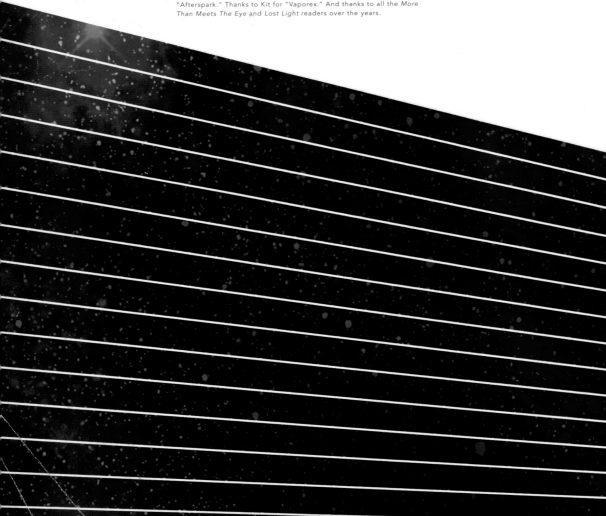

TRANSFORMERS
LOST LIGHT
VOLUME 4

WRITTEN BY **JAMES ROBERTS**

ART BY **E.J. SU** (#19)
CASEY W. COLLER (#20)
JACK LAWRENCE (#21, 23, & 25)
BRENDAN CAHILL (#22 & 24)

COLORS BY **JOANA LAFUENTE**

LETTERS BY **TOM B. LONG**

SERIES EDITS BY **DAVID MARIOTTE**

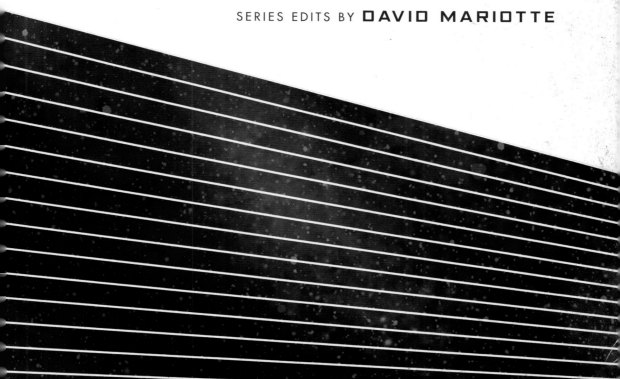

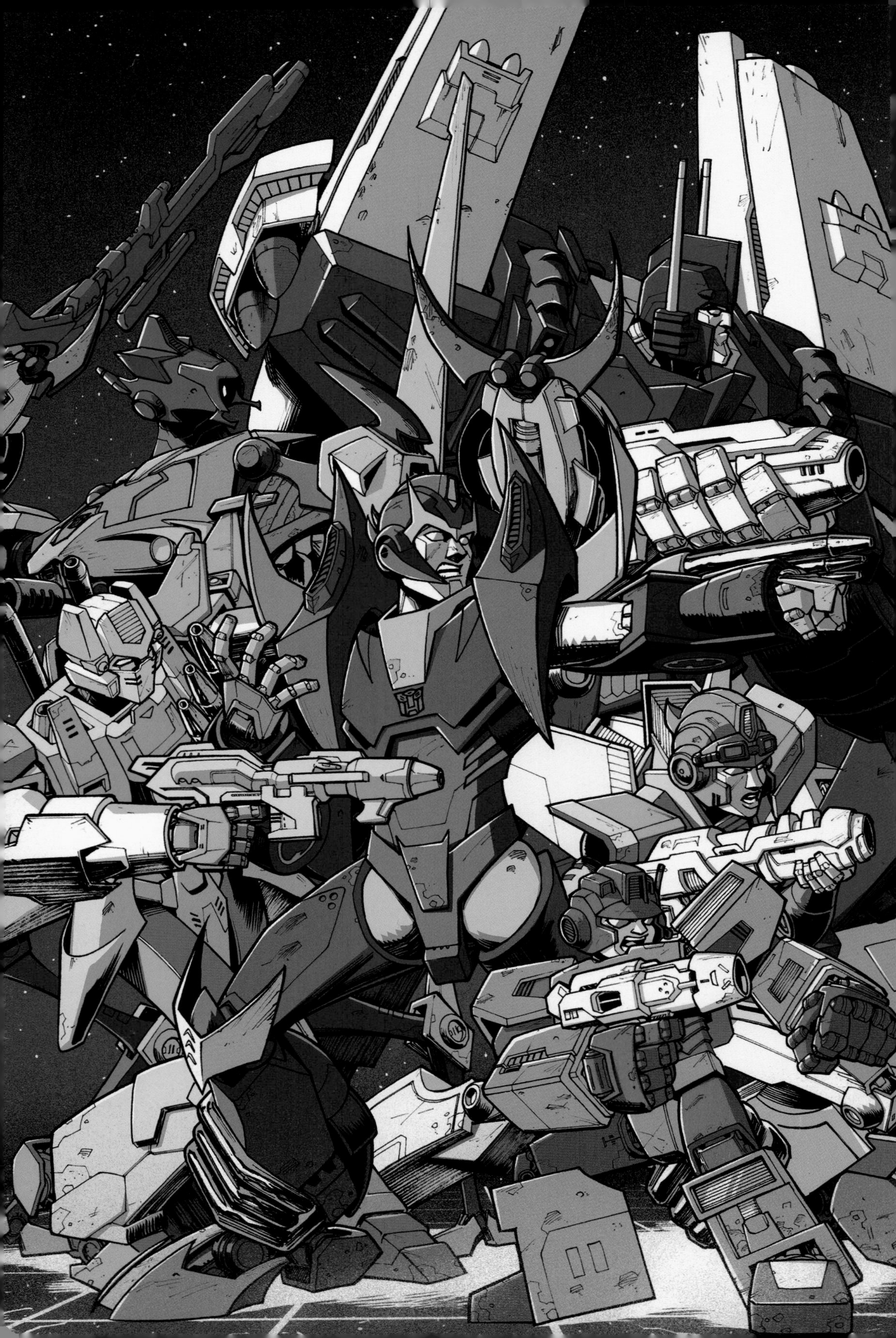

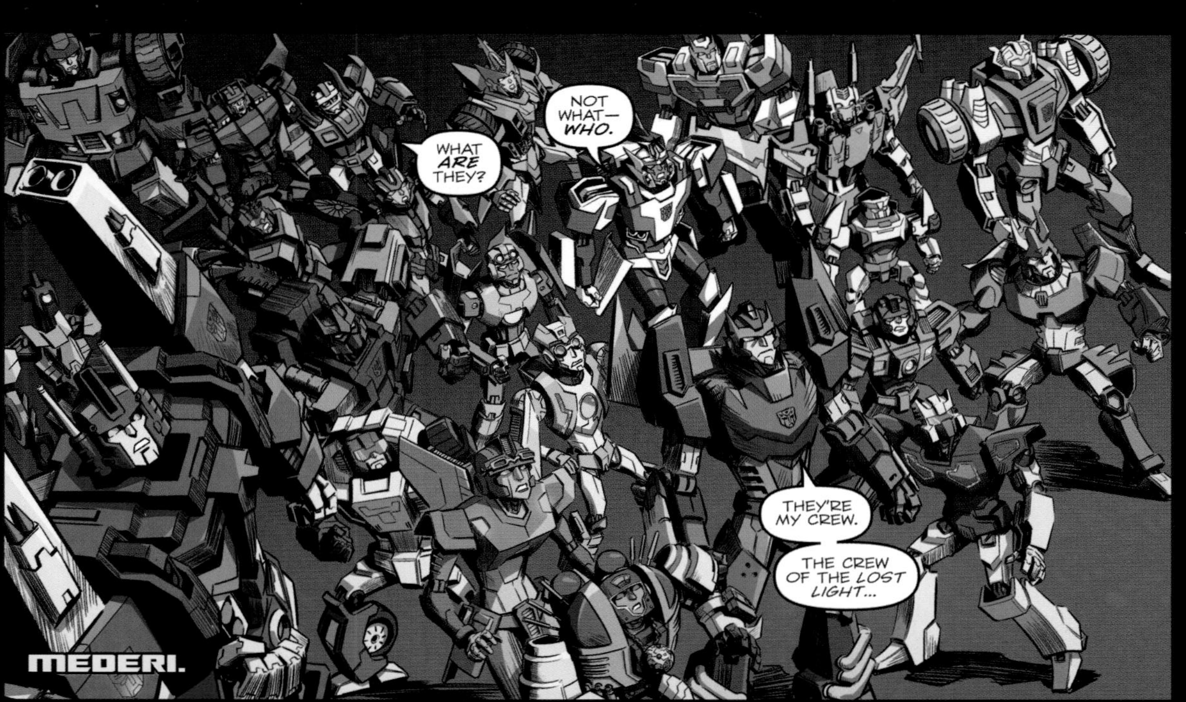
WHAT ARE THEY?
NOT WHAT— WHO.
THEY'RE MY CREW.
THE CREW OF THE LOST LIGHT...
MEDERI.

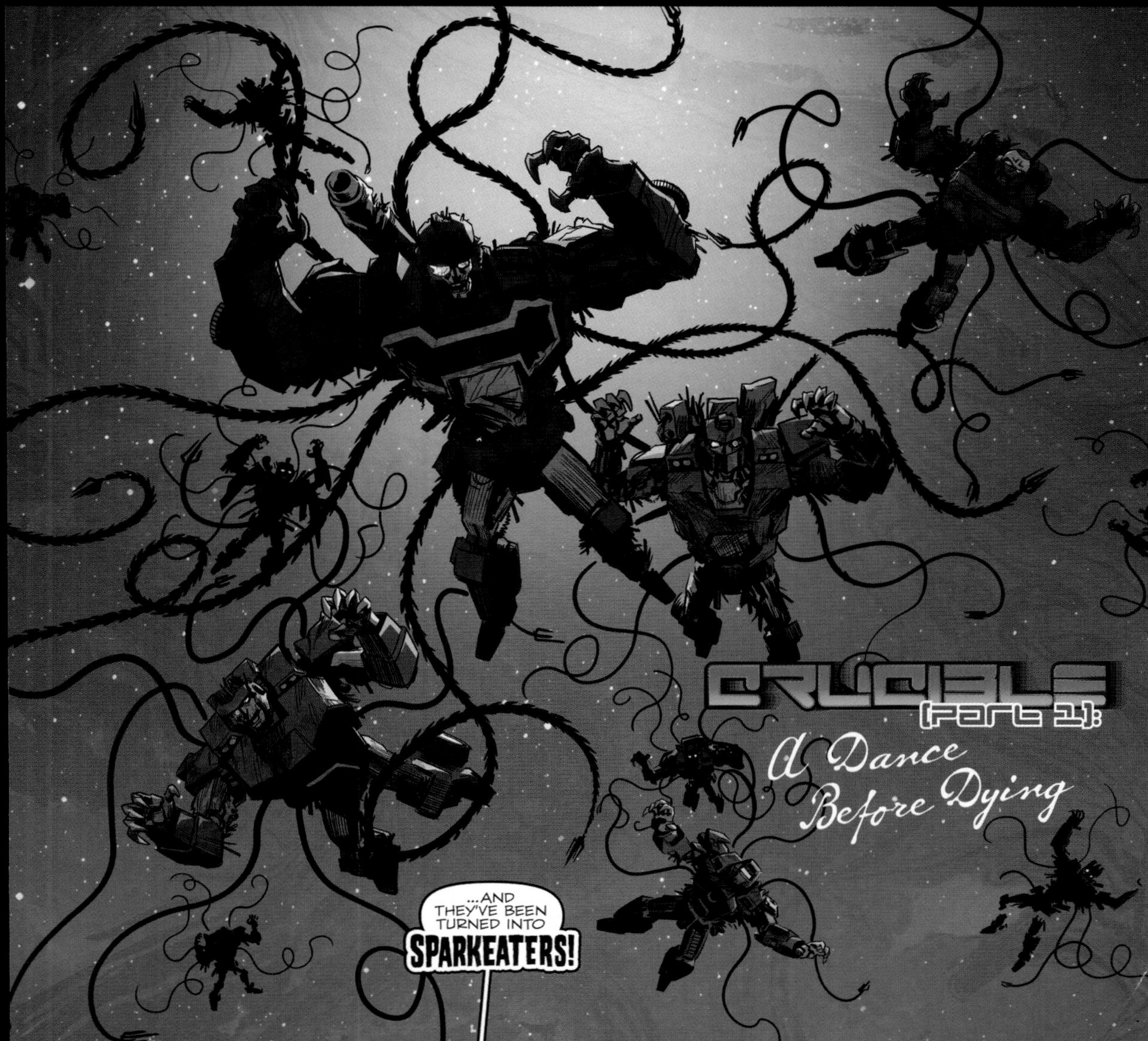
CRUCIBLE (PART 1): A Dance Before Dying
...AND THEY'VE BEEN TURNED INTO SPARKEATERS!

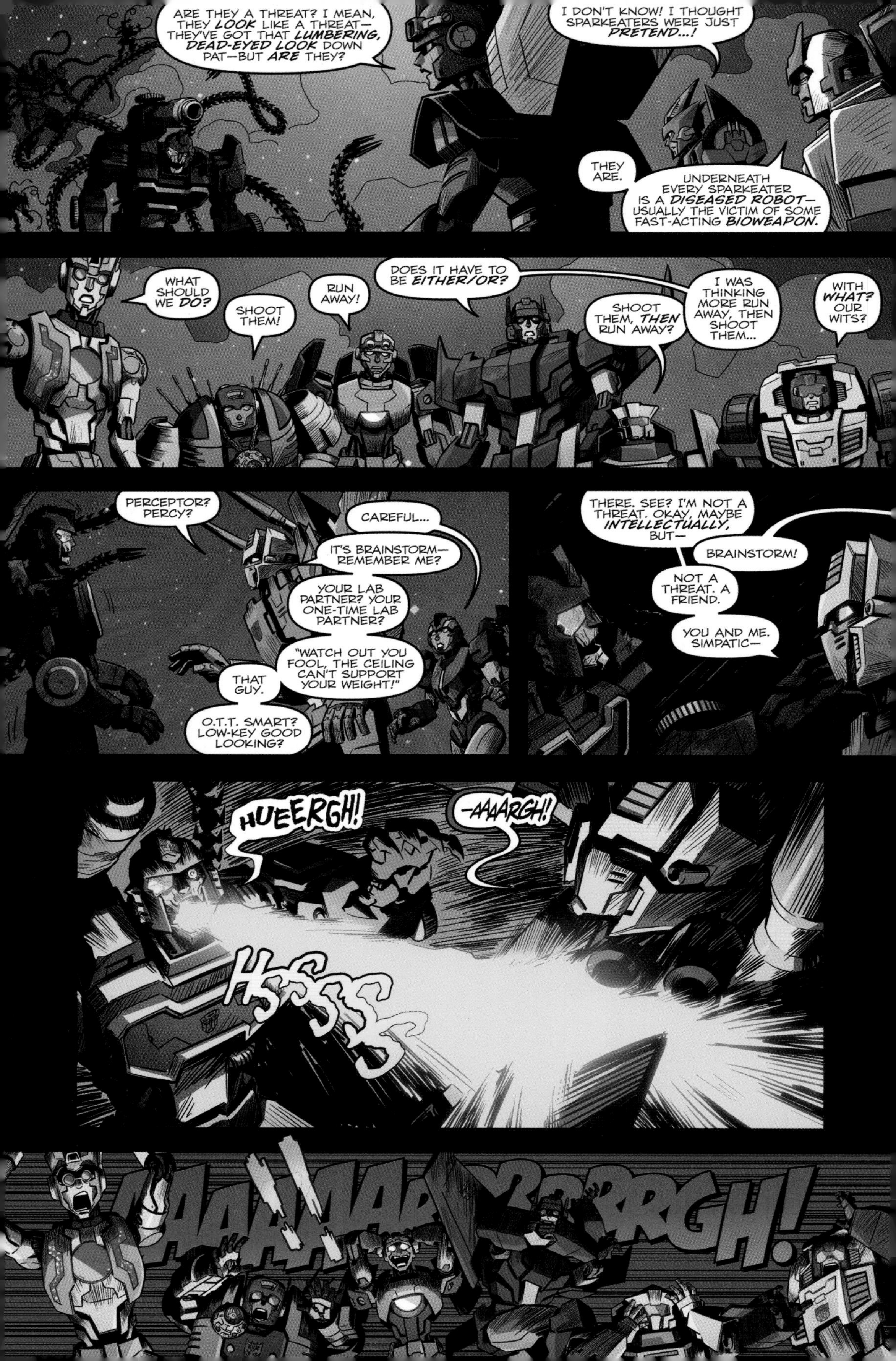
ARE THEY A THREAT? I MEAN, THEY LOOK LIKE A THREAT— THEY'VE GOT THAT LUMBERING, DEAD-EYED LOOK DOWN PAT—BUT ARE THEY?
I DON'T KNOW! I THOUGHT SPARKEATERS WERE JUST PRETEND...!
THEY ARE.
UNDERNEATH EVERY SPARKEATER IS A DISEASED ROBOT— USUALLY THE VICTIM OF SOME FAST-ACTING BIOWEAPON.
WHAT SHOULD WE DO?
SHOOT THEM!
RUN AWAY!
DOES IT HAVE TO BE EITHER/OR?
SHOOT THEM, THEN RUN AWAY?
I WAS THINKING MORE RUN AWAY, THEN SHOOT THEM...
WITH WHAT? OUR WITS?
PERCEPTOR? PERCY?
CAREFUL...
IT'S BRAINSTORM— REMEMBER ME?
YOUR LAB PARTNER? YOUR ONE-TIME LAB PARTNER?
"WATCH OUT YOU FOOL, THE CEILING CAN'T SUPPORT YOUR WEIGHT!"
THAT GUY.
O.T.T. SMART? LOW-KEY GOOD LOOKING?
THERE. SEE? I'M NOT A THREAT. OKAY, MAYBE INTELLECTUALLY, BUT—
BRAINSTORM!
NOT A THREAT. A FRIEND.
YOU AND ME. SIMPATIC—
HUEERGH!
-AAAARGH!
HSSSSS

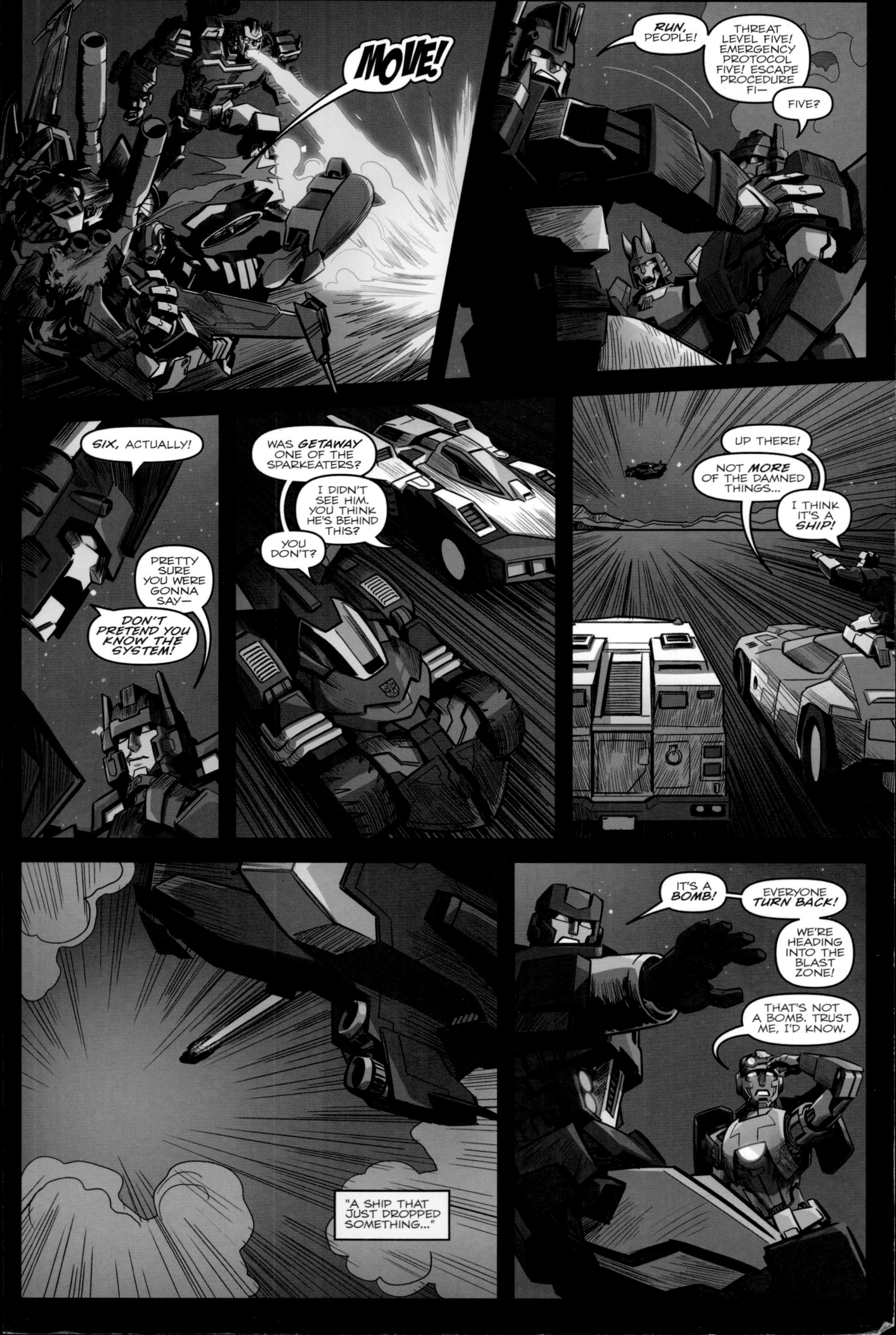
MOVE!
RUN, PEOPLE!
THREAT LEVEL FIVE! EMERGENCY PROTOCOL FIVE! ESCAPE PROCEDURE FI—
FIVE?
SIX, ACTUALLY!
PRETTY SURE YOU WERE GONNA SAY—
DON'T PRETEND YOU KNOW THE SYSTEM!
WAS GETAWAY ONE OF THE SPARKEATERS?
I DIDN'T SEE HIM. YOU THINK HE'S BEHIND THIS?
YOU DON'T?
UP THERE!
NOT MORE OF THE DAMNED THINGS...
I THINK IT'S A SHIP!
"A SHIP THAT JUST DROPPED SOMETHING..."
IT'S A BOMB!
EVERYONE TURN BACK!
WE'RE HEADING INTO THE BLAST ZONE!
THAT'S NOT A BOMB. TRUST ME, I'D KNOW.

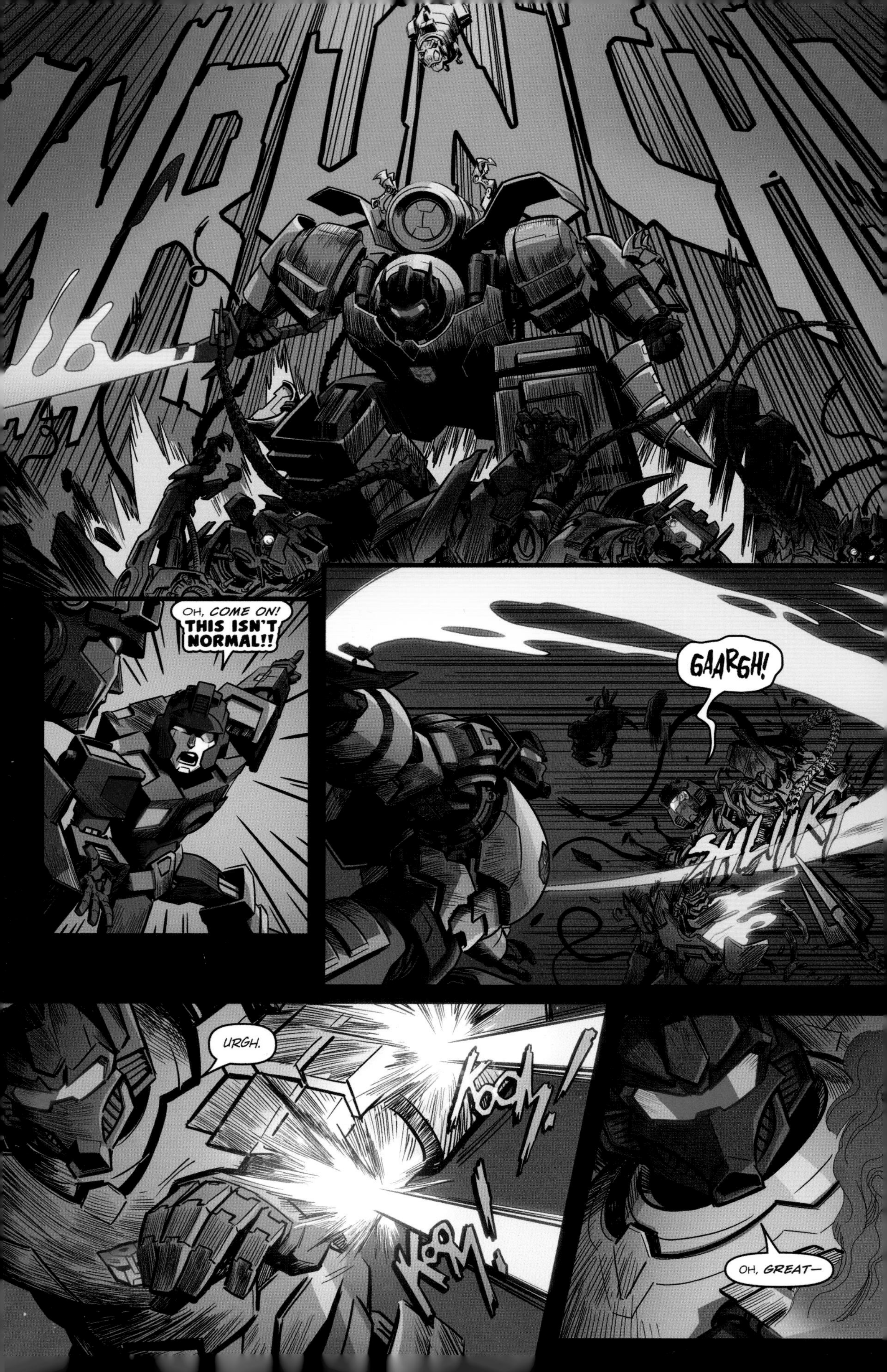
OH, COME ON! THIS ISN'T NORMAL!!
GAARGH!
SHLUKT
URGH.
KOOM!
KOOM!
OH, GREAT—

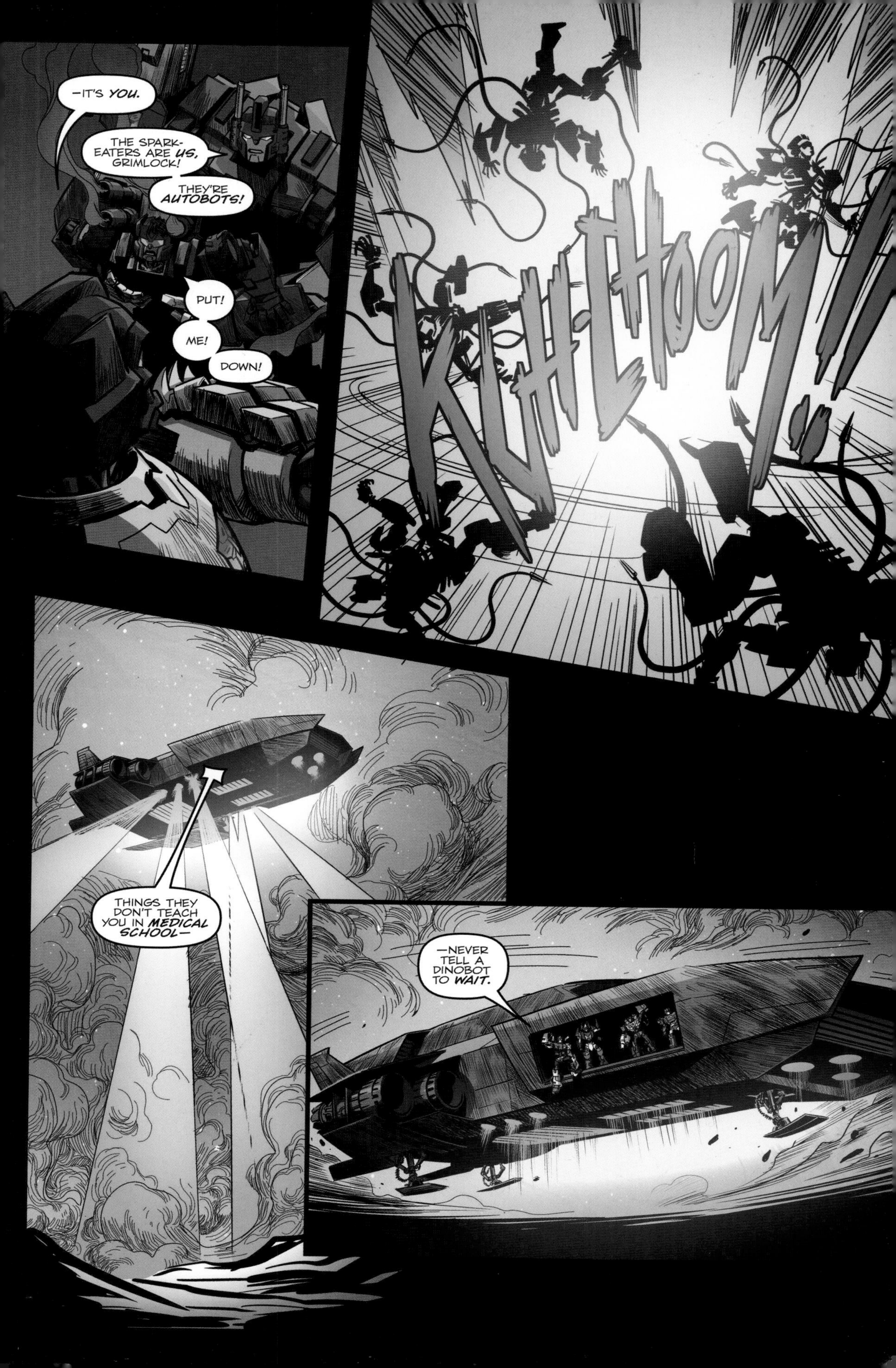
—IT'S YOU.
THE SPARK-EATERS ARE US, GRIMLOCK!
THEY'RE AUTOBOTS!
PUT!
ME!
DOWN!
KUH-CHOOM!!
THINGS THEY DON'T TEACH YOU IN MEDICAL SCHOOL—
—NEVER TELL A DINOBOT TO WAIT.

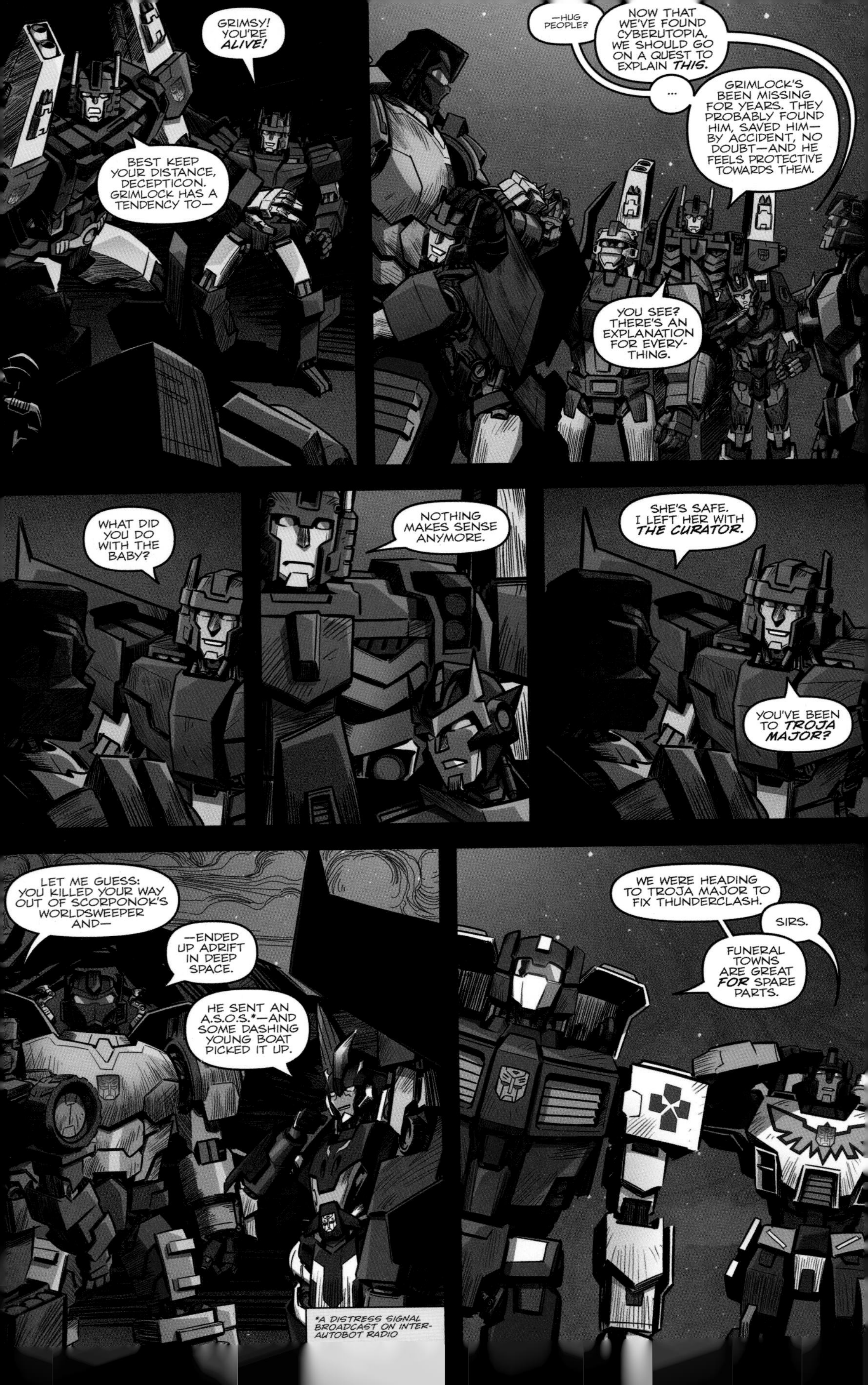
GRIMSY! YOU'RE ALIVE!
BEST KEEP YOUR DISTANCE, DECEPTICON. GRIMLOCK HAS A TENDENCY TO—
—HUG PEOPLE?
NOW THAT WE'VE FOUND CYBERUTOPIA, WE SHOULD GO ON A QUEST TO EXPLAIN THIS.
...
GRIMLOCK'S BEEN MISSING FOR YEARS. THEY PROBABLY FOUND HIM, SAVED HIM—BY ACCIDENT, NO DOUBT—AND HE FEELS PROTECTIVE TOWARDS THEM.
YOU SEE? THERE'S AN EXPLANATION FOR EVERY-THING.
WHAT DID YOU DO WITH THE BABY?
NOTHING MAKES SENSE ANYMORE.
SHE'S SAFE. I LEFT HER WITH THE CURATOR.
YOU'VE BEEN TO TROJA MAJOR?
LET ME GUESS: YOU KILLED YOUR WAY OUT OF SCORPONOK'S WORLDSWEEPER AND—
—ENDED UP ADRIFT IN DEEP SPACE.
HE SENT AN A.S.O.S.*—AND SOME DASHING YOUNG BOAT PICKED IT UP.
*A DISTRESS SIGNAL BROADCAST ON INTER-AUTOBOT RADIO
WE WERE HEADING TO TROJA MAJOR TO FIX THUNDERCLASH.
SIRS.
FUNERAL TOWNS ARE GREAT FOR SPARE PARTS.

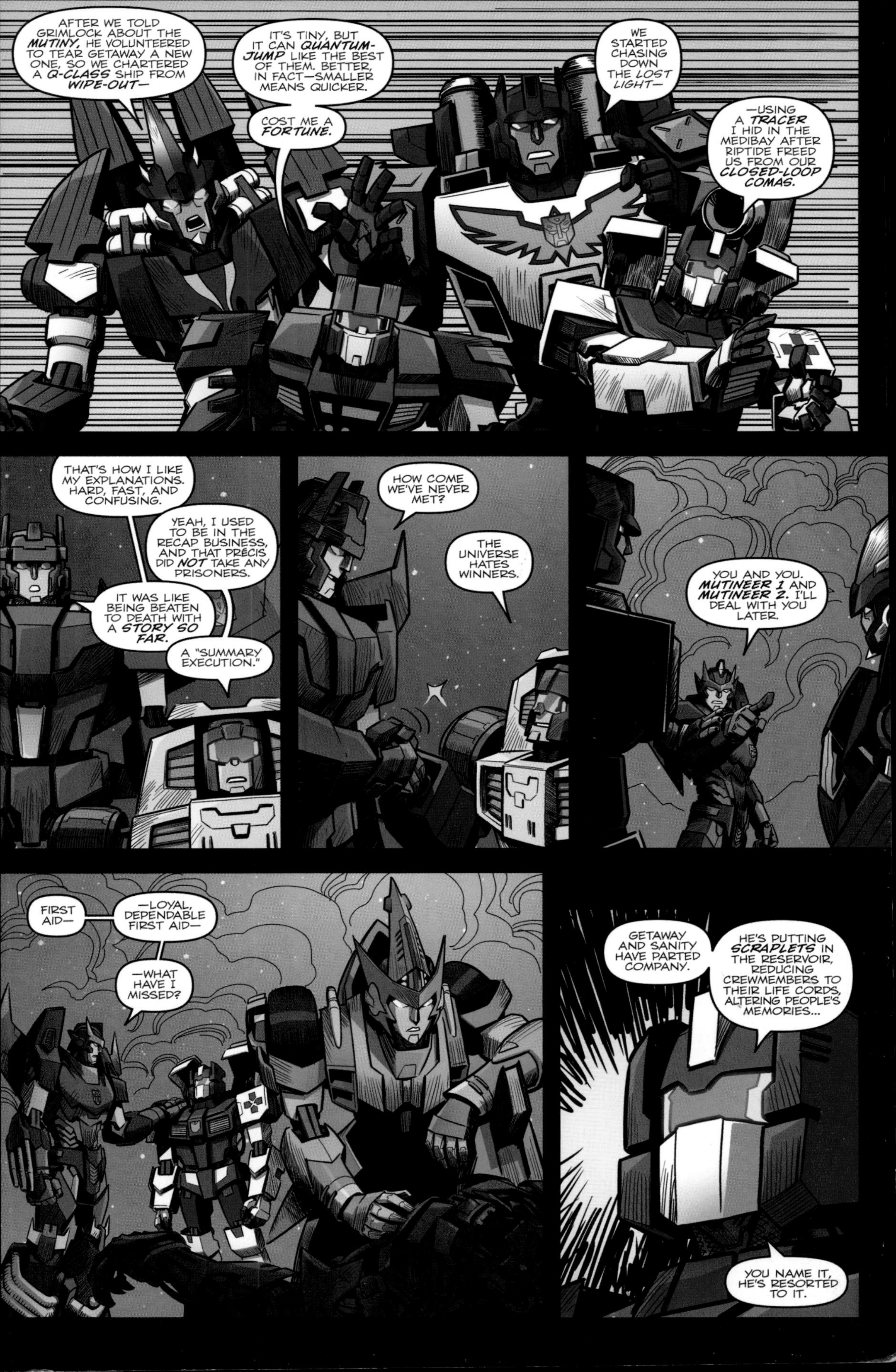

AFTER WE TOLD GRIMLOCK ABOUT THE MUTINY, HE VOLUNTEERED TO TEAR GETAWAY A NEW ONE, SO WE CHARTERED A Q-CLASS SHIP FROM WIPE-OUT—
IT'S TINY, BUT IT CAN QUANTUM-JUMP LIKE THE BEST OF THEM. BETTER, IN FACT—SMALLER MEANS QUICKER.
COST ME A FORTUNE.
WE STARTED CHASING DOWN THE LOST LIGHT—
—USING A TRACER I HID IN THE MEDIBAY AFTER RIPTIDE FREED US FROM OUR CLOSED-LOOP COMAS.
THAT'S HOW I LIKE MY EXPLANATIONS. HARD, FAST, AND CONFUSING.
YEAH, I USED TO BE IN THE RECAP BUSINESS, AND THAT PRÉCIS DID NOT TAKE ANY PRISONERS.
IT WAS LIKE BEING BEATEN TO DEATH WITH A STORY SO FAR.
A "SUMMARY EXECUTION."
HOW COME WE'VE NEVER MET?
THE UNIVERSE HATES WINNERS.
YOU AND YOU. MUTINEER 1 AND MUTINEER 2. I'LL DEAL WITH YOU LATER.
FIRST AID—
—LOYAL, DEPENDABLE FIRST AID—
—WHAT HAVE I MISSED?
GETAWAY AND SANITY HAVE PARTED COMPANY.
HE'S PUTTING SCRAPLETS IN THE RESERVOIR, REDUCING CREWMEMBERS TO THEIR LIFE CORDS, ALTERING PEOPLE'S MEMORIES...
YOU NAME IT, HE'S RESORTED TO IT.

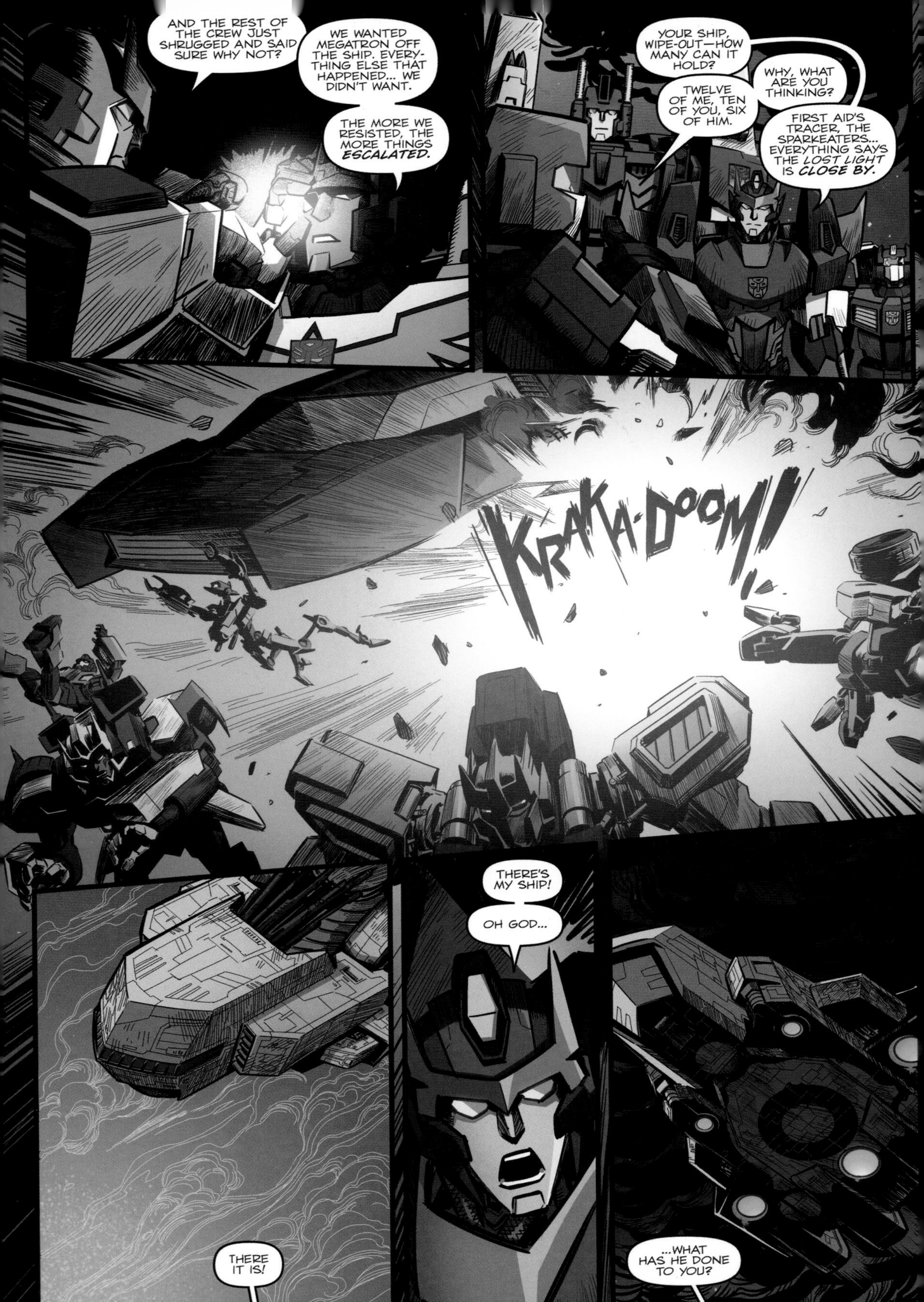
AND THE REST OF THE CREW JUST SHRUGGED AND SAID SURE WHY NOT?
WE WANTED MEGATRON OFF THE SHIP. EVERYTHING ELSE THAT HAPPENED... WE DIDN'T WANT.
THE MORE WE RESISTED, THE MORE THINGS ESCALATED.
YOUR SHIP, WIPE-OUT—HOW MANY CAN IT HOLD?
TWELVE OF ME, TEN OF YOU, SIX OF HIM.
WHY, WHAT ARE YOU THINKING?
FIRST AID'S TRACER, THE SPARKEATERS... EVERYTHING SAYS THE LOST LIGHT IS CLOSE BY.
KRAKA-DOOM!
THERE IT IS!
THERE'S MY SHIP!
OH GOD...
...WHAT HAS HE DONE TO YOU?

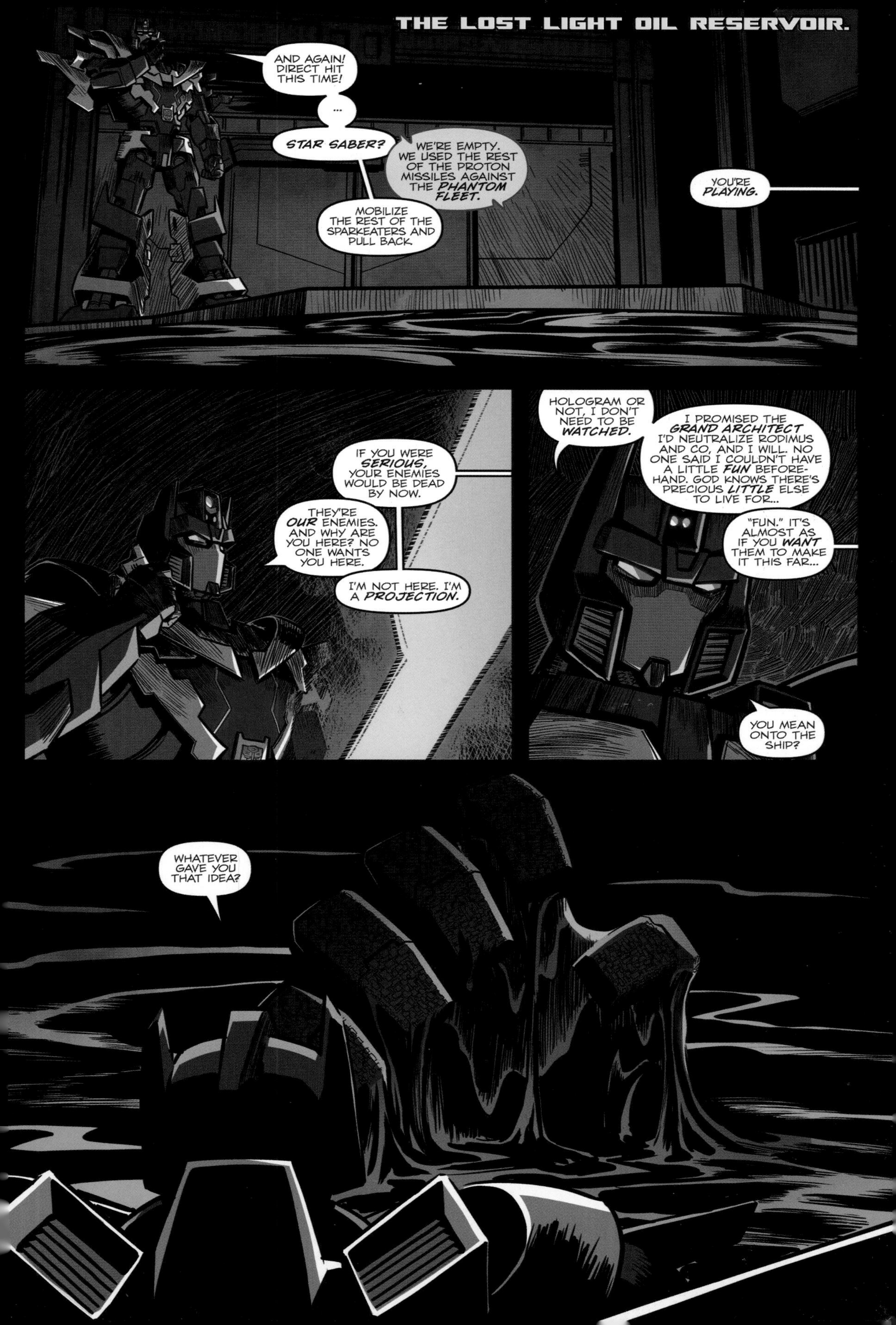
THE LOST LIGHT OIL RESERVOIR.
AND AGAIN! DIRECT HIT THIS TIME!
...
STAR SABER?
WE'RE EMPTY. WE USED THE REST OF THE PROTON MISSILES AGAINST THE PHANTOM FLEET.
MOBILIZE THE REST OF THE SPARKEATERS AND PULL BACK.
YOU'RE PLAYING.
IF YOU WERE SERIOUS, YOUR ENEMIES WOULD BE DEAD BY NOW.
THEY'RE OUR ENEMIES. AND WHY ARE YOU HERE? NO ONE WANTS YOU HERE.
I'M NOT HERE. I'M A PROJECTION.
HOLOGRAM OR NOT, I DON'T NEED TO BE WATCHED.
I PROMISED THE GRAND ARCHITECT I'D NEUTRALIZE RODIMUS AND CO, AND I WILL. NO ONE SAID I COULDN'T HAVE A LITTLE FUN BEFOREHAND. GOD KNOWS THERE'S PRECIOUS LITTLE ELSE TO LIVE FOR...
"FUN." IT'S ALMOST AS IF YOU WANT THEM TO MAKE IT THIS FAR...
YOU MEAN ONTO THE SHIP?
WHATEVER GAVE YOU THAT IDEA?

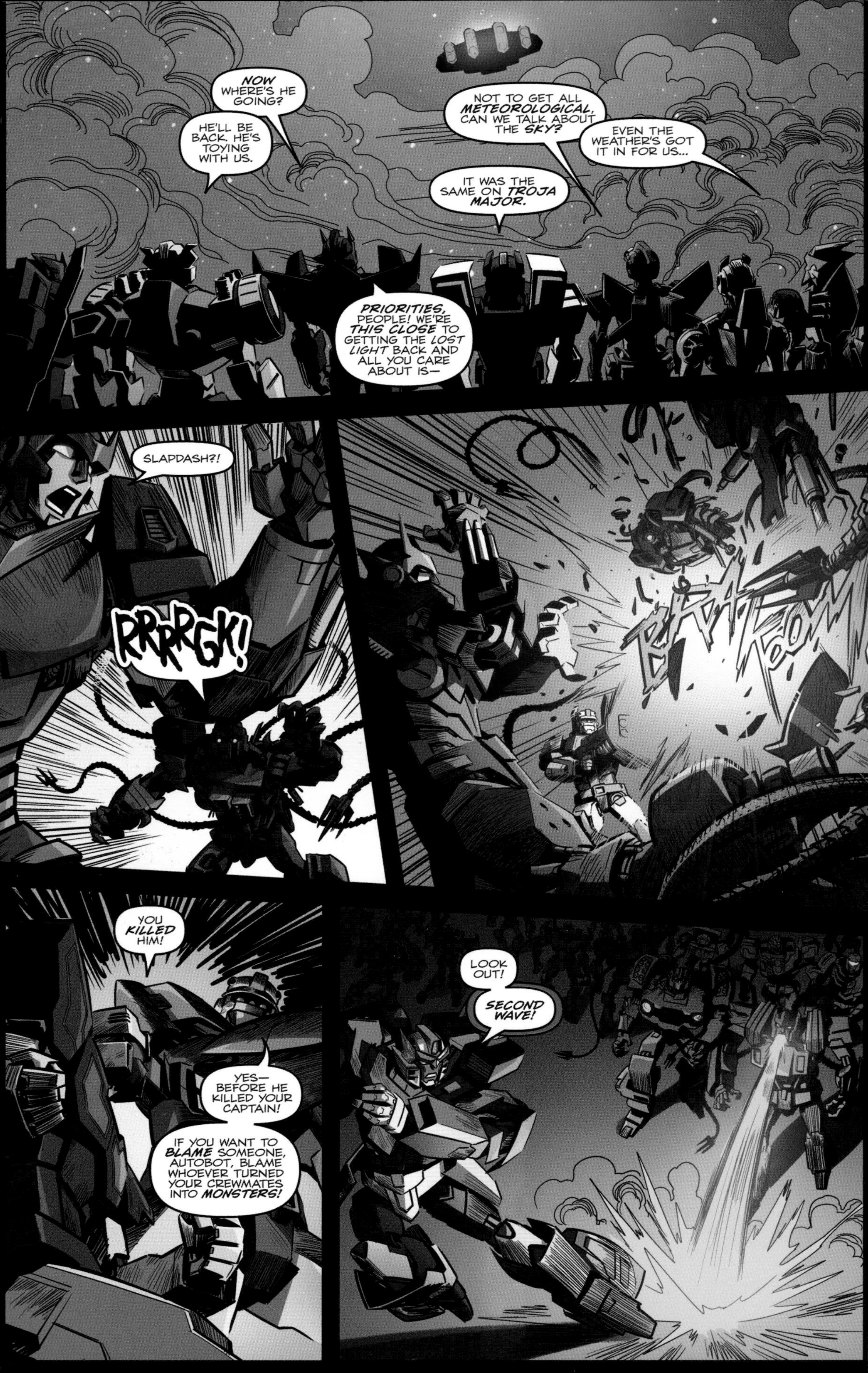
NOW WHERE'S HE GOING?
HE'LL BE BACK. HE'S TOYING WITH US.
NOT TO GET ALL METEOROLOGICAL, CAN WE TALK ABOUT THE SKY?
EVEN THE WEATHER'S GOT IT IN FOR US...
IT WAS THE SAME ON TROJA MAJOR.
PRIORITIES, PEOPLE! WE'RE THIS CLOSE TO GETTING THE LOST LIGHT BACK AND ALL YOU CARE ABOUT IS—
SLAPDASH?!
RRRRGK!
YOU KILLED HIM!
YES— BEFORE HE KILLED YOUR CAPTAIN!
IF YOU WANT TO BLAME SOMEONE, AUTOBOT, BLAME WHOEVER TURNED YOUR CREWMATES INTO MONSTERS!
LOOK OUT!
SECOND WAVE!

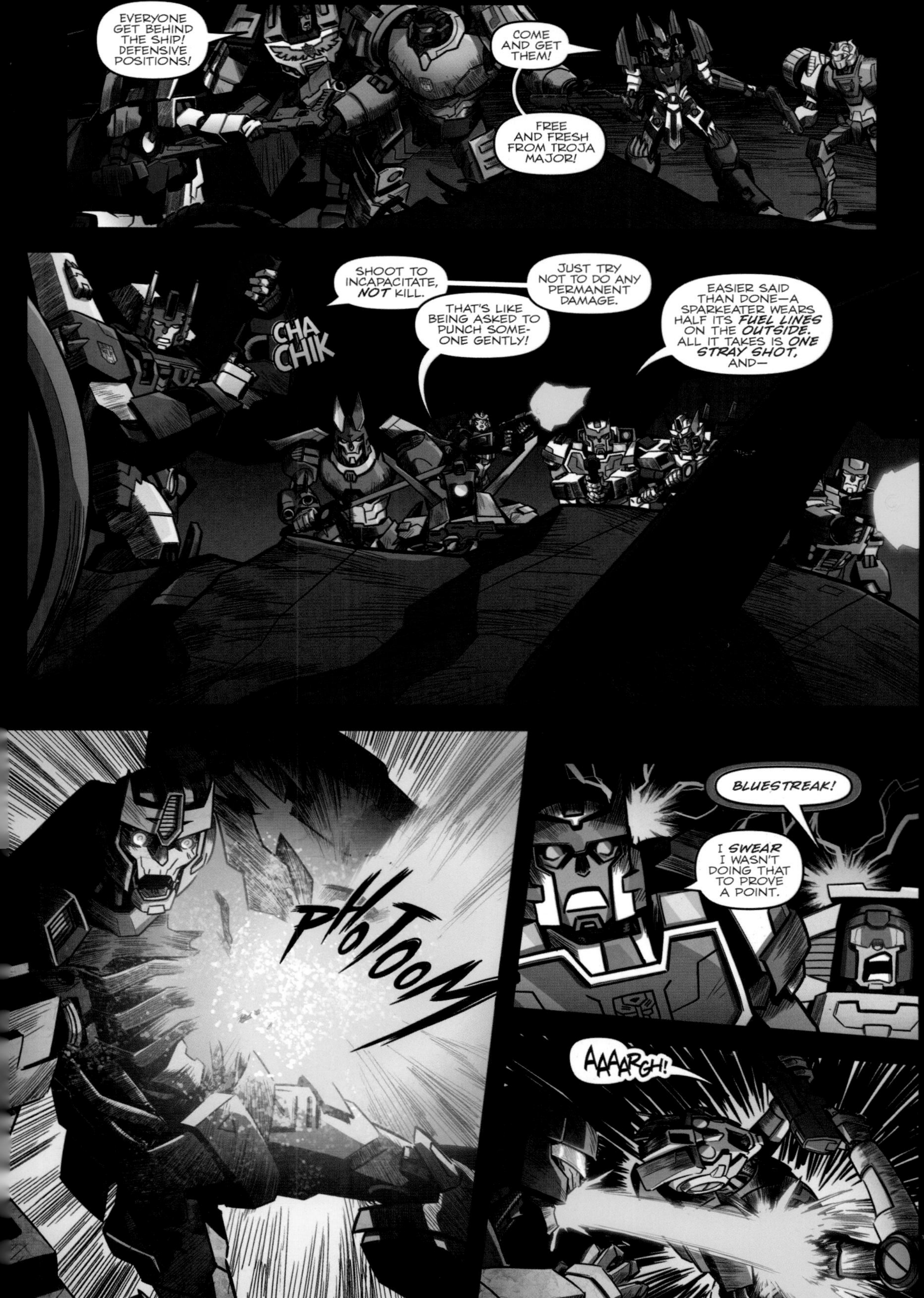
EVERYONE GET BEHIND THE SHIP! DEFENSIVE POSITIONS!
COME AND GET THEM!
FREE AND FRESH FROM TROJA MAJOR!
SHOOT TO INCAPACITATE, NOT KILL.
JUST TRY NOT TO DO ANY PERMANENT DAMAGE.
THAT'S LIKE BEING ASKED TO PUNCH SOME-ONE GENTLY!
CHA CHIK
EASIER SAID THAN DONE—A SPARKEATER WEARS HALF ITS FUEL LINES ON THE OUTSIDE. ALL IT TAKES IS ONE STRAY SHOT, AND—
PHTOOOM
BLUESTREAK!
I SWEAR I WASN'T DOING THAT TO PROVE A POINT.
AAAARGH!

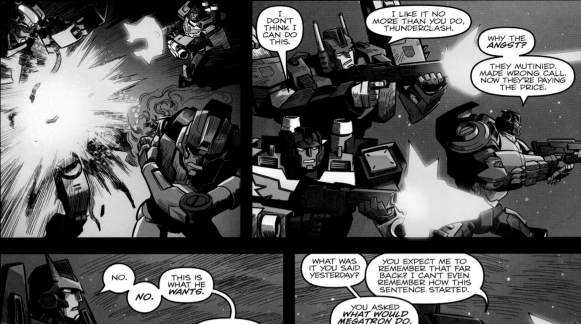

I DON'T THINK I CAN DO THIS.

I LIKE IT NO MORE THAN YOU DO, THUNDERCLASH.

WHY THE *ANGST?*

THEY MUTINIED. MADE WRONG CALL. NOW THEY'RE PAYING THE PRICE.

NO.

NO.

THIS IS WHAT HE *WANTS.*

HE KNOWS WHAT I'M LIKE— HE KNOWS I'LL *RAGE* AND *LASH OUT* AND *REACT.*

WHAT WAS IT YOU SAID YESTERDAY?

YOU EXPECT ME TO REMEMBER THAT FAR BACK? I CAN'T EVEN REMEMBER HOW THIS SENTENCE STARTED.

YOU ASKED *WHAT WOULD MEGATRON DO.* YOU SAID IT TO PISS ME OFF.

YEAH THAT DOES SOUND LIKE ME.

IF MEGATRON WAS HERE RIGHT NOW—MEGATRON AT HIS *BEST*— HE'D *THINK* HIS WAY OUT.

HE'D TAKE THE MEASURE OF THE SITUATION, WEIGH UP HIS OPTIONS, CONSIDER ALL THE VARIABLES, AND...

OKAY, EVERYONE! HERE'S WHAT WE'RE GONNA DO!

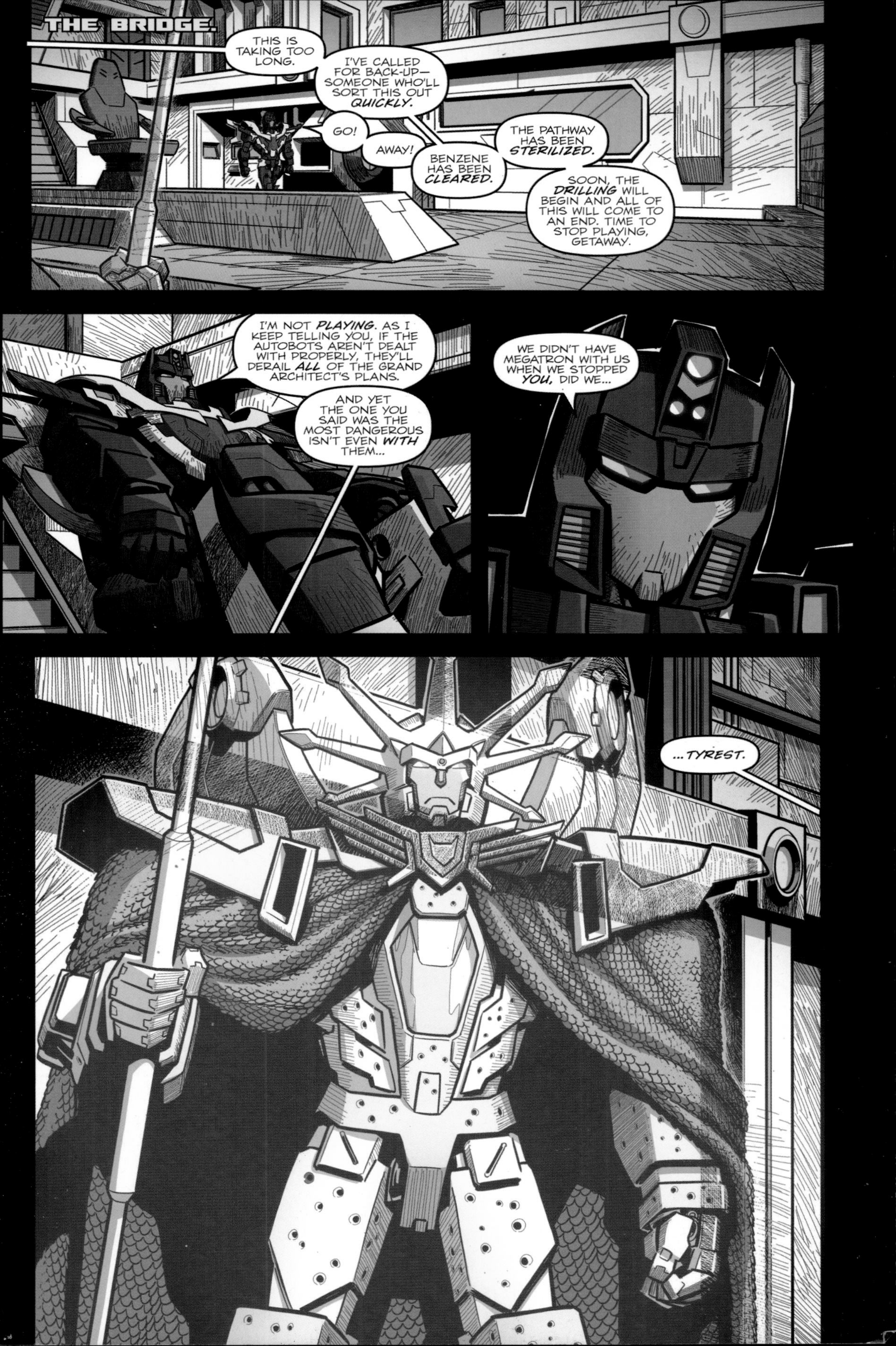
THE BRIDGE.
THIS IS TAKING TOO LONG.
I'VE CALLED FOR BACK-UP— SOMEONE WHO'LL SORT THIS OUT QUICKLY.
GO!
AWAY!
BENZENE HAS BEEN CLEARED.
THE PATHWAY HAS BEEN STERILIZED.
SOON, THE DRILLING WILL BEGIN AND ALL OF THIS WILL COME TO AN END. TIME TO STOP PLAYING, GETAWAY.
I'M NOT PLAYING. AS I KEEP TELLING YOU, IF THE AUTOBOTS AREN'T DEALT WITH PROPERLY, THEY'LL DERAIL ALL OF THE GRAND ARCHITECT'S PLANS.
AND YET THE ONE YOU SAID WAS THE MOST DANGEROUS ISN'T EVEN WITH THEM...
WE DIDN'T HAVE MEGATRON WITH US WHEN WE STOPPED YOU, DID WE...
...TYREST.

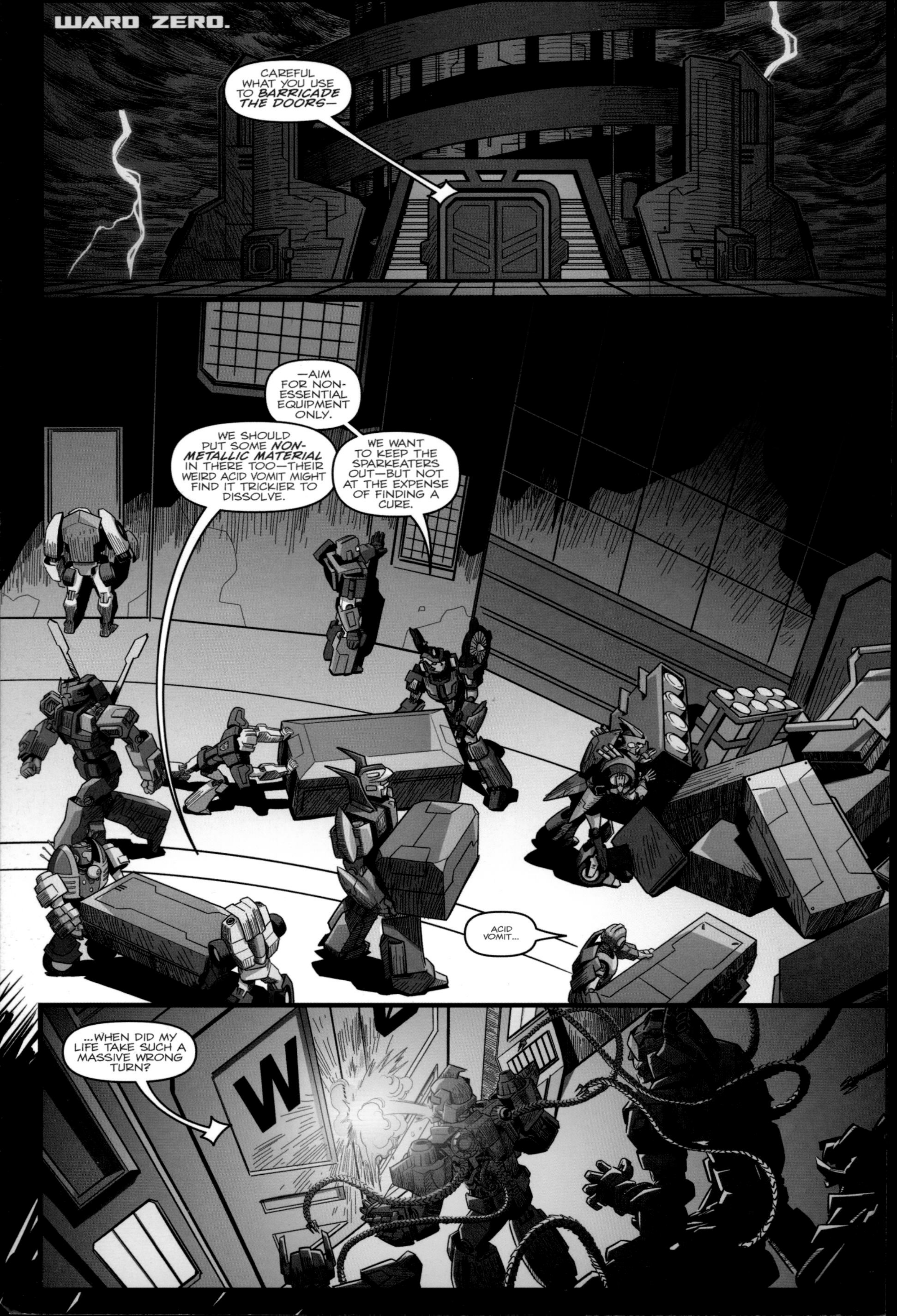
WARD ZERO.
CAREFUL WHAT YOU USE TO BARRICADE THE DOORS—
—AIM FOR NON-ESSENTIAL EQUIPMENT ONLY.
WE WANT TO KEEP THE SPARKEATERS OUT—BUT NOT AT THE EXPENSE OF FINDING A CURE.
WE SHOULD PUT SOME NON-METALLIC MATERIAL IN THERE TOO—THEIR WEIRD ACID VOMIT MIGHT FIND IT TRICKIER TO DISSOLVE.
ACID VOMIT...
...WHEN DID MY LIFE TAKE SUCH A MASSIVE WRONG TURN?
W

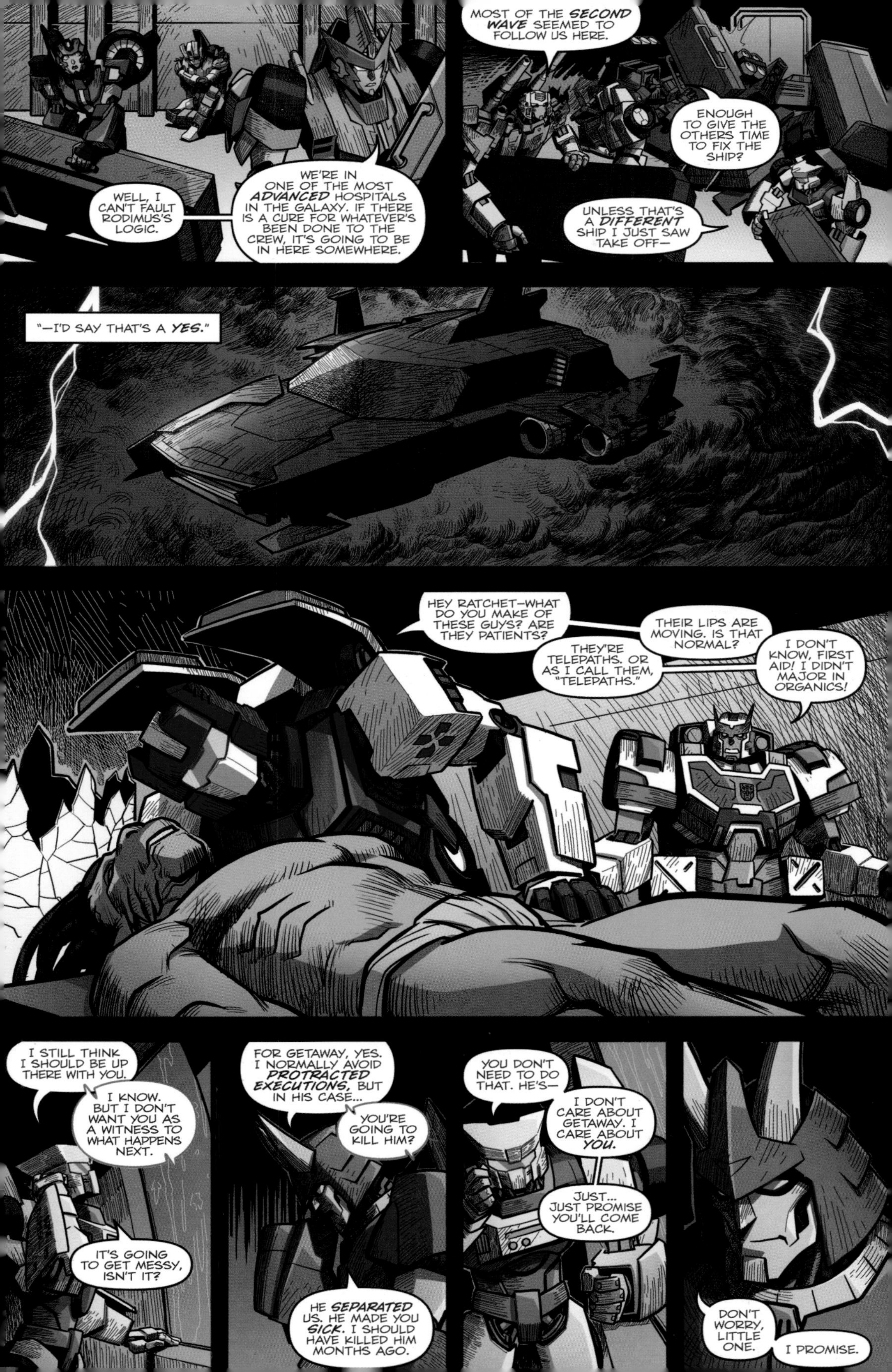
WELL, I CAN'T FAULT RODIMUS'S LOGIC.
WE'RE IN ONE OF THE MOST ADVANCED HOSPITALS IN THE GALAXY. IF THERE IS A CURE FOR WHATEVER'S BEEN DONE TO THE CREW, IT'S GOING TO BE IN HERE SOMEWHERE.
MOST OF THE SECOND WAVE SEEMED TO FOLLOW US HERE.
ENOUGH TO GIVE THE OTHERS TIME TO FIX THE SHIP?
UNLESS THAT'S A DIFFERENT SHIP I JUST SAW TAKE OFF—
"—I'D SAY THAT'S A YES."
HEY RATCHET—WHAT DO YOU MAKE OF THESE GUYS? ARE THEY PATIENTS?
THEY'RE TELEPATHS. OR AS I CALL THEM, "TELEPATHS."
THEIR LIPS ARE MOVING. IS THAT NORMAL?
I DON'T KNOW, FIRST AID! I DIDN'T MAJOR IN ORGANICS!
I STILL THINK I SHOULD BE UP THERE WITH YOU.
I KNOW. BUT I DON'T WANT YOU AS A WITNESS TO WHAT HAPPENS NEXT.
IT'S GOING TO GET MESSY, ISN'T IT?
FOR GETAWAY, YES. I NORMALLY AVOID PROTRACTED EXECUTIONS, BUT IN HIS CASE...
YOU'RE GOING TO KILL HIM?
HE SEPARATED US. HE MADE YOU SICK. I SHOULD HAVE KILLED HIM MONTHS AGO.
YOU DON'T NEED TO DO THAT. HE'S—
I DON'T CARE ABOUT GETAWAY. I CARE ABOUT YOU.
JUST... JUST PROMISE YOU'LL COME BACK.
DON'T WORRY, LITTLE ONE.
I PROMISE.

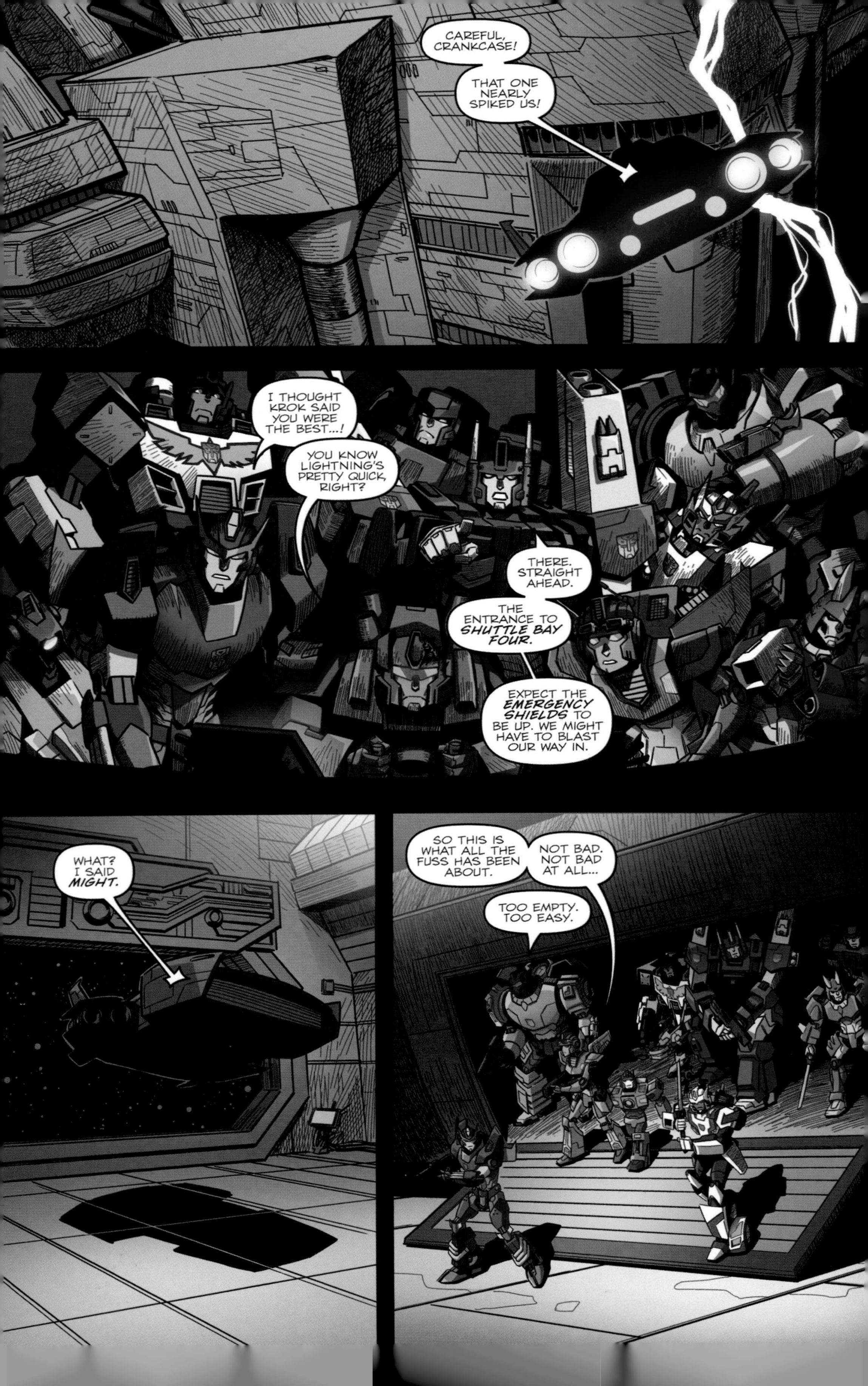
CAREFUL, CRANKCASE!
THAT ONE NEARLY SPIKED US!
I THOUGHT KROK SAID YOU WERE THE BEST...!
YOU KNOW LIGHTNING'S PRETTY QUICK, RIGHT?
THERE. STRAIGHT AHEAD.
THE ENTRANCE TO *SHUTTLE BAY FOUR.*
EXPECT THE *EMERGENCY SHIELDS* TO BE UP. WE MIGHT HAVE TO BLAST OUR WAY IN.
WHAT? I SAID *MIGHT.*
SO THIS IS WHAT ALL THE FUSS HAS BEEN ABOUT.
NOT BAD. NOT BAD AT ALL...
TOO EMPTY. TOO EASY.

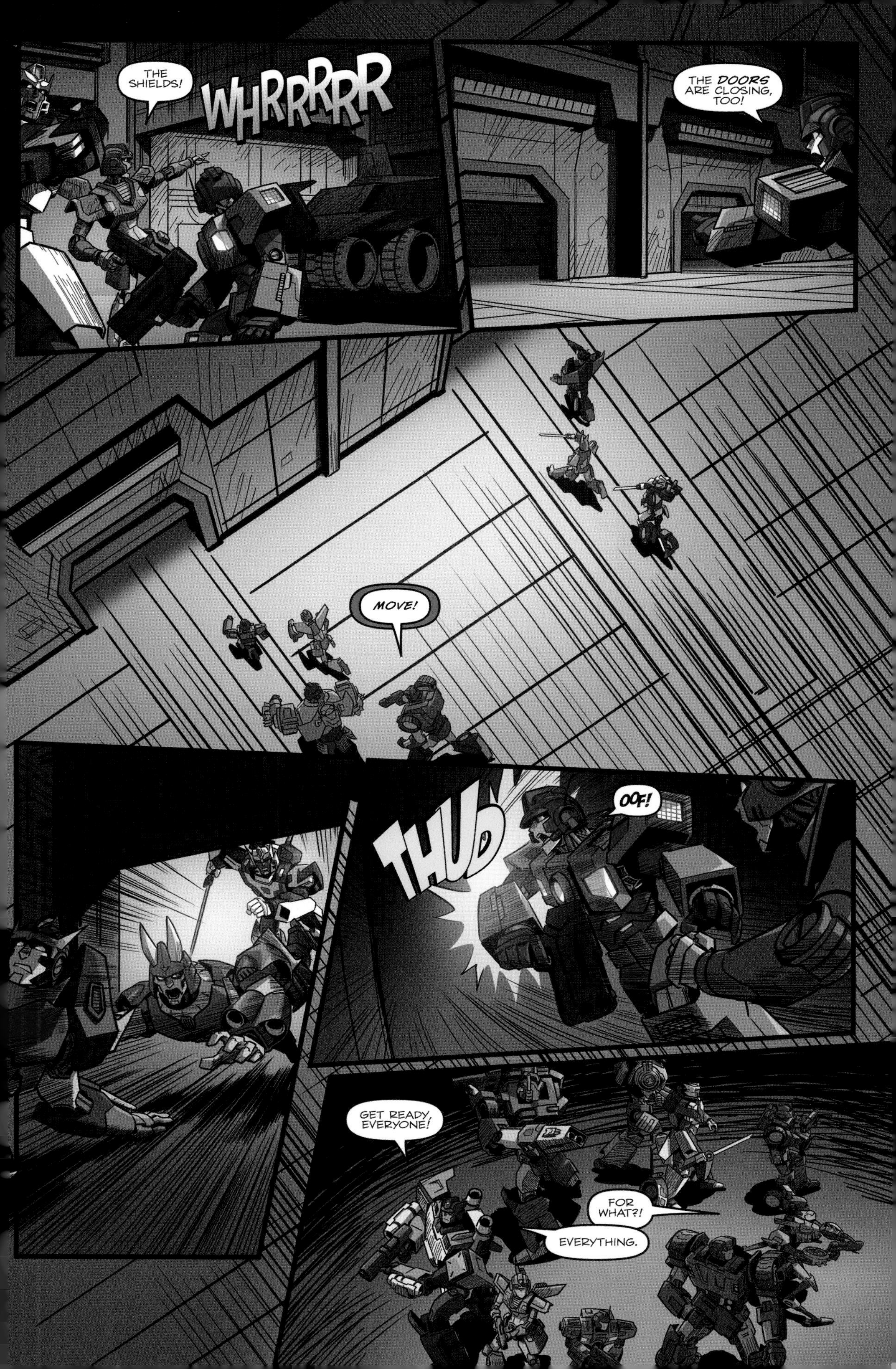
THE SHIELDS!
WHRRRRR
THE DOORS ARE CLOSING, TOO!
MOVE!
THUD
OOF!
GET READY, EVERYONE!
FOR WHAT?!
EVERYTHING.

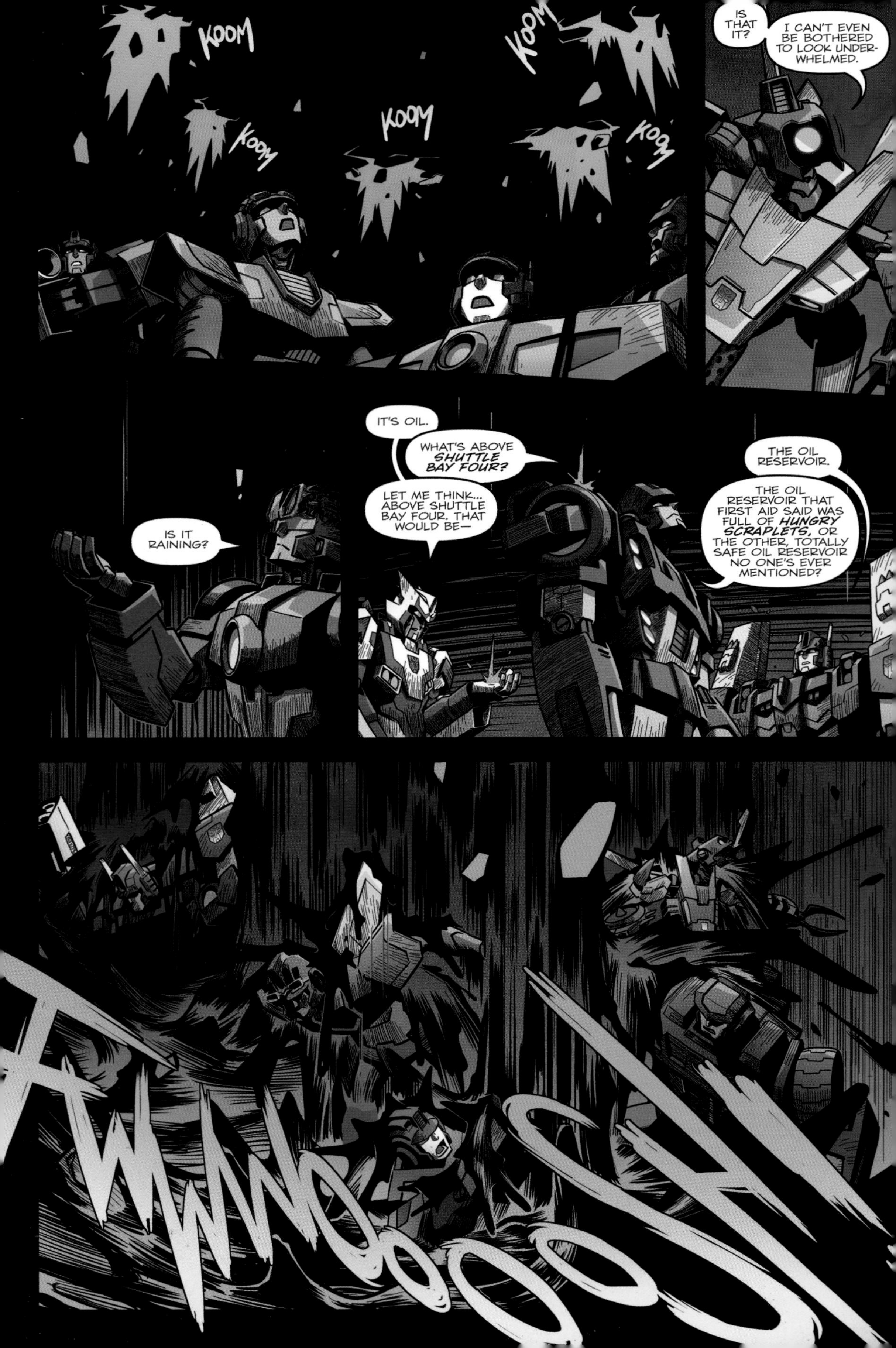
KOOM
KOOM
KOOM
KOOM
KOOM
KOOM
IS THAT IT?
I CAN'T EVEN BE BOTHERED TO LOOK UNDER-WHELMED.
IS IT RAINING?
IT'S OIL.
WHAT'S ABOVE SHUTTLE BAY FOUR?
LET ME THINK... ABOVE SHUTTLE BAY FOUR. THAT WOULD BE—
THE OIL RESERVOIR.
THE OIL RESERVOIR THAT FIRST AID SAID WAS FULL OF HUNGRY SCRAPLETS, OR THE OTHER, TOTALLY SAFE OIL RESERVOIR NO ONE'S EVER MENTIONED?

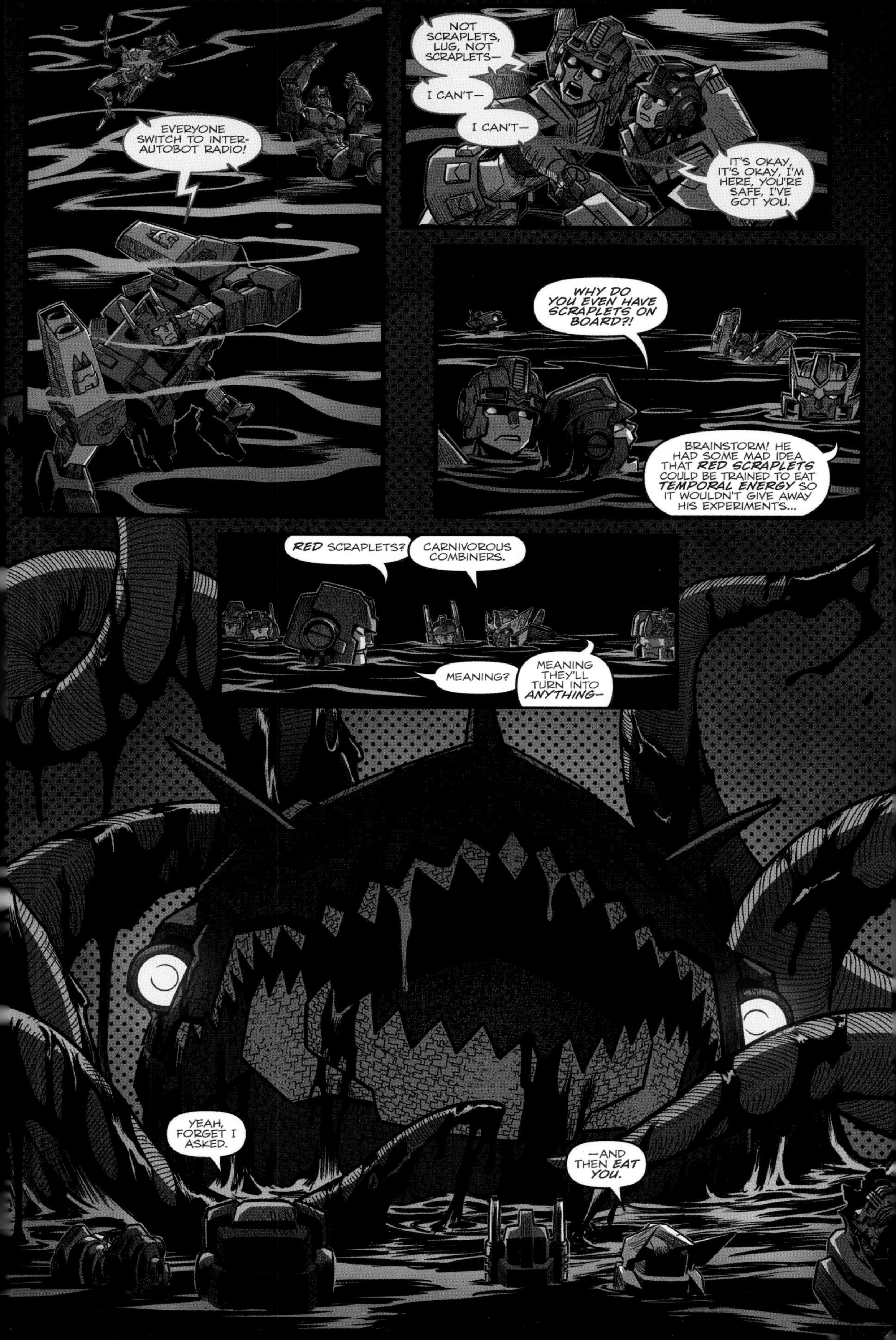
EVERYONE SWITCH TO INTER-AUTOBOT RADIO!
NOT SCRAPLETS, LUG, NOT SCRAPLETS—
I CAN'T—
I CAN'T—
IT'S OKAY, IT'S OKAY, I'M HERE, YOU'RE SAFE, I'VE GOT YOU.
WHY DO YOU EVEN HAVE SCRAPLETS ON BOARD?!
BRAINSTORM! HE HAD SOME MAD IDEA THAT RED SCRAPLETS COULD BE TRAINED TO EAT TEMPORAL ENERGY SO IT WOULDN'T GIVE AWAY HIS EXPERIMENTS...
RED SCRAPLETS?
CARNIVOROUS COMBINERS.
MEANING?
MEANING THEY'LL TURN INTO ANYTHING—
YEAH, FORGET I ASKED.
—AND THEN EAT YOU.

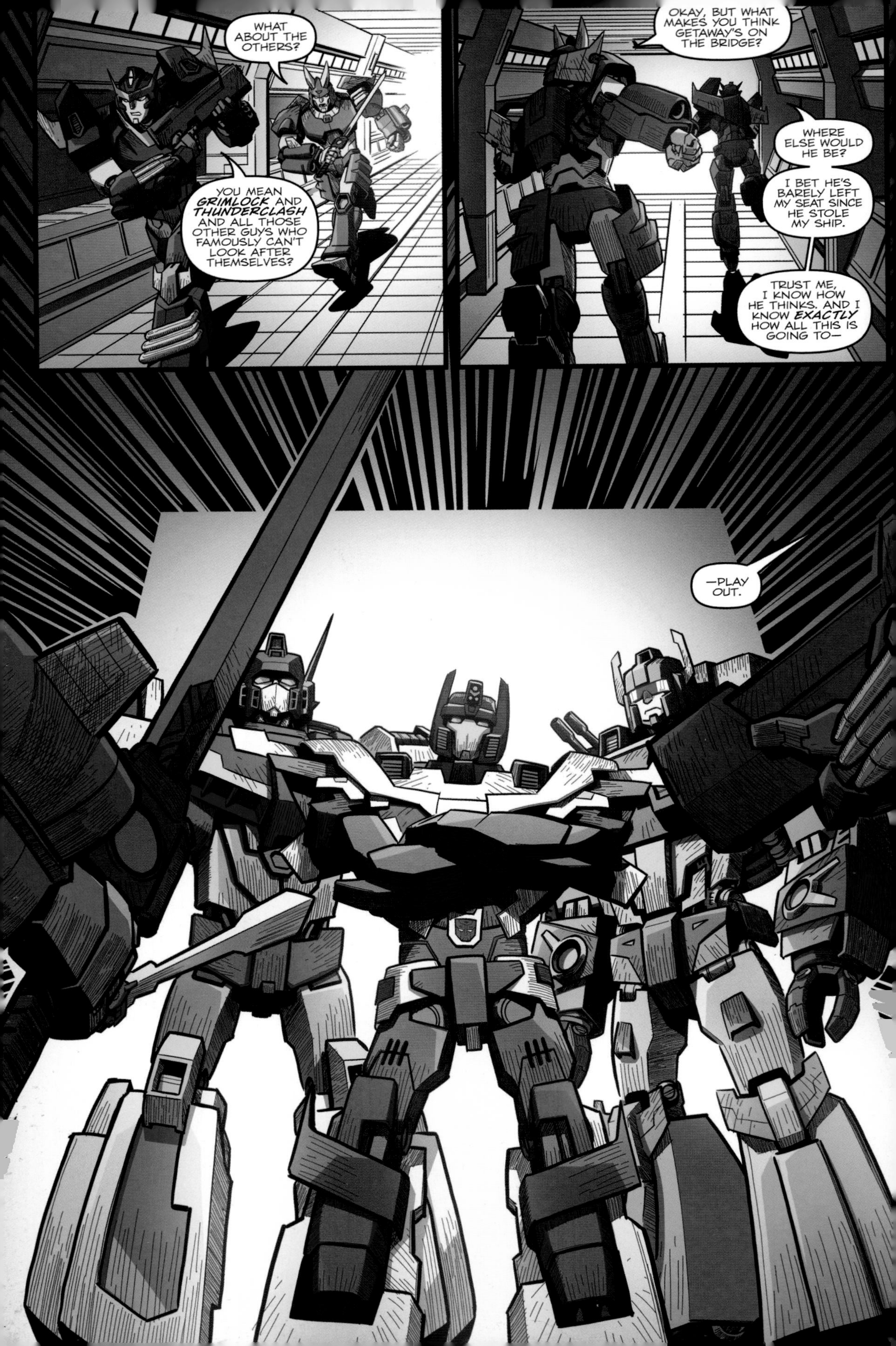
WHAT ABOUT THE OTHERS?
YOU MEAN GRIMLOCK AND THUNDERCLASH AND ALL THOSE OTHER GUYS WHO FAMOUSLY CAN'T LOOK AFTER THEMSELVES?
OKAY, BUT WHAT MAKES YOU THINK GETAWAY'S ON THE BRIDGE?
WHERE ELSE WOULD HE BE?
I BET HE'S BARELY LEFT MY SEAT SINCE HE STOLE MY SHIP.
TRUST ME, I KNOW HOW HE THINKS. AND I KNOW EXACTLY HOW ALL THIS IS GOING TO—
—PLAY OUT.

ART BY **JACK LAWRENCE**
COLORS BY **JOANA LAFUENTE**

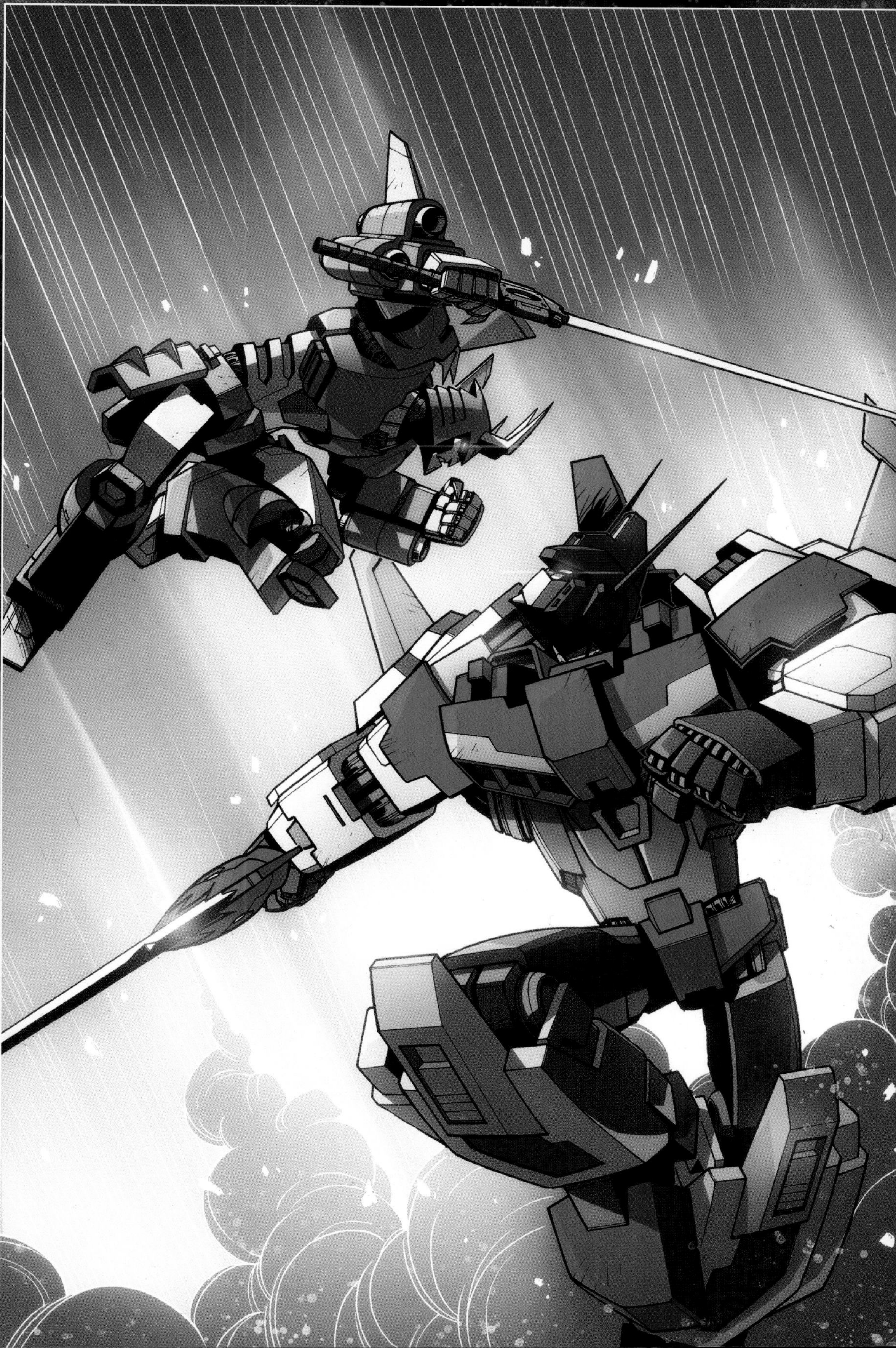

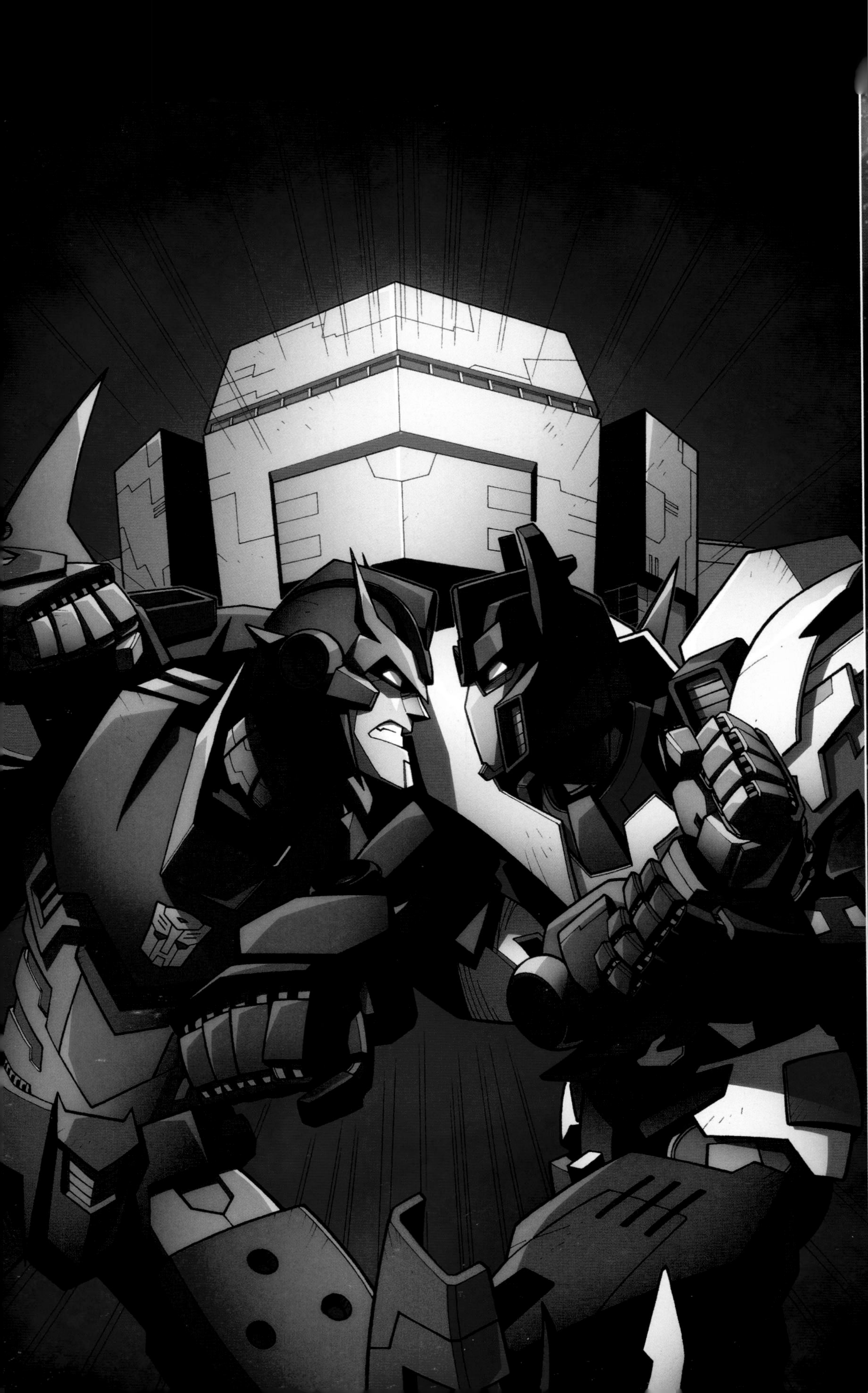

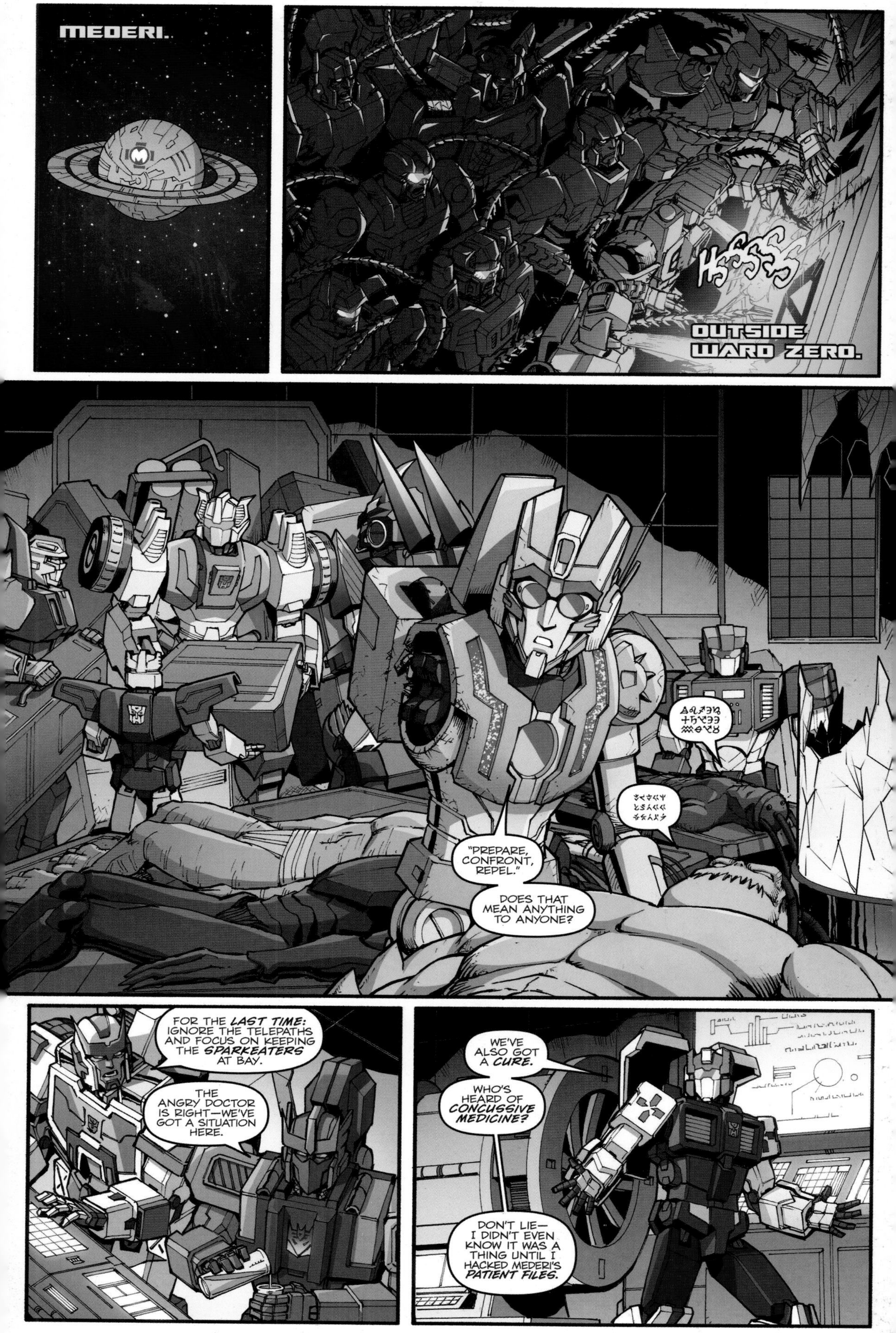
MEDERI.
HSSSSS
OUTSIDE WARD ZERO.
"PREPARE, CONFRONT, REPEL."
DOES THAT MEAN ANYTHING TO ANYONE?
FOR THE LAST TIME: IGNORE THE TELEPATHS AND FOCUS ON KEEPING THE SPARKEATERS AT BAY.
THE ANGRY DOCTOR IS RIGHT—WE'VE GOT A SITUATION HERE.
WE'VE ALSO GOT A CURE.
WHO'S HEARD OF CONCUSSIVE MEDICINE?
DON'T LIE—I DIDN'T EVEN KNOW IT WAS A THING UNTIL I HACKED MEDERI'S PATIENT FILES.

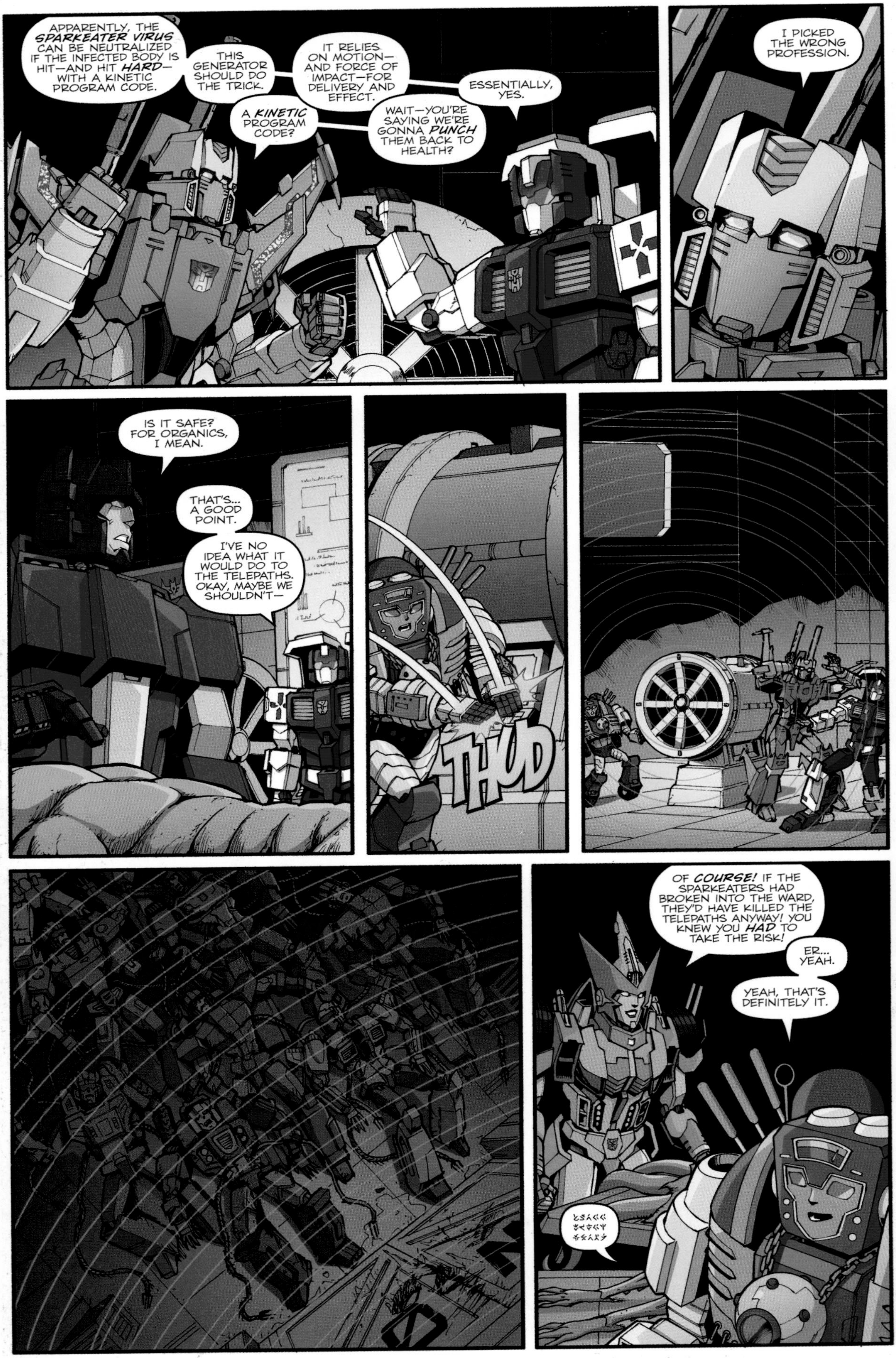
APPARENTLY, THE SPARKEATER VIRUS CAN BE NEUTRALIZED IF THE INFECTED BODY IS HIT—AND HIT HARD—WITH A KINETIC PROGRAM CODE.
THIS GENERATOR SHOULD DO THE TRICK.
A KINETIC PROGRAM CODE?
IT RELIES ON MOTION—AND FORCE OF IMPACT—FOR DELIVERY AND EFFECT.
WAIT—YOU'RE SAYING WE'RE GONNA PUNCH THEM BACK TO HEALTH?
ESSENTIALLY, YES.
I PICKED THE WRONG PROFESSION.
IS IT SAFE? FOR ORGANICS, I MEAN.
THAT'S... A GOOD POINT.
I'VE NO IDEA WHAT IT WOULD DO TO THE TELEPATHS. OKAY, MAYBE WE SHOULDN'T—
THUD
OF COURSE! IF THE SPARKEATERS HAD BROKEN INTO THE WARD, THEY'D HAVE KILLED THE TELEPATHS ANYWAY! YOU KNEW YOU HAD TO TAKE THE RISK!
ER... YEAH.
YEAH, THAT'S DEFINITELY IT.

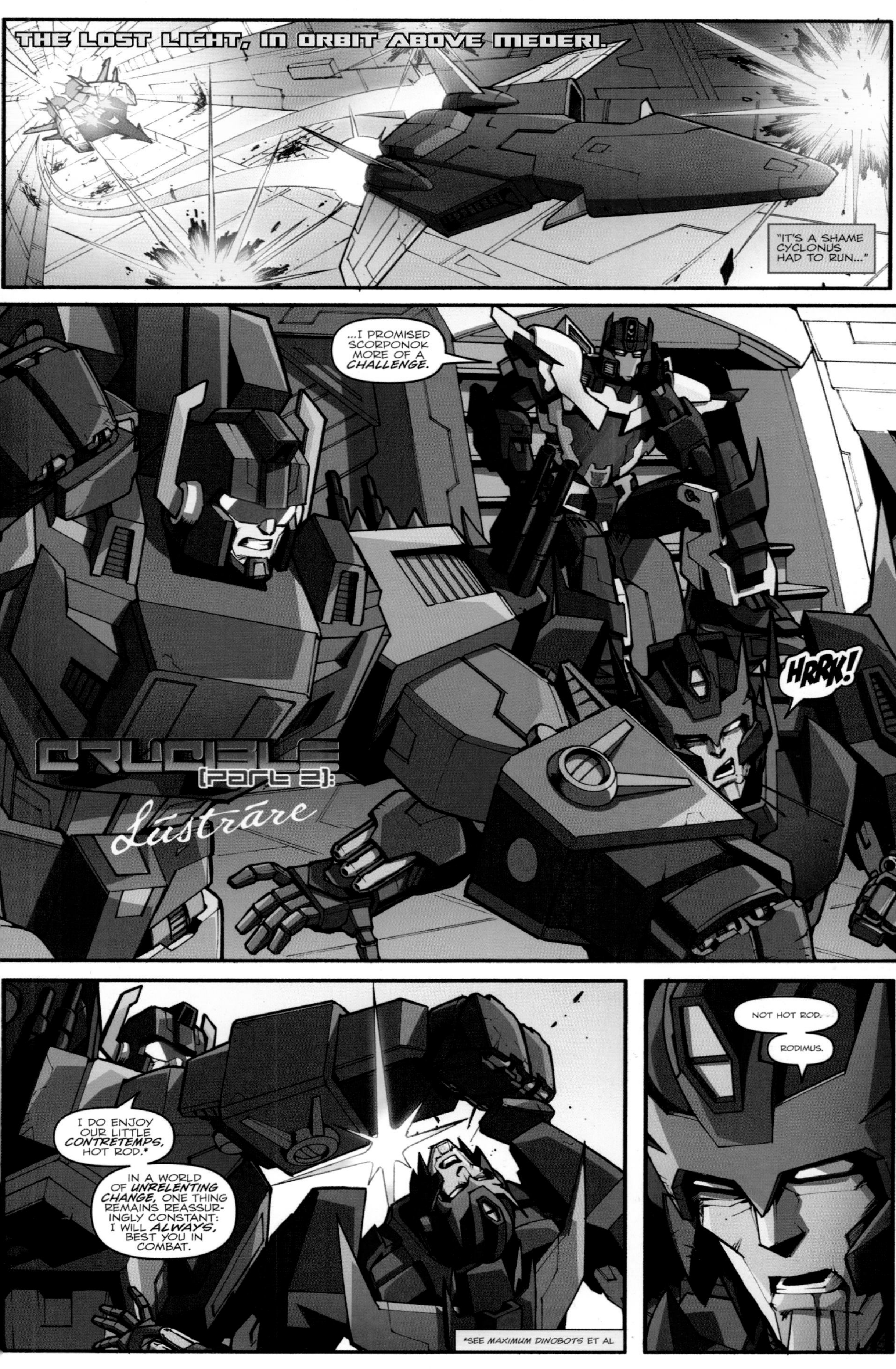
THE LOST LIGHT, IN ORBIT ABOVE MEDERI.
"IT'S A SHAME CYCLONUS HAD TO RUN..."
...I PROMISED SCORPONOK MORE OF A CHALLENGE.
HRRK!
CRUCIBLE (PART 2):
Lūstrāre
I DO ENJOY OUR LITTLE CONTRETEMPS, HOT ROD.*
IN A WORLD OF UNRELENTING CHANGE, ONE THING REMAINS REASSUR-INGLY CONSTANT: I WILL ALWAYS, BEST YOU IN COMBAT.
*SEE MAXIMUM DINOBOTS ET AL
NOT HOT ROD.
RODIMUS.

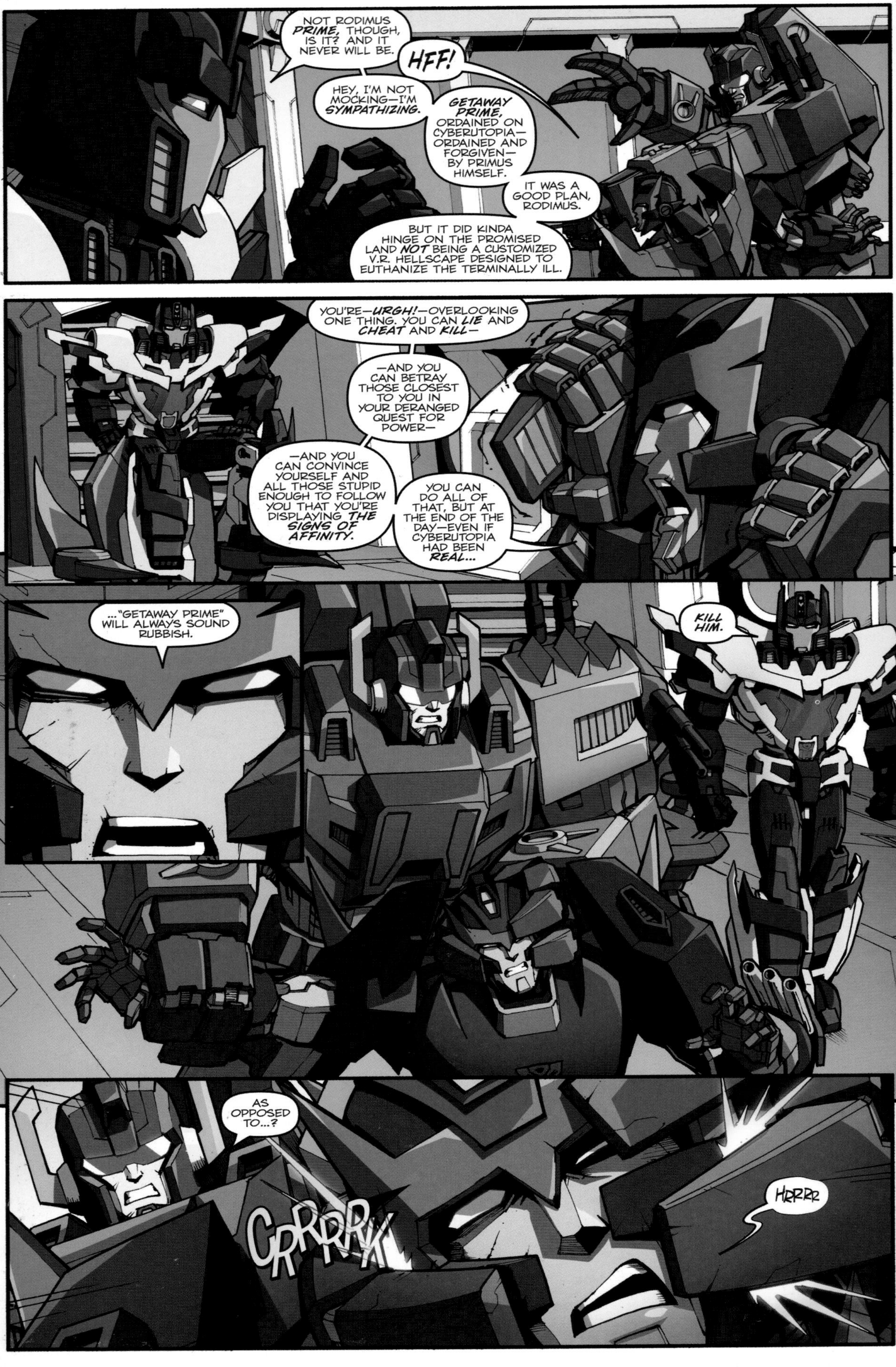
NOT RODIMUS PRIME, THOUGH, IS IT? AND IT NEVER WILL BE.
HFF!
HEY, I'M NOT MOCKING—I'M SYMPATHIZING.
GETAWAY PRIME, ORDAINED ON CYBERUTOPIA—ORDAINED AND FORGIVEN—BY PRIMUS HIMSELF.
IT WAS A GOOD PLAN, RODIMUS.
BUT IT DID KINDA HINGE ON THE PROMISED LAND NOT BEING A CUSTOMIZED V.R. HELLSCAPE DESIGNED TO EUTHANIZE THE TERMINALLY ILL.
YOU'RE—URGH!—OVERLOOKING ONE THING. YOU CAN LIE AND CHEAT AND KILL—
—AND YOU CAN BETRAY THOSE CLOSEST TO YOU IN YOUR DERANGED QUEST FOR POWER—
—AND YOU CAN CONVINCE YOURSELF AND ALL THOSE STUPID ENOUGH TO FOLLOW YOU THAT YOU'RE DISPLAYING THE SIGNS OF AFFINITY.
YOU CAN DO ALL OF THAT, BUT AT THE END OF THE DAY—EVEN IF CYBERUTOPIA HAD BEEN REAL...
..."GETAWAY PRIME" WILL ALWAYS SOUND RUBBISH.
KILL HIM.
AS OPPOSED TO...?
CRRRRK
HRRRR

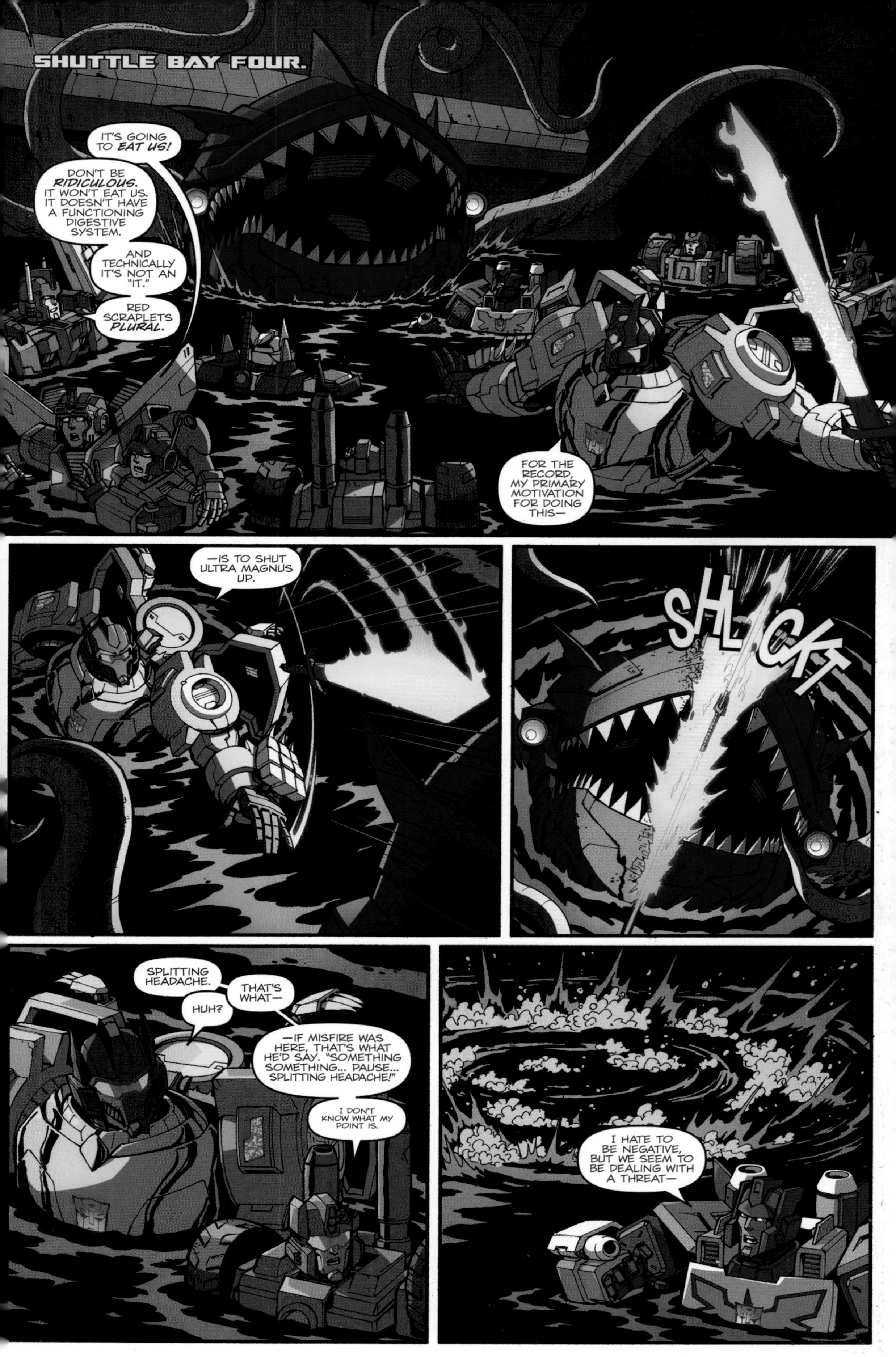
SHUTTLE BAY FOUR.
IT'S GOING TO EAT US!
DON'T BE RIDICULOUS. IT WON'T EAT US. IT DOESN'T HAVE A FUNCTIONING DIGESTIVE SYSTEM.
AND TECHNICALLY IT'S NOT AN "IT."
RED SCRAPLETS PLURAL.
FOR THE RECORD, MY PRIMARY MOTIVATION FOR DOING THIS—
—IS TO SHUT ULTRA MAGNUS UP.
SHLICKT
SPLITTING HEADACHE.
THAT'S WHAT—
HUH?
—IF MISFIRE WAS HERE, THAT'S WHAT HE'D SAY. "SOMETHING SOMETHING... PAUSE... SPLITTING HEADACHE!"
I DON'T KNOW WHAT MY POINT IS.
I HATE TO BE NEGATIVE, BUT WE SEEM TO BE DEALING WITH A THREAT—

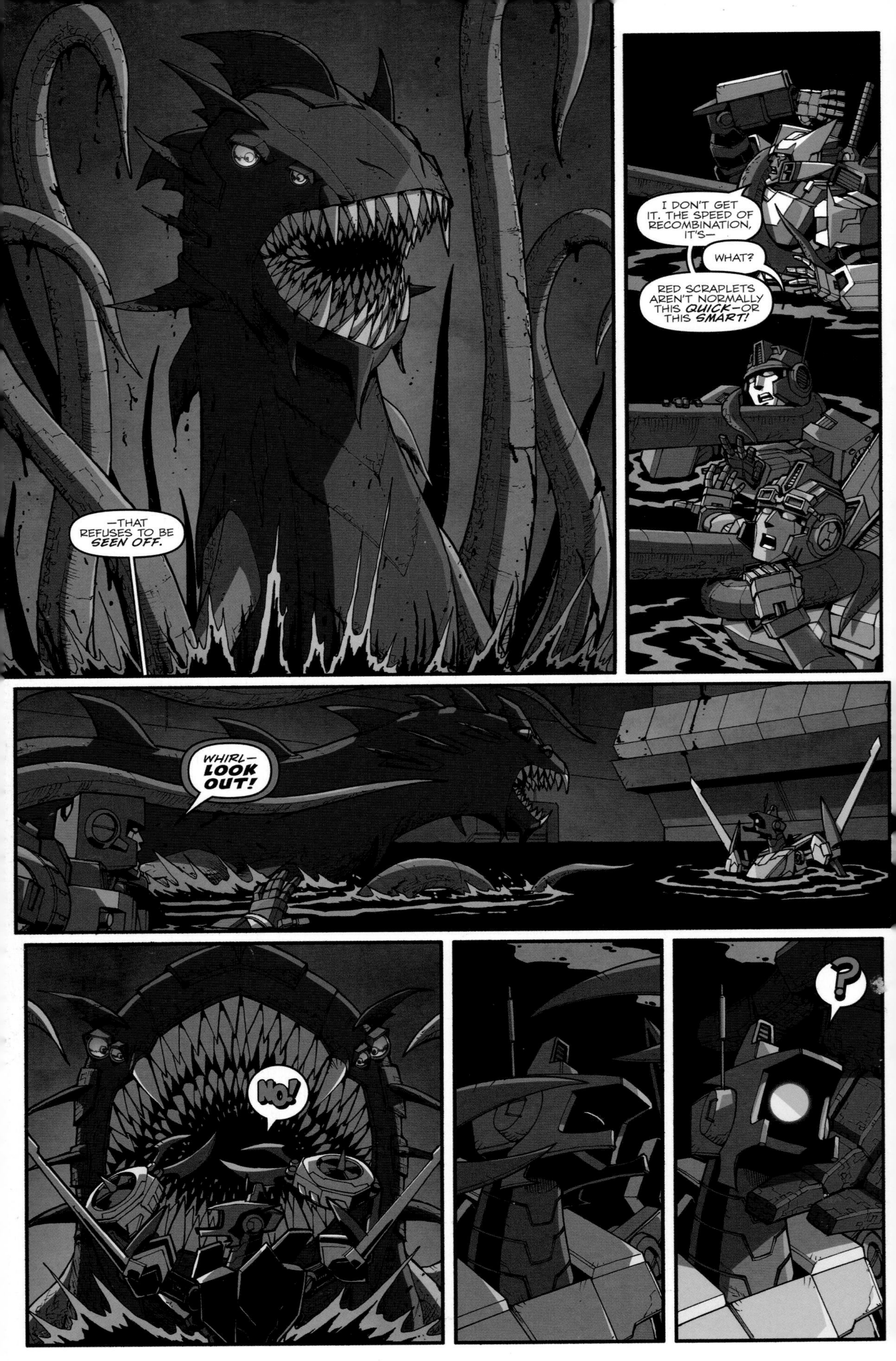

—THAT REFUSES TO BE SEEN OFF.
I DON'T GET IT. THE SPEED OF RECOMBINATION, IT'S—
WHAT?
RED SCRAPLETS AREN'T NORMALLY THIS QUICK—OR THIS SMART!
WHIRL—LOOK OUT!
NO!
?

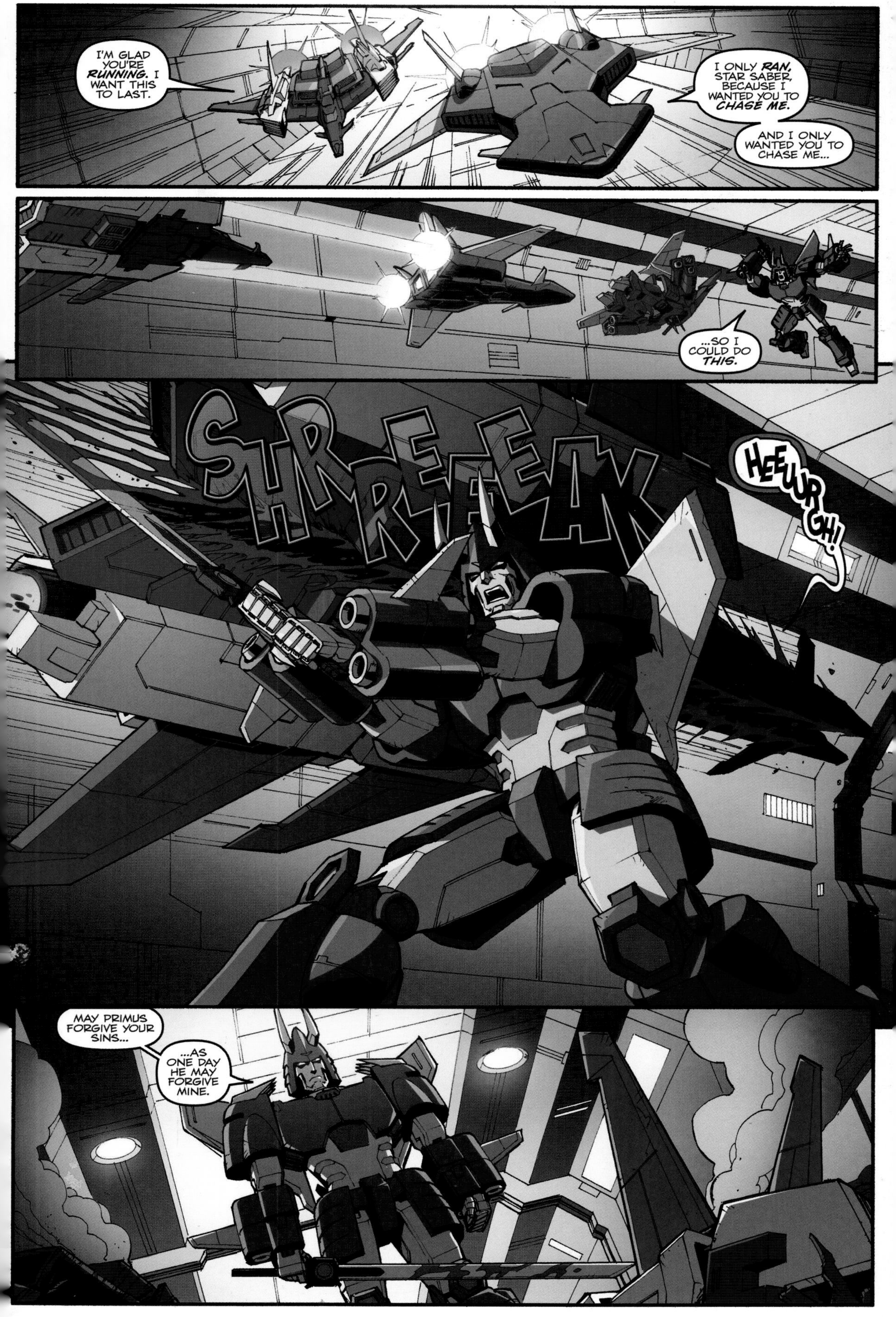

I'M GLAD YOU'RE RUNNING. I WANT THIS TO LAST.
I ONLY RAN, STAR SABER, BECAUSE I WANTED YOU TO CHASE ME.
AND I ONLY WANTED YOU TO CHASE ME...
...SO I COULD DO THIS.
SHREEEAK
HEEUURGH!
MAY PRIMUS FORGIVE YOUR SINS...
...AS ONE DAY HE MAY FORGIVE MINE.

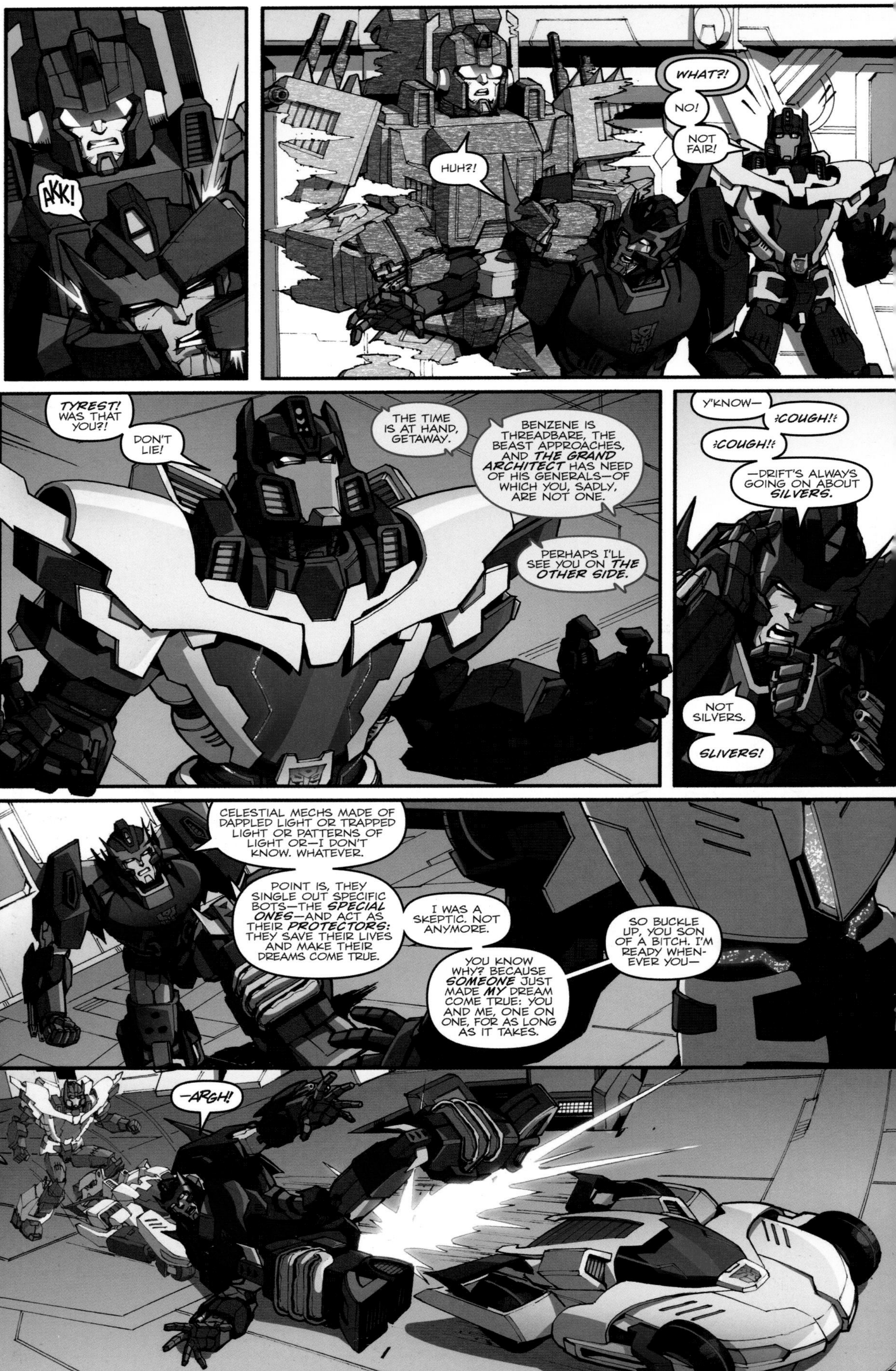
AKK!
HUH?!
WHAT?!
NO!
NOT FAIR!
TYREST! WAS THAT YOU?!
DON'T LIE!
THE TIME IS AT HAND, GETAWAY.
BENZENE IS THREADBARE, THE BEAST APPROACHES, AND THE GRAND ARCHITECT HAS NEED OF HIS GENERALS—OF WHICH YOU, SADLY, ARE NOT ONE.
PERHAPS I'LL SEE YOU ON THE OTHER SIDE.
Y'KNOW—
¡COUGH!¡
¡COUGH!¡
—DRIFT'S ALWAYS GOING ON ABOUT SILVERS.
NOT SILVERS.
SLIVERS!
CELESTIAL MECHS MADE OF DAPPLED LIGHT OR TRAPPED LIGHT OR PATTERNS OF LIGHT OR—I DON'T KNOW. WHATEVER.
POINT IS, THEY SINGLE OUT SPECIFIC BOTS—THE SPECIAL ONES—AND ACT AS THEIR PROTECTORS: THEY SAVE THEIR LIVES AND MAKE THEIR DREAMS COME TRUE.
I WAS A SKEPTIC. NOT ANYMORE.
YOU KNOW WHY? BECAUSE SOMEONE JUST MADE MY DREAM COME TRUE: YOU AND ME, ONE ON ONE, FOR AS LONG AS IT TAKES.
SO BUCKLE UP, YOU SON OF A BITCH. I'M READY WHENEVER YOU—
—ARGH!

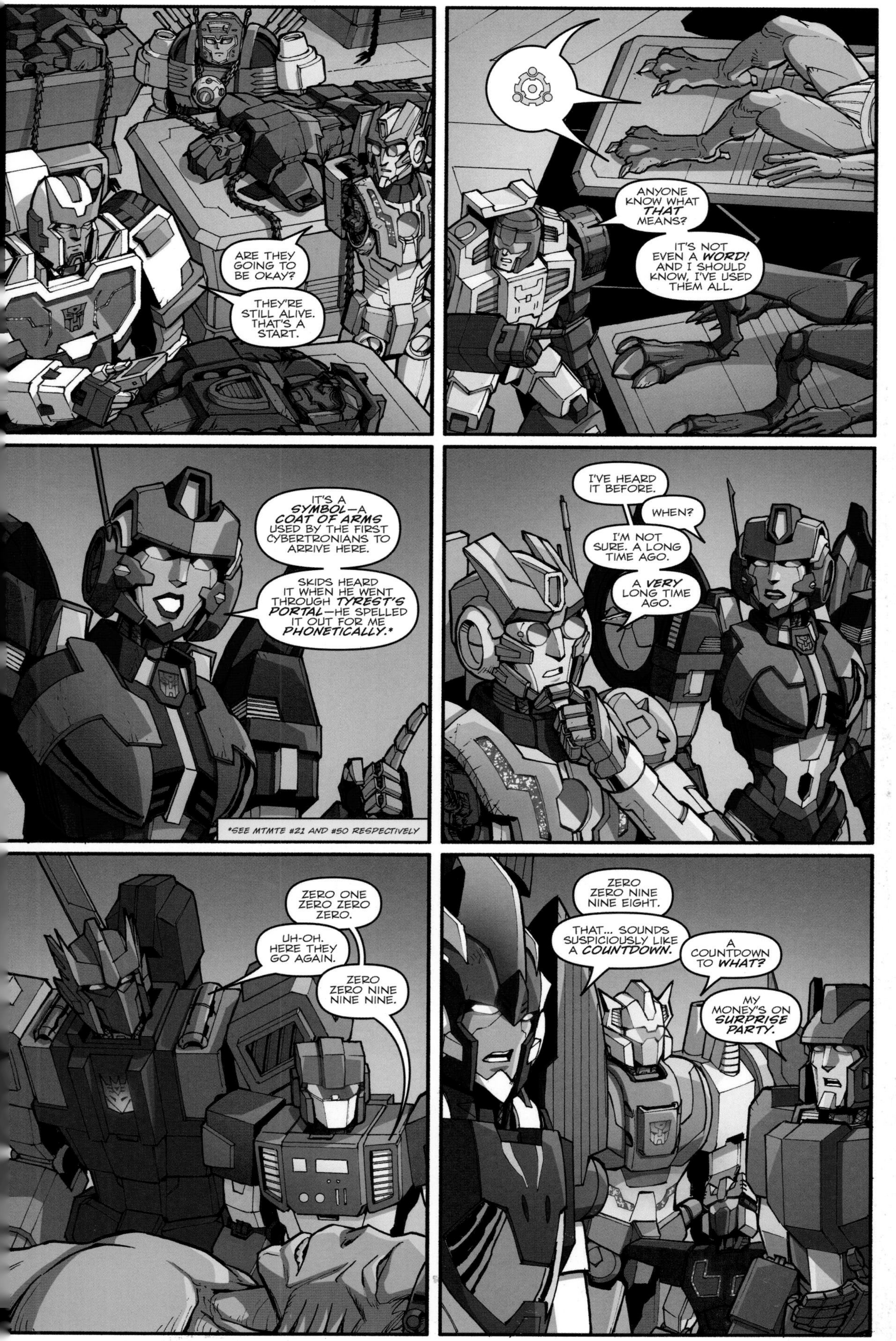
ARE THEY GOING TO BE OKAY?
THEY'RE STILL ALIVE. THAT'S A START.
ANYONE KNOW WHAT THAT MEANS?
IT'S NOT EVEN A WORD! AND I SHOULD KNOW, I'VE USED THEM ALL.
IT'S A SYMBOL—A COAT OF ARMS USED BY THE FIRST CYBERTRONIANS TO ARRIVE HERE.
SKIDS HEARD IT WHEN HE WENT THROUGH TYREST'S PORTAL—HE SPELLED IT OUT FOR ME PHONETICALLY.*
*SEE MTMTE #21 AND #50 RESPECTIVELY
I'VE HEARD IT BEFORE.
WHEN?
I'M NOT SURE. A LONG TIME AGO.
A VERY LONG TIME AGO.
ZERO ONE ZERO ZERO ZERO.
UH-OH. HERE THEY GO AGAIN.
ZERO ZERO NINE NINE NINE.
ZERO ZERO NINE NINE EIGHT.
THAT... SOUNDS SUSPICIOUSLY LIKE A COUNTDOWN.
A COUNTDOWN TO WHAT?
MY MONEY'S ON SURPRISE PARTY.

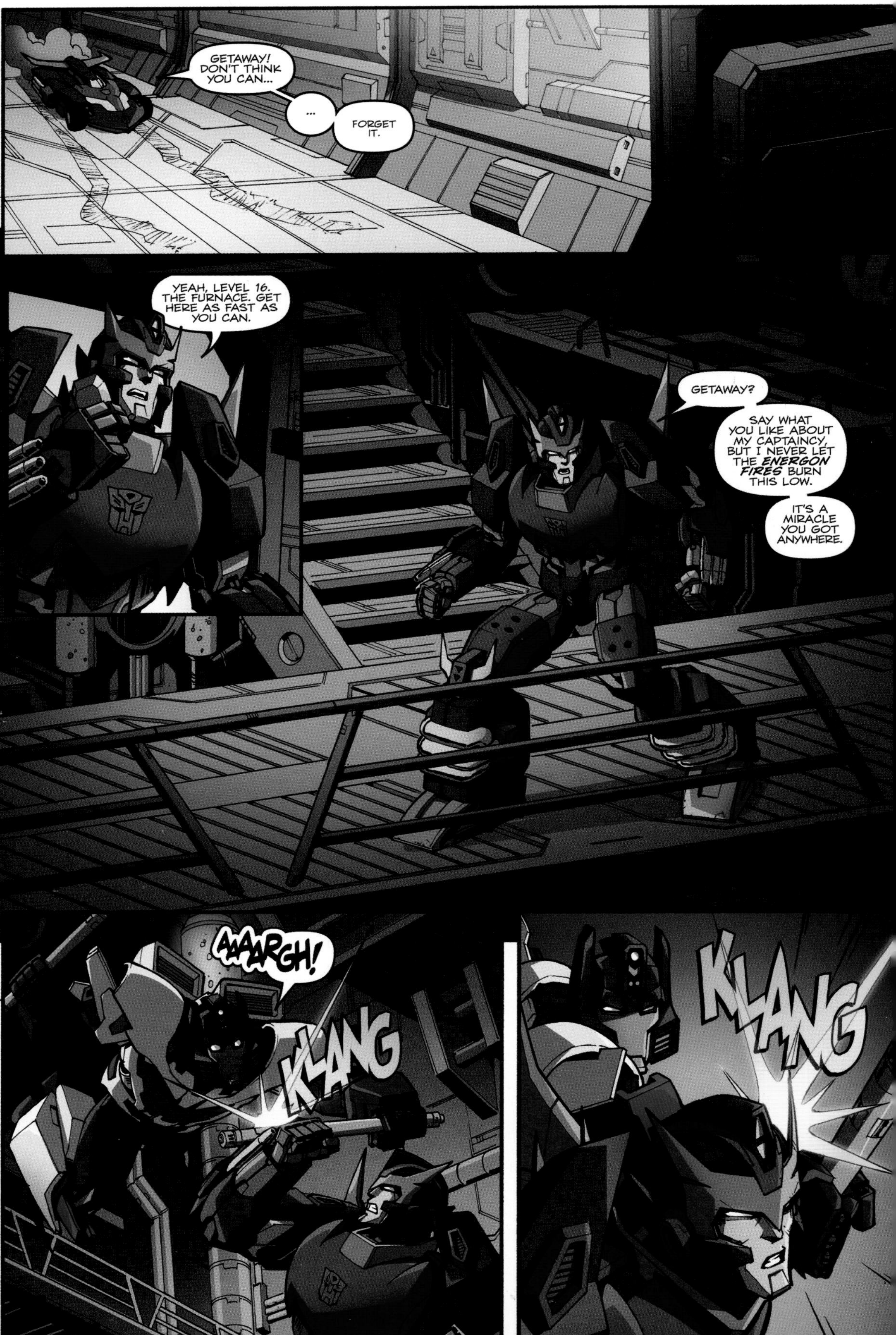
GETAWAY! DON'T THINK YOU CAN...
...
FORGET IT.
YEAH, LEVEL 16. THE FURNACE. GET HERE AS FAST AS YOU CAN.
GETAWAY?
SAY WHAT YOU LIKE ABOUT MY CAPTAINCY, BUT I NEVER LET THE ENERGON FIRES BURN THIS LOW.
IT'S A MIRACLE YOU GOT ANYWHERE.
AAAARGH!
KLANG
KLANG

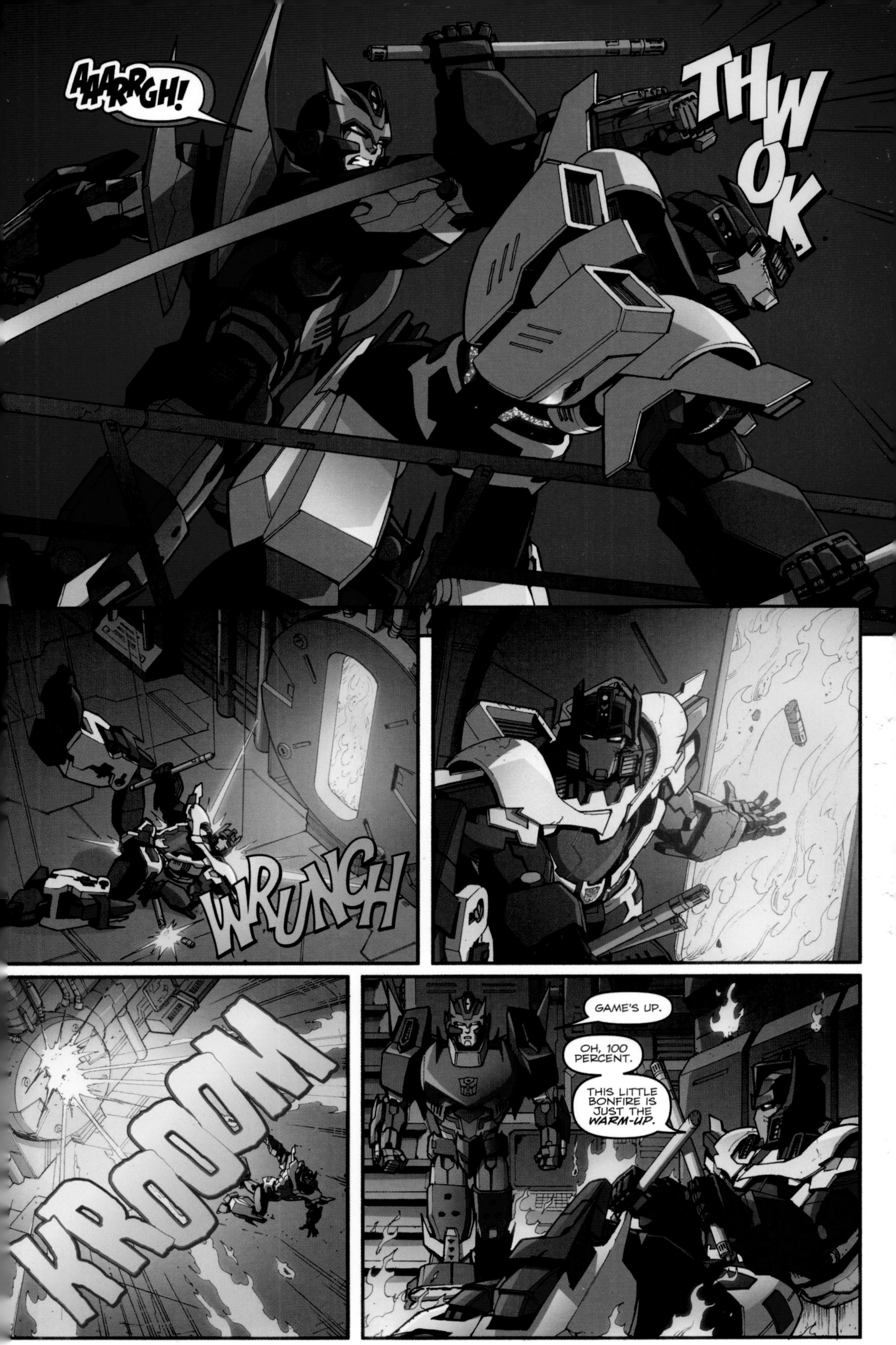

AAARRGH!
THWOK
WRUNCH
KROOOM
GAME'S UP.
OH, 100 PERCENT.
THIS LITTLE BONFIRE IS JUST THE WARM-UP.

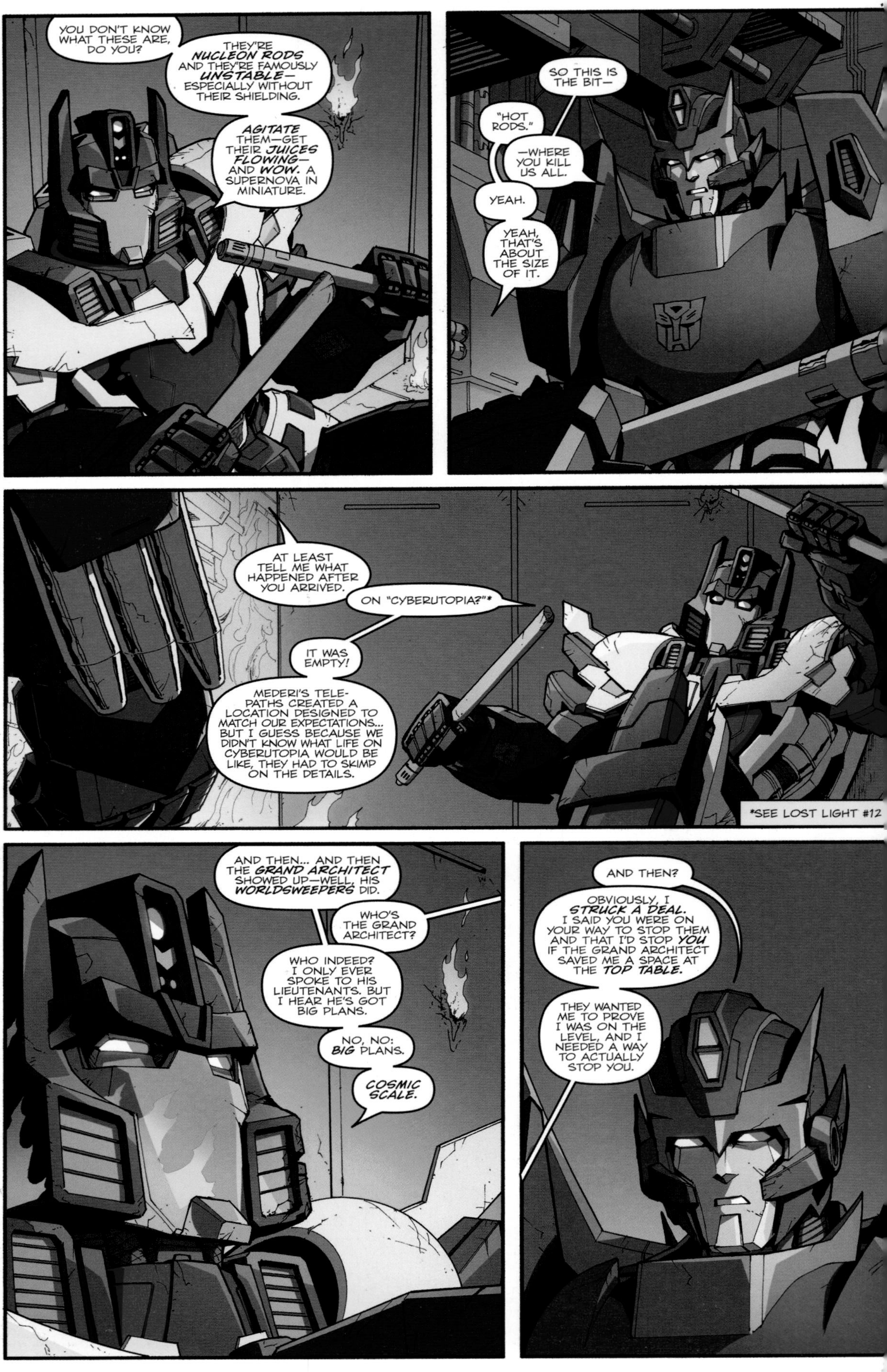
YOU DON'T KNOW WHAT THESE ARE, DO YOU?
THEY'RE NUCLEON RODS AND THEY'RE FAMOUSLY UNSTABLE— ESPECIALLY WITHOUT THEIR SHIELDING.
AGITATE THEM—GET THEIR JUICES FLOWING— AND WOW. A SUPERNOVA IN MINIATURE.
SO THIS IS THE BIT—
"HOT RODS."
—WHERE YOU KILL US ALL.
YEAH.
YEAH, THAT'S ABOUT THE SIZE OF IT.
AT LEAST TELL ME WHAT HAPPENED AFTER YOU ARRIVED.
ON "CYBERUTOPIA?"*
IT WAS EMPTY!
MEDERI'S TELE-PATHS CREATED A LOCATION DESIGNED TO MATCH OUR EXPECTATIONS... BUT I GUESS BECAUSE WE DIDN'T KNOW WHAT LIFE ON CYBERUTOPIA WOULD BE LIKE, THEY HAD TO SKIMP ON THE DETAILS.
*SEE LOST LIGHT #12
AND THEN... AND THEN THE GRAND ARCHITECT SHOWED UP—WELL, HIS WORLDSWEEPERS DID.
WHO'S THE GRAND ARCHITECT?
WHO INDEED? I ONLY EVER SPOKE TO HIS LIEUTENANTS. BUT I HEAR HE'S GOT BIG PLANS.
NO, NO: BIG PLANS.
COSMIC SCALE.
AND THEN?
OBVIOUSLY, I STRUCK A DEAL. I SAID YOU WERE ON YOUR WAY TO STOP THEM AND THAT I'D STOP YOU IF THE GRAND ARCHITECT SAVED ME A SPACE AT THE TOP TABLE.
THEY WANTED ME TO PROVE I WAS ON THE LEVEL, AND I NEEDED A WAY TO ACTUALLY STOP YOU.

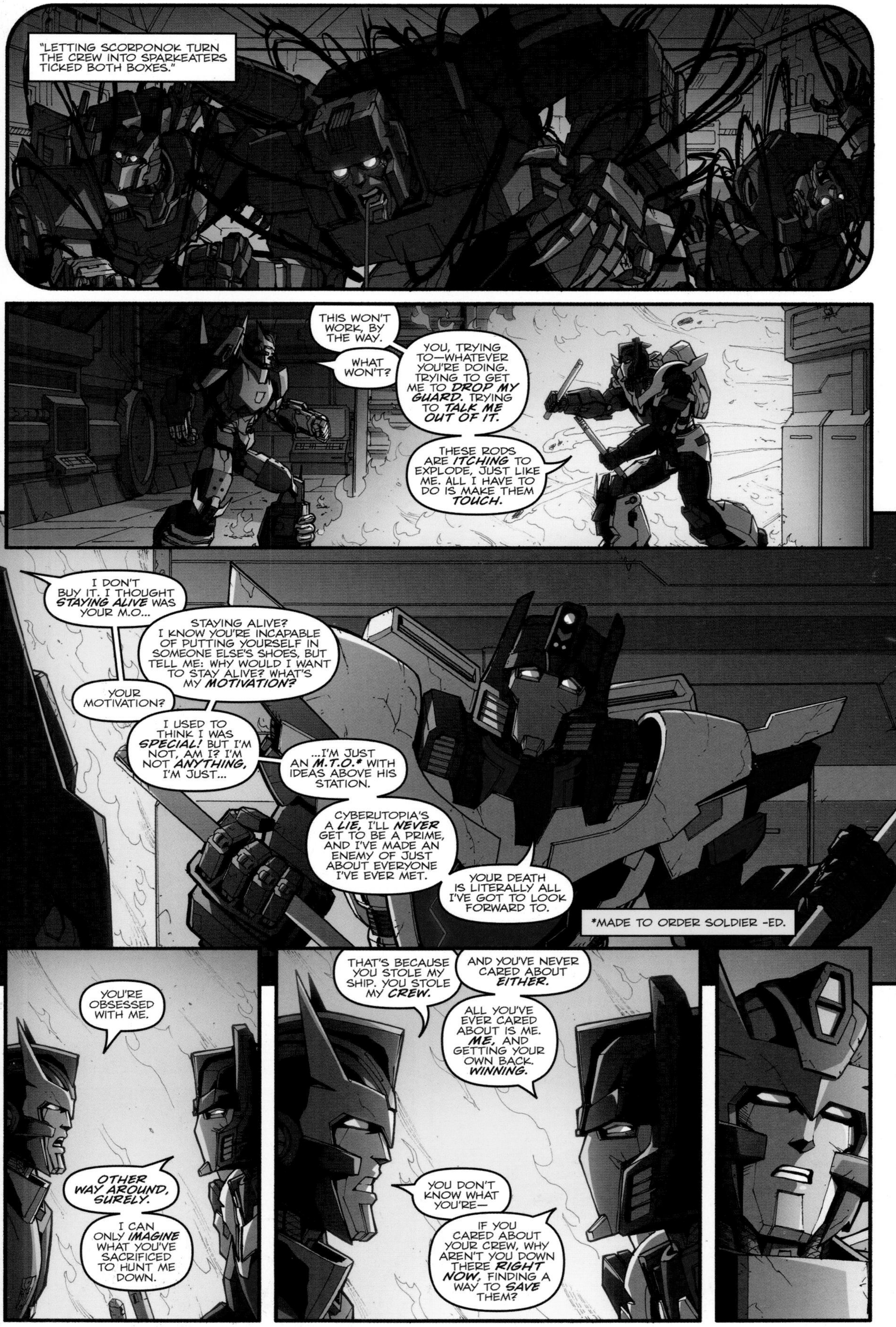
"LETTING SCORPONOK TURN THE CREW INTO SPARKEATERS TICKED BOTH BOXES."
THIS WON'T WORK, BY THE WAY.
WHAT WON'T?
YOU, TRYING TO—WHATEVER YOU'RE DOING. TRYING TO GET ME TO DROP MY GUARD. TRYING TO TALK ME OUT OF IT.
THESE RODS ARE ITCHING TO EXPLODE, JUST LIKE ME. ALL I HAVE TO DO IS MAKE THEM TOUCH.
I DON'T BUY IT. I THOUGHT STAYING ALIVE WAS YOUR M.O...
STAYING ALIVE? I KNOW YOU'RE INCAPABLE OF PUTTING YOURSELF IN SOMEONE ELSE'S SHOES, BUT TELL ME: WHY WOULD I WANT TO STAY ALIVE? WHAT'S MY MOTIVATION?
YOUR MOTIVATION?
I USED TO THINK I WAS SPECIAL! BUT I'M NOT, AM I? I'M NOT ANYTHING, I'M JUST...
...I'M JUST AN M.T.O.* WITH IDEAS ABOVE HIS STATION.
CYBERUTOPIA'S A LIE, I'LL NEVER GET TO BE A PRIME, AND I'VE MADE AN ENEMY OF JUST ABOUT EVERYONE I'VE EVER MET.
YOUR DEATH IS LITERALLY ALL I'VE GOT TO LOOK FORWARD TO.
*MADE TO ORDER SOLDIER -ED.
YOU'RE OBSESSED WITH ME.
OTHER WAY AROUND, SURELY.
I CAN ONLY IMAGINE WHAT YOU'VE SACRIFICED TO HUNT ME DOWN.
THAT'S BECAUSE YOU STOLE MY SHIP. YOU STOLE MY CREW.
AND YOU'VE NEVER CARED ABOUT EITHER.
ALL YOU'VE EVER CARED ABOUT IS ME. ME, AND GETTING YOUR OWN BACK. WINNING.
YOU DON'T KNOW WHAT YOU'RE—
IF YOU CARED ABOUT YOUR CREW, WHY AREN'T YOU DOWN THERE RIGHT NOW, FINDING A WAY TO SAVE THEM?

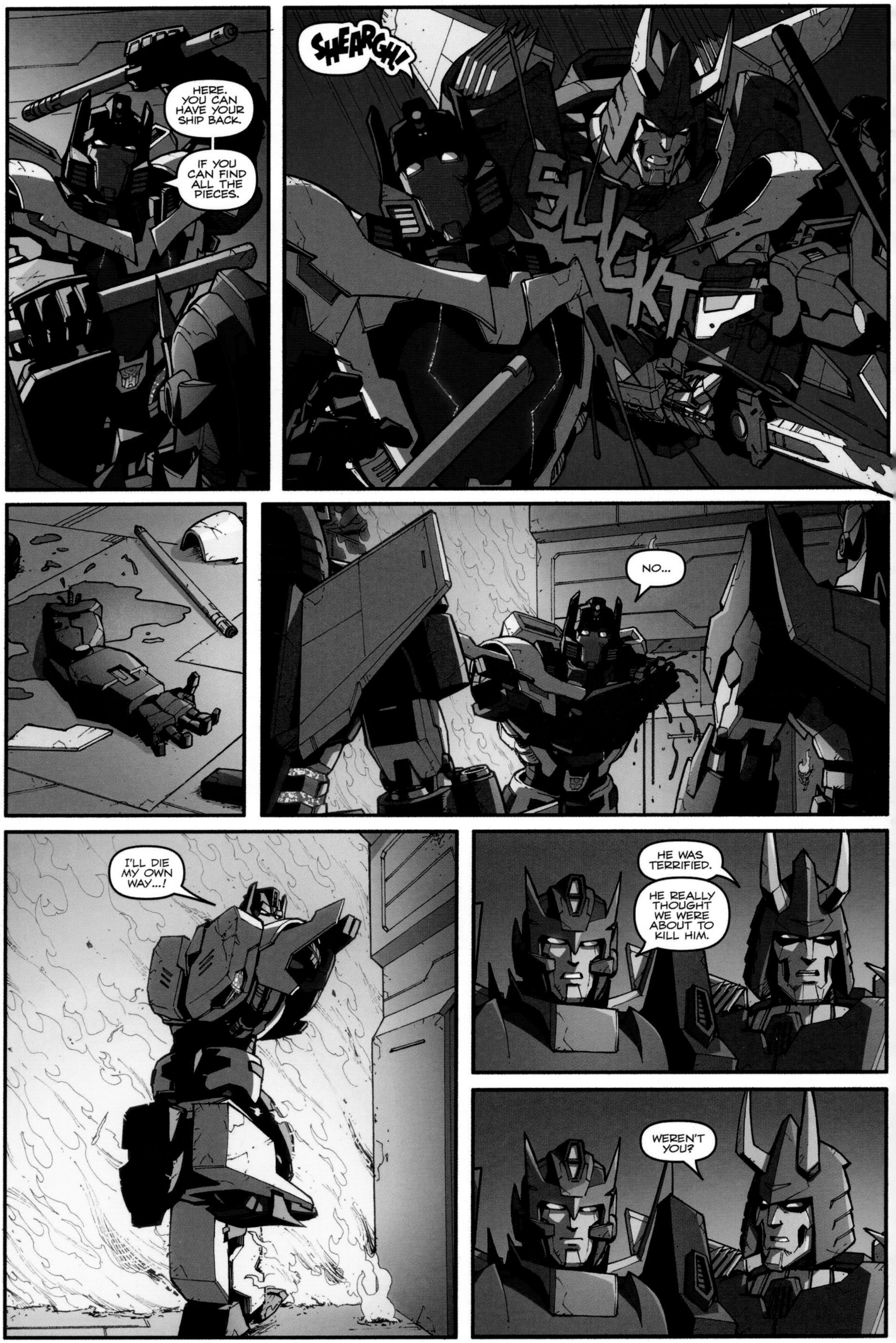
HERE. YOU CAN HAVE YOUR SHIP BACK.
IF YOU CAN FIND ALL THE PIECES.
SHEARGH!
SLICKT
NO...
I'LL DIE MY OWN WAY...!
HE WAS TERRIFIED.
HE REALLY THOUGHT WE WERE ABOUT TO KILL HIM.
WEREN'T YOU?

GETAWAY!

RODIMUS!
IT'S NOT SAFE!

KA-
KOOM

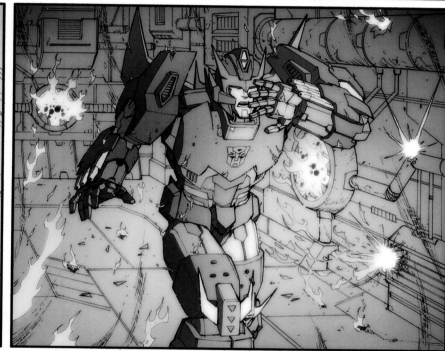

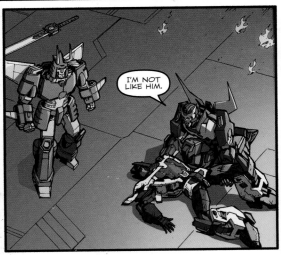

I'M NOT LIKE HIM.

THE SPRINKLERS SHOULD'VE KICKED IN BY NOW. MUST'VE BEEN DAMAGED BY THE FIRE...

...CAN YOU SAY "DESIGN FLAW"?

IS THERE NO BACK-UP SYSTEM?

SOMEWHERE...

I'LL TELL YOU WHO'D KNOW *EXACTLY* HOW THE SPRINKLER SYSTEM WORKS: ULTRA MAGNUS. HE'S *OBSESSED* WITH THEM! SWERVE SAYS HE WRITES SPRINKLER *FAN FICTION.*

I DON'T UNDERSTAND HALF OF WHAT SWERVE SAYS.

I DON'T *LISTEN* TO HALF OF WHAT SWERVE SAYS.

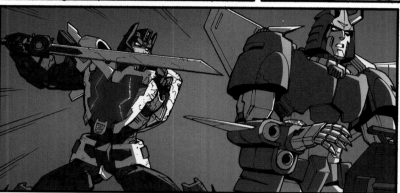

PRIMUS...?

IS—IS THIS IT? ARE YOU MAKING ME A *PRIME?*

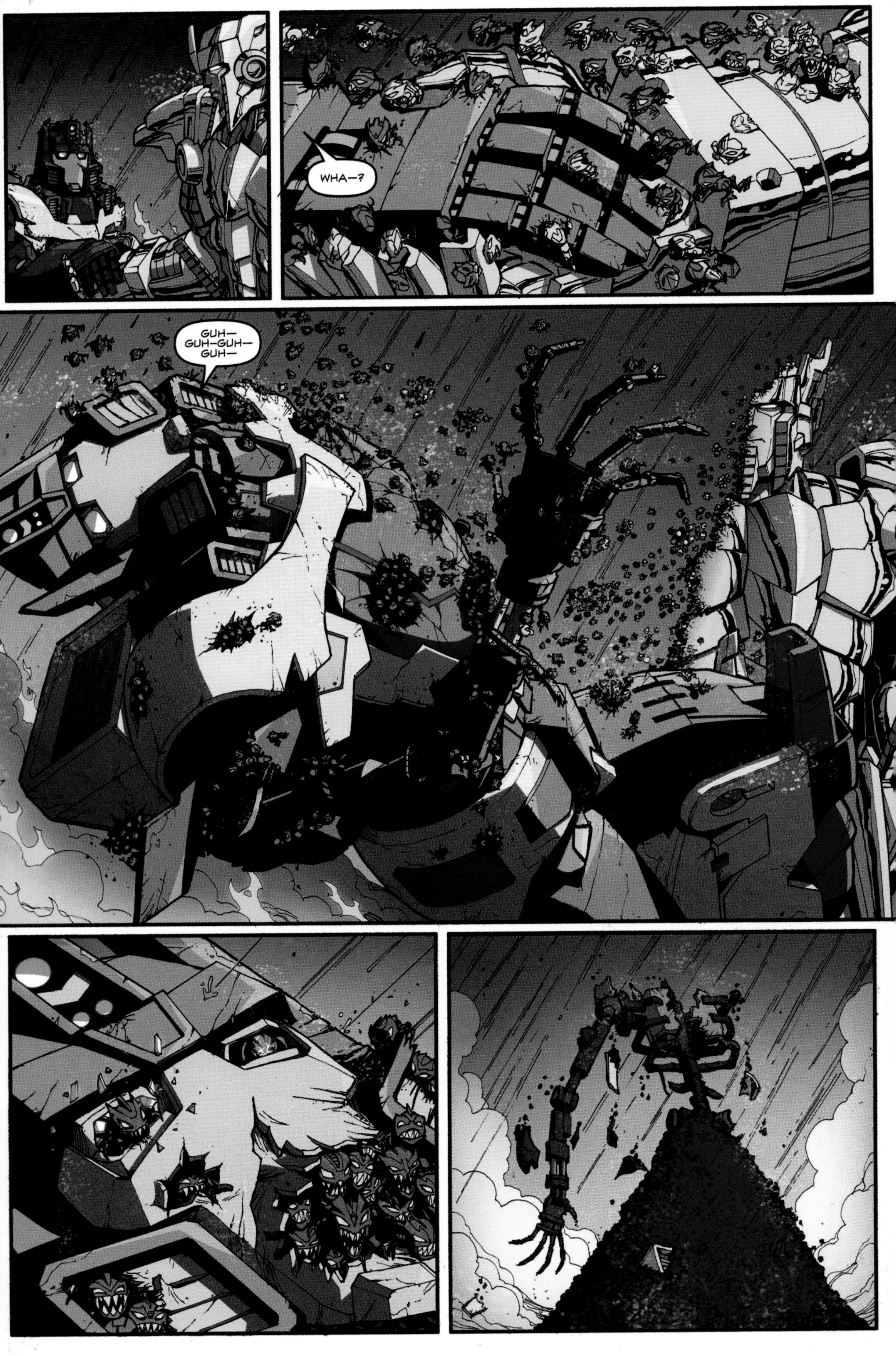
WHA—?
GUH— GUH-GUH-GUH— GUH—

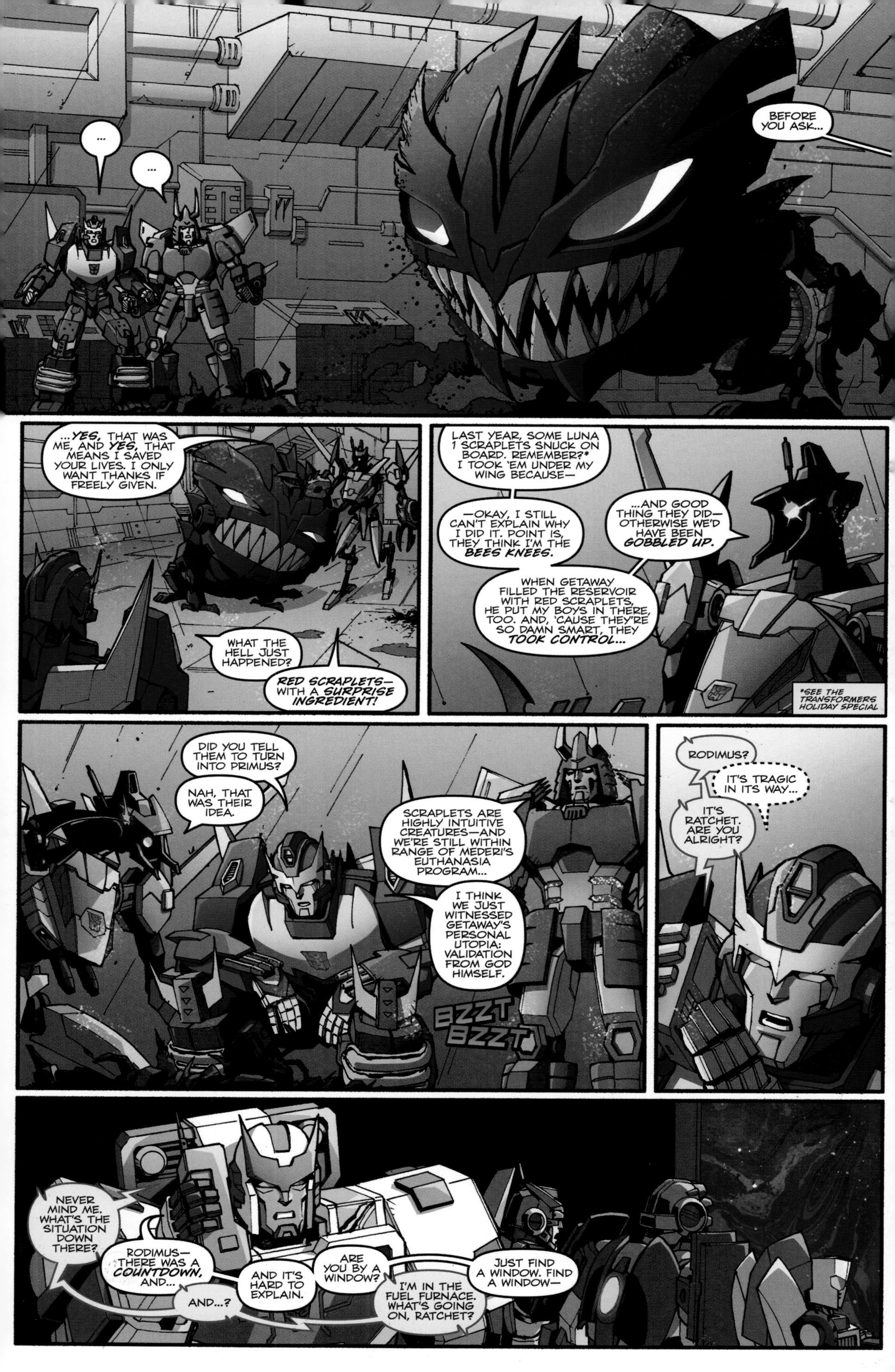

...
...
BEFORE YOU ASK...
...YES, THAT WAS ME, AND YES, THAT MEANS I SAVED YOUR LIVES. I ONLY WANT THANKS IF FREELY GIVEN.
WHAT THE HELL JUST HAPPENED?
RED SCRAPLETS—WITH A SURPRISE INGREDIENT!
LAST YEAR, SOME LUNA 1 SCRAPLETS SNUCK ON BOARD. REMEMBER?* I TOOK 'EM UNDER MY WING BECAUSE—
—OKAY, I STILL CAN'T EXPLAIN WHY I DID IT. POINT IS, THEY THINK I'M THE BEES KNEES.
WHEN GETAWAY FILLED THE RESERVOIR WITH RED SCRAPLETS, HE PUT MY BOYS IN THERE, TOO. AND, 'CAUSE THEY'RE SO DAMN SMART, THEY TOOK CONTROL...
...AND GOOD THING THEY DID—OTHERWISE WE'D HAVE BEEN GOBBLED UP.
*SEE THE TRANSFORMERS HOLIDAY SPECIAL
DID YOU TELL THEM TO TURN INTO PRIMUS?
NAH, THAT WAS THEIR IDEA.
SCRAPLETS ARE HIGHLY INTUITIVE CREATURES—AND WE'RE STILL WITHIN RANGE OF MEDERI'S EUTHANASIA PROGRAM...
I THINK WE JUST WITNESSED GETAWAY'S PERSONAL UTOPIA: VALIDATION FROM GOD HIMSELF.
BZZT BZZT
RODIMUS?
IT'S TRAGIC IN ITS WAY...
IT'S RATCHET. ARE YOU ALRIGHT?
NEVER MIND ME. WHAT'S THE SITUATION DOWN THERE?
RODIMUS—THERE WAS A COUNTDOWN, AND...
AND...?
AND IT'S HARD TO EXPLAIN.
ARE YOU BY A WINDOW?
I'M IN THE FUEL FURNACE. WHAT'S GOING ON, RATCHET?
JUST FIND A WINDOW. FIND A WINDOW—

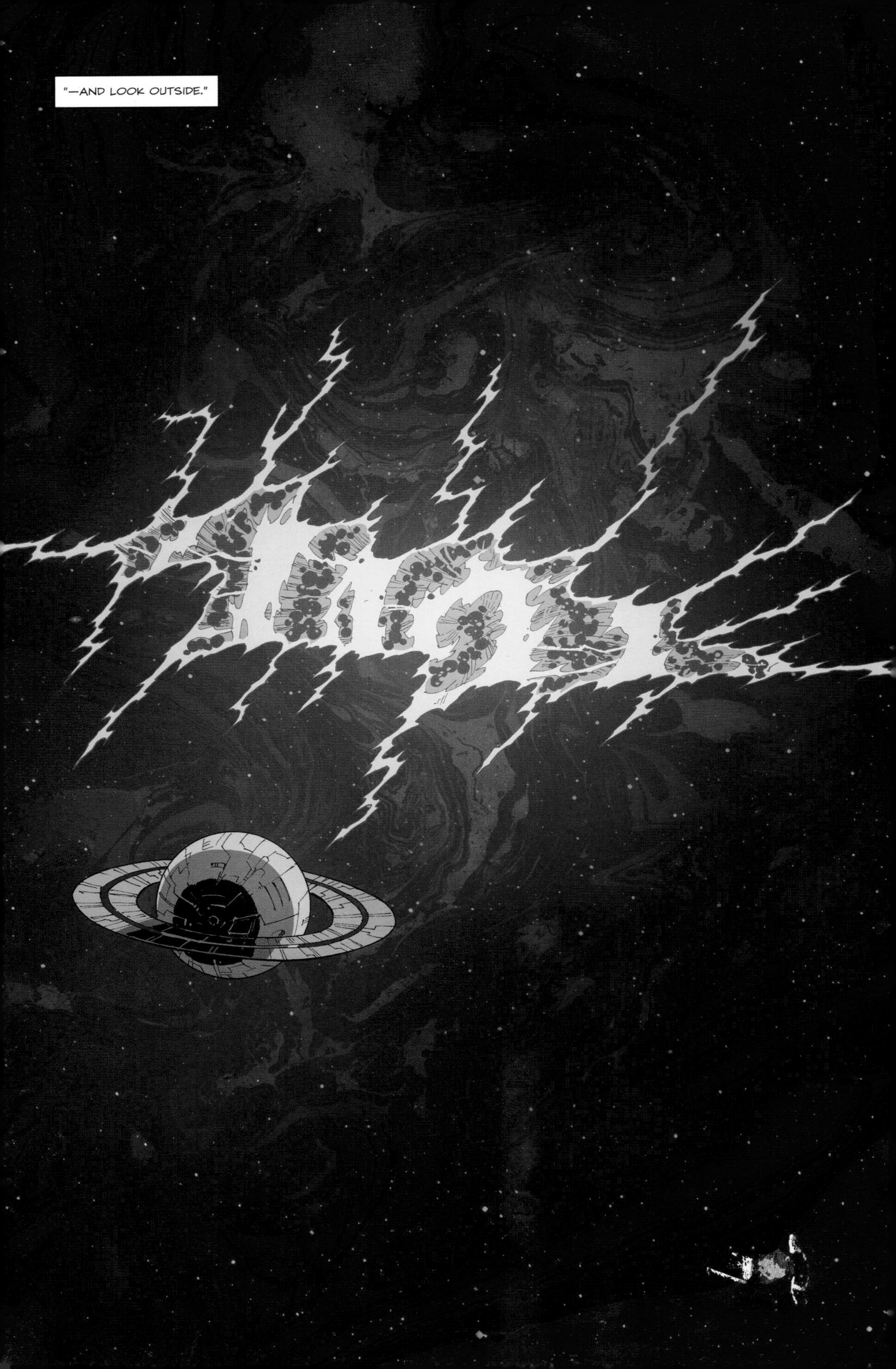
"—AND LOOK OUTSIDE."

ART BY **GEOFF SENIOR**
COLORS BY **JOSH BURCHAM**

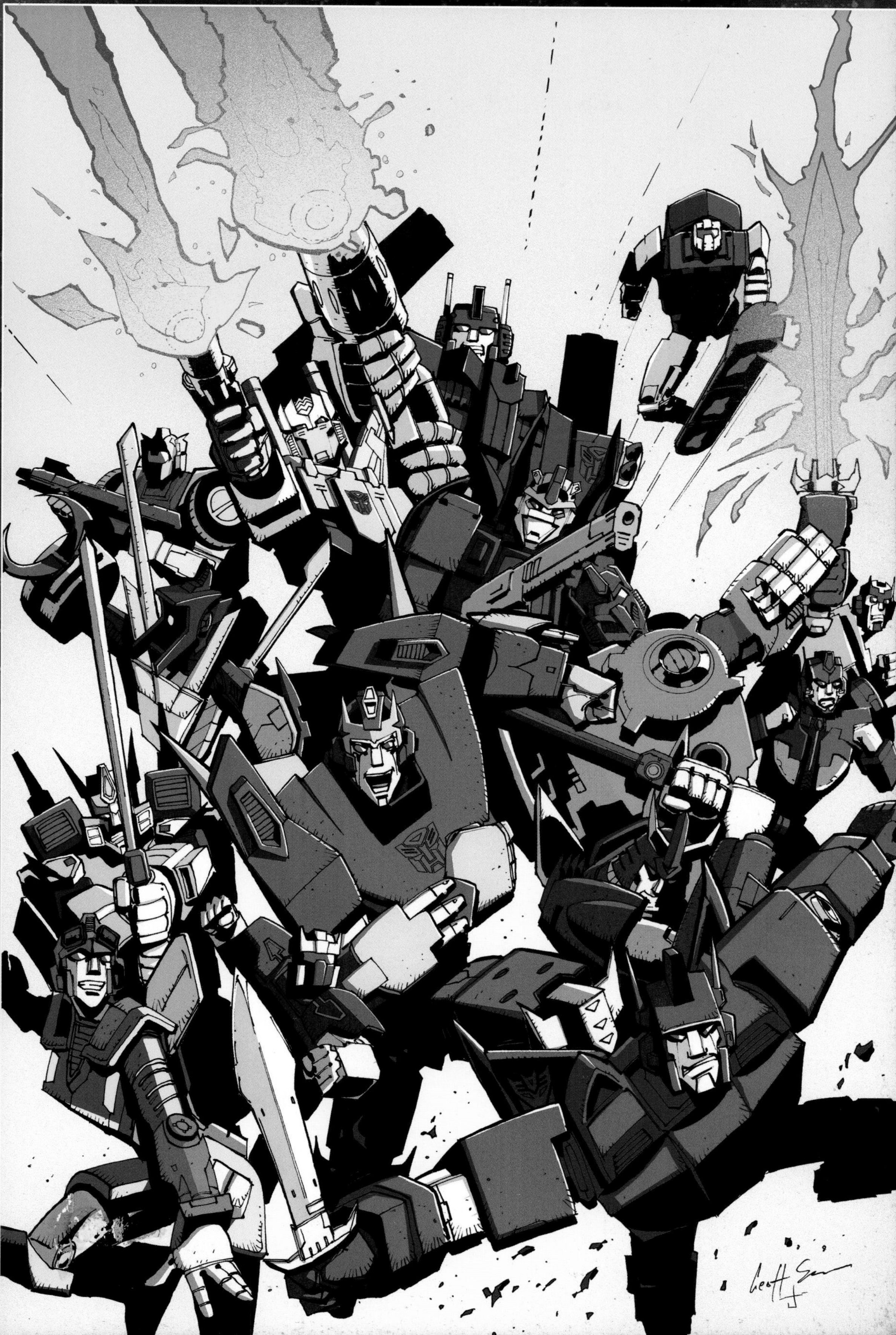

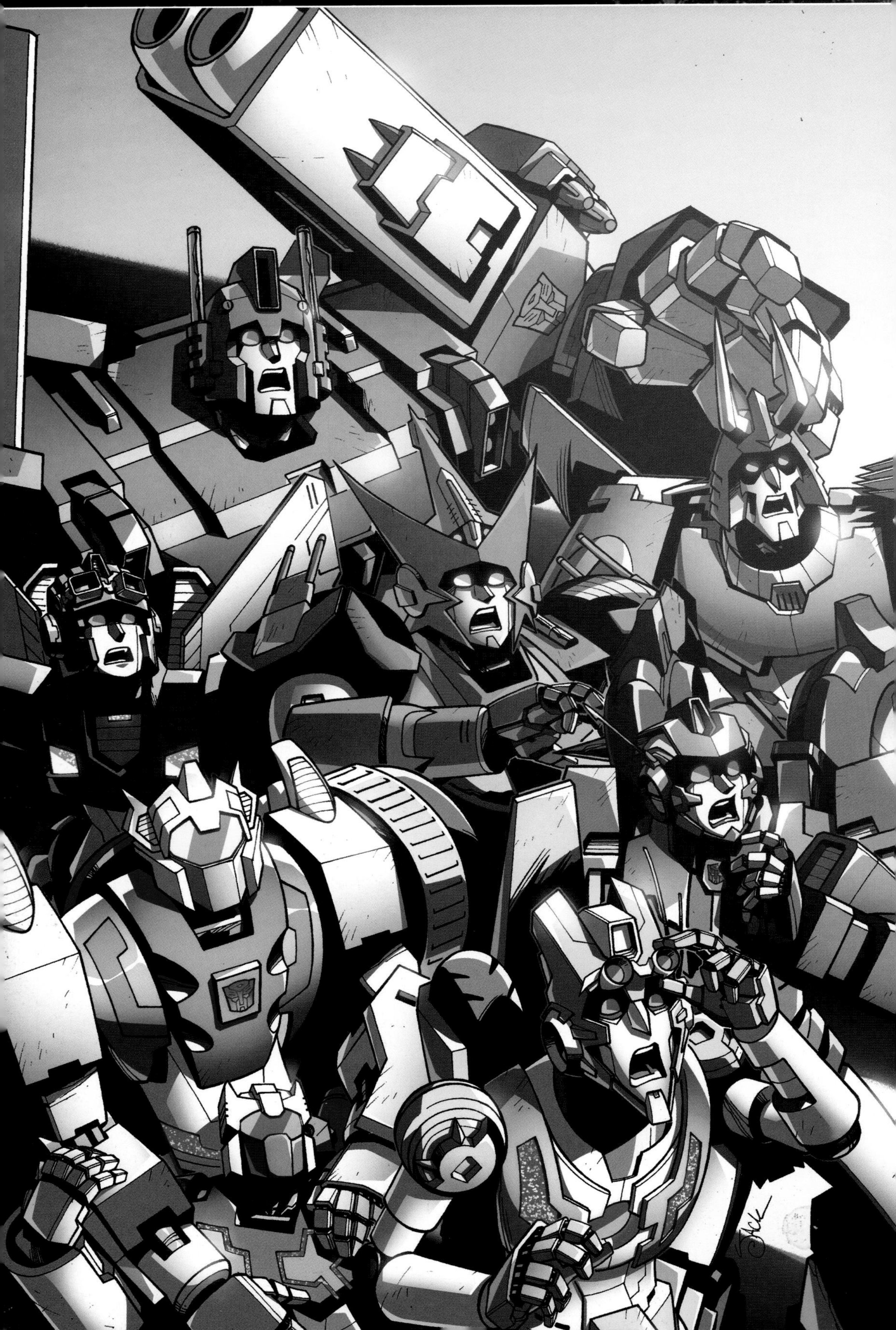

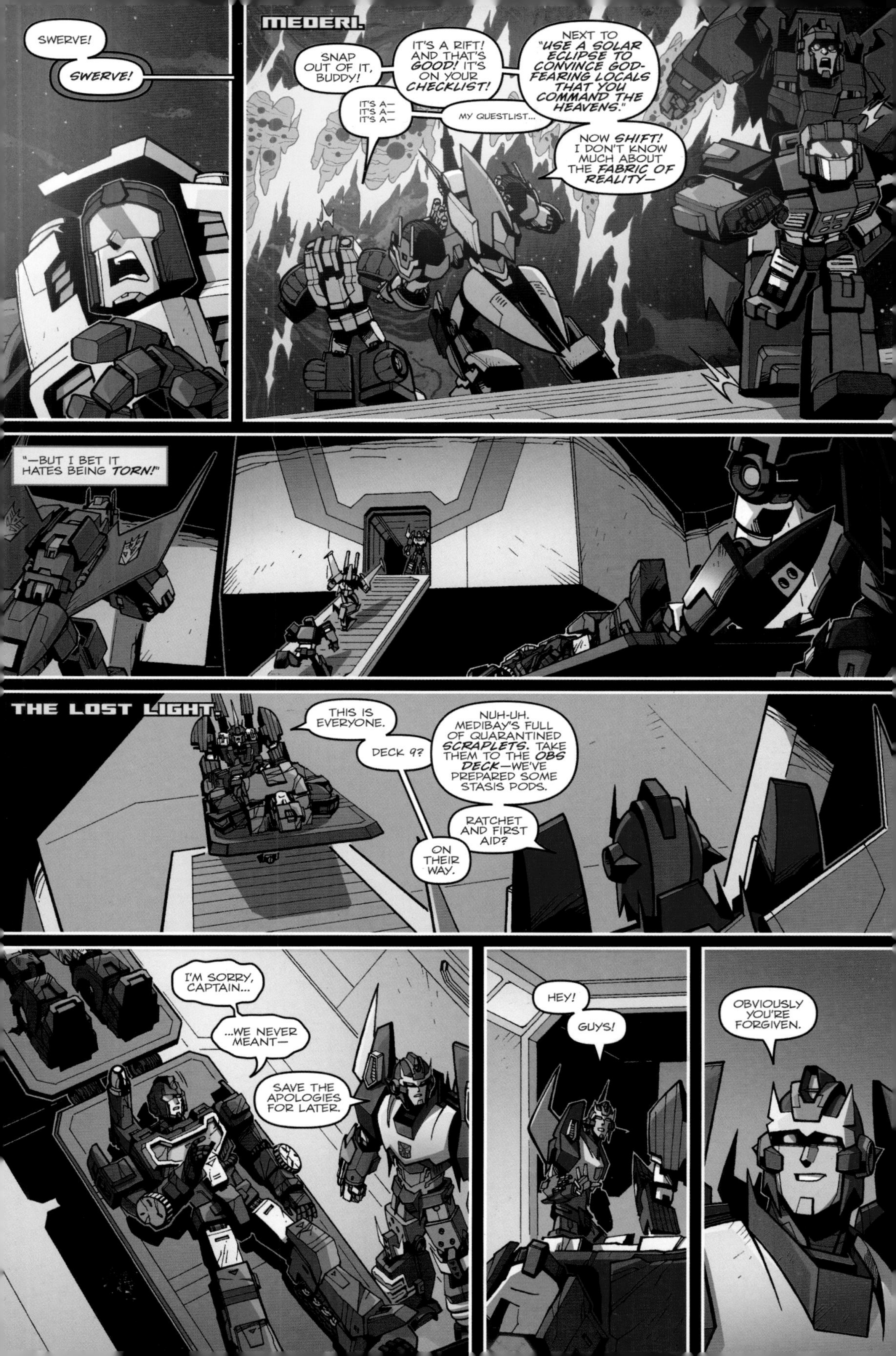
SWERVE!
SWERVE!
MEDERI.
SNAP OUT OF IT, BUDDY!
IT'S A RIFT! AND THAT'S GOOD! IT'S ON YOUR CHECKLIST!
NEXT TO "USE A SOLAR ECLIPSE TO CONVINCE GOD-FEARING LOCALS THAT YOU COMMAND THE HEAVENS."
IT'S A— IT'S A— IT'S A—
MY QUESTLIST...
NOW SHIFT! I DON'T KNOW MUCH ABOUT THE FABRIC OF REALITY—
"—BUT I BET IT HATES BEING TORN!"
THE LOST LIGHT.
THIS IS EVERYONE.
DECK 9?
NUH-UH. MEDIBAY'S FULL OF QUARANTINED SCRAPLETS. TAKE THEM TO THE OBS DECK—WE'VE PREPARED SOME STASIS PODS.
RATCHET AND FIRST AID?
ON THEIR WAY.
I'M SORRY, CAPTAIN...
...WE NEVER MEANT—
SAVE THE APOLOGIES FOR LATER.
HEY!
GUYS!
OBVIOUSLY YOU'RE FORGIVEN.

I DON'T KNOW IF THE "TELEPATHS" CAN SURVIVE OUTSIDE OF *WARD ZERO*, BUT WE CAN'T LEAVE THEM HERE.

THE DECEPTICON WITH THE MOUTH— THE RED ONE...

FLYHIGH? MISFIRE?

HE SEEMS TO KNOW A THING OR TWO ABOUT ORGANICS. ASK HIM.

ANYONE ELSE SEEN THIS? I'M PRETTY SURE IT WASN'T HERE FIVE MINUTES AG—

—OWWW!

IT'S CALLED A *GEOBOMB*. YOU CAN WORK OUT THE REST.

GREAT...

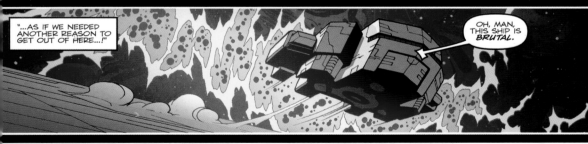

"...AS IF WE NEEDED ANOTHER REASON TO GET OUT OF HERE...!"

OH, MAN, THIS SHIP IS *BRUTAL*.

SERIOUSLY, IT HANDLES LIKE A *DREAM!*

IF YOU GET US CLEAR OF THE RIFT, YOU CAN KEEP IT.

REALLY?!

NO.

SORRY.

TIMES LIKE THESE, I SAY THE FIRST THING THAT COMES INTO MY HEAD.

"TIMES LIKE THESE..."

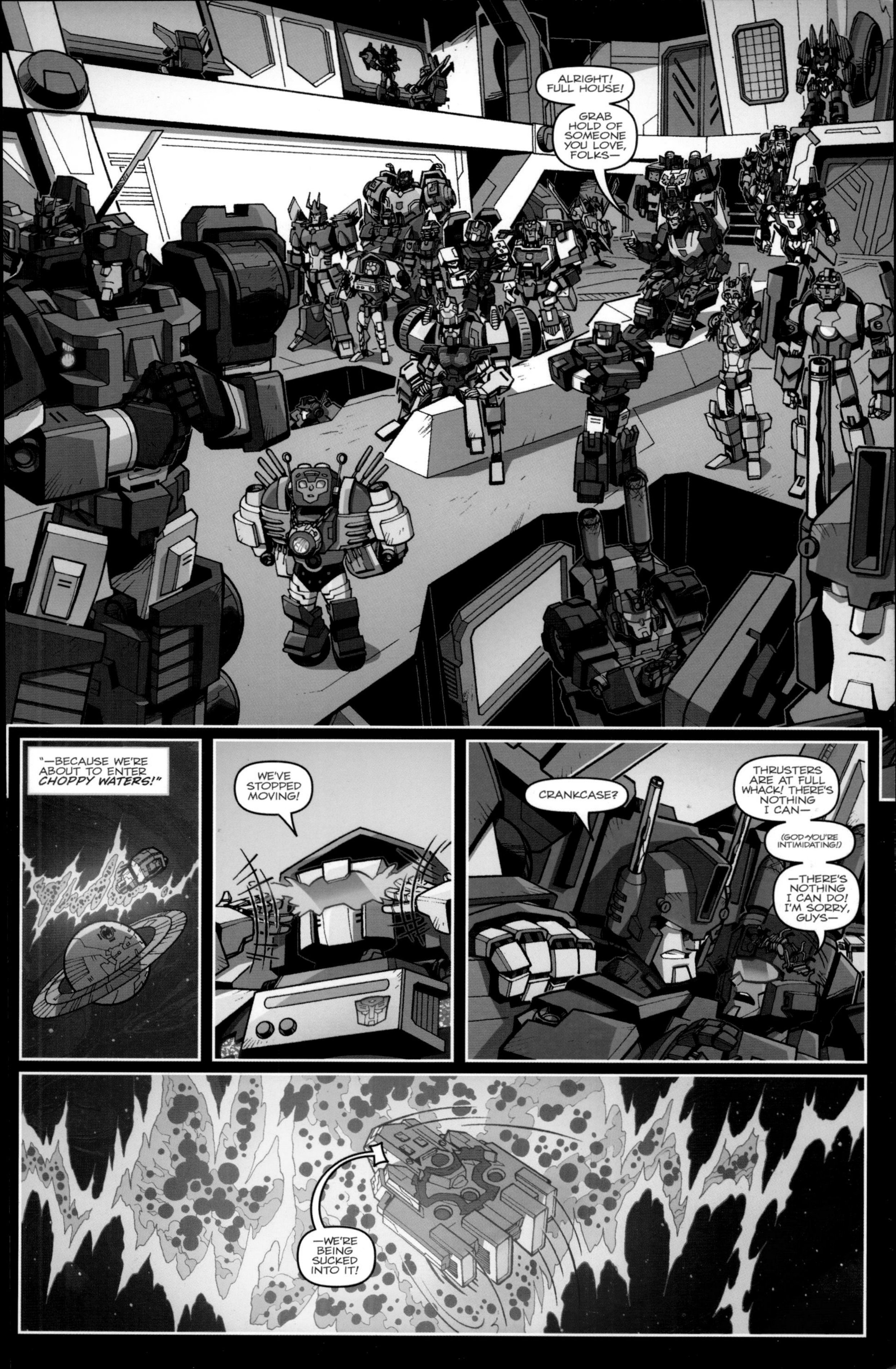
ALRIGHT! FULL HOUSE!
GRAB HOLD OF SOMEONE YOU LOVE, FOLKS—
"—BECAUSE WE'RE ABOUT TO ENTER CHOPPY WATERS!"
WE'VE STOPPED MOVING!
CRANKCASE?
THRUSTERS ARE AT FULL WHACK! THERE'S NOTHING I CAN—
(GOD—YOU'RE INTIMIDATING!)
—THERE'S NOTHING I CAN DO! I'M SORRY, GUYS—
—WE'RE BEING SUCKED INTO IT!

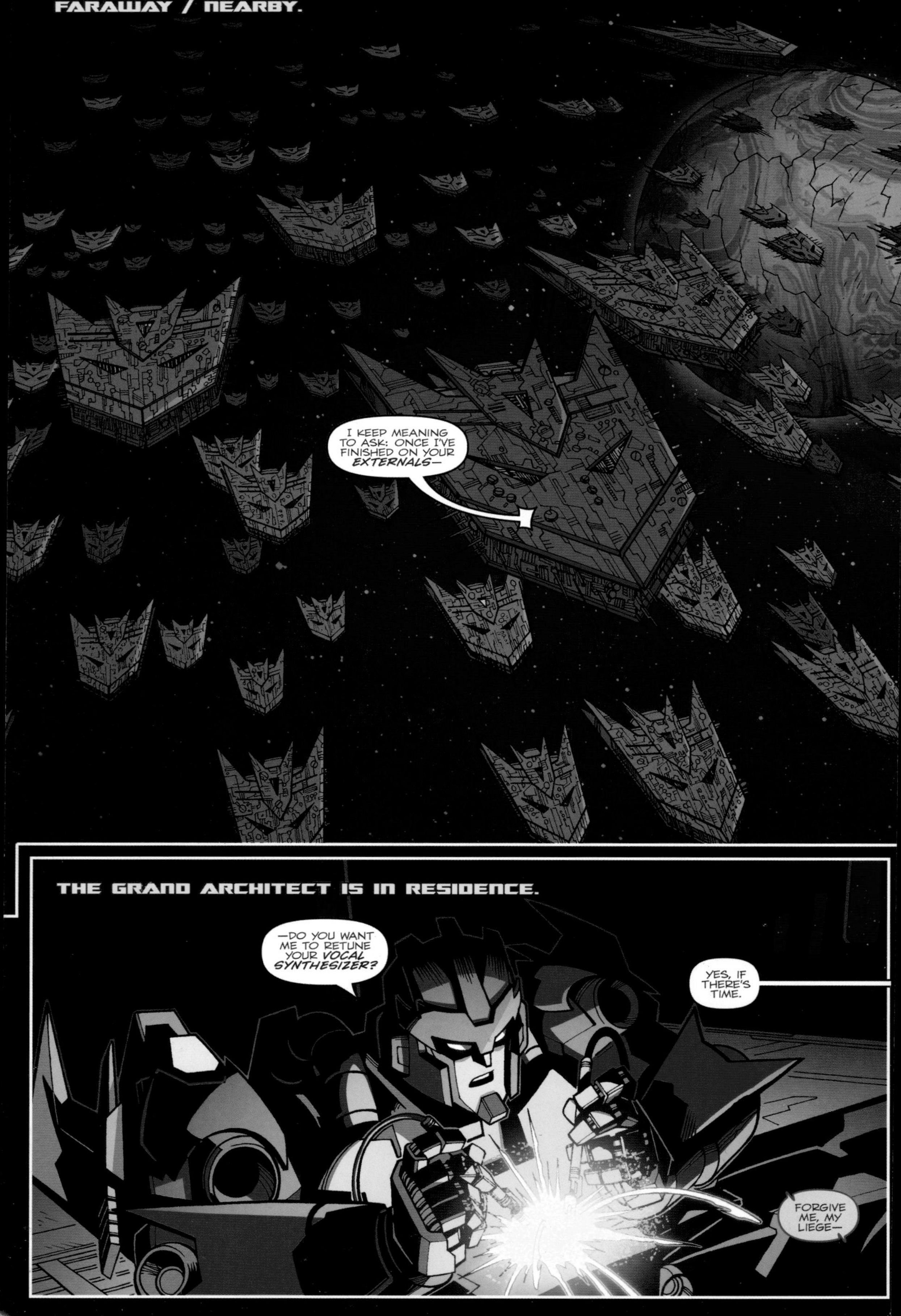
FARAWAY / NEARBY.
I KEEP MEANING TO ASK: ONCE I'VE FINISHED ON YOUR *EXTERNALS*—
THE GRAND ARCHITECT IS IN RESIDENCE.
—DO YOU WANT ME TO RETUNE YOUR *VOCAL SYNTHESIZER?*
YES, IF THERE'S TIME.
FORGIVE ME, MY LIEGE—

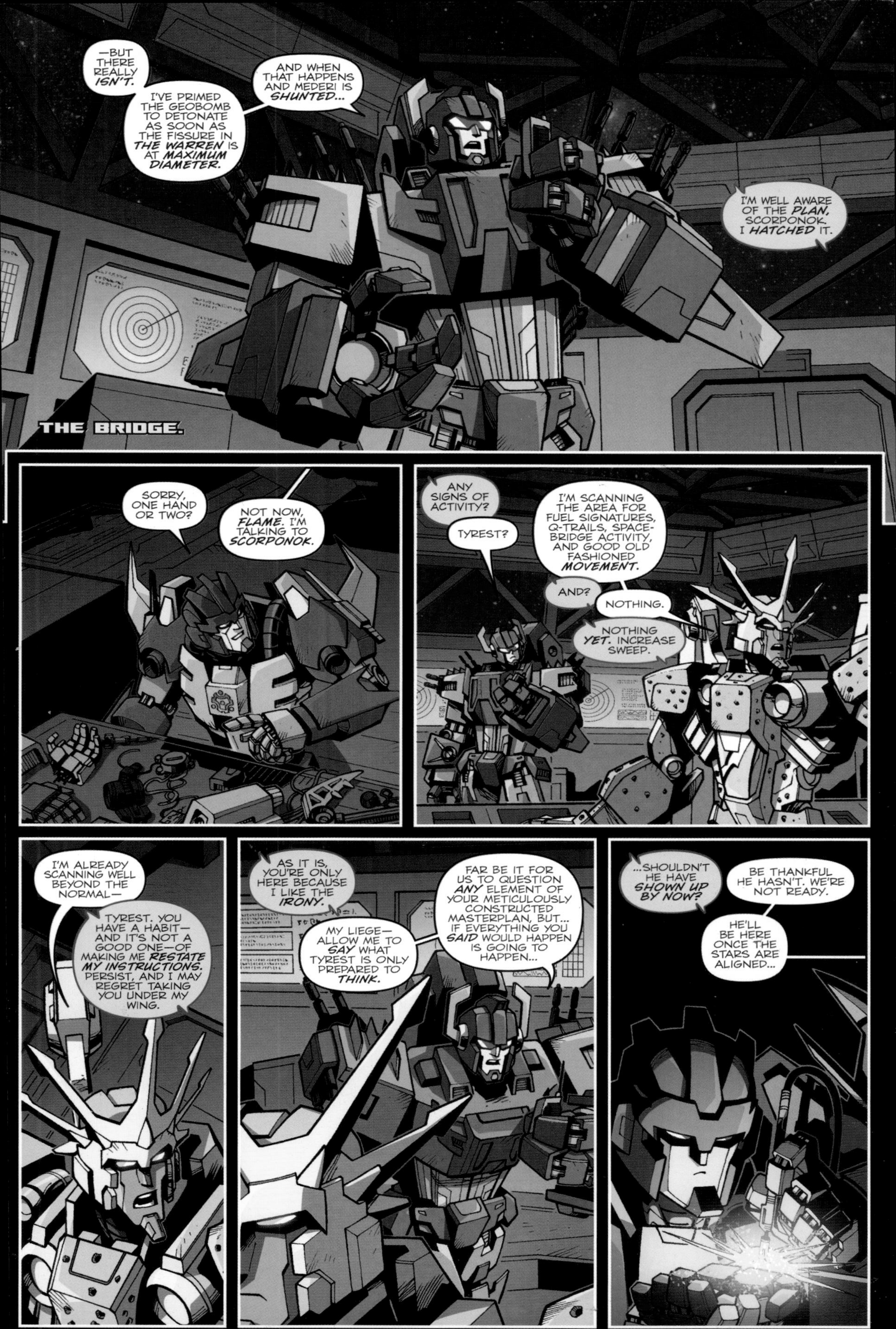
—BUT THERE REALLY ISN'T.
I'VE PRIMED THE GEOBOMB TO DETONATE AS SOON AS THE FISSURE IN THE WARREN IS AT MAXIMUM DIAMETER.
AND WHEN THAT HAPPENS AND MEDERI IS SHUNTED...
I'M WELL AWARE OF THE PLAN, SCORPONOK. I HATCHED IT.
THE BRIDGE.
SORRY, ONE HAND OR TWO?
NOT NOW, FLAME. I'M TALKING TO SCORPONOK.
ANY SIGNS OF ACTIVITY?
TYREST?
I'M SCANNING THE AREA FOR FUEL SIGNATURES, Q-TRAILS, SPACE-BRIDGE ACTIVITY, AND GOOD OLD FASHIONED MOVEMENT.
AND?
NOTHING.
NOTHING YET. INCREASE SWEEP.
I'M ALREADY SCANNING WELL BEYOND THE NORMAL—
TYREST. YOU HAVE A HABIT—AND IT'S NOT A GOOD ONE—OF MAKING ME RESTATE MY INSTRUCTIONS. PERSIST, AND I MAY REGRET TAKING YOU UNDER MY WING.
AS IT IS, YOU'RE ONLY HERE BECAUSE I LIKE THE IRONY.
MY LIEGE—ALLOW ME TO SAY WHAT TYREST IS ONLY PREPARED TO THINK.
FAR BE IT FOR US TO QUESTION ANY ELEMENT OF YOUR METICULOUSLY CONSTRUCTED MASTERPLAN, BUT... IF EVERYTHING YOU SAID WOULD HAPPEN IS GOING TO HAPPEN...
...SHOULDN'T HE HAVE SHOWN UP BY NOW?
BE THANKFUL HE HASN'T. WE'RE NOT READY.
HE'LL BE HERE ONCE THE STARS ARE ALIGNED...

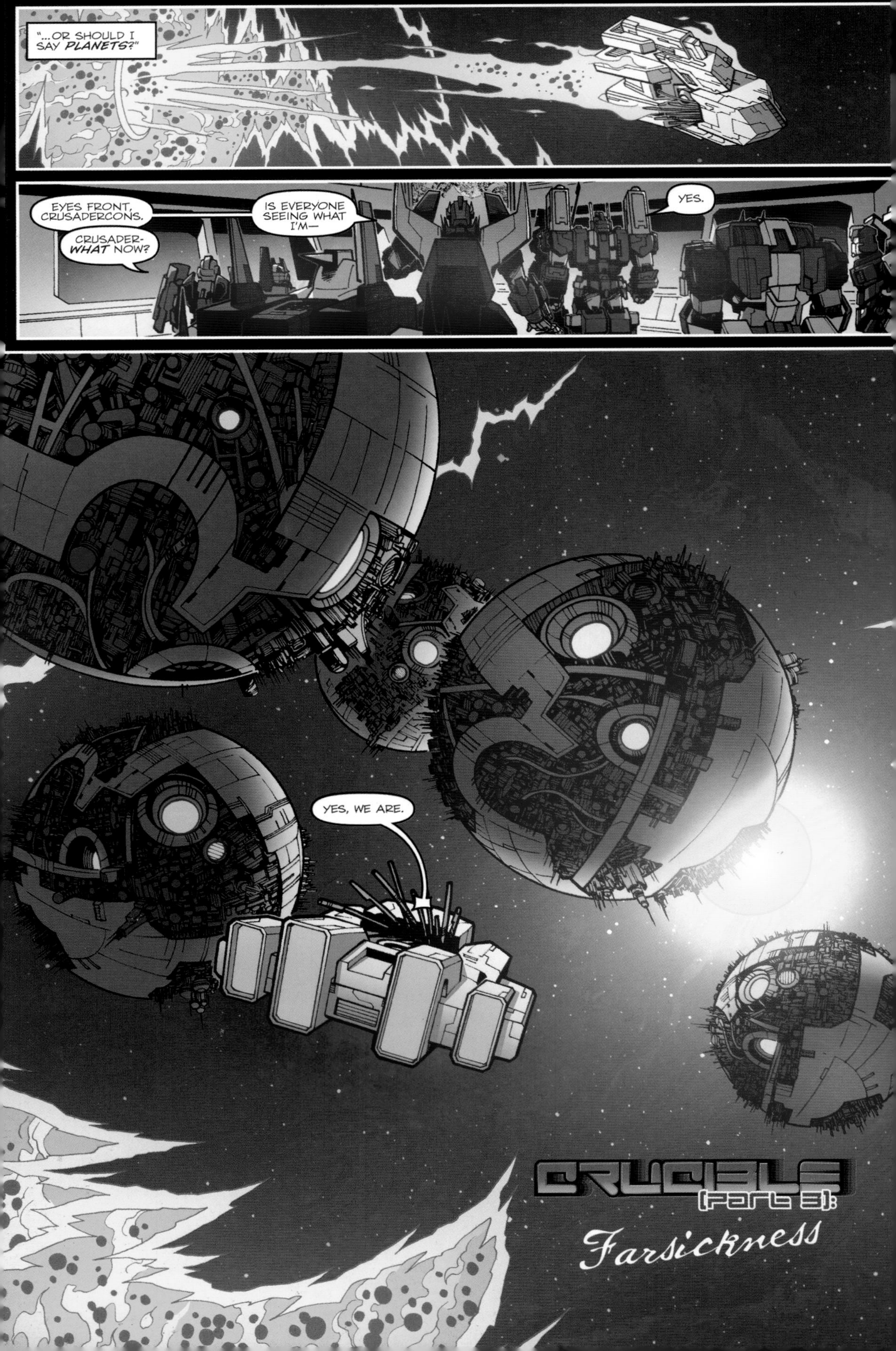
"...OR SHOULD I SAY *PLANETS?*"
EYES FRONT, CRUSADERCONS.
CRUSADER-*WHAT* NOW?
IS EVERYONE SEEING WHAT I'M—
YES.
YES, WE ARE.
CRUCIBLE
(PART 3):
Farsickness

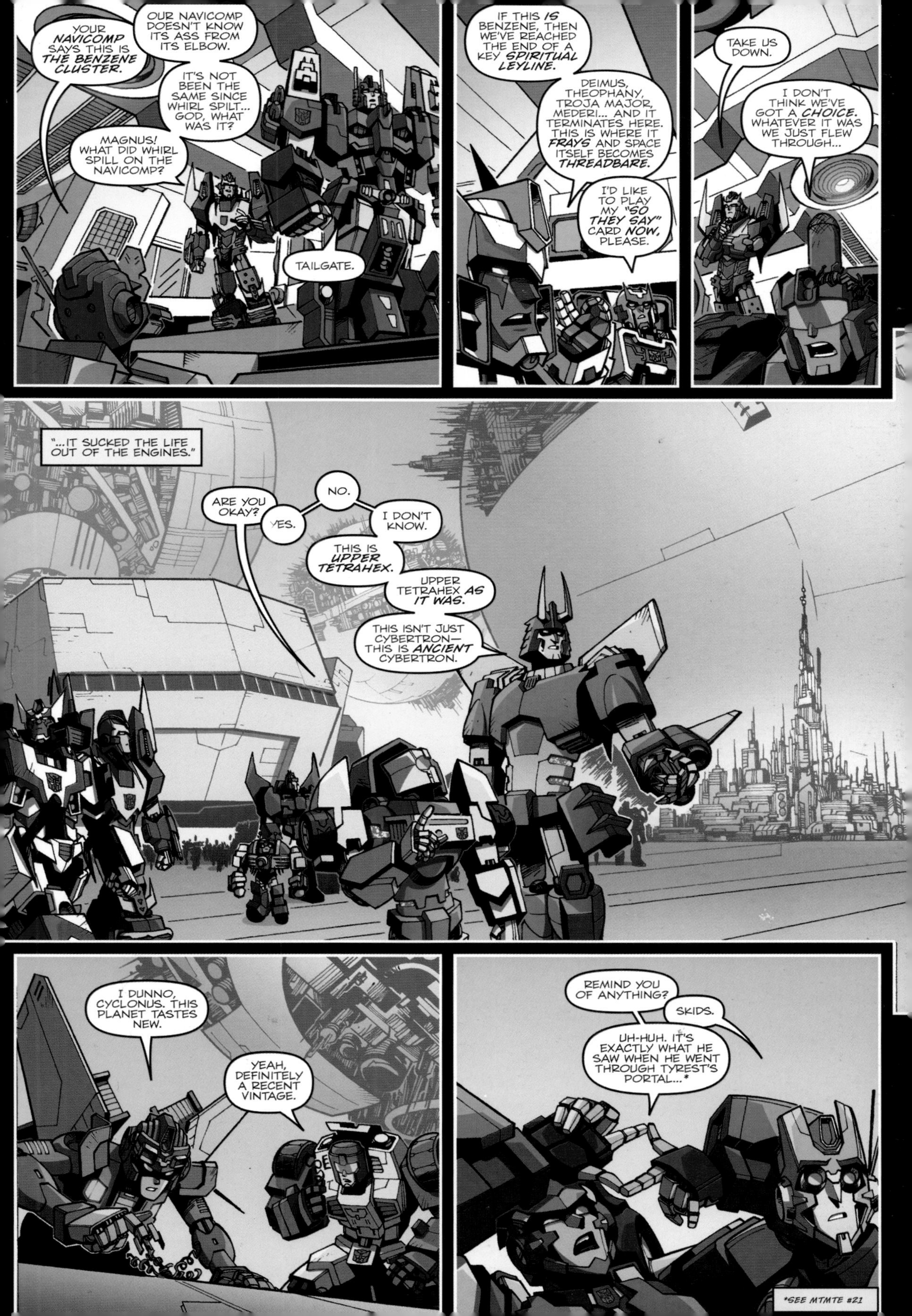
YOUR NAVICOMP SAYS THIS IS THE BENZENE CLUSTER.
OUR NAVICOMP DOESN'T KNOW ITS ASS FROM ITS ELBOW.
IT'S NOT BEEN THE SAME SINCE WHIRL SPILT... GOD, WHAT WAS IT?
MAGNUS! WHAT DID WHIRL SPILL ON THE NAVICOMP?
TAILGATE.
IF THIS IS BENZENE, THEN WE'VE REACHED THE END OF A KEY SPIRITUAL LEYLINE.
DEIMUS, THEOPHANY, TROJA MAJOR, MEDERI... AND IT TERMINATES HERE. THIS IS WHERE IT FRAYS AND SPACE ITSELF BECOMES THREADBARE.
I'D LIKE TO PLAY MY "SO THEY SAY" CARD NOW, PLEASE.
TAKE US DOWN.
I DON'T THINK WE'VE GOT A CHOICE. WHATEVER IT WAS WE JUST FLEW THROUGH...
"...IT SUCKED THE LIFE OUT OF THE ENGINES."
ARE YOU OKAY?
NO.
YES.
I DON'T KNOW.
THIS IS UPPER TETRAHEX.
UPPER TETRAHEX AS IT WAS.
THIS ISN'T JUST CYBERTRON— THIS IS ANCIENT CYBERTRON.
I DUNNO, CYCLONUS. THIS PLANET TASTES NEW.
YEAH, DEFINITELY A RECENT VINTAGE.
REMIND YOU OF ANYTHING?
SKIDS.
UH-HUH. IT'S EXACTLY WHAT HE SAW WHEN HE WENT THROUGH TYREST'S PORTAL...*
*SEE MTMTE #21

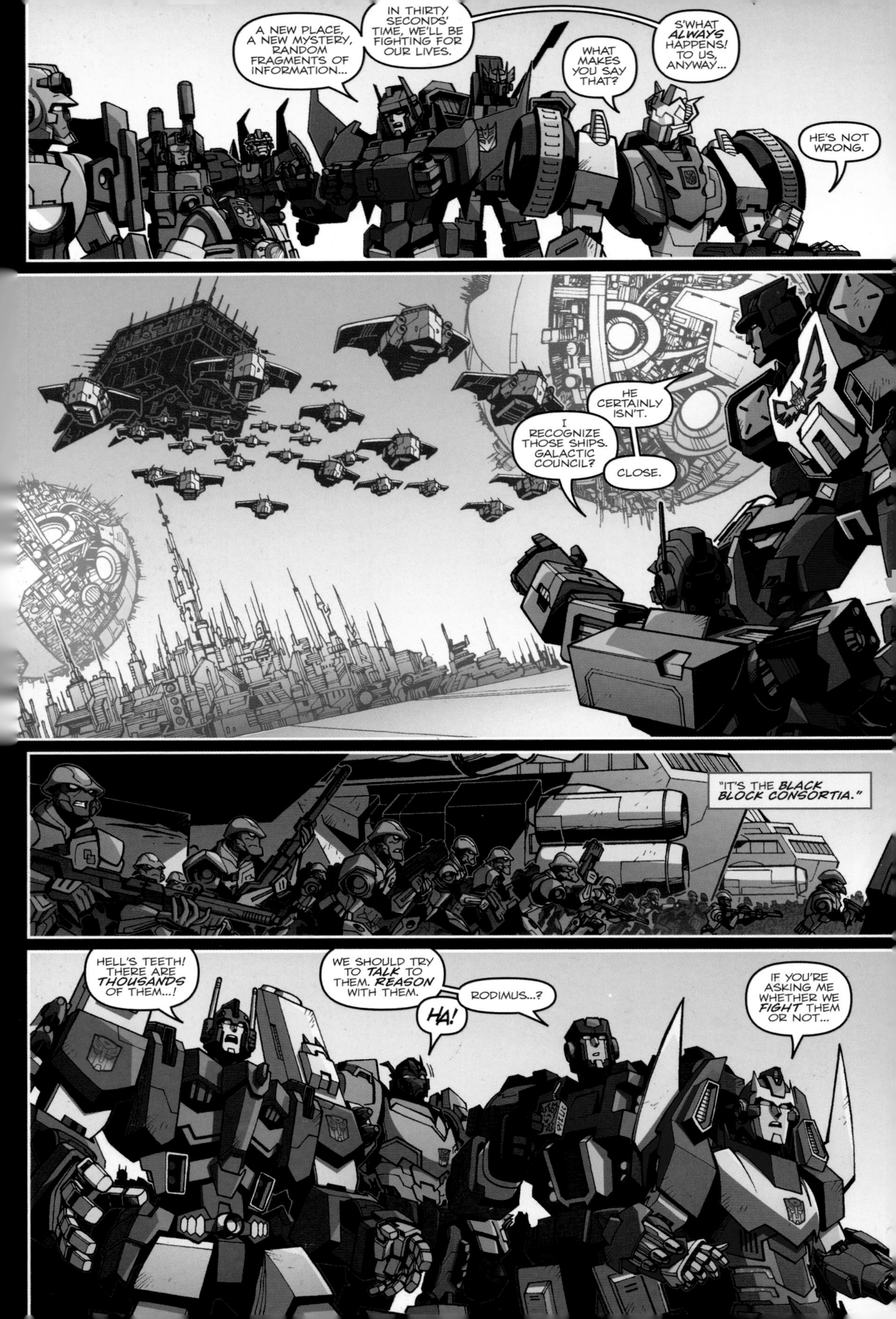

A NEW PLACE, A NEW MYSTERY, RANDOM FRAGMENTS OF INFORMATION...
IN THIRTY SECONDS' TIME, WE'LL BE FIGHTING FOR OUR LIVES.
WHAT MAKES YOU SAY THAT?
S'WHAT *ALWAYS* HAPPENS! TO US, ANYWAY...
HE'S NOT WRONG.
HE CERTAINLY ISN'T.
I RECOGNIZE THOSE SHIPS. GALACTIC COUNCIL?
CLOSE.
"IT'S THE *BLACK BLOCK CONSORTIA.*"
HELL'S TEETH! THERE ARE *THOUSANDS* OF THEM...!
WE SHOULD TRY TO *TALK* TO THEM. *REASON* WITH THEM.
HA!
RODIMUS...?
IF YOU'RE ASKING ME WHETHER WE *FIGHT* THEM OR NOT...

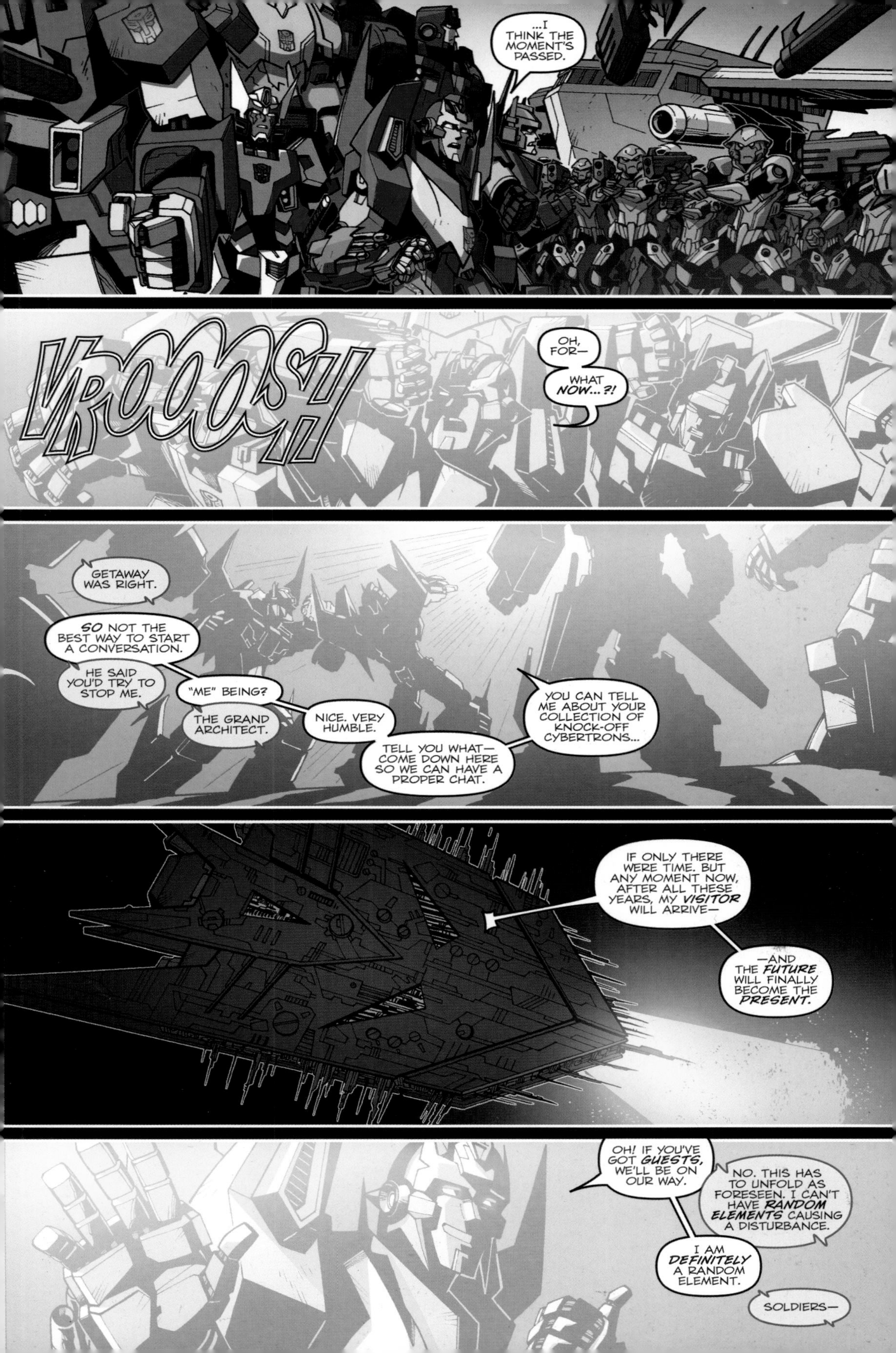
...I THINK THE MOMENT'S PASSED.
VROOOOSH
OH, FOR—
WHAT NOW...?!
GETAWAY WAS RIGHT.
SO NOT THE BEST WAY TO START A CONVERSATION.
HE SAID YOU'D TRY TO STOP ME.
"ME" BEING?
THE GRAND ARCHITECT.
NICE. VERY HUMBLE.
TELL YOU WHAT—COME DOWN HERE SO WE CAN HAVE A PROPER CHAT.
YOU CAN TELL ME ABOUT YOUR COLLECTION OF KNOCK-OFF CYBERTRONS...
IF ONLY THERE WERE TIME. BUT ANY MOMENT NOW, AFTER ALL THESE YEARS, MY VISITOR WILL ARRIVE—
—AND THE FUTURE WILL FINALLY BECOME THE PRESENT.
OH! IF YOU'VE GOT GUESTS, WE'LL BE ON OUR WAY.
NO. THIS HAS TO UNFOLD AS FORESEEN. I CAN'T HAVE RANDOM ELEMENTS CAUSING A DISTURBANCE.
I AM DEFINITELY A RANDOM ELEMENT.
SOLDIERS—

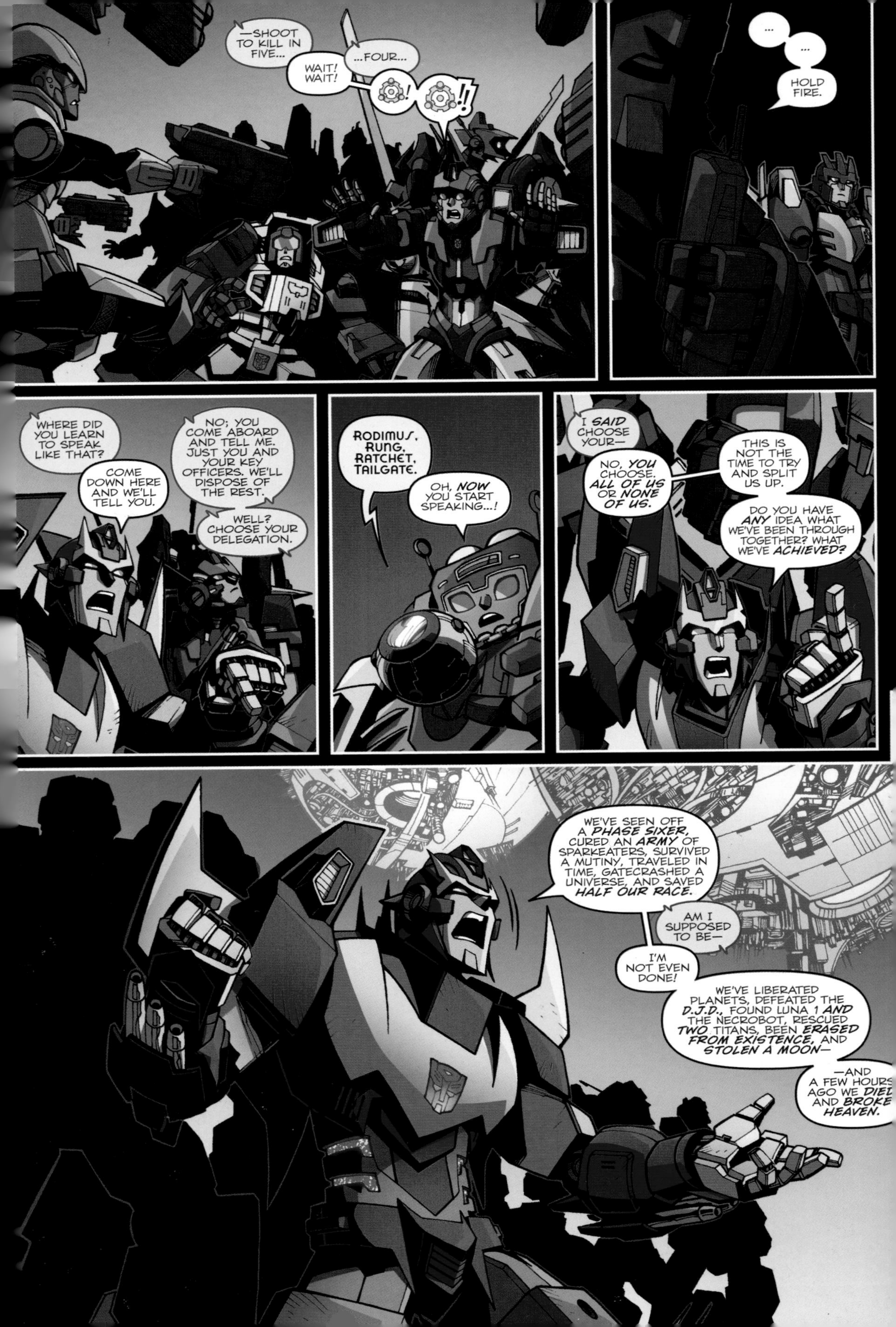
—SHOOT TO KILL IN FIVE...
WAIT! WAIT!
...FOUR...
!
!!
...
...
HOLD FIRE.
WHERE DID YOU LEARN TO SPEAK LIKE THAT?
NO; YOU COME ABOARD AND TELL ME. JUST YOU AND YOUR KEY OFFICERS. WE'LL DISPOSE OF THE REST.
COME DOWN HERE AND WE'LL TELL YOU.
WELL? CHOOSE YOUR DELEGATION.
RODIMUS. RUNG. RATCHET. TAILGATE.
OH, NOW YOU START SPEAKING...!
I SAID CHOOSE YOUR—
NO, YOU CHOOSE. ALL OF US OR NONE OF US.
THIS IS NOT THE TIME TO TRY AND SPLIT US UP.
DO YOU HAVE ANY IDEA WHAT WE'VE BEEN THROUGH TOGETHER? WHAT WE'VE ACHIEVED?
WE'VE SEEN OFF A PHASE SIXER, CURED AN ARMY OF SPARKEATERS, SURVIVED A MUTINY, TRAVELED IN TIME, GATECRASHED A UNIVERSE, AND SAVED HALF OUR RACE.
AM I SUPPOSED TO BE—
I'M NOT EVEN DONE!
WE'VE LIBERATED PLANETS, DEFEATED THE D.J.D., FOUND LUNA 1 AND THE NECROBOT, RESCUED TWO TITANS, BEEN ERASED FROM EXISTENCE, AND STOLEN A MOON—
—AND A FEW HOURS AGO WE DIED AND BROKE HEAVEN.

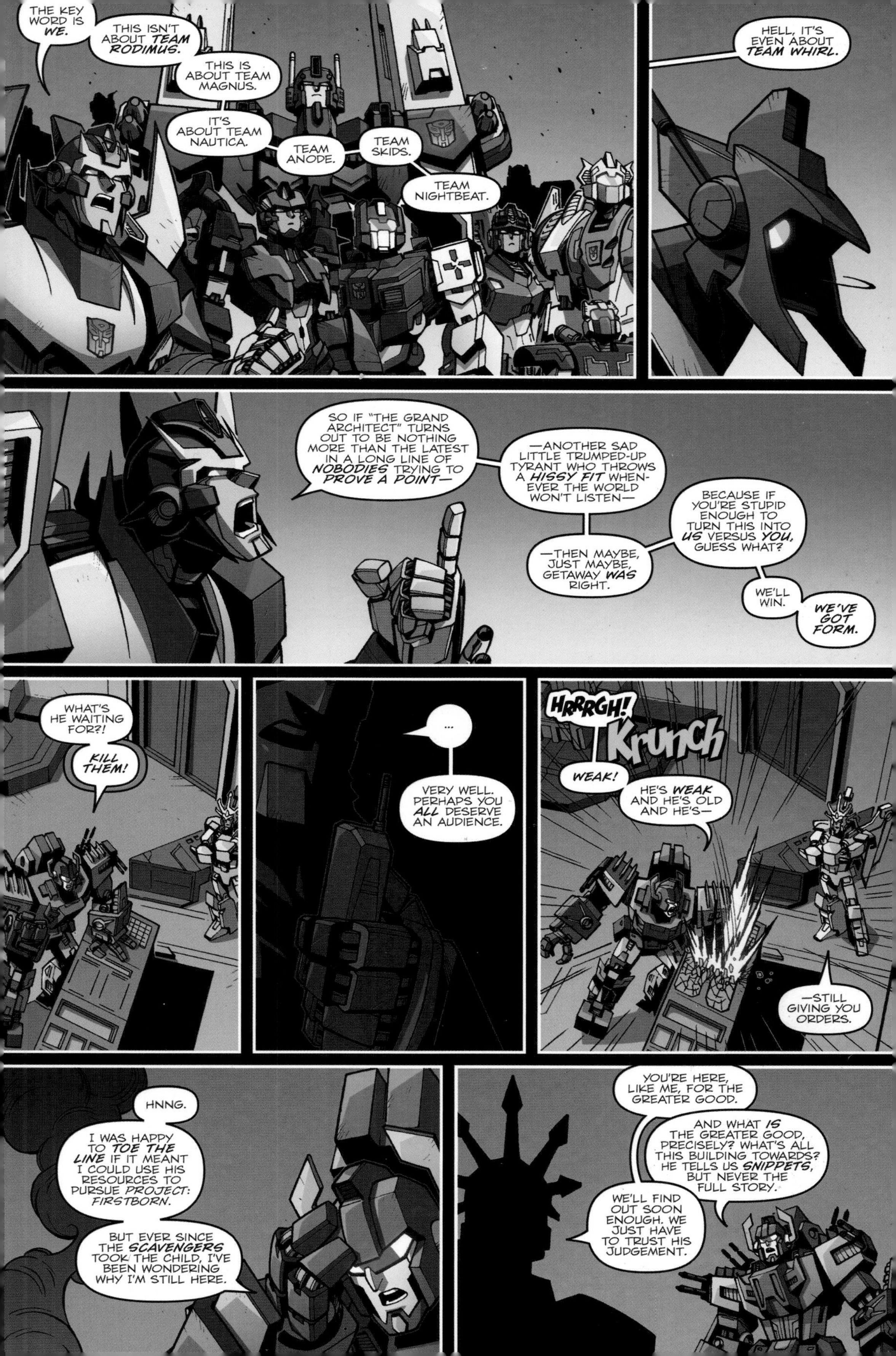
THE KEY WORD IS *WE.*
THIS ISN'T ABOUT *TEAM RODIMUS.*
THIS IS ABOUT TEAM MAGNUS.
IT'S ABOUT TEAM NAUTICA.
TEAM ANODE.
TEAM SKIDS.
TEAM NIGHTBEAT.
HELL, IT'S EVEN ABOUT *TEAM WHIRL.*
SO IF "THE GRAND ARCHITECT" TURNS OUT TO BE NOTHING MORE THAN THE LATEST IN A LONG LINE OF *NOBODIES* TRYING TO *PROVE A POINT*—
—ANOTHER SAD LITTLE TRUMPED-UP TYRANT WHO THROWS A *HISSY FIT* WHENEVER THE WORLD WON'T LISTEN—
—THEN MAYBE, JUST MAYBE, GETAWAY *WAS* RIGHT.
BECAUSE IF YOU'RE STUPID ENOUGH TO TURN THIS INTO *US* VERSUS *YOU,* GUESS WHAT?
WE'LL WIN.
WE'VE GOT FORM.
WHAT'S HE WAITING FOR?!
KILL THEM!
...
VERY WELL. PERHAPS YOU *ALL* DESERVE AN AUDIENCE.
HRRRGH!
Krunch
WEAK!
HE'S *WEAK* AND HE'S OLD AND HE'S—
—STILL GIVING YOU ORDERS.
HNNG.
I WAS HAPPY TO *TOE THE LINE* IF IT MEANT I COULD USE HIS RESOURCES TO PURSUE *PROJECT: FIRSTBORN.*
BUT EVER SINCE THE *SCAVENGERS* TOOK THE CHILD, I'VE BEEN WONDERING WHY I'M STILL HERE.
YOU'RE HERE, LIKE ME, FOR THE GREATER GOOD.
AND WHAT *IS* THE GREATER GOOD, PRECISELY? WHAT'S ALL THIS BUILDING TOWARDS? HE TELLS US *SNIPPETS,* BUT NEVER THE FULL STORY.
WE'LL FIND OUT SOON ENOUGH. WE JUST HAVE TO TRUST HIS JUDGEMENT.

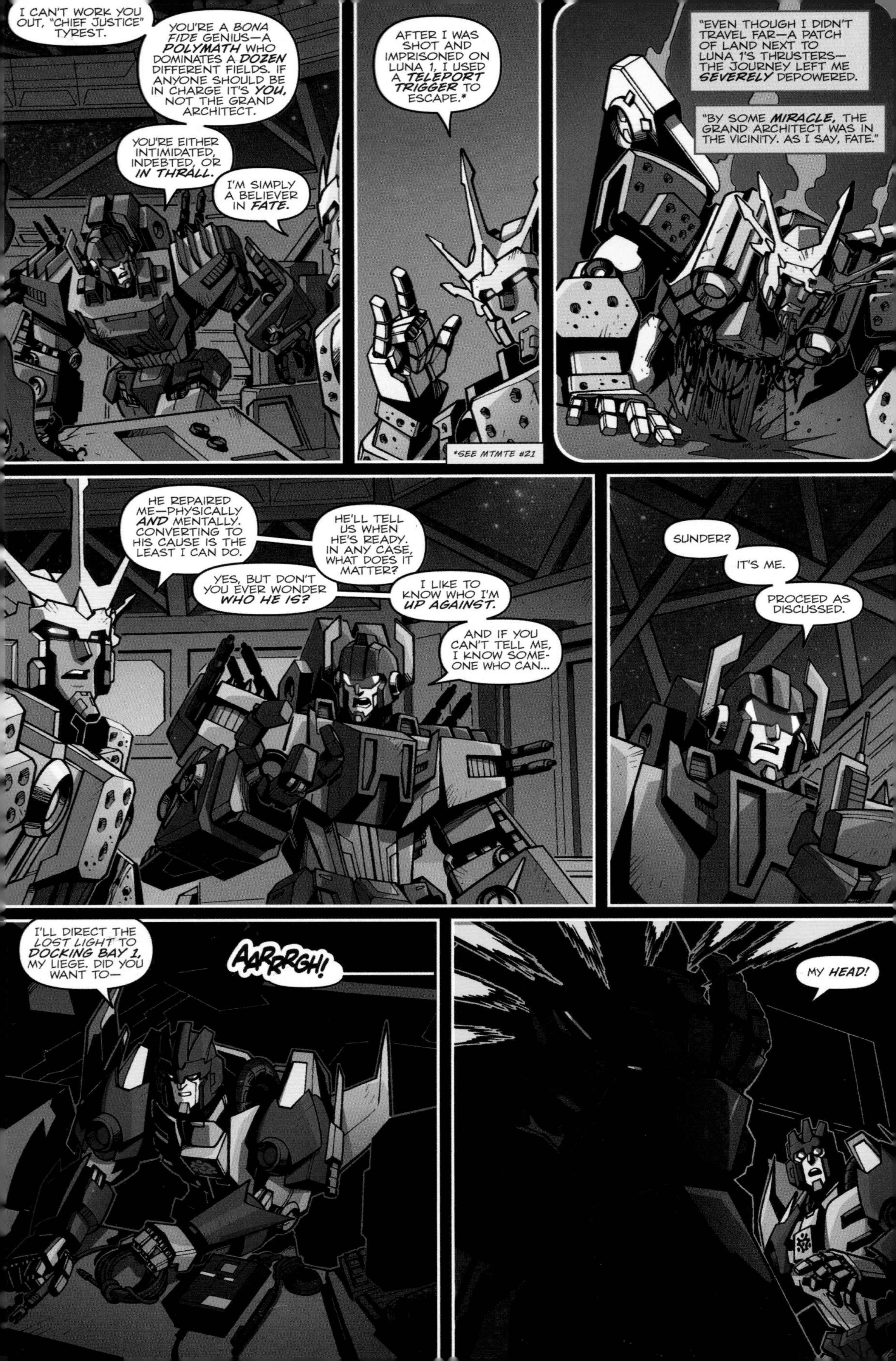
I CAN'T WORK YOU OUT, "CHIEF JUSTICE" TYREST.
YOU'RE A *BONA FIDE* GENIUS—A ***POLYMATH*** WHO DOMINATES A ***DOZEN*** DIFFERENT FIELDS. IF ANYONE SHOULD BE IN CHARGE IT'S ***YOU,*** NOT THE GRAND ARCHITECT.
YOU'RE EITHER INTIMIDATED, INDEBTED, OR ***IN THRALL.***
I'M SIMPLY A BELIEVER IN ***FATE.***
AFTER I WAS SHOT AND IMPRISONED ON LUNA 1, I USED A ***TELEPORT TRIGGER*** TO ESCAPE.*
*SEE MTMTE #21
"EVEN THOUGH I DIDN'T TRAVEL FAR—A PATCH OF LAND NEXT TO LUNA 1'S THRUSTERS—THE JOURNEY LEFT ME ***SEVERELY*** DEPOWERED.
"BY SOME ***MIRACLE,*** THE GRAND ARCHITECT WAS IN THE VICINITY. AS I SAY, FATE."
HE REPAIRED ME—PHYSICALLY ***AND*** MENTALLY. CONVERTING TO HIS CAUSE IS THE LEAST I CAN DO.
HE'LL TELL US WHEN HE'S READY. IN ANY CASE, WHAT DOES IT MATTER?
YES, BUT DON'T YOU EVER WONDER ***WHO HE IS?***
I LIKE TO KNOW WHO I'M ***UP AGAINST.***
AND IF YOU CAN'T TELL ME, I KNOW SOME-ONE WHO CAN...
SUNDER?
IT'S ME.
PROCEED AS DISCUSSED.
I'LL DIRECT THE *LOST LIGHT* TO ***DOCKING BAY 1,*** MY LIEGE. DID YOU WANT TO—
AARRRGH!
MY ***HEAD!***

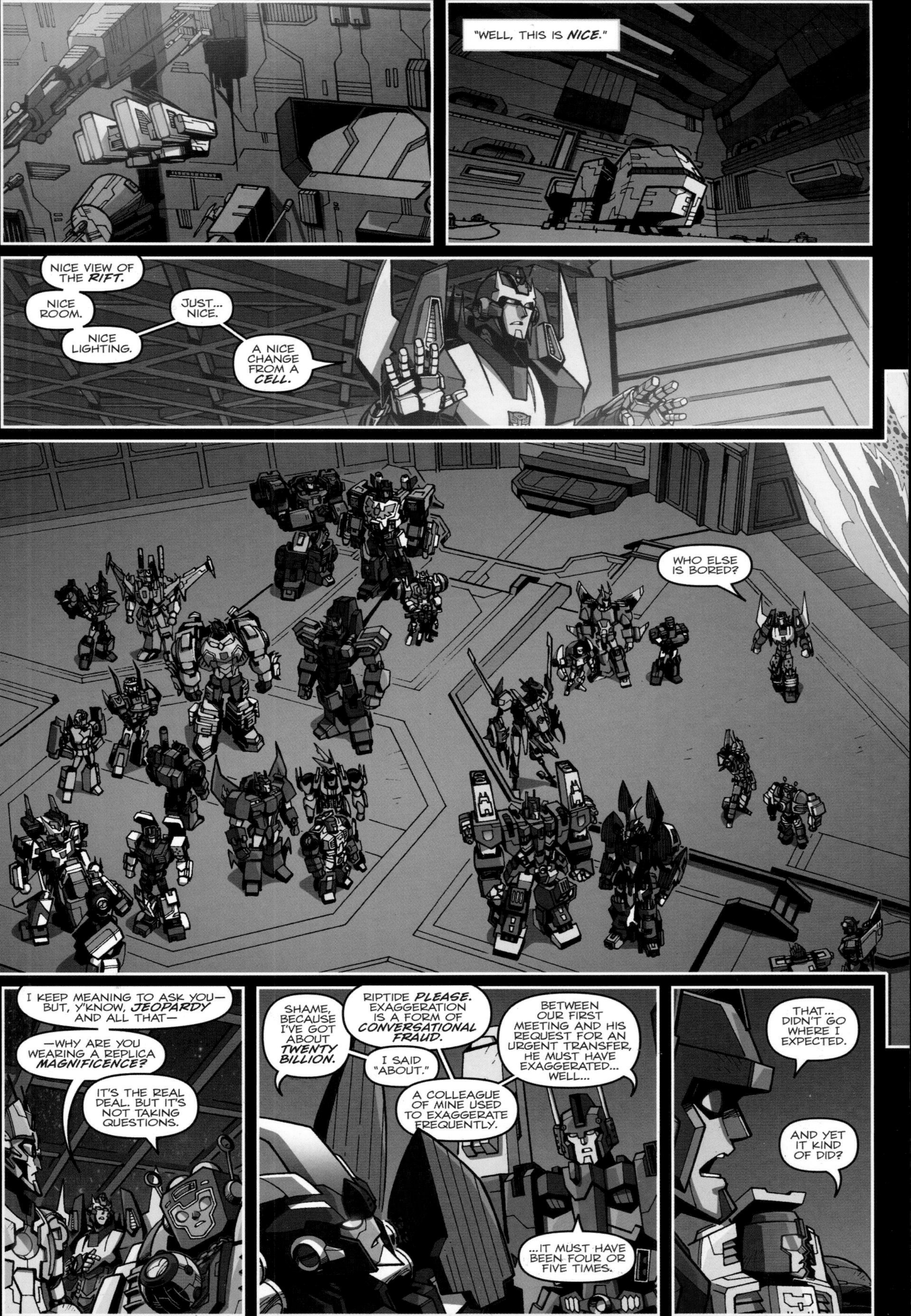
"WELL, THIS IS NICE."
NICE VIEW OF THE RIFT.
NICE ROOM.
NICE LIGHTING.
JUST... NICE.
A NICE CHANGE FROM A CELL.
WHO ELSE IS BORED?
I KEEP MEANING TO ASK YOU—BUT, Y'KNOW, JEOPARDY AND ALL THAT—
—WHY ARE YOU WEARING A REPLICA MAGNIFICENCE?
IT'S THE REAL DEAL. BUT IT'S NOT TAKING QUESTIONS.
SHAME, BECAUSE I'VE GOT ABOUT TWENTY BILLION.
RIPTIDE PLEASE. EXAGGERATION IS A FORM OF CONVERSATIONAL FRAUD.
I SAID "ABOUT."
A COLLEAGUE OF MINE USED TO EXAGGERATE FREQUENTLY.
BETWEEN OUR FIRST MEETING AND HIS REQUEST FOR AN URGENT TRANSFER, HE MUST HAVE EXAGGERATED... WELL...
...IT MUST HAVE BEEN FOUR OR FIVE TIMES.
THAT... DIDN'T GO WHERE I EXPECTED.
AND YET IT KIND OF DID?

I'M SORRY, BUT—

DID IT JUST *SAY SOMETHING?*

EH?

THE MAGNIFICENCE. I THOUGHT IT SAID MY NAME.

I DIDN'T HEAR ANY-THING.

HOW ODD.

DO YOU MIND IF I...?

TSCHE-CHU-CHU-CHU-TSCHE!

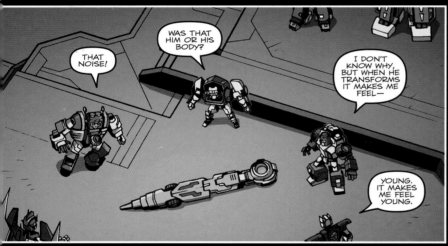

THAT NOISE!

WAS THAT HIM OR HIS BODY?

I DON'T KNOW WHY, BUT WHEN HE TRANSFORMS IT MAKES ME FEEL—

YOUNG. IT MAKES ME FEEL YOUNG.

HEY, RODIMUS. CHECK THIS OUT.

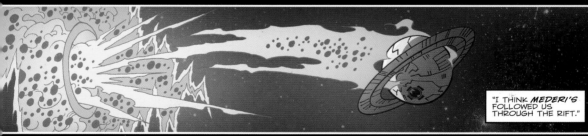

"I THINK *MEDERI'S* FOLLOWED US THROUGH THE RIFT."

THE RIFT WHICH *FINALLY* SEEMS TO BE *RE-SEALING* ITSELF...

IT MAKES YOU WONDER WHETHER THE RIFT WAS REALLY A RIFT... OR JUST A WAY OF BRINGING MEDERI HERE.

OH, *BRAVO!* GOOD GUESS!

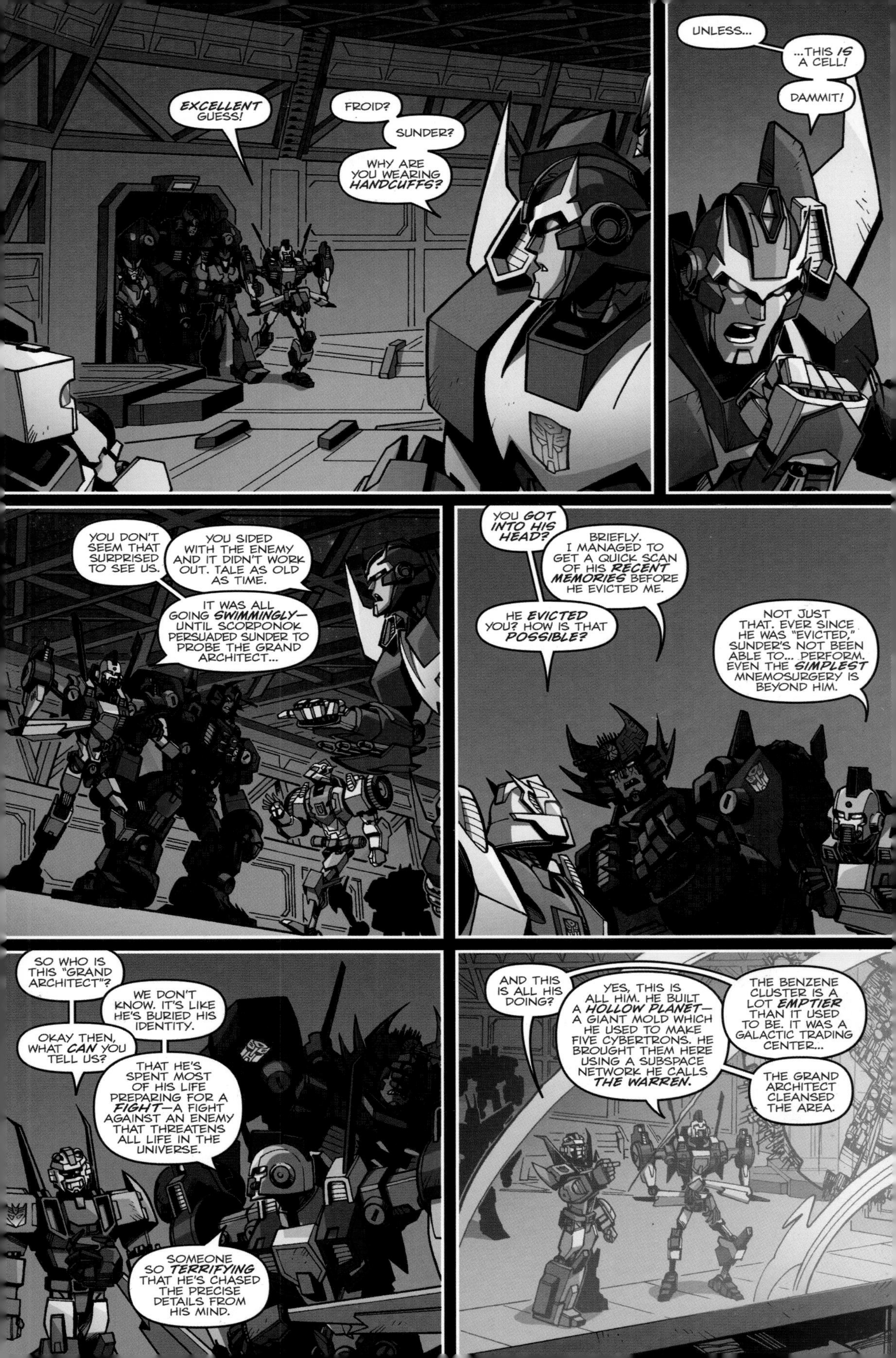
EXCELLENT GUESS!
FROID?
SUNDER?
WHY ARE YOU WEARING HANDCUFFS?
UNLESS...
...THIS IS A CELL!
DAMMIT!
YOU DON'T SEEM THAT SURPRISED TO SEE US.
YOU SIDED WITH THE ENEMY AND IT DIDN'T WORK OUT. TALE AS OLD AS TIME.
IT WAS ALL GOING SWIMMINGLY—UNTIL SCORPONOK PERSUADED SUNDER TO PROBE THE GRAND ARCHITECT...
YOU GOT INTO HIS HEAD?
BRIEFLY. I MANAGED TO GET A QUICK SCAN OF HIS RECENT MEMORIES BEFORE HE EVICTED ME.
HE EVICTED YOU? HOW IS THAT POSSIBLE?
NOT JUST THAT. EVER SINCE HE WAS "EVICTED," SUNDER'S NOT BEEN ABLE TO... PERFORM. EVEN THE SIMPLEST MNEMOSURGERY IS BEYOND HIM.
SO WHO IS THIS "GRAND ARCHITECT"?
WE DON'T KNOW. IT'S LIKE HE'S BURIED HIS IDENTITY.
OKAY THEN, WHAT CAN YOU TELL US?
THAT HE'S SPENT MOST OF HIS LIFE PREPARING FOR A FIGHT—A FIGHT AGAINST AN ENEMY THAT THREATENS ALL LIFE IN THE UNIVERSE.
SOMEONE SO TERRIFYING THAT HE'S CHASED THE PRECISE DETAILS FROM HIS MIND.
AND THIS IS ALL HIS DOING?
YES, THIS IS ALL HIM. HE BUILT A HOLLOW PLANET—A GIANT MOLD WHICH HE USED TO MAKE FIVE CYBERTRONS. HE BROUGHT THEM HERE USING A SUBSPACE NETWORK HE CALLS THE WARREN.
THE BENZENE CLUSTER IS A LOT EMPTIER THAN IT USED TO BE. IT WAS A GALACTIC TRADING CENTER...
THE GRAND ARCHITECT CLEANSED THE AREA.

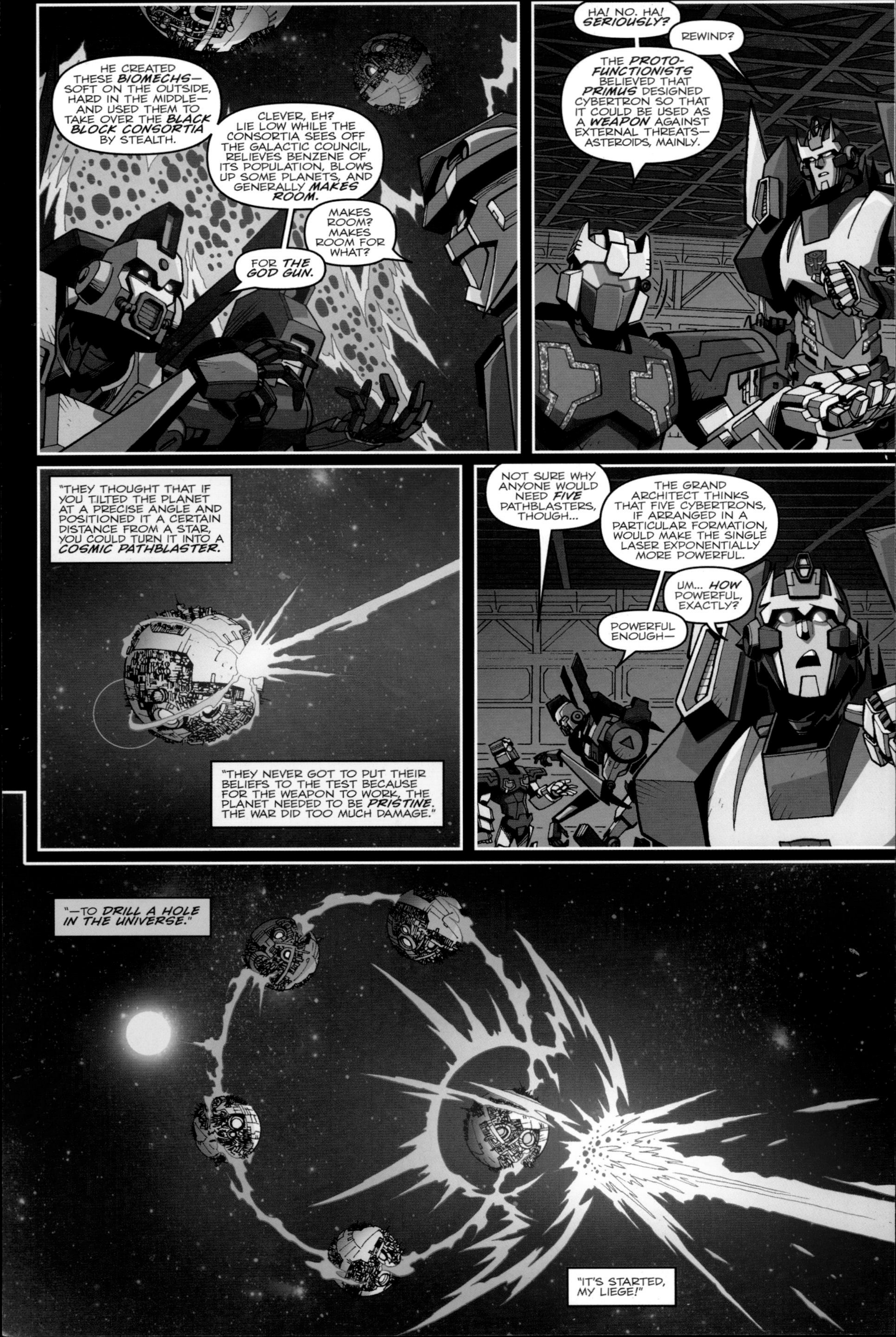

HE CREATED THESE BIOMECHS— SOFT ON THE OUTSIDE, HARD IN THE MIDDLE— AND USED THEM TO TAKE OVER THE BLACK BLOCK CONSORTIA BY STEALTH.
CLEVER, EH? LIE LOW WHILE THE CONSORTIA SEES OFF THE GALACTIC COUNCIL, RELIEVES BENZENE OF ITS POPULATION, BLOWS UP SOME PLANETS, AND GENERALLY MAKES ROOM.
MAKES ROOM? MAKES ROOM FOR WHAT?
FOR THE GOD GUN.
HA! NO. HA! SERIOUSLY?
REWIND?
THE PROTO-FUNCTIONISTS BELIEVED THAT PRIMUS DESIGNED CYBERTRON SO THAT IT COULD BE USED AS A WEAPON AGAINST EXTERNAL THREATS— ASTEROIDS, MAINLY.
"THEY THOUGHT THAT IF YOU TILTED THE PLANET AT A PRECISE ANGLE AND POSITIONED IT A CERTAIN DISTANCE FROM A STAR, YOU COULD TURN IT INTO A COSMIC PATHBLASTER.
"THEY NEVER GOT TO PUT THEIR BELIEFS TO THE TEST BECAUSE FOR THE WEAPON TO WORK, THE PLANET NEEDED TO BE PRISTINE. THE WAR DID TOO MUCH DAMAGE."
NOT SURE WHY ANYONE WOULD NEED FIVE PATHBLASTERS, THOUGH...
THE GRAND ARCHITECT THINKS THAT FIVE CYBERTRONS, IF ARRANGED IN A PARTICULAR FORMATION, WOULD MAKE THE SINGLE LASER EXPONENTIALLY MORE POWERFUL.
UM... HOW POWERFUL, EXACTLY?
POWERFUL ENOUGH—
"—TO DRILL A HOLE IN THE UNIVERSE."
"IT'S STARTED, MY LIEGE!"

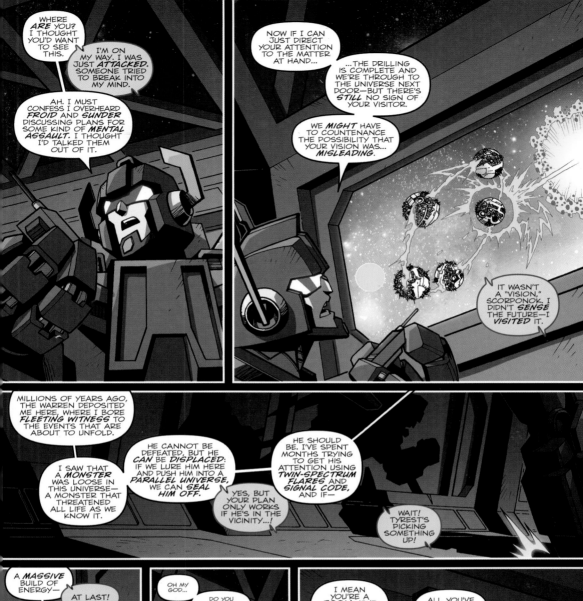

WHERE *ARE* YOU? I THOUGHT YOU'D WANT TO SEE THIS.

I'M ON MY WAY. I WAS JUST *ATTACKED.* SOMEONE TRIED TO BREAK INTO MY MIND.

AH. I MUST CONFESS I OVERHEARD *FROID* AND *SUNDER* DISCUSSING PLANS FOR SOME KIND OF *MENTAL ASSAULT.* I THOUGHT I'D TALKED THEM OUT OF IT.

NOW IF I CAN JUST DIRECT YOUR ATTENTION TO THE MATTER AT HAND...

...THE DRILLING IS COMPLETE AND WE'RE THROUGH TO THE UNIVERSE NEXT DOOR—BUT THERE'S *STILL* NO SIGN OF YOUR VISITOR.

WE *MIGHT* HAVE TO COUNTENANCE THE POSSIBILITY THAT YOUR VISION WAS... *MISLEADING.*

IT WASN'T A "VISION," SCORPONOK. I DIDN'T *SENSE* THE FUTURE—I *VISITED* IT.

MILLIONS OF YEARS AGO, THE WARREN DEPOSITED ME HERE, WHERE I BORE *FLEETING WITNESS* TO THE EVENTS THAT ARE ABOUT TO UNFOLD.

I SAW THAT A *MONSTER* WAS LOOSE IN THIS UNIVERSE— A MONSTER THAT THREATENED ALL LIFE AS WE KNOW IT.

HE CANNOT BE DEFEATED, BUT HE *CAN* BE *DISPLACED:* IF WE LURE HIM HERE AND PUSH HIM INTO A *PARALLEL UNIVERSE,* WE CAN *SEAL HIM OFF.*

YES, BUT YOUR PLAN ONLY WORKS IF HE'S IN THE VICINITY...!

HE SHOULD BE. I'VE SPENT MONTHS TRYING TO GET HIS ATTENTION USING *TWIN-SPECTRUM FLARES* AND *SIGNAL CODE,* AND IF—

WAIT! TYREST'S PICKING SOMETHING UP!

A *MASSIVE* BUILD OF ENERGY—

AT LAST!

—ON THE *OTHER SIDE* OF THE PORTAL!

OH MY GOD...

DO YOU REALIZE WHAT YOU'VE DONE?

IN PREPARING TO CONFRONT THE FUTURE, YOU MADE IT COME TO PASS!

WHAT DO YOU MEAN?

I MEAN YOU'RE A *FOOL!* YOUR "MONSTER" WAS *ALREADY IN* THE NEXT UNIVERSE!

ALL YOU'VE DONE... *IS INVITE HIM INTO OURS!*

SWUSH

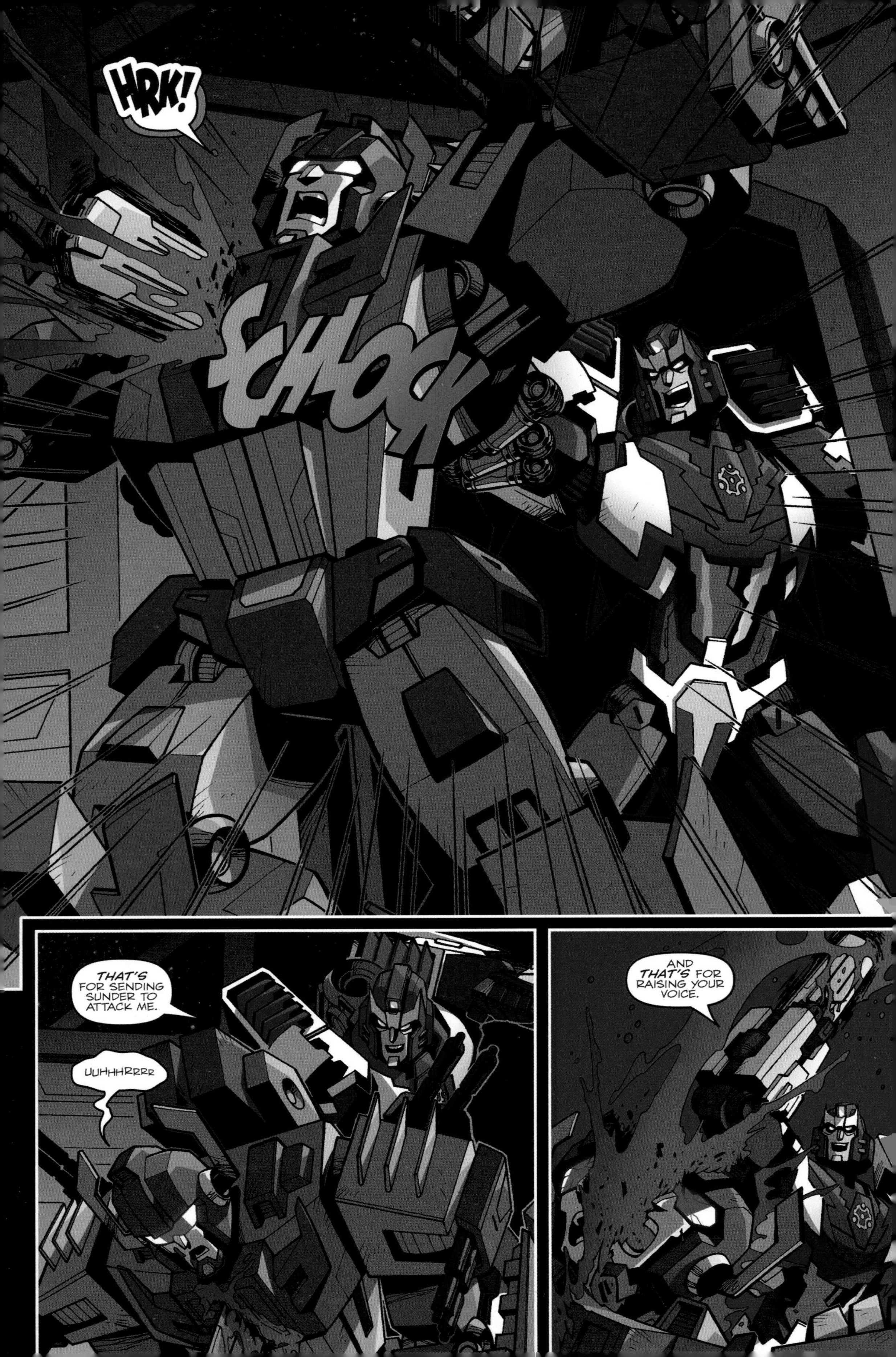
HRK!
SHOCK
THAT'S FOR SENDING SUNDER TO ATTACK ME.
UUHHHRRRR
AND THAT'S FOR RAISING YOUR VOICE.

HEY LOTTY— I'D LIKE TO PUT *"RIFT"* BACK ON MY LIST SO I CAN *CROSS IT OFF AGAIN*—

—BECAUSE LOOK AT *THAT!*

ISN'T THAT MORE OF A PORTAL?

EITHER WAY, WE'RE ABOUT TO SEE WHAT THE GRAND ARCHITECT HAS DEDICATED HIS LIFE TO *STOPPING.*

ALL THIS PLANNING, ALL THIS EFFORT— JUST TO SEE OFF A *SINGLE ENEMY.*

WHO COULD POSE A THREAT TO THE *ENTIRE UNIVERSE?* WHO'S *THAT* DANGEROUS?

LOOK— SOMETHING'S COMING THROUGH!

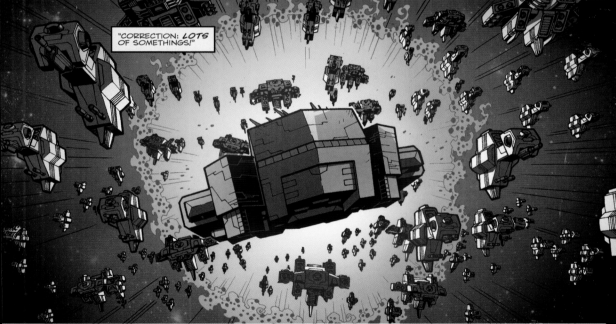

"CORRECTION: *LOTS* OF SOMETHINGS!"

EH? WHY WOULD SOMEONE CALL BOTH OF US—

—AT THE SAME TIME?

BZZZ

BZZZ

HELLO.

YOU?!

YOU.

OF COURSE IT'S ME...

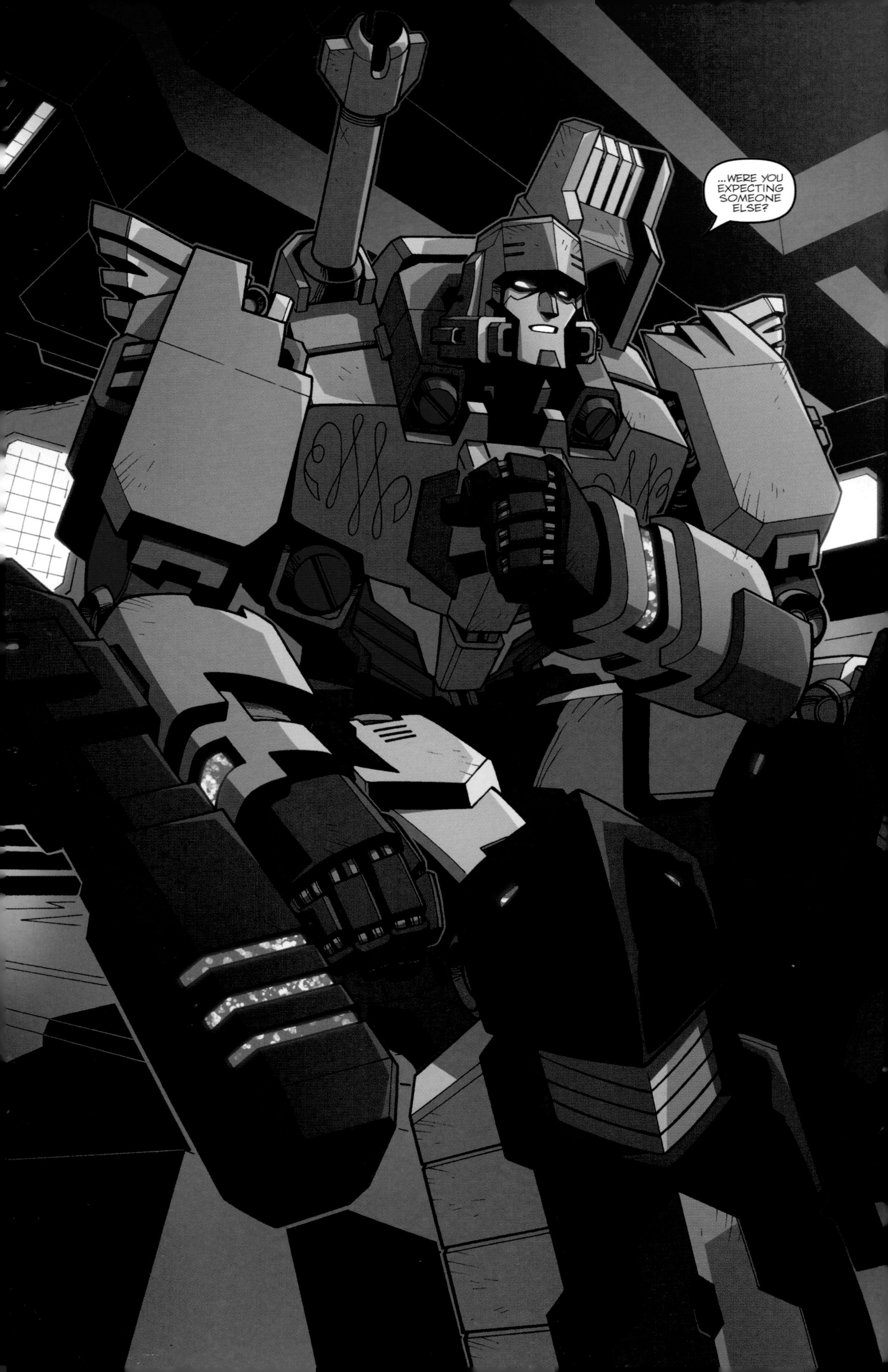
...WERE YOU EXPECTING SOMEONE ELSE?

ART BY **GEOFF SENIOR**
COLORS BY **JOSH BURCHAM**

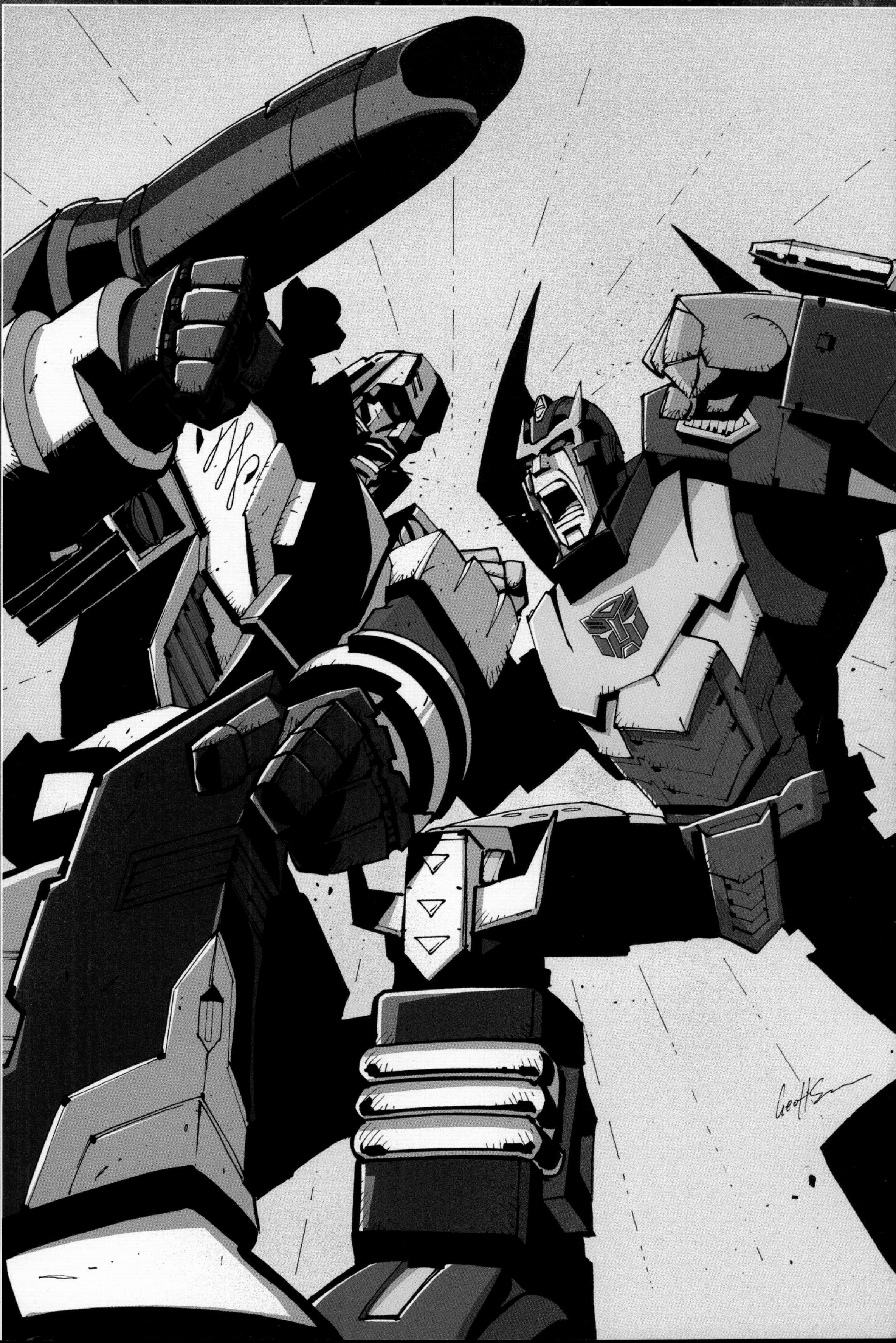

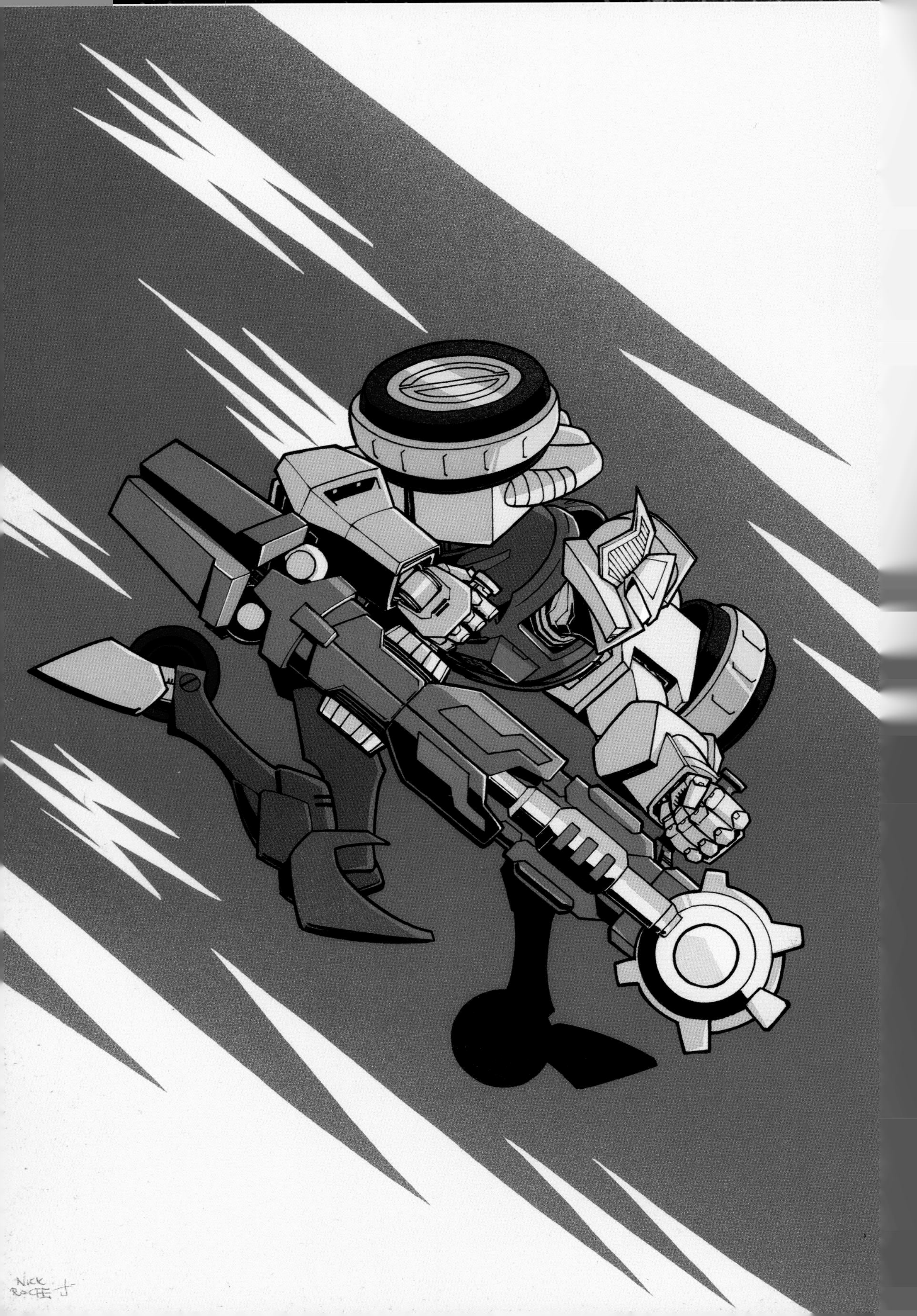
NICK
ROCHE

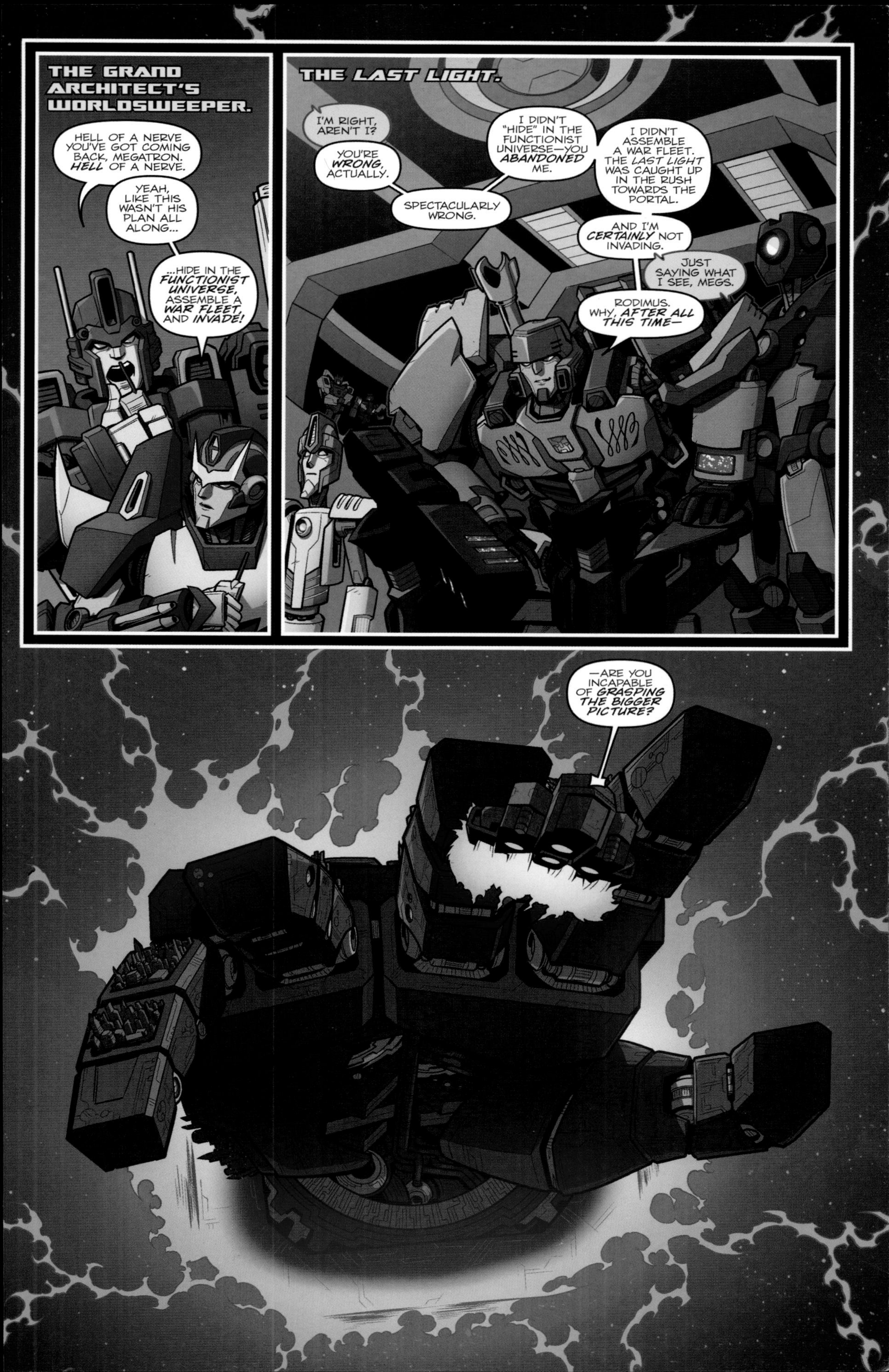
THE GRAND ARCHITECT'S WORLDSWEEPER.
HELL OF A NERVE YOU'VE GOT COMING BACK, MEGATRON. HELL OF A NERVE.
YEAH, LIKE THIS WASN'T HIS PLAN ALL ALONG...
...HIDE IN THE FUNCTIONIST UNIVERSE, ASSEMBLE A WAR FLEET, AND INVADE!
THE LAST LIGHT.
I'M RIGHT, AREN'T I?
YOU'RE WRONG, ACTUALLY.
SPECTACULARLY WRONG.
I DIDN'T "HIDE" IN THE FUNCTIONIST UNIVERSE—YOU ABANDONED ME.
I DIDN'T ASSEMBLE A WAR FLEET. THE LAST LIGHT WAS CAUGHT UP IN THE RUSH TOWARDS THE PORTAL.
AND I'M CERTAINLY NOT INVADING.
JUST SAYING WHAT I SEE, MEGS.
RODIMUS. WHY, AFTER ALL THIS TIME—
—ARE YOU INCAPABLE OF GRASPING THE BIGGER PICTURE?

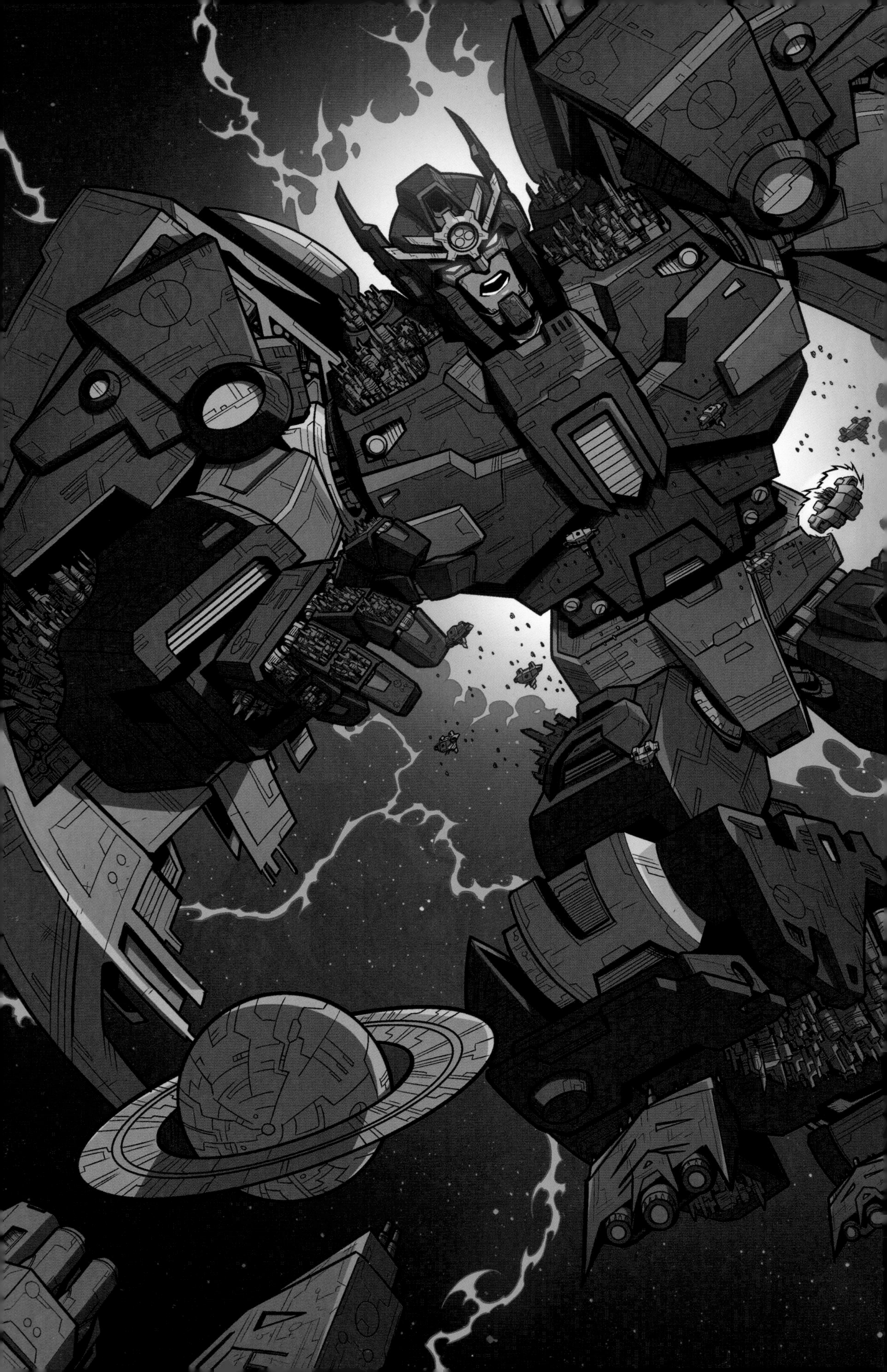

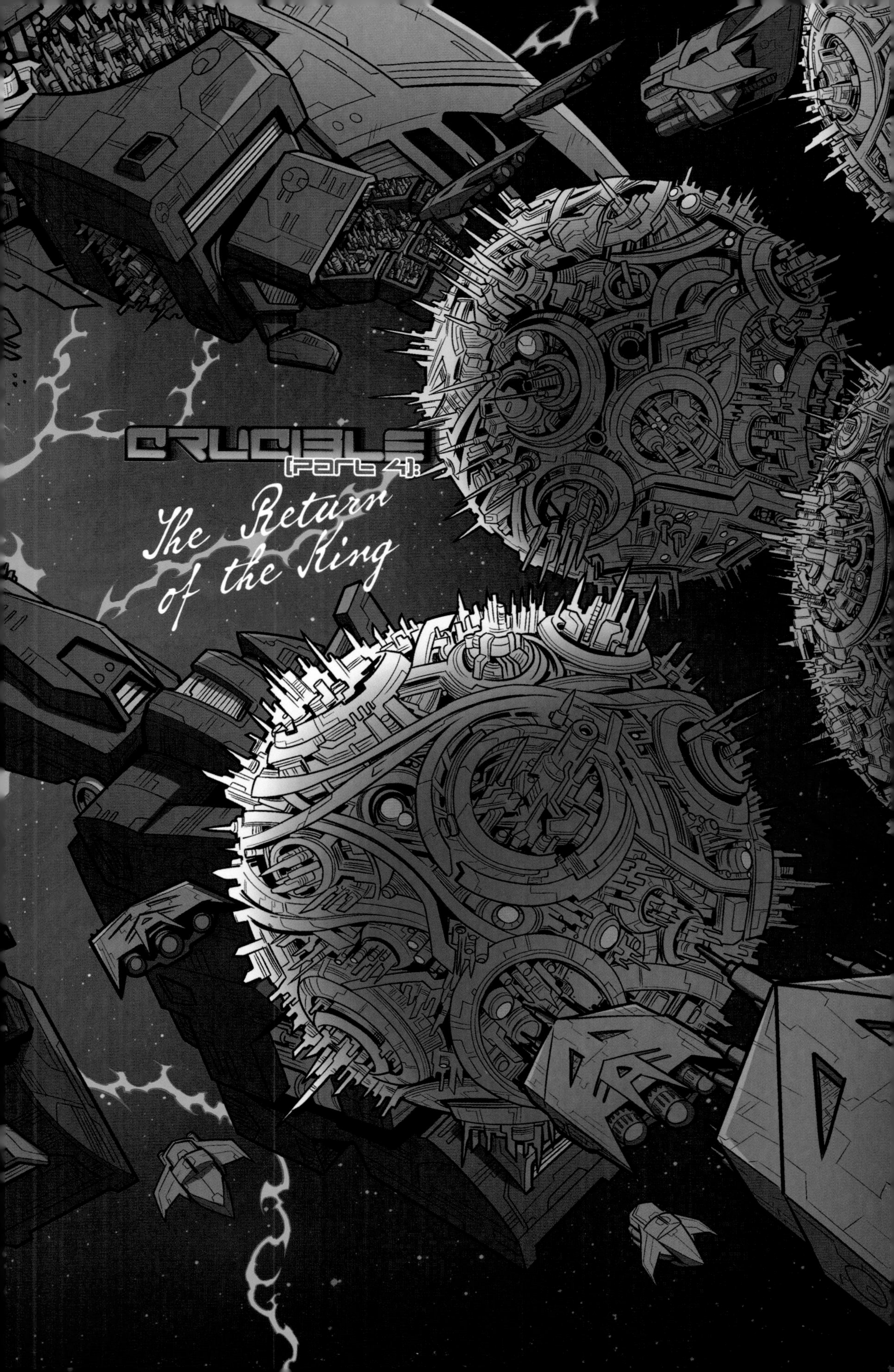
CRUCIBLE
(Part 4):
The Return of the King

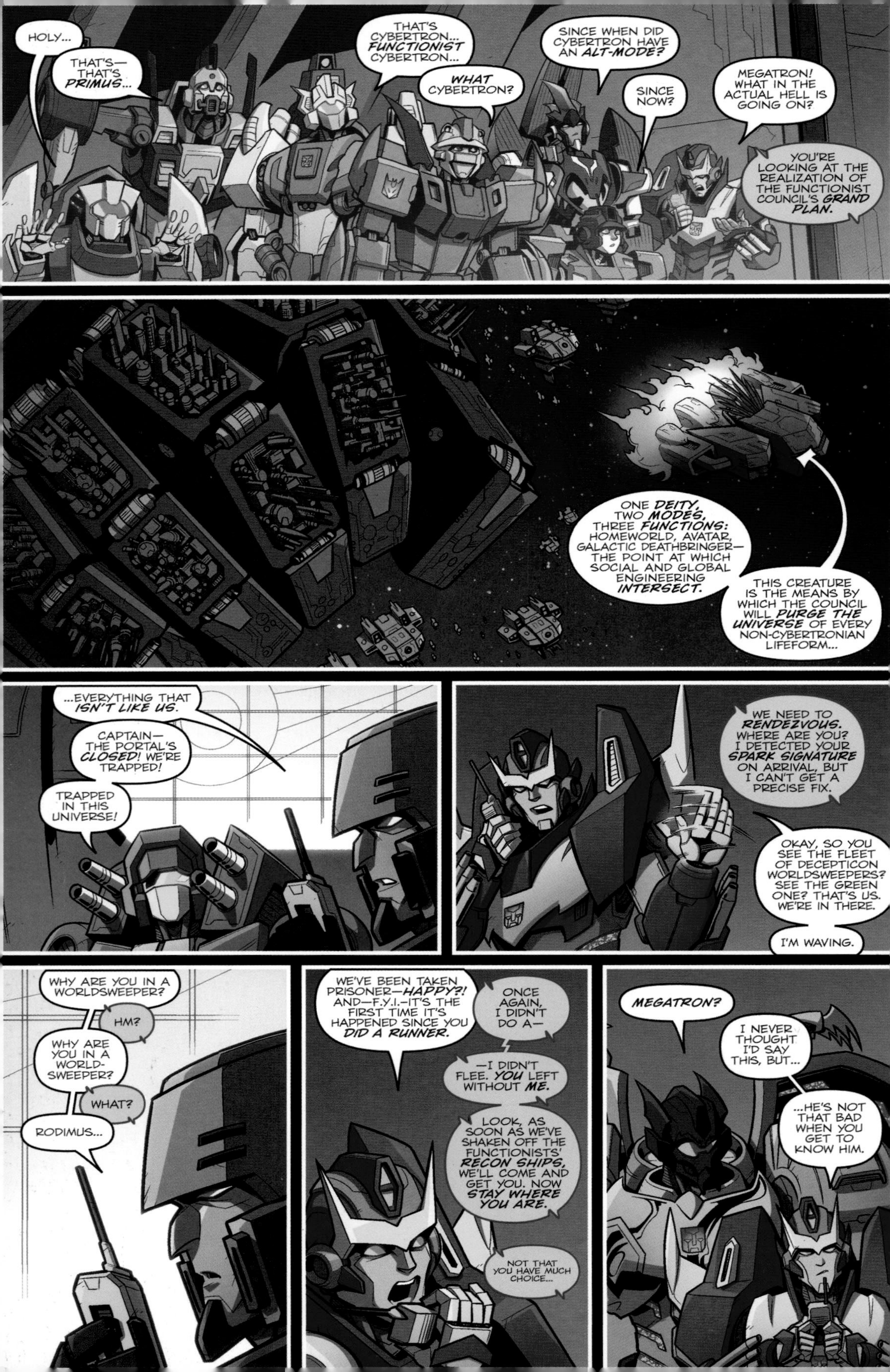
HOLY...
THAT'S— THAT'S PRIMUS...
THAT'S CYBERTRON... FUNCTIONIST CYBERTRON...
WHAT CYBERTRON?
SINCE WHEN DID CYBERTRON HAVE AN ALT-MODE?
SINCE NOW?
MEGATRON! WHAT IN THE ACTUAL HELL IS GOING ON?
YOU'RE LOOKING AT THE REALIZATION OF THE FUNCTIONIST COUNCIL'S GRAND PLAN.
ONE DEITY, TWO MODES, THREE FUNCTIONS: HOMEWORLD, AVATAR, GALACTIC DEATHBRINGER— THE POINT AT WHICH SOCIAL AND GLOBAL ENGINEERING INTERSECT.
THIS CREATURE IS THE MEANS BY WHICH THE COUNCIL WILL PURGE THE UNIVERSE OF EVERY NON-CYBERTRONIAN LIFEFORM...
...EVERYTHING THAT ISN'T LIKE US.
CAPTAIN— THE PORTAL'S CLOSED! WE'RE TRAPPED!
TRAPPED IN THIS UNIVERSE!
WE NEED TO RENDEZVOUS. WHERE ARE YOU? I DETECTED YOUR SPARK SIGNATURE ON ARRIVAL, BUT I CAN'T GET A PRECISE FIX.
OKAY, SO YOU SEE THE FLEET OF DECEPTICON WORLDSWEEPERS? SEE THE GREEN ONE? THAT'S US. WE'RE IN THERE.
I'M WAVING.
WHY ARE YOU IN A WORLDSWEEPER?
HM?
WHY ARE YOU IN A WORLD-SWEEPER?
WHAT?
RODIMUS...
WE'VE BEEN TAKEN PRISONER—HAPPY?! AND—F.Y.I.—IT'S THE FIRST TIME IT'S HAPPENED SINCE YOU DID A RUNNER.
ONCE AGAIN, I DIDN'T DO A—
—I DIDN'T FLEE. YOU LEFT WITHOUT ME.
LOOK, AS SOON AS WE'VE SHAKEN OFF THE FUNCTIONISTS' RECON SHIPS, WE'LL COME AND GET YOU. NOW STAY WHERE YOU ARE.
NOT THAT YOU HAVE MUCH CHOICE...
MEGATRON?
I NEVER THOUGHT I'D SAY THIS, BUT...
...HE'S NOT THAT BAD WHEN YOU GET TO KNOW HIM.

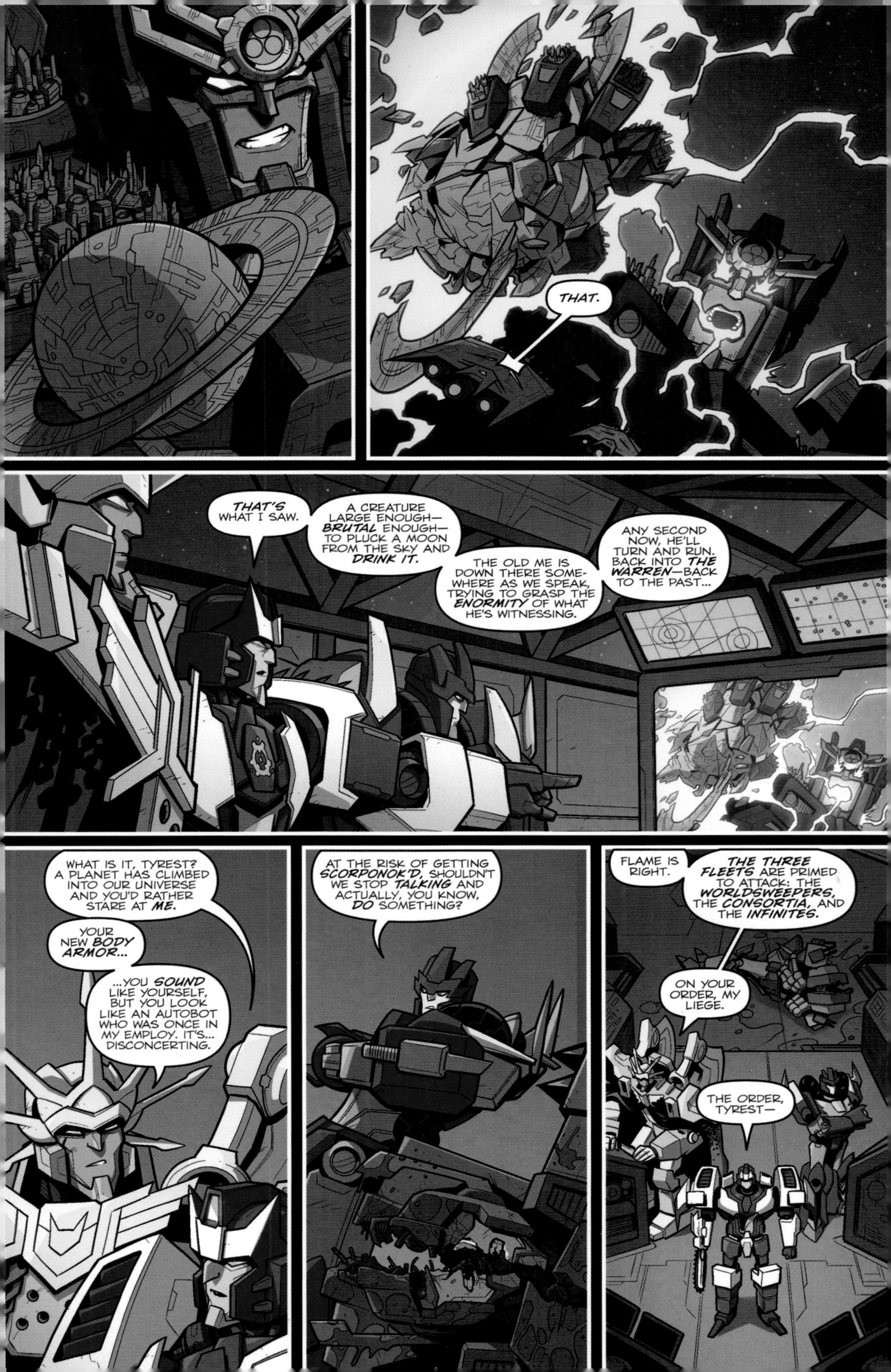
THAT.
THAT'S WHAT I SAW.
A CREATURE LARGE ENOUGH—BRUTAL ENOUGH—TO PLUCK A MOON FROM THE SKY AND DRINK IT.
THE OLD ME IS DOWN THERE SOMEWHERE AS WE SPEAK, TRYING TO GRASP THE ENORMITY OF WHAT HE'S WITNESSING.
ANY SECOND NOW, HE'LL TURN AND RUN. BACK INTO THE WARREN—BACK TO THE PAST...
WHAT IS IT, TYREST? A PLANET HAS CLIMBED INTO OUR UNIVERSE AND YOU'D RATHER STARE AT ME.
YOUR NEW BODY ARMOR...
...YOU SOUND LIKE YOURSELF, BUT YOU LOOK LIKE AN AUTOBOT WHO WAS ONCE IN MY EMPLOY. IT'S... DISCONCERTING.
AT THE RISK OF GETTING SCORPONOK'D, SHOULDN'T WE STOP TALKING AND ACTUALLY, YOU KNOW, DO SOMETHING?
FLAME IS RIGHT.
THE THREE FLEETS ARE PRIMED TO ATTACK: THE WORLDSWEEPERS, THE CONSORTIA, AND THE INFINITES.
ON YOUR ORDER, MY LIEGE.
THE ORDER, TYREST—

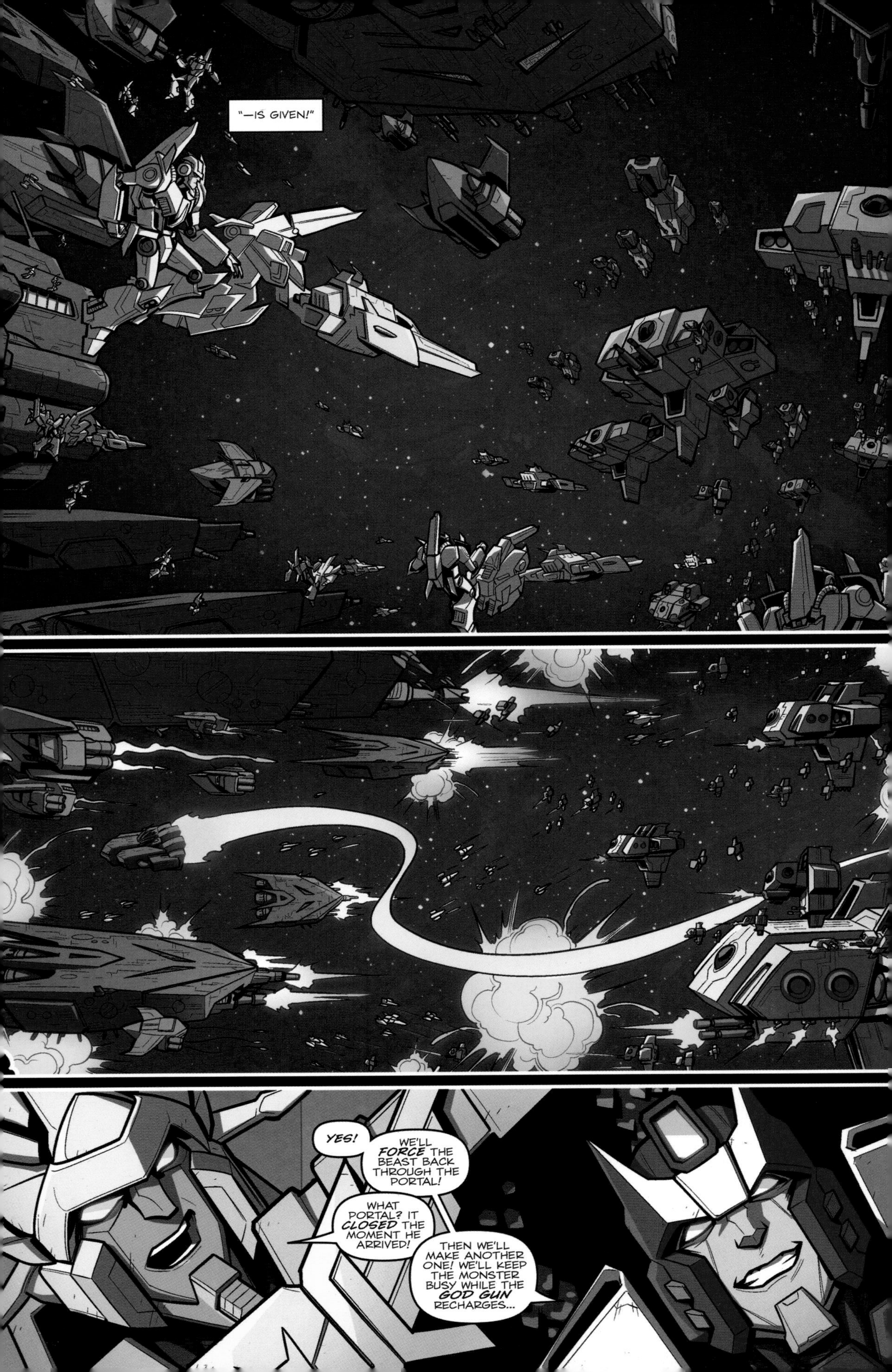
"—IS GIVEN!"
YES!
WE'LL FORCE THE BEAST BACK THROUGH THE PORTAL!
WHAT PORTAL? IT CLOSED THE MOMENT HE ARRIVED!
THEN WE'LL MAKE ANOTHER ONE! WE'LL KEEP THE MONSTER BUSY WHILE THE GOD GUN RECHARGES...

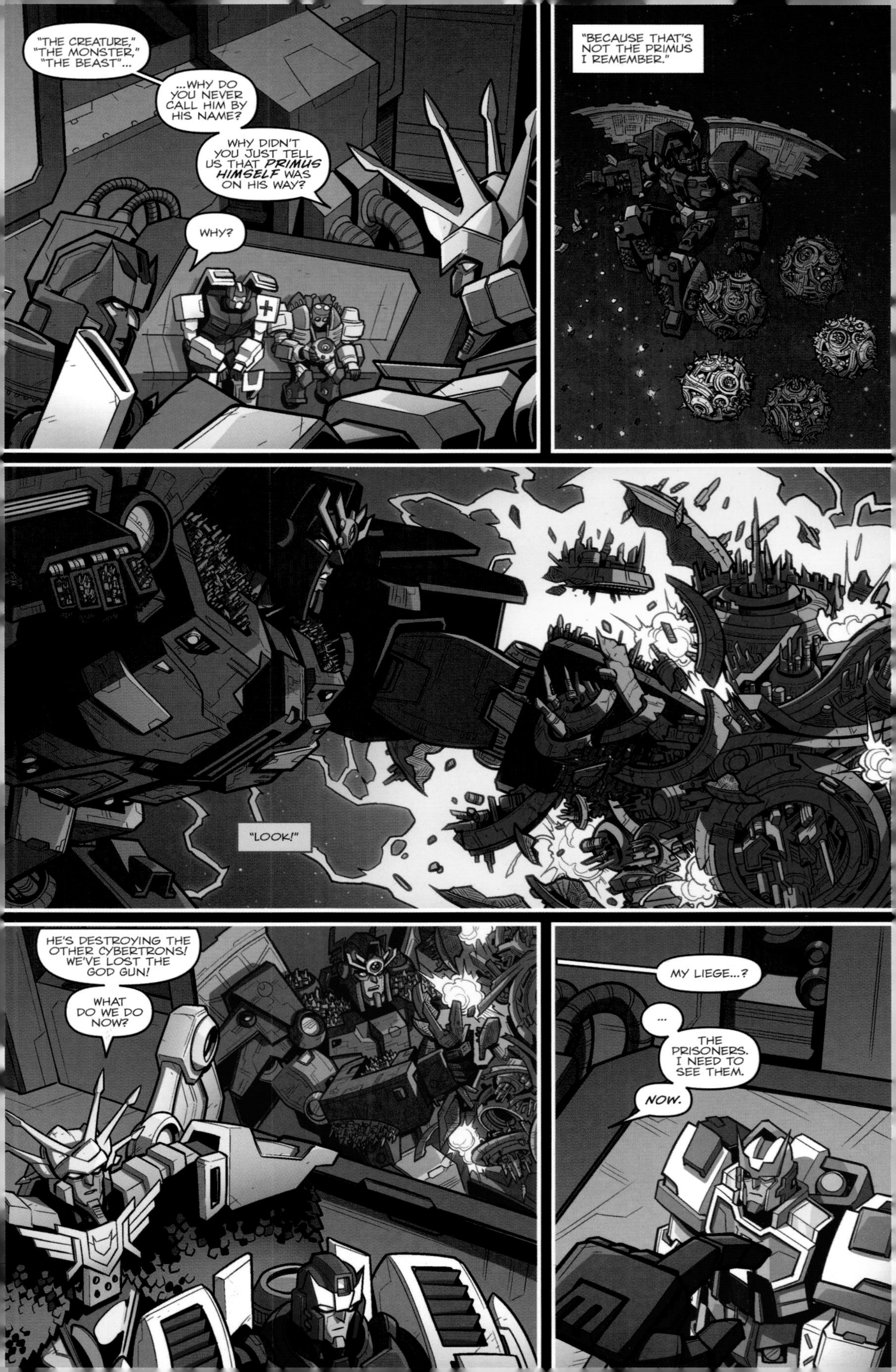
"THE CREATURE," "THE MONSTER," "THE BEAST"...
...WHY DO YOU NEVER CALL HIM BY HIS NAME?
WHY DIDN'T YOU JUST TELL US THAT *PRIMUS HIMSELF* WAS ON HIS WAY?
WHY?
"BECAUSE THAT'S NOT THE PRIMUS I REMEMBER."
"LOOK!"
HE'S DESTROYING THE OTHER CYBERTRONS! WE'VE LOST THE GOD GUN!
WHAT DO WE DO NOW?
MY LIEGE...?
...
THE PRISONERS. I NEED TO SEE THEM.
NOW.

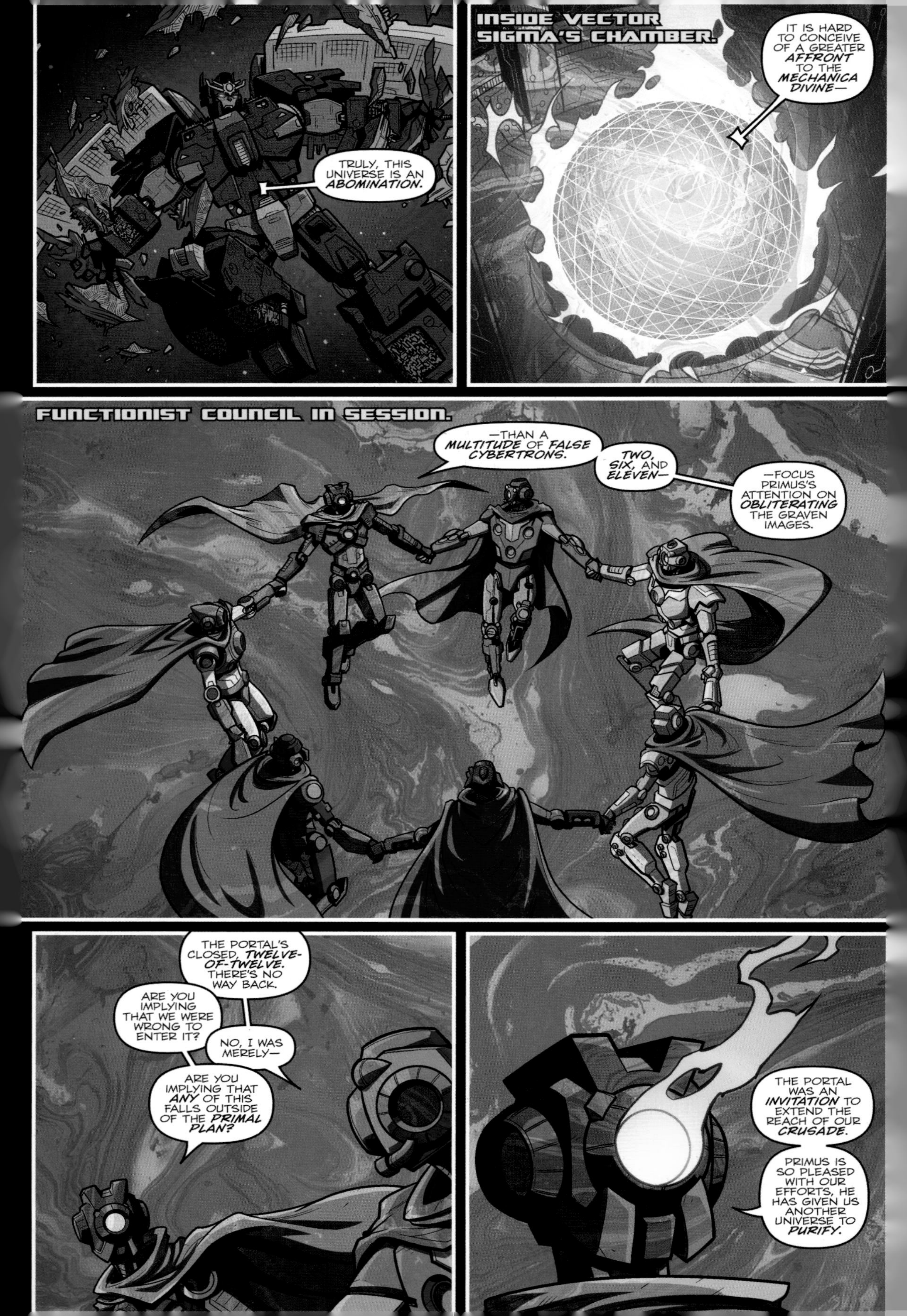
TRULY, THIS UNIVERSE IS AN ABOMINATION.
INSIDE VECTOR SIGMA'S CHAMBER.
IT IS HARD TO CONCEIVE OF A GREATER AFFRONT TO THE MECHANICA DIVINE—
FUNCTIONIST COUNCIL IN SESSION.
—THAN A MULTITUDE OF FALSE CYBERTRONS.
TWO, SIX, AND ELEVEN—
—FOCUS PRIMUS'S ATTENTION ON OBLITERATING THE GRAVEN IMAGES.
THE PORTAL'S CLOSED, TWELVE-OF-TWELVE. THERE'S NO WAY BACK.
ARE YOU IMPLYING THAT WE WERE WRONG TO ENTER IT?
NO, I WAS MERELY—
ARE YOU IMPLYING THAT ANY OF THIS FALLS OUTSIDE OF THE PRIMAL PLAN?
THE PORTAL WAS AN INVITATION TO EXTEND THE REACH OF OUR CRUSADE.
PRIMUS IS SO PLEASED WITH OUR EFFORTS, HE HAS GIVEN US ANOTHER UNIVERSE TO PURIFY.

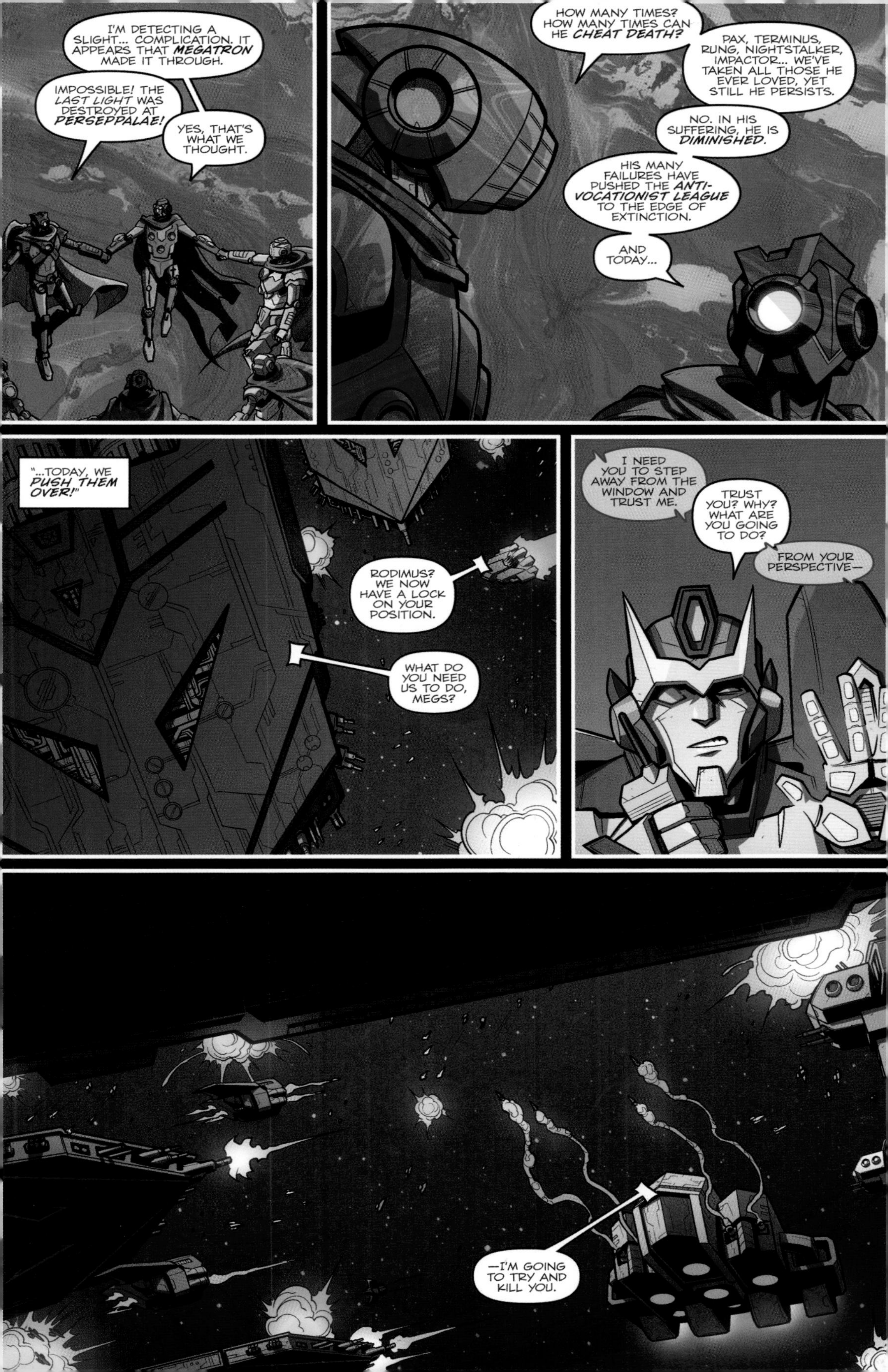

I'M DETECTING A SLIGHT... COMPLICATION. IT APPEARS THAT MEGATRON MADE IT THROUGH.
IMPOSSIBLE! THE LAST LIGHT WAS DESTROYED AT PERSEPPALAE!
YES, THAT'S WHAT WE THOUGHT.
HOW MANY TIMES? HOW MANY TIMES CAN HE CHEAT DEATH?
PAX, TERMINUS, RUNG, NIGHTSTALKER, IMPACTOR... WE'VE TAKEN ALL THOSE HE EVER LOVED, YET STILL HE PERSISTS.
NO. IN HIS SUFFERING, HE IS DIMINISHED.
HIS MANY FAILURES HAVE PUSHED THE ANTI-VOCATIONIST LEAGUE TO THE EDGE OF EXTINCTION.
AND TODAY...
"...TODAY, WE PUSH THEM OVER!"
RODIMUS? WE NOW HAVE A LOCK ON YOUR POSITION.
WHAT DO YOU NEED US TO DO, MEGS?
I NEED YOU TO STEP AWAY FROM THE WINDOW AND TRUST ME.
TRUST YOU? WHY? WHAT ARE YOU GOING TO DO?
FROM YOUR PERSPECTIVE—
—I'M GOING TO TRY AND KILL YOU.

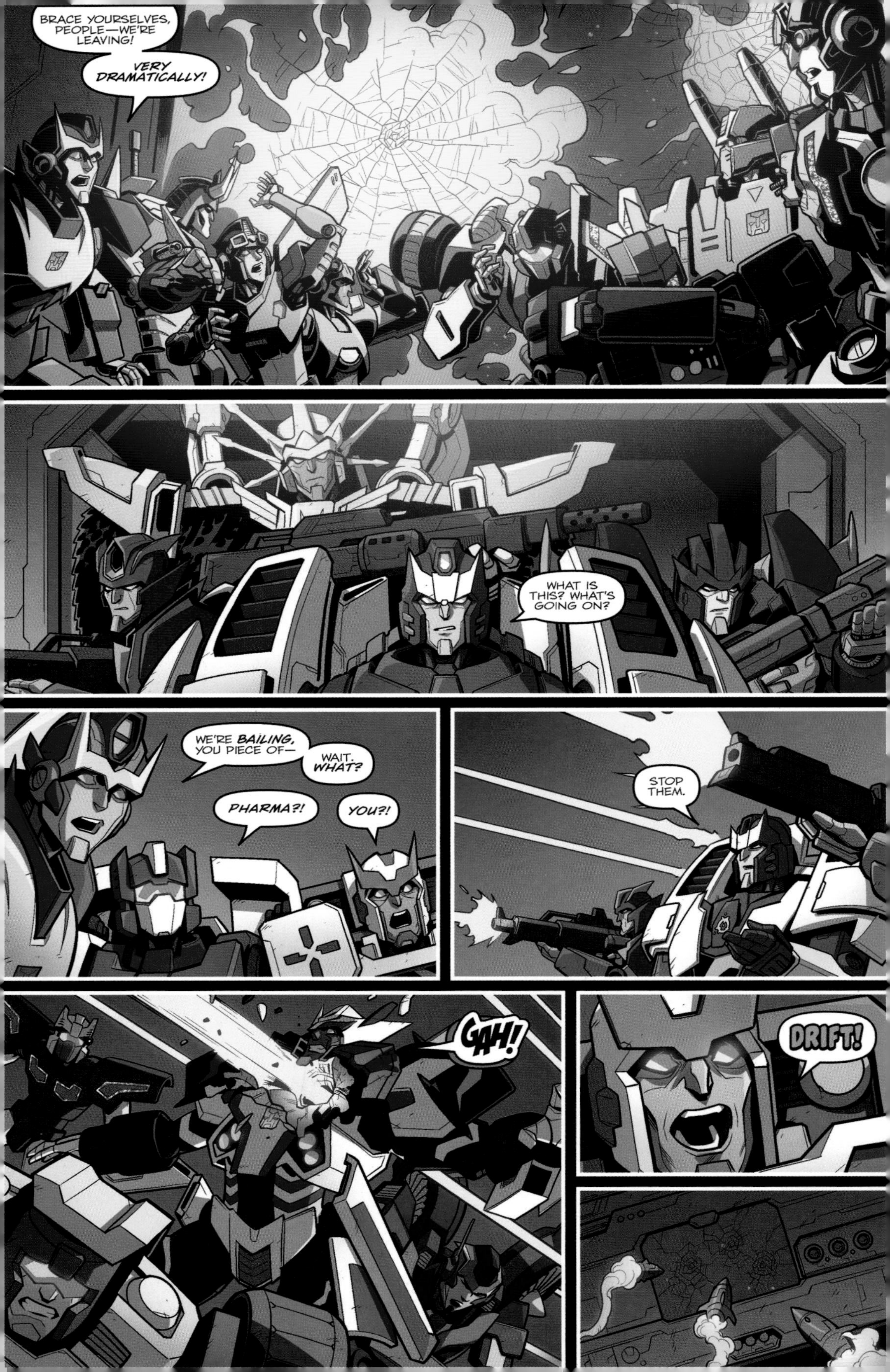

BRACE YOURSELVES, PEOPLE—WE'RE LEAVING!
VERY DRAMATICALLY!
WHAT IS THIS? WHAT'S GOING ON?
WE'RE BAILING, YOU PIECE OF—
WAIT. WHAT?
PHARMA?!
YOU?!
STOP THEM.
GAH!
DRIFT!

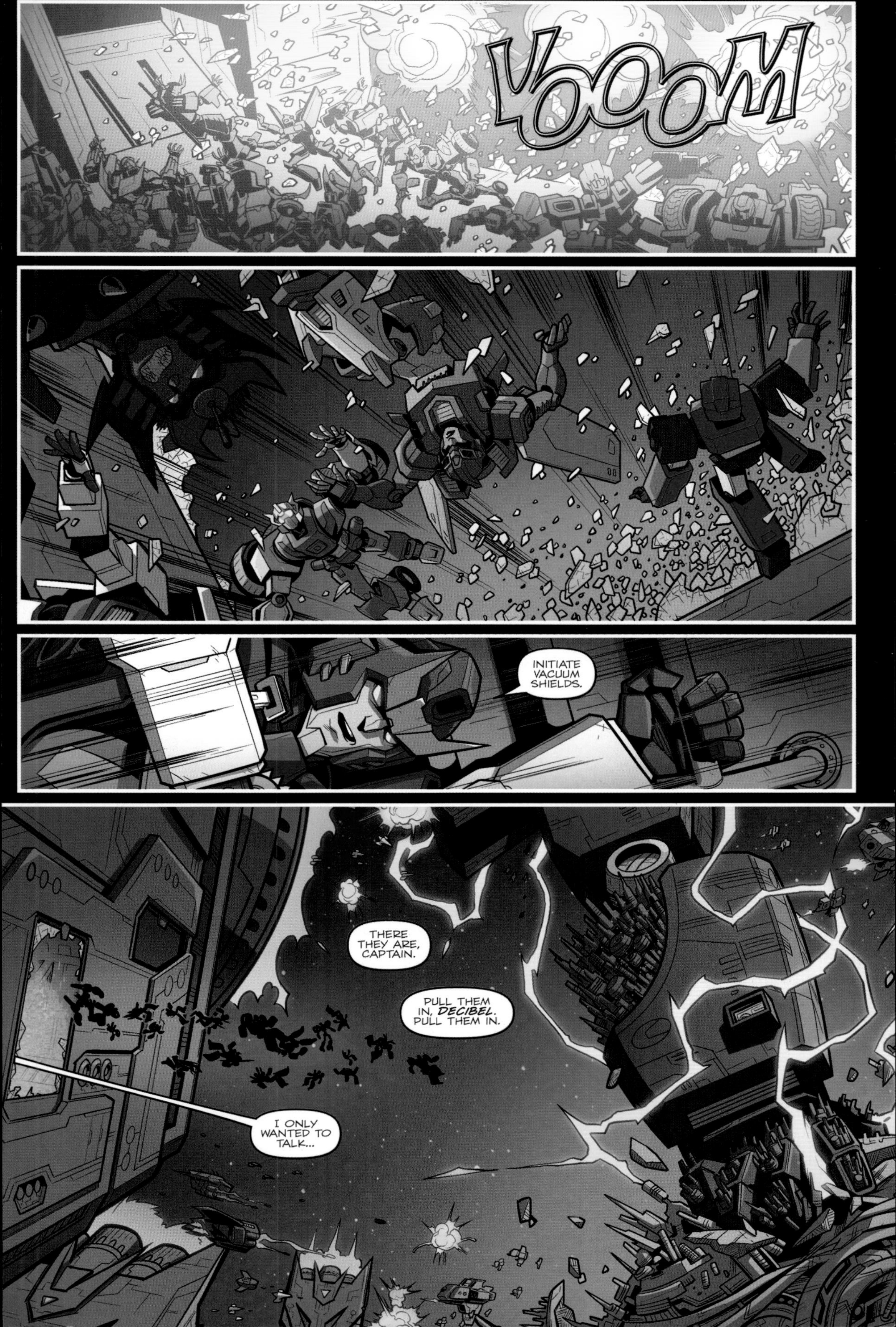
VOOOOM
INITIATE VACUUM SHIELDS.
THERE THEY ARE, CAPTAIN.
PULL THEM IN, *DECIBEL*. PULL THEM IN.
I ONLY WANTED TO TALK...

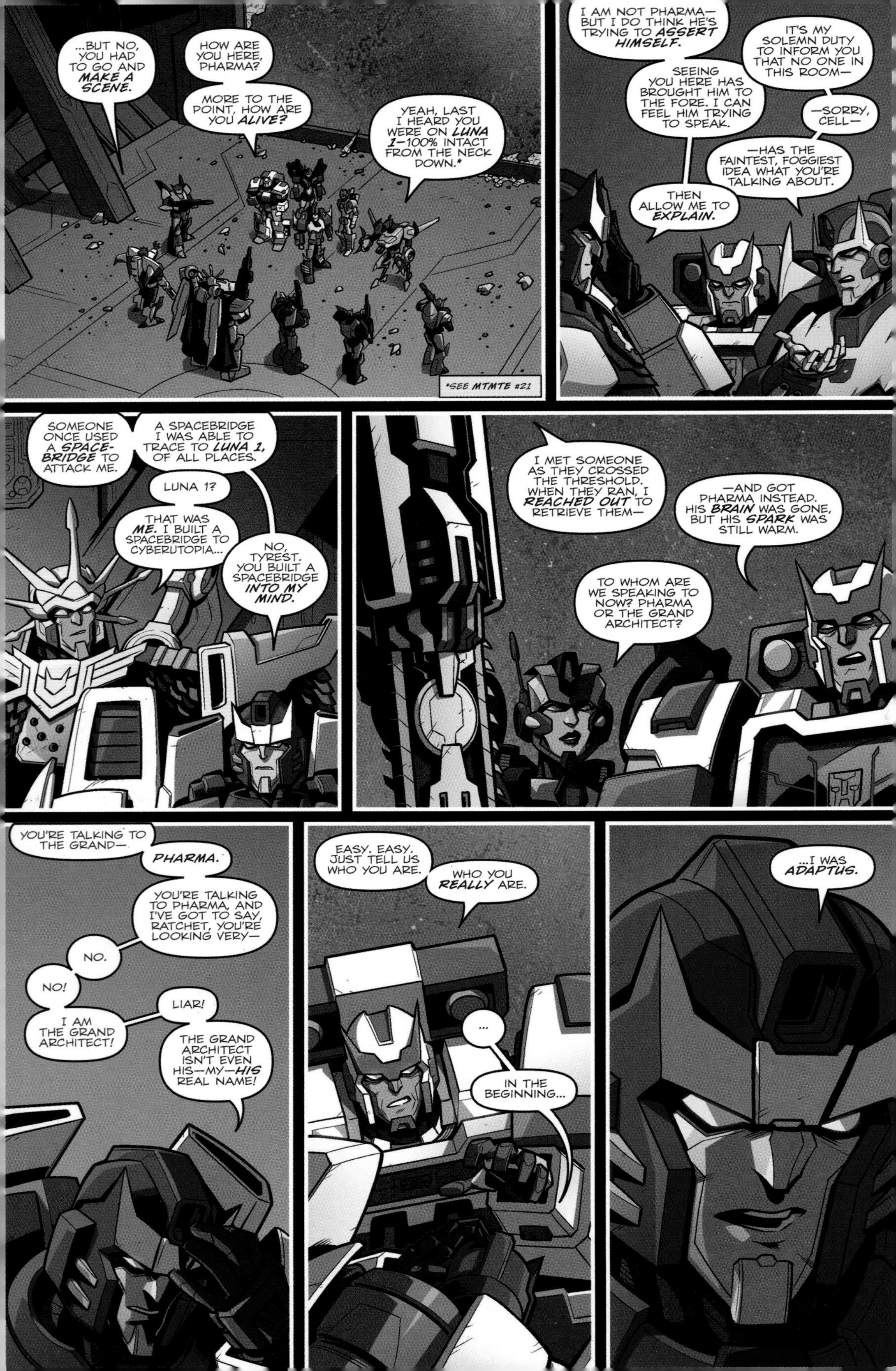
...BUT NO, YOU HAD TO GO AND MAKE A SCENE.
HOW ARE YOU HERE, PHARMA?
MORE TO THE POINT, HOW ARE YOU ALIVE?
YEAH, LAST I HEARD YOU WERE ON LUNA 1—100% INTACT FROM THE NECK DOWN.*
*SEE MTMTE #21
I AM NOT PHARMA—BUT I DO THINK HE'S TRYING TO ASSERT HIMSELF.
SEEING YOU HERE HAS BROUGHT HIM TO THE FORE. I CAN FEEL HIM TRYING TO SPEAK.
IT'S MY SOLEMN DUTY TO INFORM YOU THAT NO ONE IN THIS ROOM—
—SORRY, CELL—
—HAS THE FAINTEST, FOGGIEST IDEA WHAT YOU'RE TALKING ABOUT.
THEN ALLOW ME TO EXPLAIN.
SOMEONE ONCE USED A SPACE-BRIDGE TO ATTACK ME.
A SPACEBRIDGE I WAS ABLE TO TRACE TO LUNA 1, OF ALL PLACES.
LUNA 1?
THAT WAS ME. I BUILT A SPACEBRIDGE TO CYBERUTOPIA...
NO, TYREST. YOU BUILT A SPACEBRIDGE INTO MY MIND.
I MET SOMEONE AS THEY CROSSED THE THRESHOLD. WHEN THEY RAN, I REACHED OUT TO RETRIEVE THEM—
—AND GOT PHARMA INSTEAD. HIS BRAIN WAS GONE, BUT HIS SPARK WAS STILL WARM.
TO WHOM ARE WE SPEAKING TO NOW? PHARMA OR THE GRAND ARCHITECT?
YOU'RE TALKING TO THE GRAND—
PHARMA.
YOU'RE TALKING TO PHARMA, AND I'VE GOT TO SAY, RATCHET, YOU'RE LOOKING VERY—
NO.
NO!
I AM THE GRAND ARCHITECT!
LIAR!
THE GRAND ARCHITECT ISN'T EVEN HIS—MY—HIS REAL NAME!
EASY. EASY. JUST TELL US WHO YOU ARE.
WHO YOU REALLY ARE.
...
IN THE BEGINNING...
...I WAS ADAPTUS.

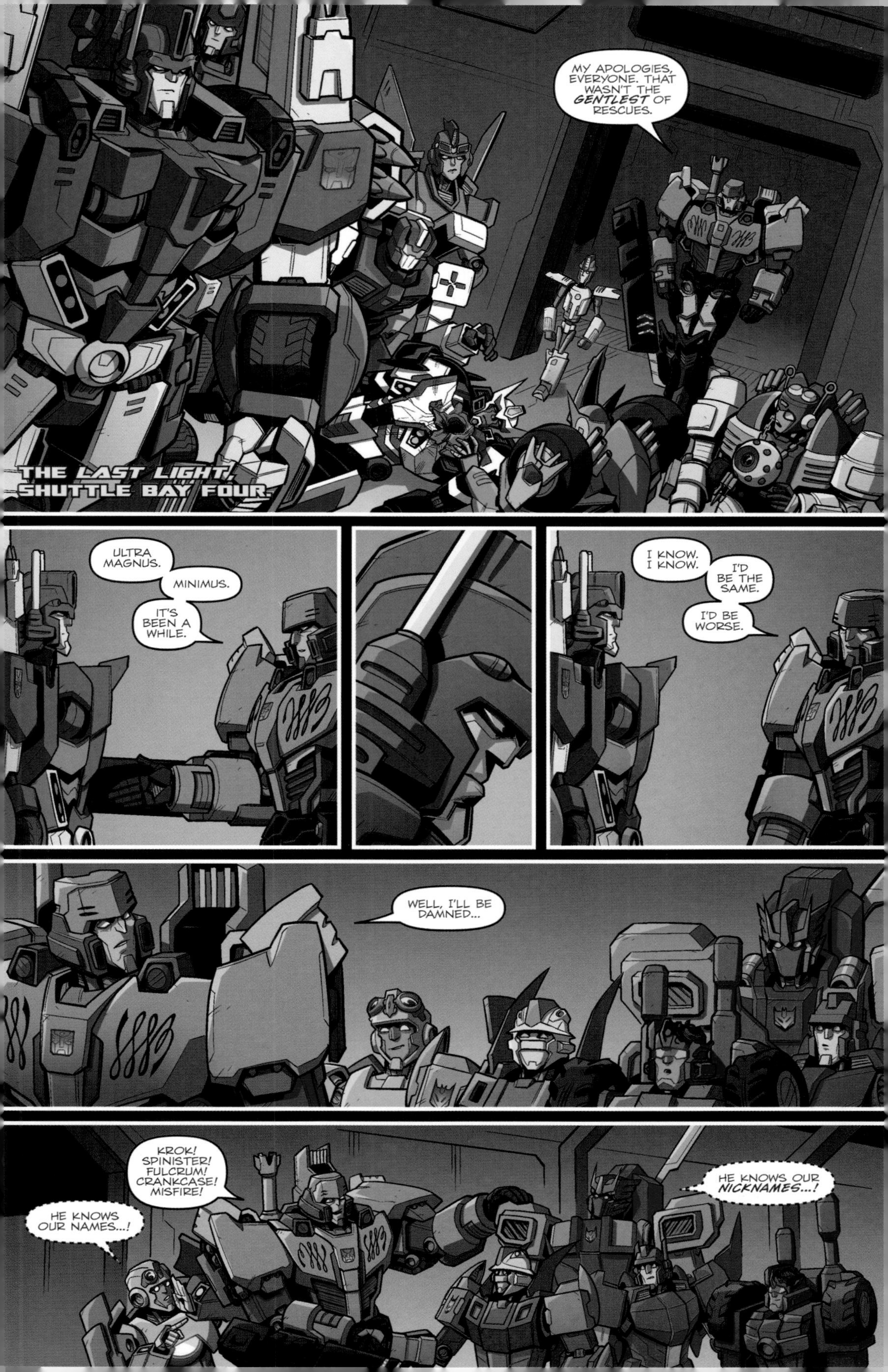
MY APOLOGIES, EVERYONE. THAT WASN'T THE GENTLEST OF RESCUES.
THE LAST LIGHT, SHUTTLE BAY FOUR.
ULTRA MAGNUS.
MINIMUS.
IT'S BEEN A WHILE.
I KNOW. I KNOW.
I'D BE THE SAME.
I'D BE WORSE.
WELL, I'LL BE DAMNED...
KROK! SPINISTER! FULCRUM! CRANKCASE! MISFIRE!
HE KNOWS OUR NAMES...!
HE KNOWS OUR NICKNAMES...!

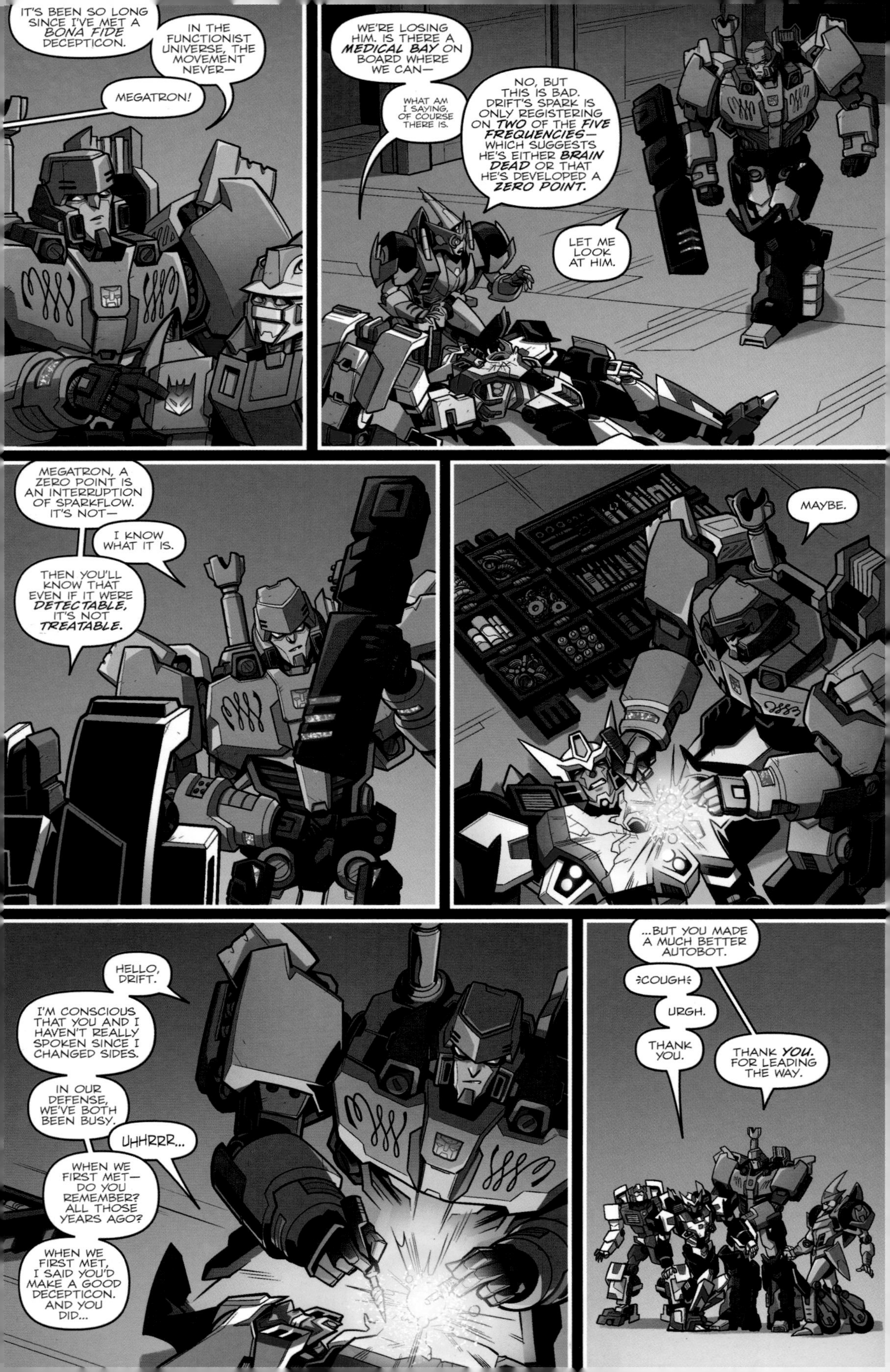
IT'S BEEN SO LONG SINCE I'VE MET A *BONA FIDE* DECEPTICON.
IN THE FUNCTIONIST UNIVERSE, THE MOVEMENT NEVER—
MEGATRON!
WE'RE LOSING HIM. IS THERE A *MEDICAL BAY* ON BOARD WHERE WE CAN—
WHAT AM I SAYING, OF COURSE THERE IS.
NO, BUT THIS IS BAD. DRIFT'S SPARK IS ONLY REGISTERING ON *TWO* OF THE *FIVE FREQUENCIES*— WHICH SUGGESTS HE'S EITHER *BRAIN DEAD* OR THAT HE'S DEVELOPED A *ZERO POINT.*
LET ME LOOK AT HIM.
MEGATRON, A ZERO POINT IS AN INTERRUPTION OF SPARKFLOW. IT'S NOT—
I KNOW WHAT IT IS.
THEN YOU'LL KNOW THAT EVEN IF IT WERE *DETECTABLE,* IT'S NOT *TREATABLE.*
MAYBE.
HELLO, DRIFT.
I'M CONSCIOUS THAT YOU AND I HAVEN'T REALLY SPOKEN SINCE I CHANGED SIDES.
IN OUR DEFENSE, WE'VE BOTH BEEN BUSY.
UHHRRR...
WHEN WE FIRST MET— DO YOU REMEMBER? ALL THOSE YEARS AGO?
WHEN WE FIRST MET, I SAID YOU'D MAKE A GOOD DECEPTICON. AND YOU DID...
...BUT YOU MADE A MUCH BETTER AUTOBOT.
COUGH
URGH.
THANK YOU.
THANK *YOU.* FOR LEADING THE WAY.

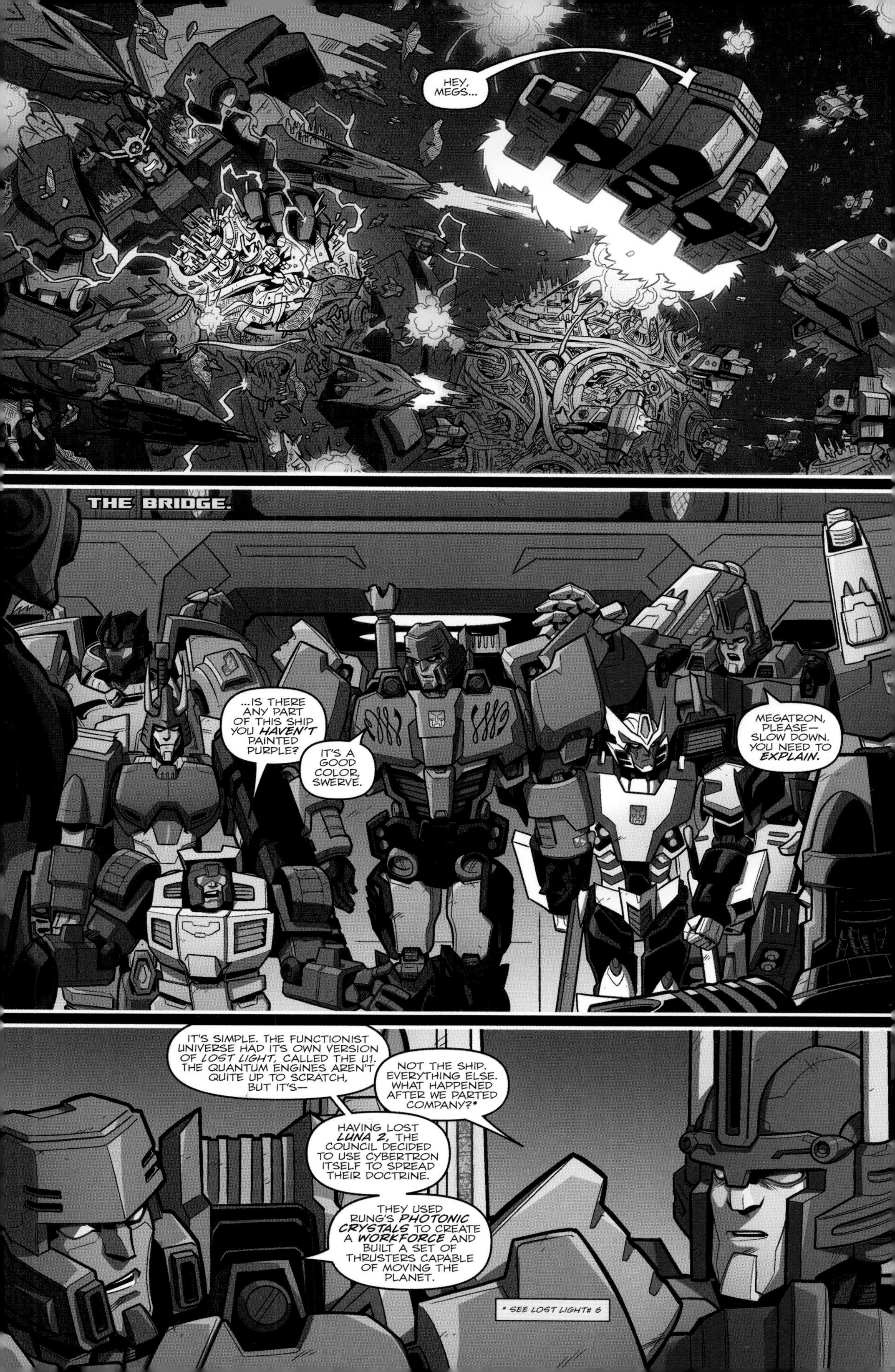
HEY, MEGS...
THE BRIDGE.
...IS THERE ANY PART OF THIS SHIP YOU *HAVEN'T* PAINTED PURPLE?
IT'S A GOOD COLOR, SWERVE.
MEGATRON, PLEASE— SLOW DOWN. YOU NEED TO *EXPLAIN.*
IT'S SIMPLE. THE FUNCTIONIST UNIVERSE HAD ITS OWN VERSION OF *LOST LIGHT,* CALLED THE U1. THE QUANTUM ENGINES AREN'T QUITE UP TO SCRATCH, BUT IT'S—
NOT THE SHIP. EVERYTHING ELSE. WHAT HAPPENED AFTER WE PARTED COMPANY?*
HAVING LOST *LUNA 2,* THE COUNCIL DECIDED TO USE CYBERTRON ITSELF TO SPREAD THEIR DOCTRINE.
THEY USED RUNG'S *PHOTONIC CRYSTALS* TO CREATE A *WORKFORCE* AND BUILT A SET OF THRUSTERS CAPABLE OF MOVING THE PLANET.
* SEE LOST LIGHT# 6

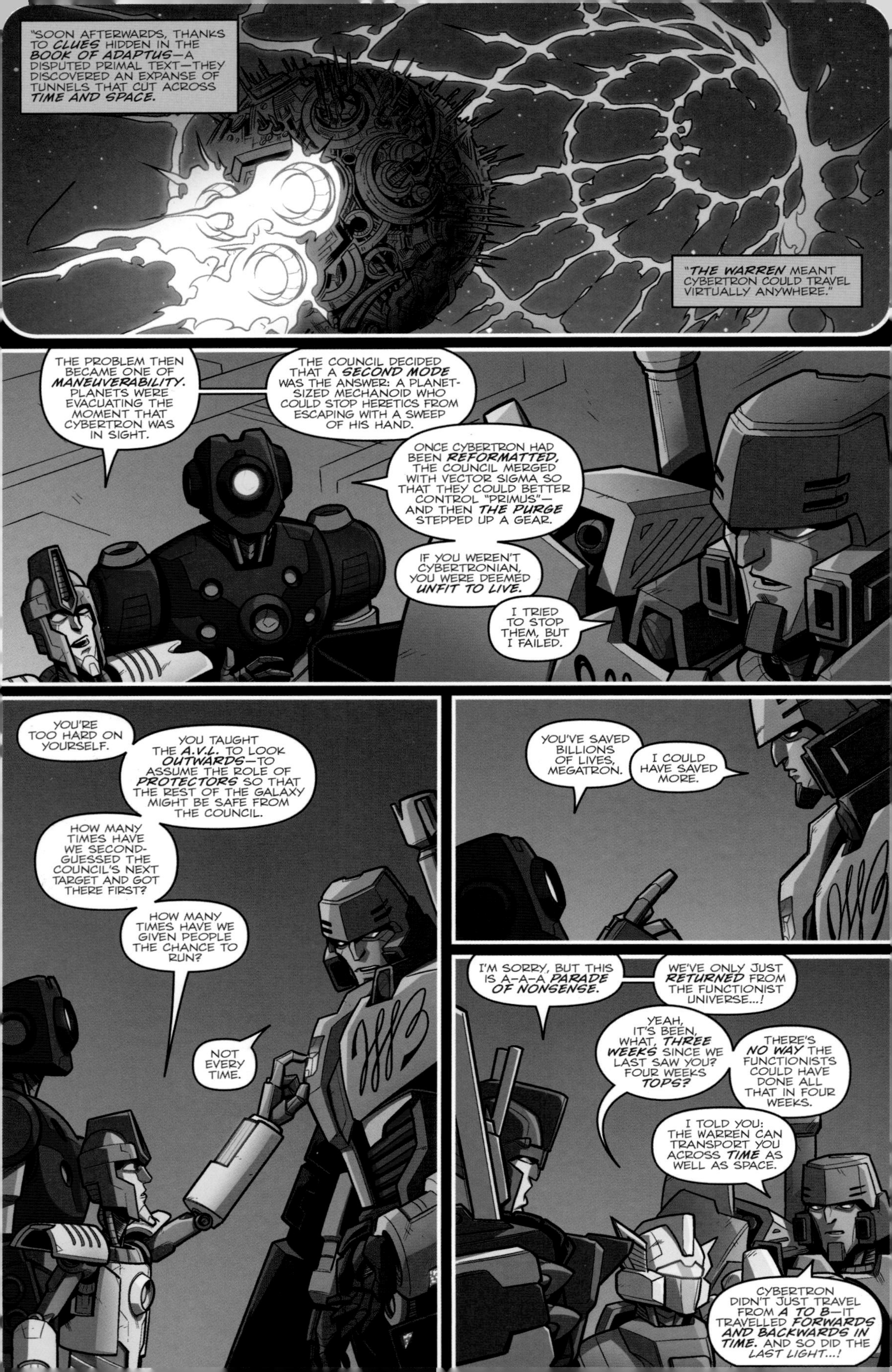
"SOON AFTERWARDS, THANKS TO CLUES HIDDEN IN THE BOOK OF ADAPTUS—A DISPUTED PRIMAL TEXT—THEY DISCOVERED AN EXPANSE OF TUNNELS THAT CUT ACROSS TIME AND SPACE.
"THE WARREN MEANT CYBERTRON COULD TRAVEL VIRTUALLY ANYWHERE."
THE PROBLEM THEN BECAME ONE OF MANEUVERABILITY. PLANETS WERE EVACUATING THE MOMENT THAT CYBERTRON WAS IN SIGHT.
THE COUNCIL DECIDED THAT A SECOND MODE WAS THE ANSWER: A PLANET-SIZED MECHANOID WHO COULD STOP HERETICS FROM ESCAPING WITH A SWEEP OF HIS HAND.
ONCE CYBERTRON HAD BEEN REFORMATTED, THE COUNCIL MERGED WITH VECTOR SIGMA SO THAT THEY COULD BETTER CONTROL "PRIMUS"—AND THEN THE PURGE STEPPED UP A GEAR.
IF YOU WEREN'T CYBERTRONIAN, YOU WERE DEEMED UNFIT TO LIVE.
I TRIED TO STOP THEM, BUT I FAILED.
YOU'RE TOO HARD ON YOURSELF.
YOU TAUGHT THE A.V.L. TO LOOK OUTWARDS—TO ASSUME THE ROLE OF PROTECTORS SO THAT THE REST OF THE GALAXY MIGHT BE SAFE FROM THE COUNCIL.
HOW MANY TIMES HAVE WE SECOND-GUESSED THE COUNCIL'S NEXT TARGET AND GOT THERE FIRST?
HOW MANY TIMES HAVE WE GIVEN PEOPLE THE CHANCE TO RUN?
NOT EVERY TIME.
YOU'VE SAVED BILLIONS OF LIVES, MEGATRON.
I COULD HAVE SAVED MORE.
I'M SORRY, BUT THIS IS A-A-A PARADE OF NONSENSE.
WE'VE ONLY JUST RETURNED FROM THE FUNCTIONIST UNIVERSE...!
YEAH, IT'S BEEN, WHAT, THREE WEEKS SINCE WE LAST SAW YOU? FOUR WEEKS TOPS?
THERE'S NO WAY THE FUNCTIONISTS COULD HAVE DONE ALL THAT IN FOUR WEEKS.
I TOLD YOU: THE WARREN CAN TRANSPORT YOU ACROSS TIME AS WELL AS SPACE.
CYBERTRON DIDN'T JUST TRAVEL FROM A TO B—IT TRAVELLED FORWARDS AND BACKWARDS IN TIME. AND SO DID THE LAST LIGHT...!

"FOUR WEEKS..."

MINIMUS, I'VE NOT SEEN YOU IN **CENTURIES**.

LOOK, I'M GLAD EVERYONE'S ON THE **SAME PAGE**...

...BUT IT'S THE LAST PAGE IN A BOOK CALLED **WE'RE ALL GOING TO DIE.**

WHAT? THAT'S NOT EVEN CLEVER.

I LOVE IT.

CON'S GOT A POINT, THOUGH. HOW DO WE STOP PRIMUS FROM SCREWING UP ANOTHER UNIVERSE?

WE BLOW HIM UP.

WE BLOW HIM UP. THAT'S YOUR PLAN.

WHAT'S **YOUR** PLAN, WE **DON'T** BLOW HIM UP?

GRIMLOCK'S RIGHT: YOU **SHOULD** BLOW HIM UP. YOU'RE **DESTINED** TO.

Y'KNOW, THAT THING'S KIND OF **SELECTIVE** WITH ITS INTER-JECTIONS...

DESTINED TO...?

TAILGATE'S HERE, BUT IT'S IMPERATIVE WE FIND RATCHET, RUNG, AND RODIMUS.

BECAUSE ALLITERATION?

WE ARE NOT BLOWING UP PRIMUS.

WELL NO, NOT WITH **THAT** ATTITUDE...

WHEN THE COUNCIL BEGAN **THE PURGE,** WHAT DO YOU THINK HAPPENED TO THE REST OF THE CYBERTRONIAN RACE? NOT THE SOLDIERS, THE **CITIZENS.** WHERE DO YOU THINK THEY WENT?

THEY WENT **NOWHERE.** THEY STAYED ON CYBERTRON. THEY HAD NO CHOICE.

ENLIGHTEN US.

AH.

PRECISELY. WE CAN'T BLOW UP PRIMUS—

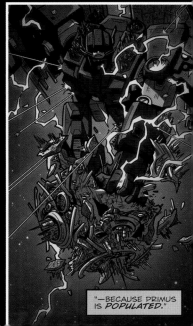

"—BECAUSE PRIMUS IS **POPULATED.**"

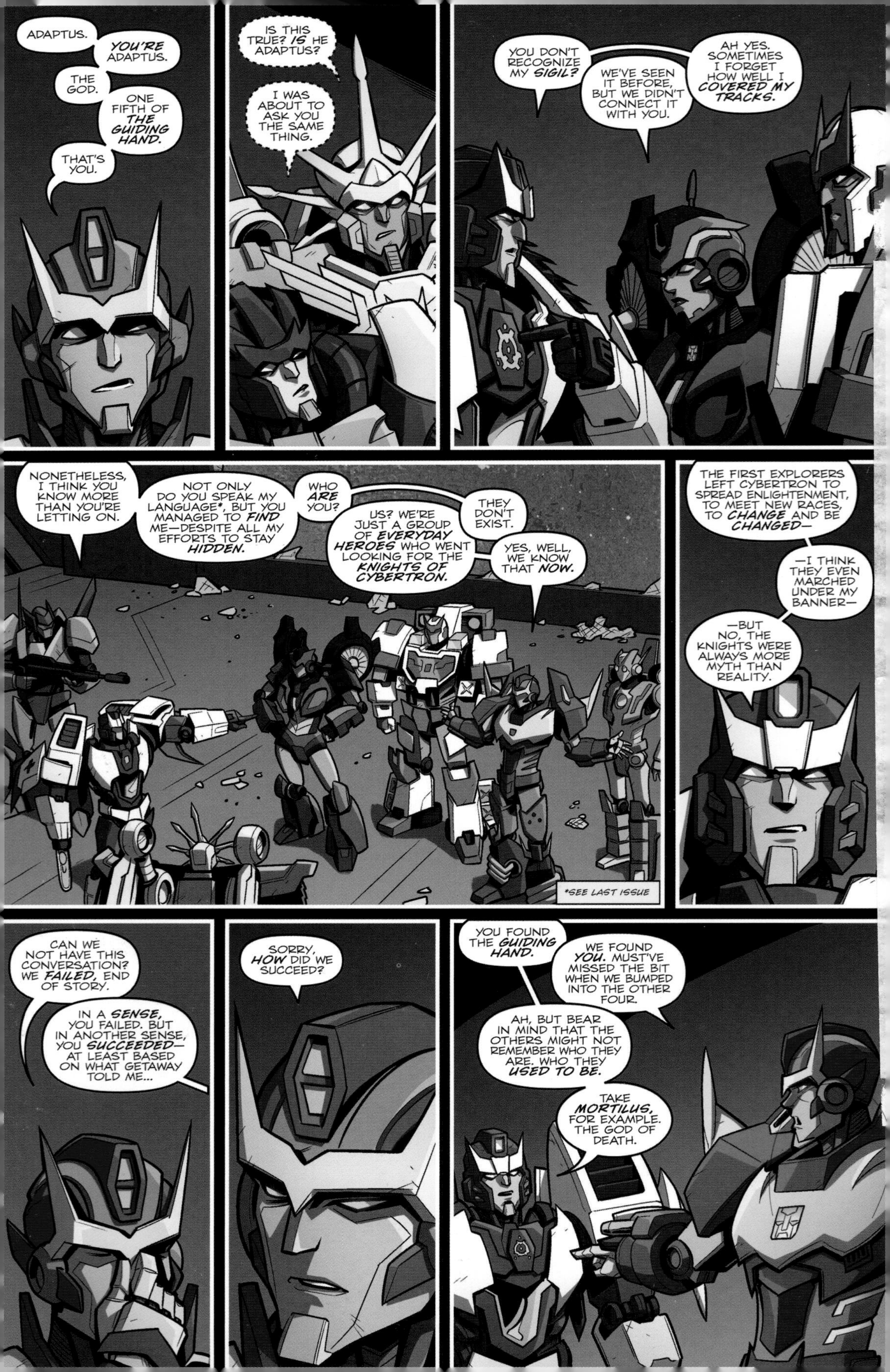
ADAPTUS.
YOU'RE ADAPTUS.
THE GOD.
ONE FIFTH OF THE GUIDING HAND.
THAT'S YOU.
IS THIS TRUE? IS HE ADAPTUS?
I WAS ABOUT TO ASK YOU THE SAME THING.
YOU DON'T RECOGNIZE MY SIGIL?
WE'VE SEEN IT BEFORE, BUT WE DIDN'T CONNECT IT WITH YOU.
AH YES. SOMETIMES I FORGET HOW WELL I COVERED MY TRACKS.
NONETHELESS, I THINK YOU KNOW MORE THAN YOU'RE LETTING ON.
NOT ONLY DO YOU SPEAK MY LANGUAGE*, BUT YOU MANAGED TO FIND ME—DESPITE ALL MY EFFORTS TO STAY HIDDEN.
WHO ARE YOU?
US? WE'RE JUST A GROUP OF EVERYDAY HEROES WHO WENT LOOKING FOR THE KNIGHTS OF CYBERTRON.
THEY DON'T EXIST.
YES, WELL, WE KNOW THAT NOW.
*SEE LAST ISSUE
THE FIRST EXPLORERS LEFT CYBERTRON TO SPREAD ENLIGHTENMENT, TO MEET NEW RACES, TO CHANGE AND BE CHANGED—
—I THINK THEY EVEN MARCHED UNDER MY BANNER—
—BUT NO, THE KNIGHTS WERE ALWAYS MORE MYTH THAN REALITY.
CAN WE NOT HAVE THIS CONVERSATION? WE FAILED, END OF STORY.
IN A SENSE, YOU FAILED. BUT IN ANOTHER SENSE, YOU SUCCEEDED—AT LEAST BASED ON WHAT GETAWAY TOLD ME...
SORRY, HOW DID WE SUCCEED?
YOU FOUND THE GUIDING HAND.
WE FOUND YOU. MUST'VE MISSED THE BIT WHEN WE BUMPED INTO THE OTHER FOUR.
AH, BUT BEAR IN MIND THAT THE OTHERS MIGHT NOT REMEMBER WHO THEY ARE. WHO THEY USED TO BE.
TAKE MORTILUS, FOR EXAMPLE. THE GOD OF DEATH.

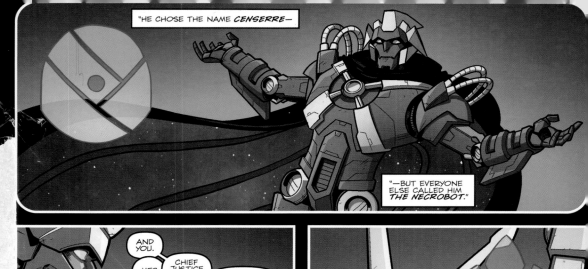

"HE CHOSE THE NAME *CENSERRE*—

"—BUT EVERYONE ELSE CALLED HIM *THE NECROBOT.*"

AND YOU.

ME?

CHIEF JUSTICE TYREST.

ARBITRATOR, MEDIATOR, NEGOTIATOR.

WISDOM INCARNATE.

TO ME, YOU'LL ALWAYS BE *SOLOMUS.*

"AND ONE OF YOU EVEN CARRIES *EPISTEMUS* AROUND THEIR NECK...!

"THE *FONT OF ALL KNOWLEDGE,* REDUCED TO A *BAUBLE.*"

"NOT QUITE AS *MAGNIFICENT* AS THE NAME SUGGESTS."

AND I GUESS OLD *PRIMUS* MAKES FIVE...

HAH! NO, NO, NO.

THAT'S NOT *PRIMUS...*

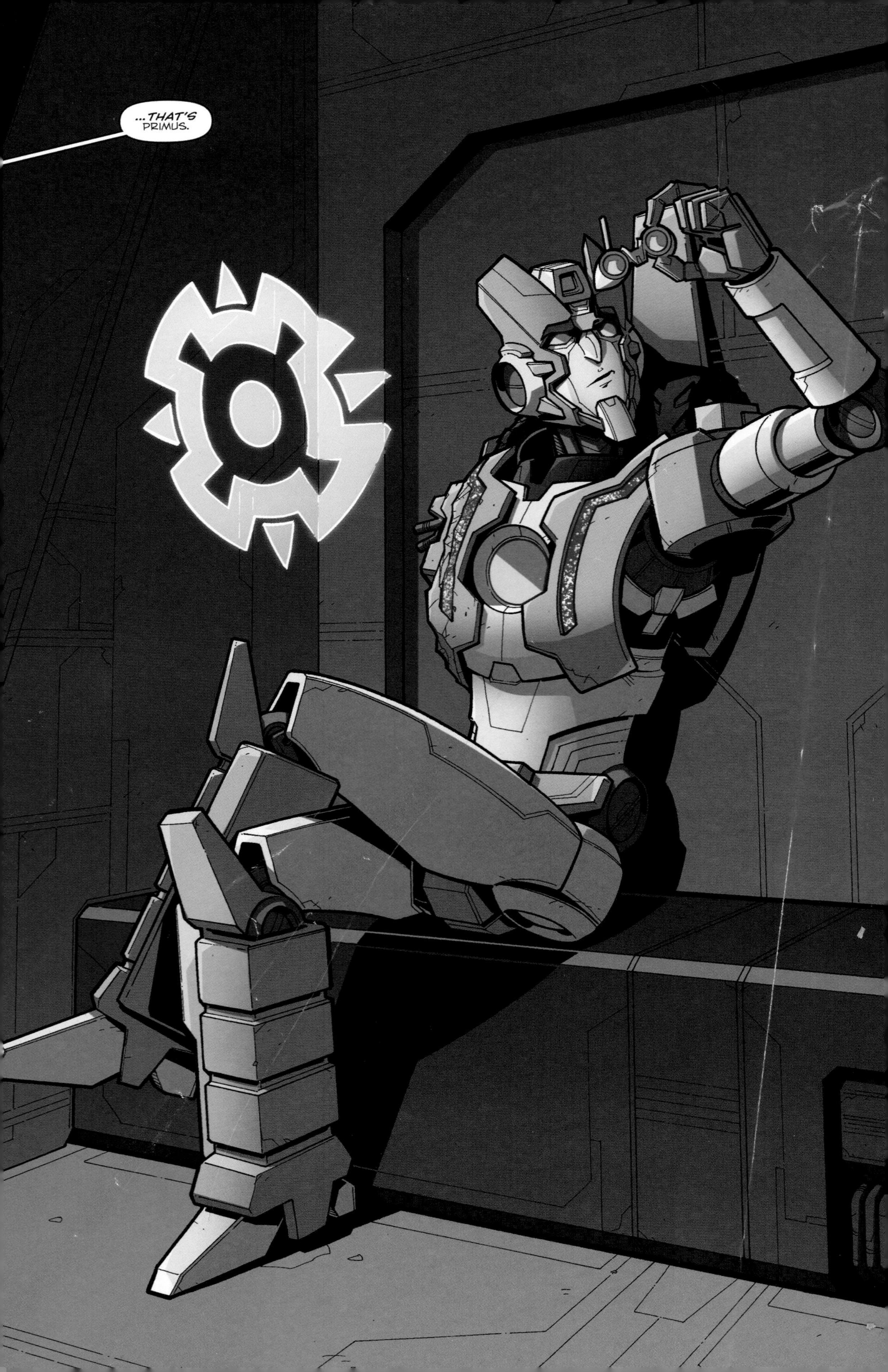
...THAT'S PRIMUS.

ART BY **GEOFF SENIOR**
COLORS BY **JOSH BURCHAM**

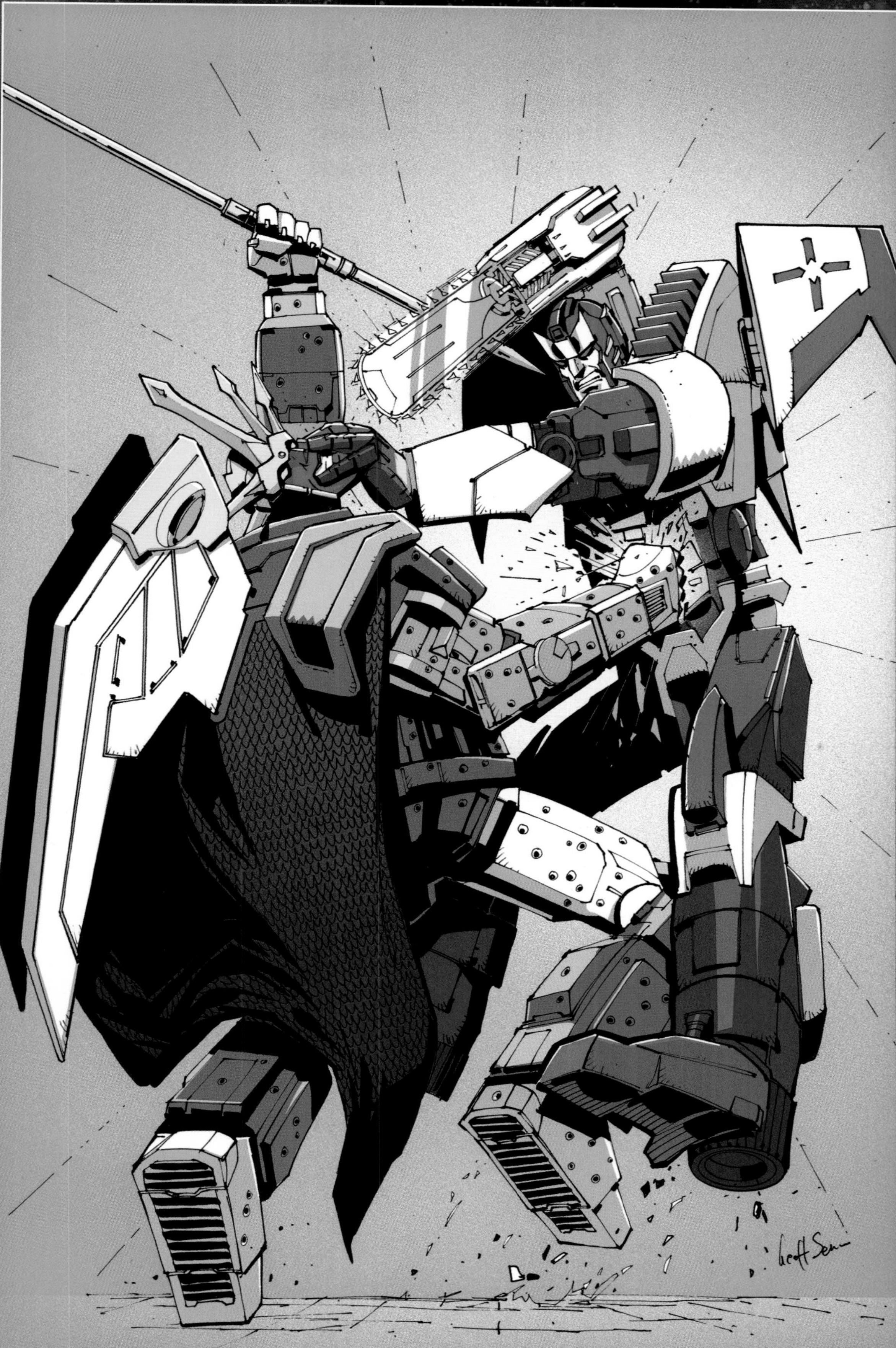

Z3

ART BY **JACK LAWRENCE**
COLORS BY **JOANA LAFUENTE**

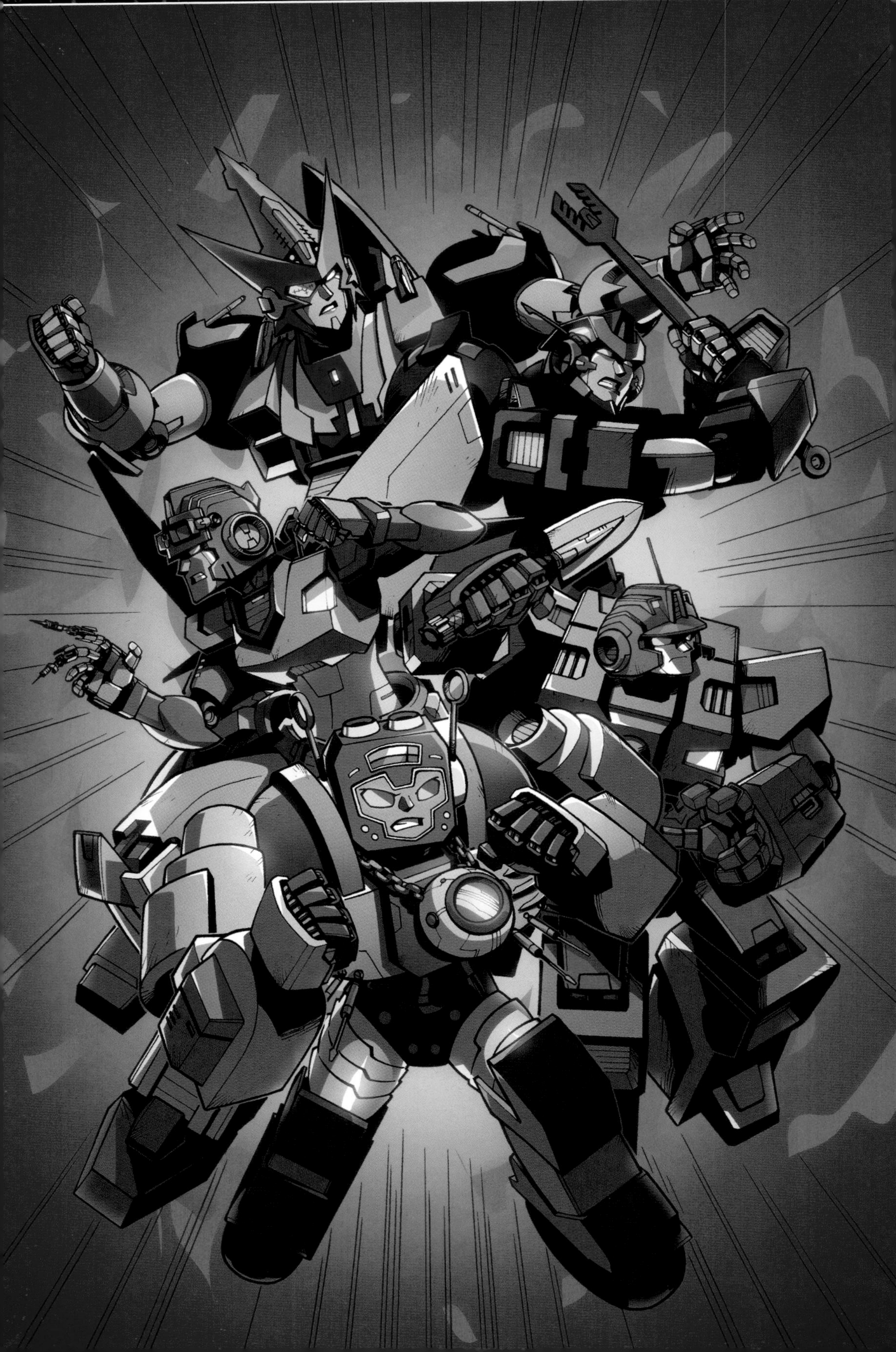

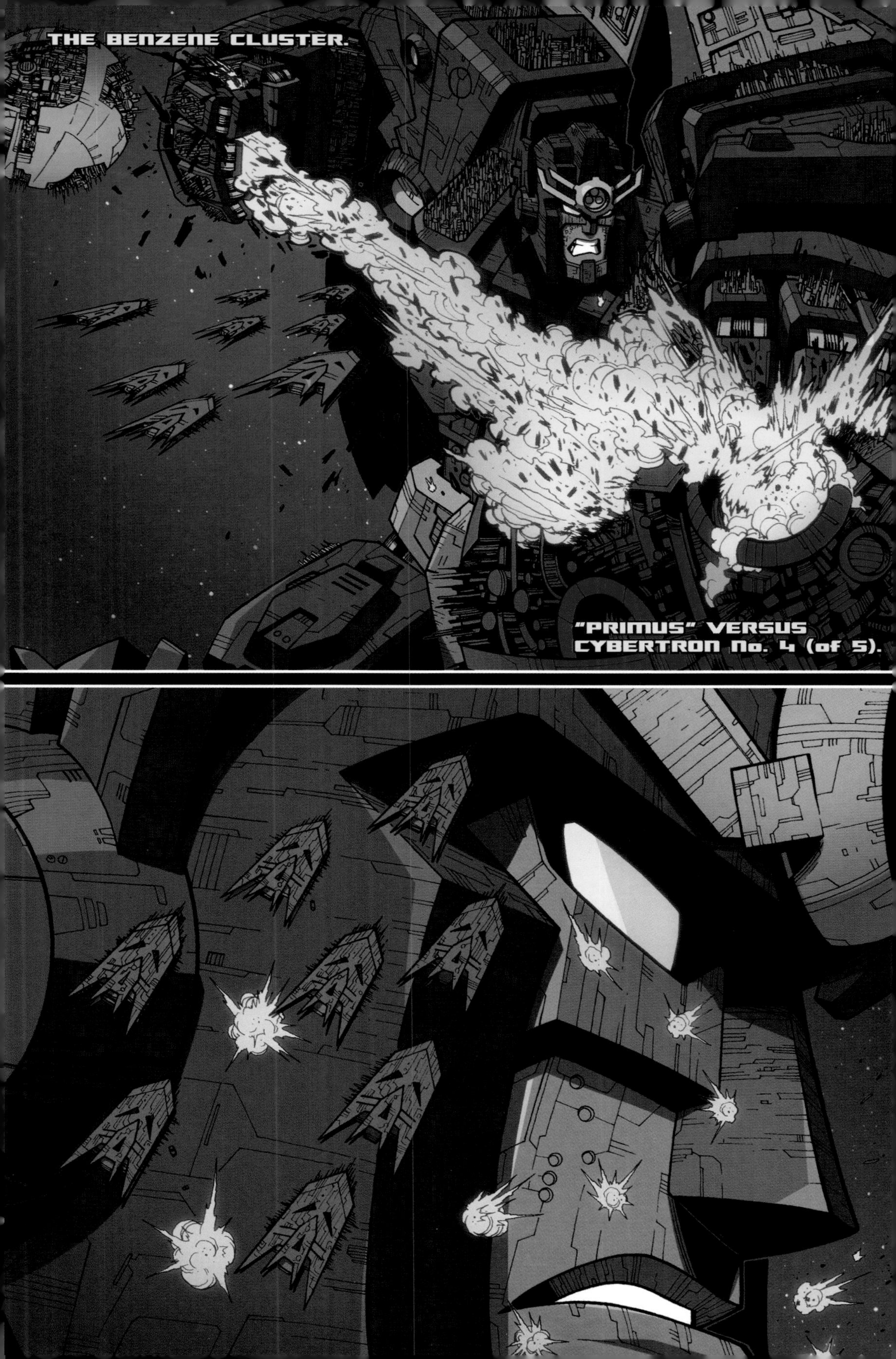
THE BENZENE CLUSTER.
"PRIMUS" VERSUS
CYBERTRON No. 4 (of 5).

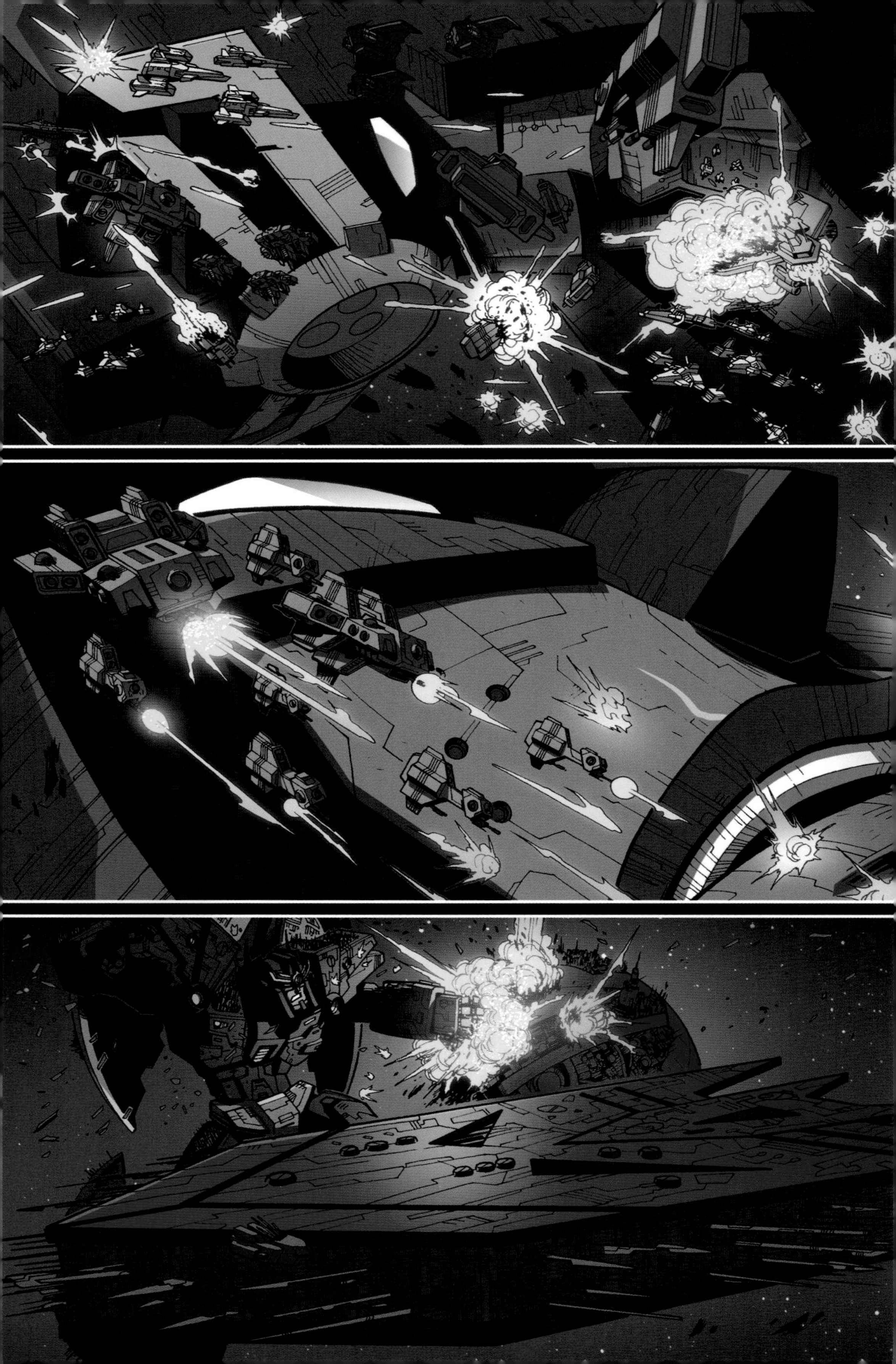

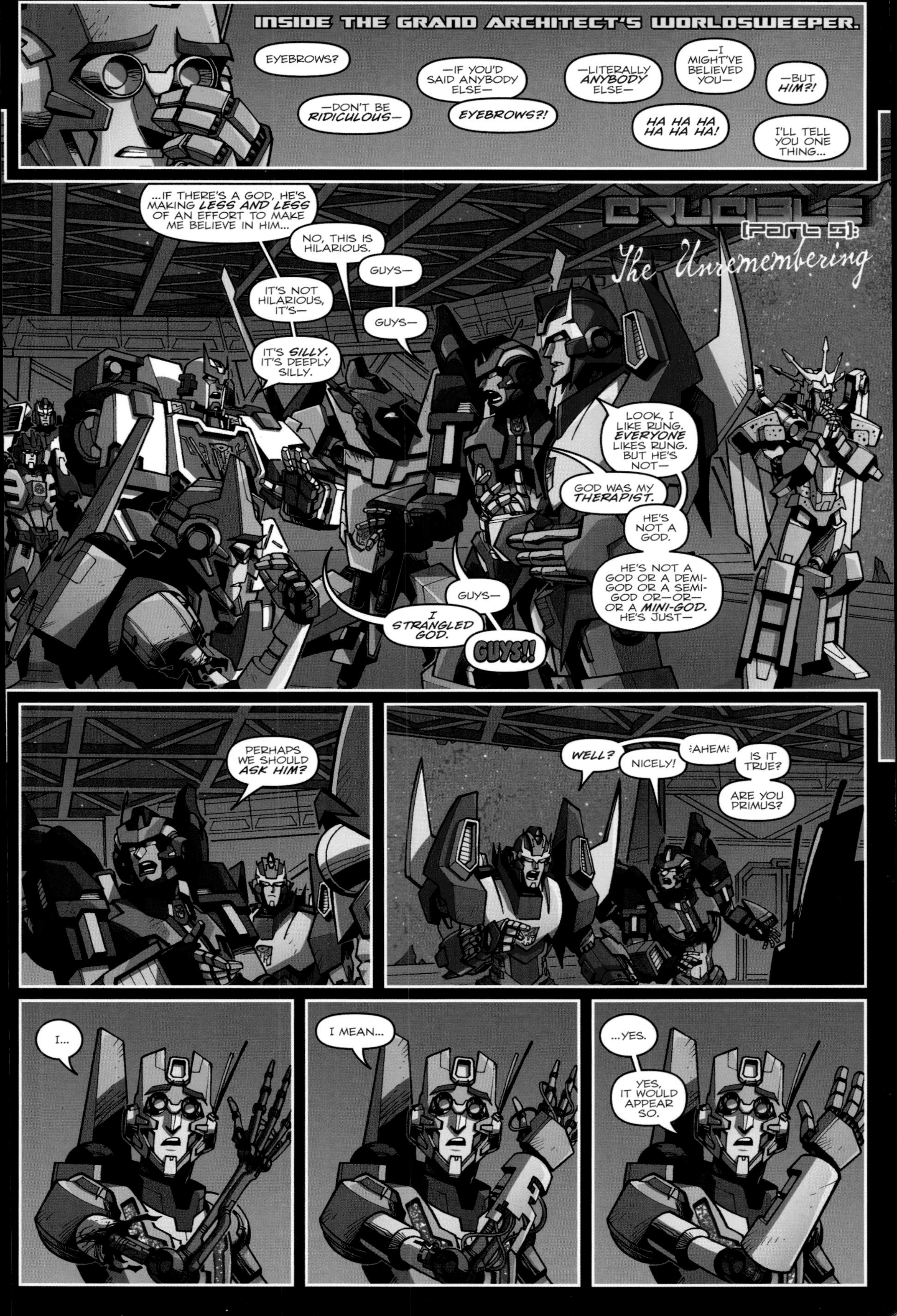

INSIDE THE GRAND ARCHITECT'S WORLDSWEEPER.
EYEBROWS?
—DON'T BE RIDICULOUS—
—IF YOU'D SAID ANYBODY ELSE—
EYEBROWS?!
—LITERALLY ANYBODY ELSE—
—I MIGHT'VE BELIEVED YOU—
HA HA HA HA HA HA!
—BUT HIM?!
I'LL TELL YOU ONE THING...
...IF THERE'S A GOD, HE'S MAKING LESS AND LESS OF AN EFFORT TO MAKE ME BELIEVE IN HIM...
CRUCIBLE (PART 5): The Unremembering
NO, THIS IS HILARIOUS.
GUYS—
IT'S NOT HILARIOUS, IT'S—
GUYS—
IT'S SILLY. IT'S DEEPLY SILLY.
LOOK, I LIKE RUNG. EVERYONE LIKES RUNG. BUT HE'S NOT—
GOD WAS MY THERAPIST.
HE'S NOT A GOD.
HE'S NOT A GOD OR A DEMI-GOD OR A SEMI-GOD OR—OR—OR A MINI-GOD. HE'S JUST—
GUYS—
I STRANGLED GOD.
GUYS!!
PERHAPS WE SHOULD ASK HIM?
WELL?
NICELY!
AHEM
IS IT TRUE?
ARE YOU PRIMUS?
I...
I MEAN...
...YES.
YES, IT WOULD APPEAR SO.

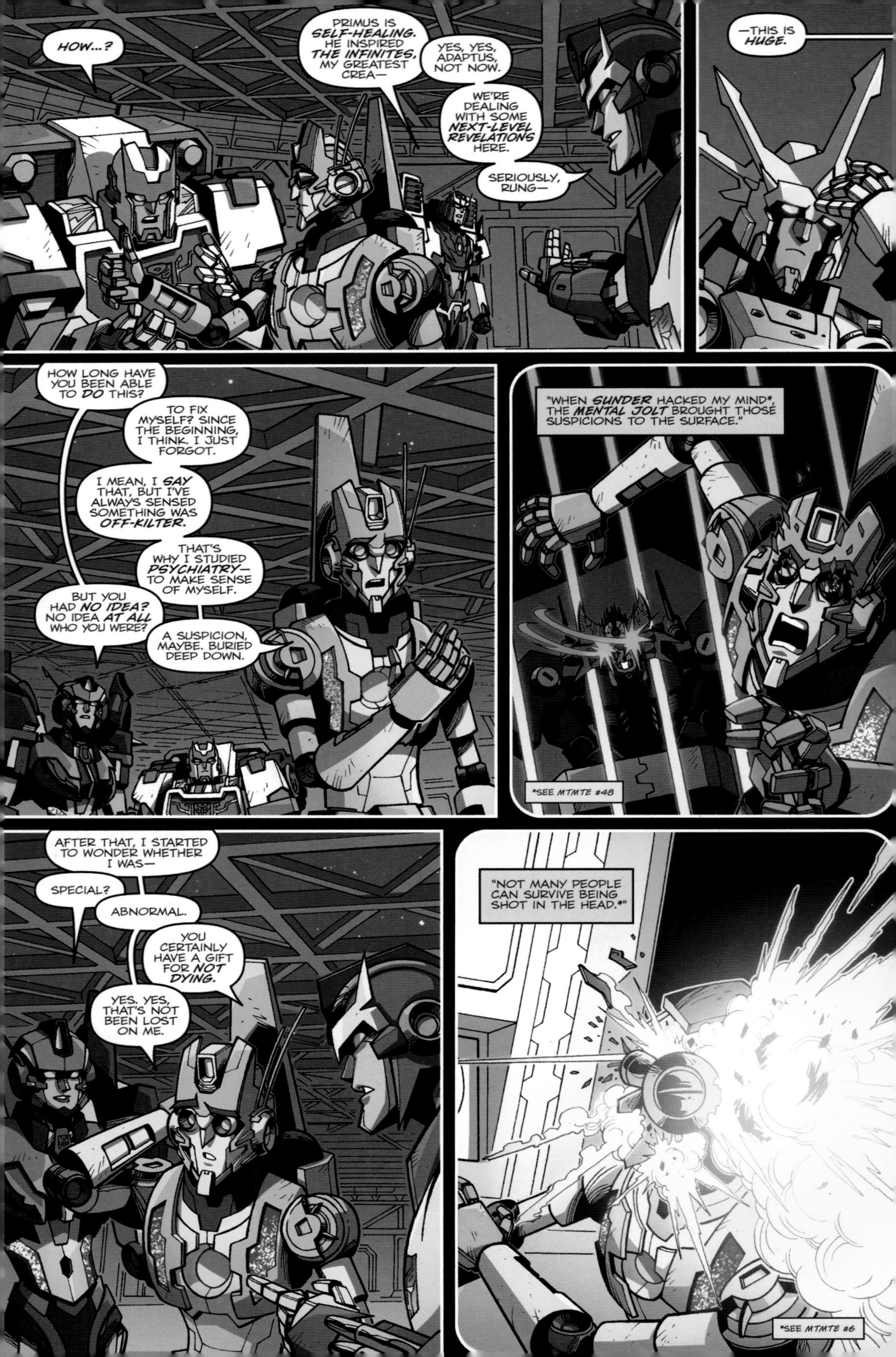

HOW...?
PRIMUS IS SELF-HEALING. HE INSPIRED THE INFINITES, MY GREATEST CREA—
YES, YES, ADAPTUS, NOT NOW.
WE'RE DEALING WITH SOME NEXT-LEVEL REVELATIONS HERE.
SERIOUSLY, RUNG—
—THIS IS HUGE.
HOW LONG HAVE YOU BEEN ABLE TO DO THIS?
TO FIX MYSELF? SINCE THE BEGINNING, I THINK. I JUST FORGOT.
I MEAN, I SAY THAT, BUT I'VE ALWAYS SENSED SOMETHING WAS OFF-KILTER.
THAT'S WHY I STUDIED PSYCHIATRY— TO MAKE SENSE OF MYSELF.
BUT YOU HAD NO IDEA? NO IDEA AT ALL WHO YOU WERE?
A SUSPICION, MAYBE. BURIED DEEP DOWN.
"WHEN SUNDER HACKED MY MIND*, THE MENTAL JOLT BROUGHT THOSE SUSPICIONS TO THE SURFACE."
*SEE MTMTE #48
AFTER THAT, I STARTED TO WONDER WHETHER I WAS—
SPECIAL?
ABNORMAL.
YOU CERTAINLY HAVE A GIFT FOR NOT DYING.
YES, YES, THAT'S NOT BEEN LOST ON ME.
"NOT MANY PEOPLE CAN SURVIVE BEING SHOT IN THE HEAD.*"
*SEE MTMTE #6

"AND I'VE LOST COUNT OF THE NUMBER OF TIMES I'VE WALKED AWAY FROM A *CRASH* OR AN *EXPLOSION* OR AN *ACCIDENT*."

THE FATEFUL ARCHETYPE

SO YOU'RE *THE FIRST.* THE FIRST OF OUR KIND.

I'M NO MORE INCLINED TO TRUST *ADAPTUS* THAN YOU ARE... BUT I KNOW THAT WHAT HE'S SAYING IS TRUE.

BEING *NAMED*— BEING *RECOGNIZED*... IT'S BROUGHT EVERY-THING BACK.

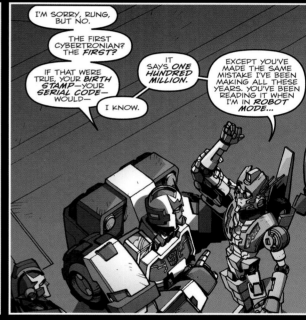

I'M SORRY, RUNG, BUT NO.

THE FIRST CYBERTRONIAN? THE *FIRST?*

IF THAT WERE TRUE, YOUR *BIRTH STAMP*—YOUR *SERIAL CODE*—WOULD—

IT SAYS *ONE HUNDRED MILLION.*

I KNOW.

EXCEPT YOU'VE MADE THE SAME MISTAKE I'VE BEEN MAKING ALL THESE YEARS. YOU'VE BEEN READING IT WHEN I'M IN *ROBOT MODE...*

...WHEN IT'S *UPSIDE DOWN.*

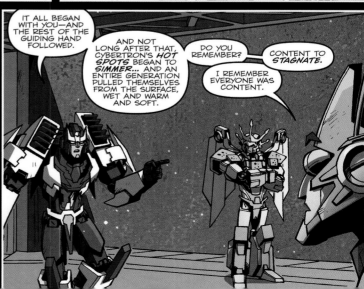

IT ALL BEGAN WITH YOU—AND THE REST OF THE *GUIDING HAND* FOLLOWED.

AND NOT LONG AFTER THAT, CYBERTRON'S *HOT SPOTS* BEGAN TO *SIMMER*... AND AN ENTIRE GENERATION PULLED THEMSELVES FROM THE SURFACE, WET AND WARM AND SOFT.

DO YOU REMEMBER?

CONTENT TO *STAGNATE.*

I REMEMBER EVERYONE WAS CONTENT.

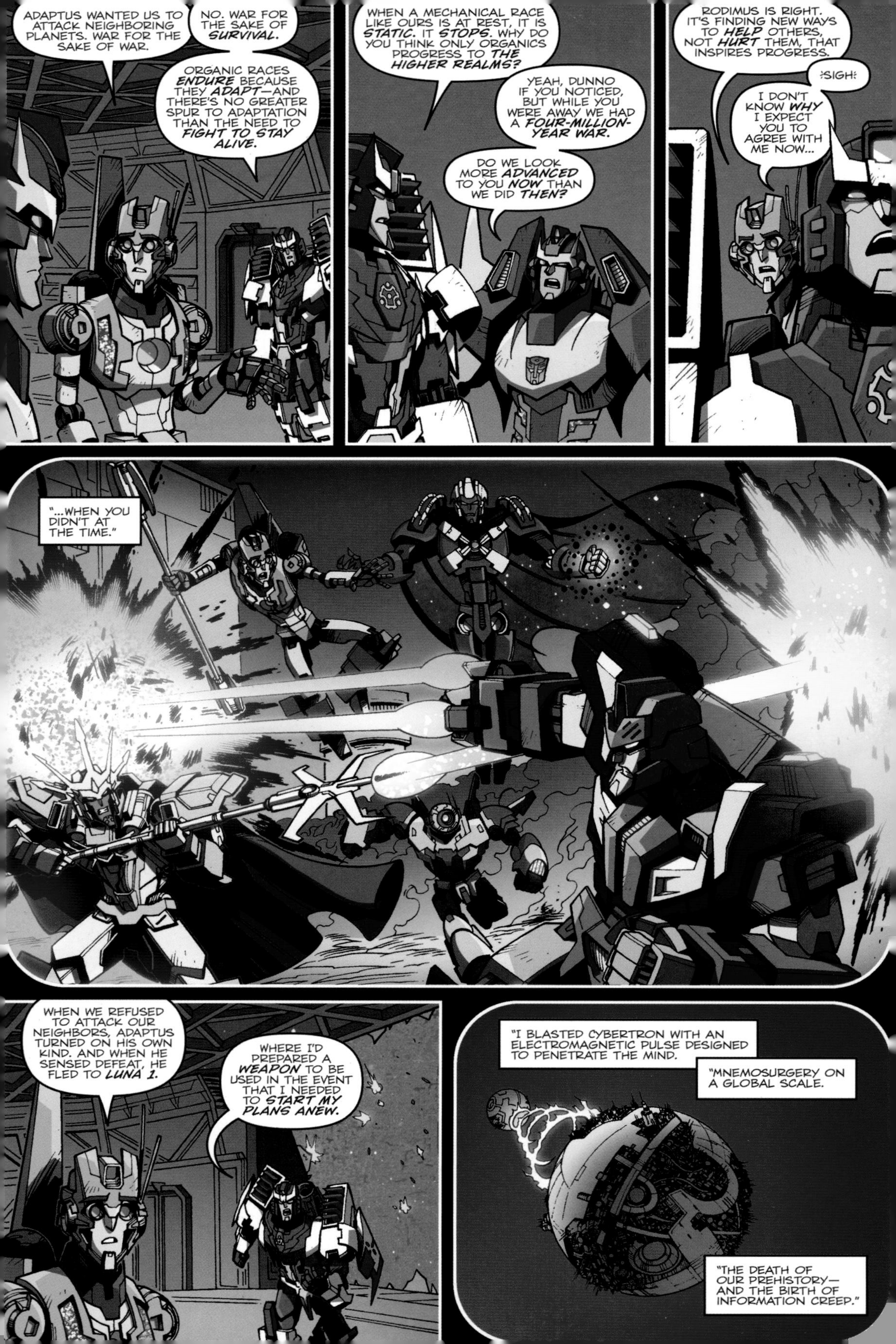
ADAPTUS WANTED US TO ATTACK NEIGHBORING PLANETS. WAR FOR THE SAKE OF WAR.
NO. WAR FOR THE SAKE OF SURVIVAL.
ORGANIC RACES ENDURE BECAUSE THEY ADAPT—AND THERE'S NO GREATER SPUR TO ADAPTATION THAN THE NEED TO FIGHT TO STAY ALIVE.
WHEN A MECHANICAL RACE LIKE OURS IS AT REST, IT IS STATIC. IT STOPS. WHY DO YOU THINK ONLY ORGANICS PROGRESS TO THE HIGHER REALMS?
YEAH, DUNNO IF YOU NOTICED, BUT WHILE YOU WERE AWAY WE HAD A FOUR-MILLION-YEAR WAR.
DO WE LOOK MORE ADVANCED TO YOU NOW THAN WE DID THEN?
RODIMUS IS RIGHT. IT'S FINDING NEW WAYS TO HELP OTHERS, NOT HURT THEM, THAT INSPIRES PROGRESS.
:SIGH:
I DON'T KNOW WHY I EXPECT YOU TO AGREE WITH ME NOW...
"...WHEN YOU DIDN'T AT THE TIME."
WHEN WE REFUSED TO ATTACK OUR NEIGHBORS, ADAPTUS TURNED ON HIS OWN KIND. AND WHEN HE SENSED DEFEAT, HE FLED TO LUNA 1.
WHERE I'D PREPARED A WEAPON TO BE USED IN THE EVENT THAT I NEEDED TO START MY PLANS ANEW.
"I BLASTED CYBERTRON WITH AN ELECTROMAGNETIC PULSE DESIGNED TO PENETRATE THE MIND.
"MNEMOSURGERY ON A GLOBAL SCALE.
"THE DEATH OF OUR PREHISTORY—AND THE BIRTH OF INFORMATION CREEP."

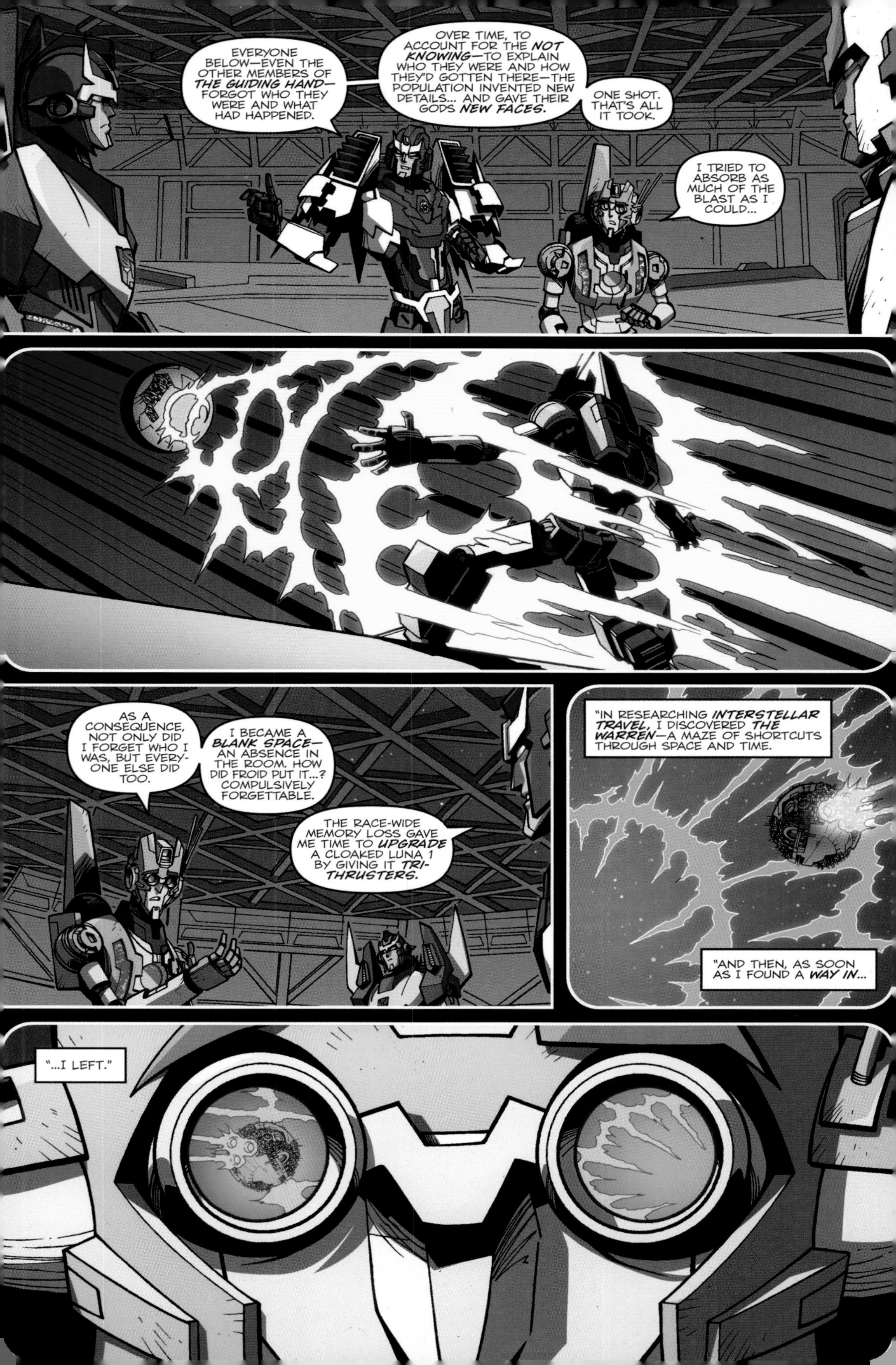

EVERYONE BELOW—EVEN THE OTHER MEMBERS OF *THE GUIDING HAND*—FORGOT WHO THEY WERE AND WHAT HAD HAPPENED.
OVER TIME, TO ACCOUNT FOR THE *NOT KNOWING*—TO EXPLAIN WHO THEY WERE AND HOW THEY'D GOTTEN THERE—THE POPULATION INVENTED NEW DETAILS... AND GAVE THEIR GODS *NEW FACES.*
ONE SHOT. THAT'S ALL IT TOOK.
I TRIED TO ABSORB AS MUCH OF THE BLAST AS I COULD...
AS A CONSEQUENCE, NOT ONLY DID I FORGET WHO I WAS, BUT EVERY-ONE ELSE DID TOO.
I BECAME A *BLANK SPACE*—AN ABSENCE IN THE ROOM. HOW DID FROID PUT IT...? COMPULSIVELY FORGETTABLE.
THE RACE-WIDE MEMORY LOSS GAVE ME TIME TO *UPGRADE* A CLOAKED LUNA 1 BY GIVING IT *TRI-THRUSTERS.*
"IN RESEARCHING *INTERSTELLAR TRAVEL,* I DISCOVERED *THE WARREN*—A MAZE OF SHORTCUTS THROUGH SPACE AND TIME.
"AND THEN, AS SOON AS I FOUND A *WAY IN*...
"...I LEFT."

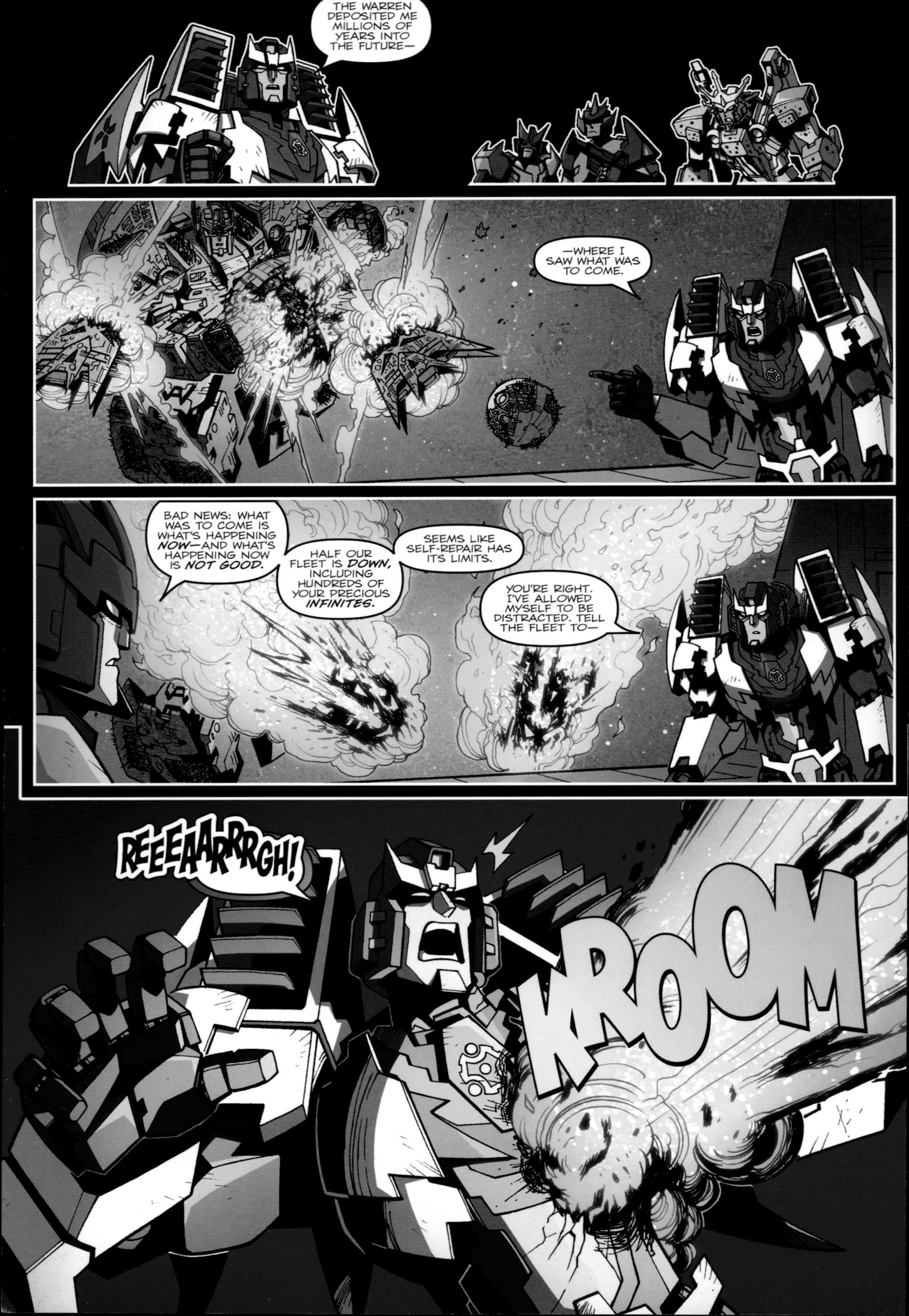
THE WARREN DEPOSITED ME MILLIONS OF YEARS INTO THE FUTURE—
—WHERE I SAW WHAT WAS TO COME.
BAD NEWS: WHAT WAS TO COME IS WHAT'S HAPPENING NOW—AND WHAT'S HAPPENING NOW IS NOT GOOD.
HALF OUR FLEET IS DOWN, INCLUDING HUNDREDS OF YOUR PRECIOUS INFINITES.
SEEMS LIKE SELF-REPAIR HAS ITS LIMITS.
YOU'RE RIGHT. I'VE ALLOWED MYSELF TO BE DISTRACTED. TELL THE FLEET TO—
REEEAARRRGH!
KROOM

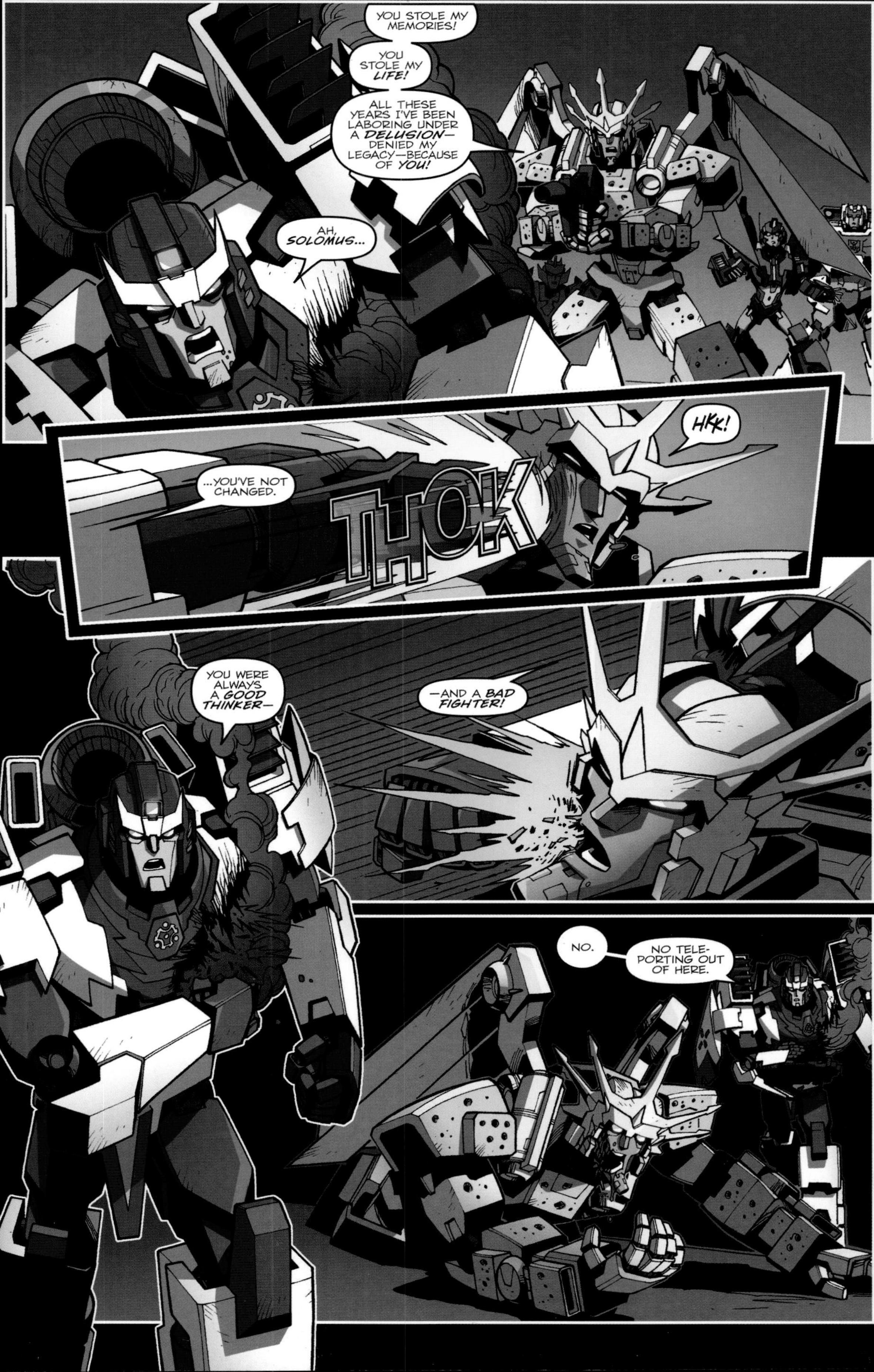

YOU STOLE MY MEMORIES!
YOU STOLE MY LIFE!
ALL THESE YEARS I'VE BEEN LABORING UNDER A DELUSION—DENIED MY LEGACY—BECAUSE OF YOU!
AH, SOLOMUS...
...YOU'VE NOT CHANGED.
THOK
HKK!
YOU WERE ALWAYS A GOOD THINKER—
—AND A BAD FIGHTER!
NO.
NO TELE-PORTING OUT OF HERE.

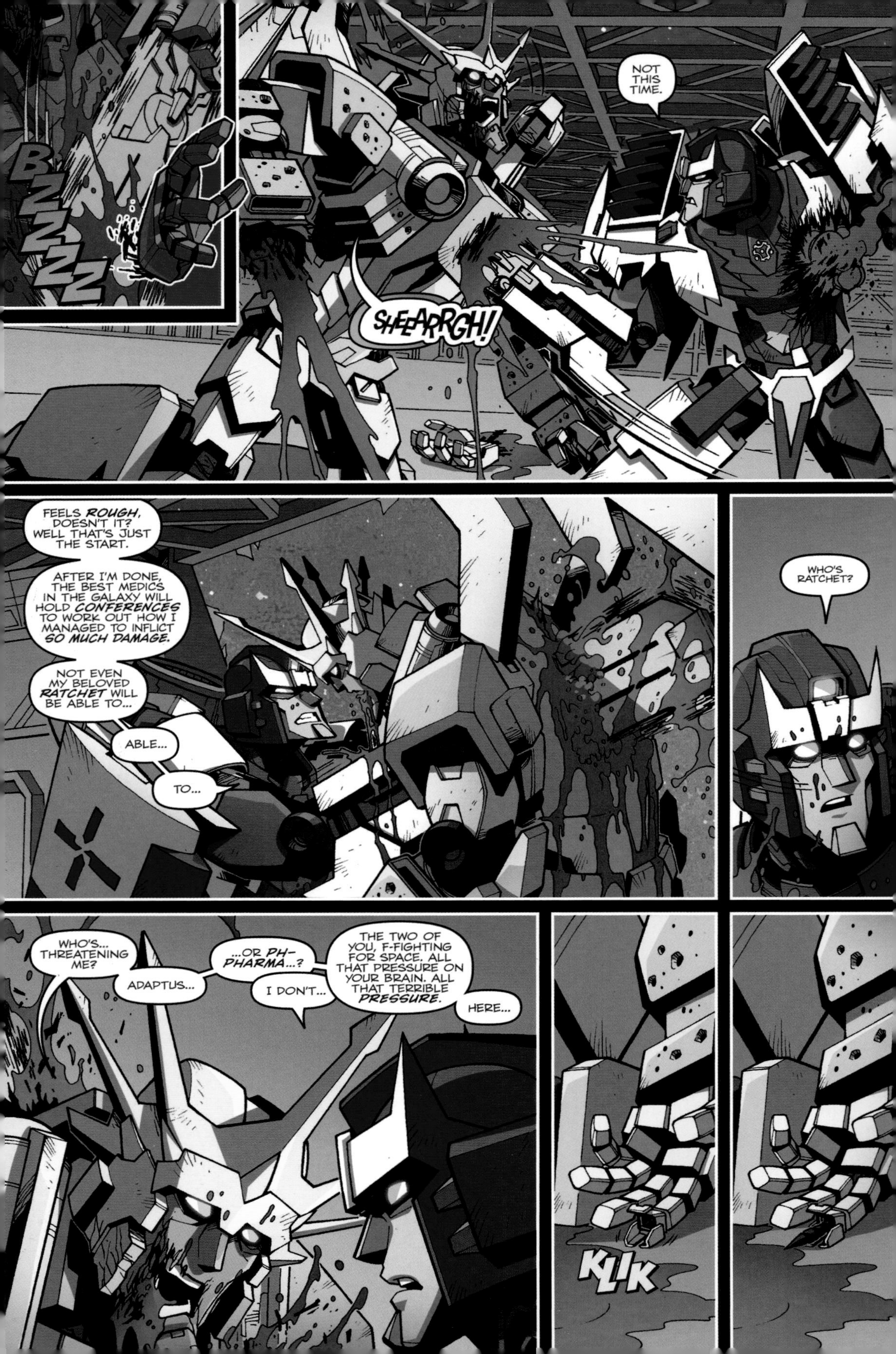
BZZZZZ
NOT THIS TIME.
SHEEARRGH!
FEELS ROUGH, DOESN'T IT? WELL THAT'S JUST THE START.
AFTER I'M DONE, THE BEST MEDICS IN THE GALAXY WILL HOLD CONFERENCES TO WORK OUT HOW I MANAGED TO INFLICT SO MUCH DAMAGE.
NOT EVEN MY BELOVED RATCHET WILL BE ABLE TO...
ABLE...
TO...
WHO'S RATCHET?
WHO'S... THREATENING ME?
ADAPTUS...
...OR PH-PHARMA...?
I DON'T...
THE TWO OF YOU, F-FIGHTING FOR SPACE. ALL THAT PRESSURE ON YOUR BRAIN. ALL THAT TERRIBLE PRESSURE.
HERE...
KLIK

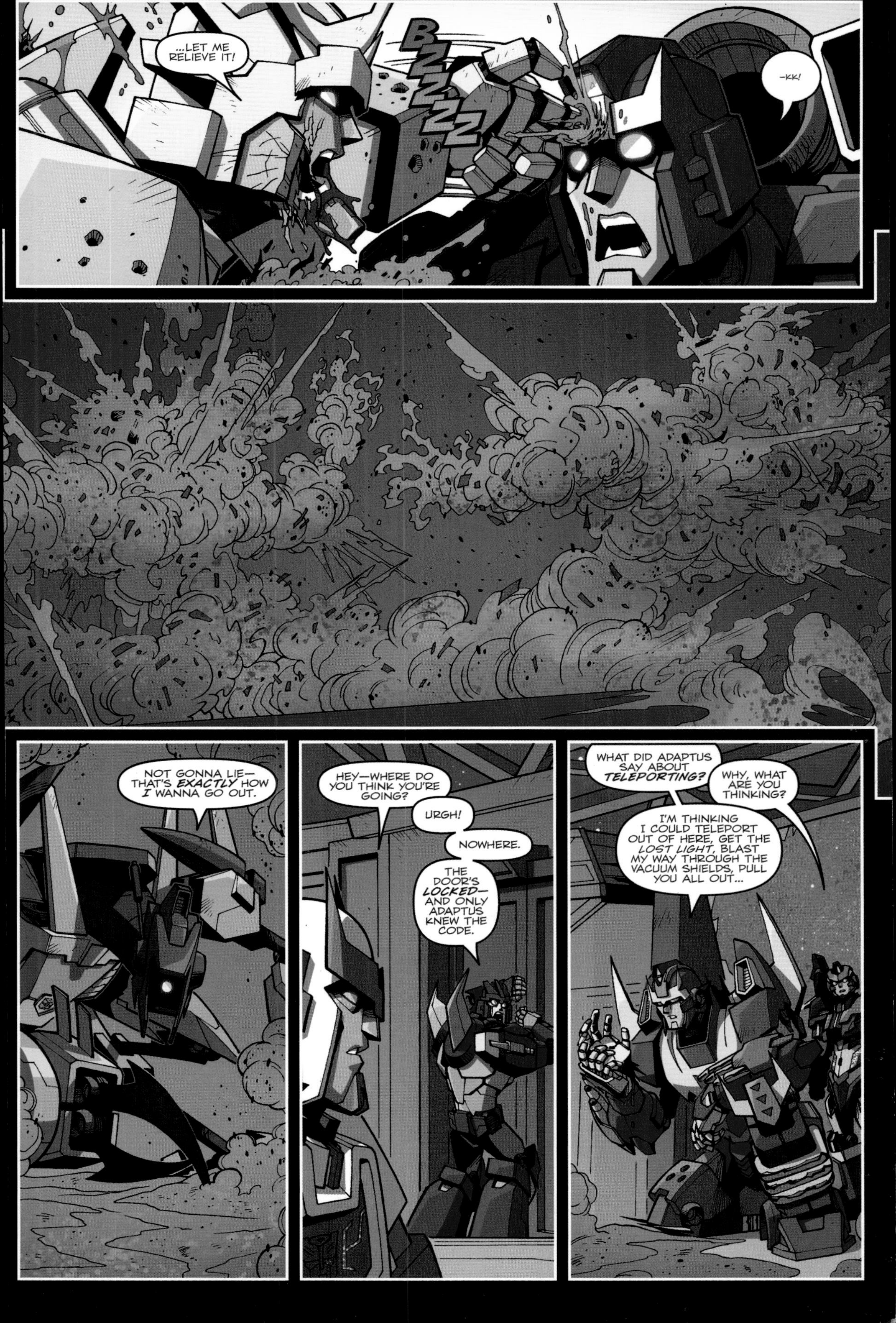
...LET ME RELIEVE IT!
BZZZZZ
-KK!
NOT GONNA LIE–THAT'S EXACTLY HOW I WANNA GO OUT.
HEY—WHERE DO YOU THINK YOU'RE GOING?
URGH!
NOWHERE.
THE DOOR'S LOCKED—AND ONLY ADAPTUS KNEW THE CODE.
WHAT DID ADAPTUS SAY ABOUT TELEPORTING?
WHY, WHAT ARE YOU THINKING?
I'M THINKING I COULD TELEPORT OUT OF HERE, GET THE LOST LIGHT, BLAST MY WAY THROUGH THE VACUUM SHIELDS, PULL YOU ALL OUT...

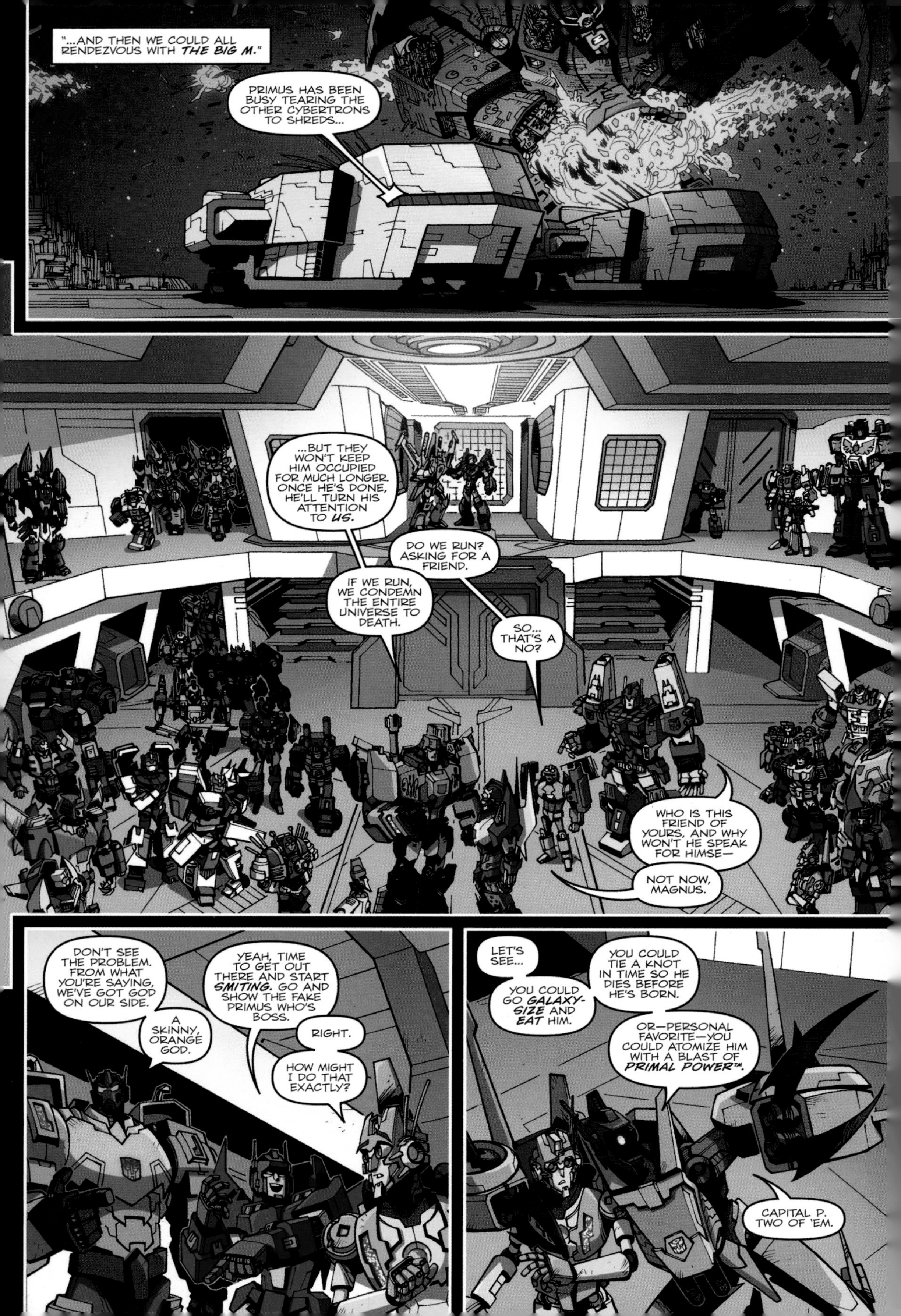

"...AND THEN WE COULD ALL RENDEZVOUS WITH THE BIG M."
PRIMUS HAS BEEN BUSY TEARING THE OTHER CYBERTRONS TO SHREDS...
...BUT THEY WON'T KEEP HIM OCCUPIED FOR MUCH LONGER. ONCE HE'S DONE, HE'LL TURN HIS ATTENTION TO US.
DO WE RUN? ASKING FOR A FRIEND.
IF WE RUN, WE CONDEMN THE ENTIRE UNIVERSE TO DEATH.
SO... THAT'S A NO?
WHO IS THIS FRIEND OF YOURS, AND WHY WON'T HE SPEAK FOR HIMSE—
NOT NOW, MAGNUS.
DON'T SEE THE PROBLEM. FROM WHAT YOU'RE SAYING, WE'VE GOT GOD ON OUR SIDE.
A SKINNY, ORANGE GOD.
YEAH, TIME TO GET OUT THERE AND START SMITING. GO AND SHOW THE FAKE PRIMUS WHO'S BOSS.
RIGHT.
HOW MIGHT I DO THAT EXACTLY?
LET'S SEE...
YOU COULD GO GALAXY-SIZE AND EAT HIM.
YOU COULD TIE A KNOT IN TIME SO HE DIES BEFORE HE'S BORN.
OR—PERSONAL FAVORITE—YOU COULD ATOMIZE HIM WITH A BLAST OF PRIMAL POWER™.
CAPITAL P. TWO OF 'EM.

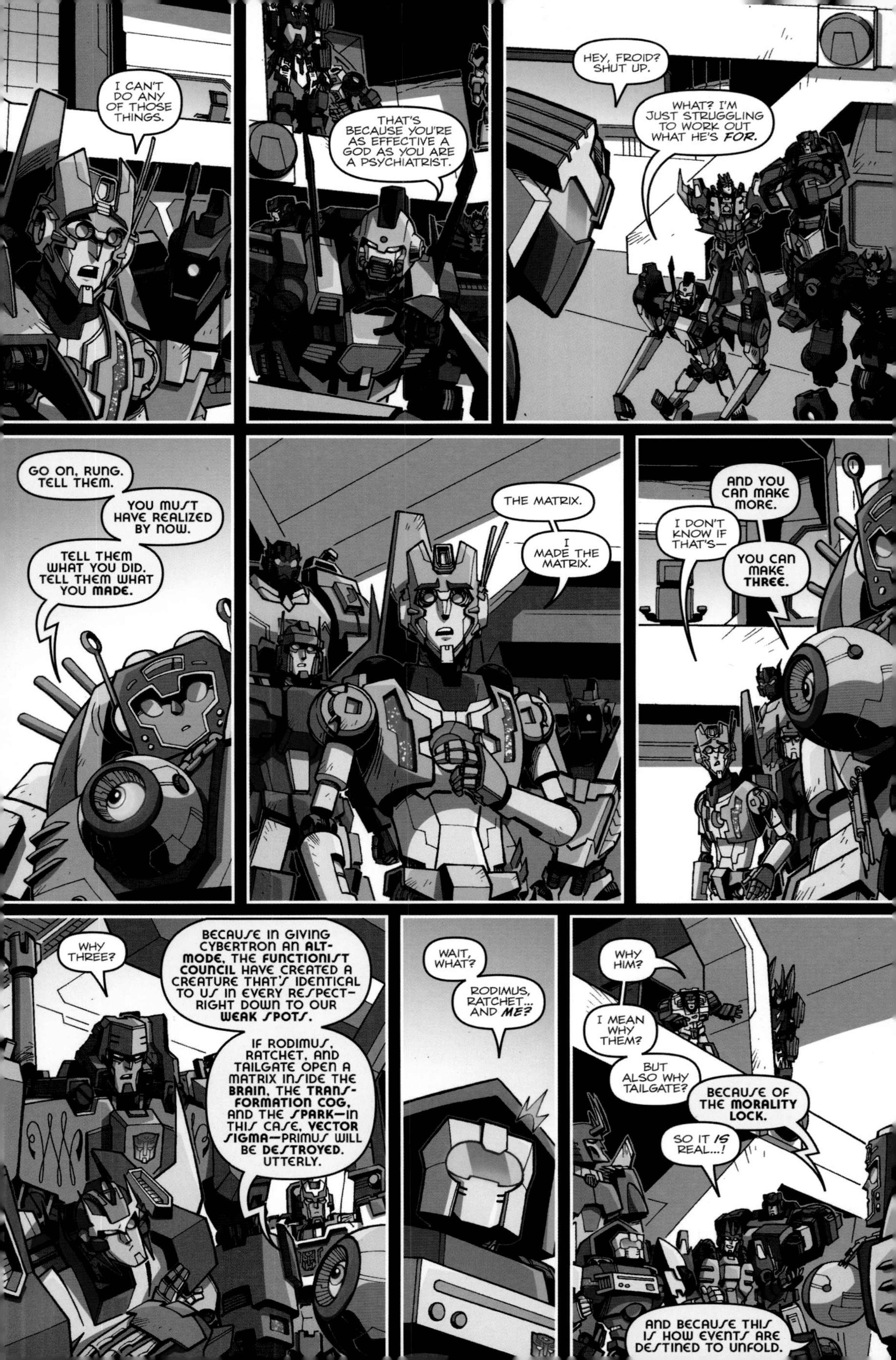
I CAN'T DO ANY OF THOSE THINGS.
THAT'S BECAUSE YOU'RE AS EFFECTIVE A GOD AS YOU ARE A PSYCHIATRIST.
HEY, FROID? SHUT UP.
WHAT? I'M JUST STRUGGLING TO WORK OUT WHAT HE'S FOR.
GO ON, RUNG. TELL THEM.
YOU MUST HAVE REALIZED BY NOW.
TELL THEM WHAT YOU DID. TELL THEM WHAT YOU MADE.
THE MATRIX.
I MADE THE MATRIX.
AND YOU CAN MAKE MORE.
I DON'T KNOW IF THAT'S—
YOU CAN MAKE THREE.
WHY THREE?
BECAUSE IN GIVING CYBERTRON AN ALT-MODE, THE FUNCTIONIST COUNCIL HAVE CREATED A CREATURE THAT'S IDENTICAL TO US IN EVERY RESPECT-RIGHT DOWN TO OUR WEAK SPOTS.
IF RODIMUS, RATCHET, AND TAILGATE OPEN A MATRIX INSIDE THE BRAIN, THE TRANSFORMATION COG, AND THE SPARK—IN THIS CASE, VECTOR SIGMA—PRIMUS WILL BE DESTROYED. UTTERLY.
WAIT, WHAT?
RODIMUS, RATCHET... AND ME?
WHY HIM?
I MEAN WHY THEM?
BUT ALSO WHY TAILGATE?
BECAUSE OF THE MORALITY LOCK.
SO IT IS REAL...!
AND BECAUSE THIS IS HOW EVENTS ARE DESTINED TO UNFOLD.

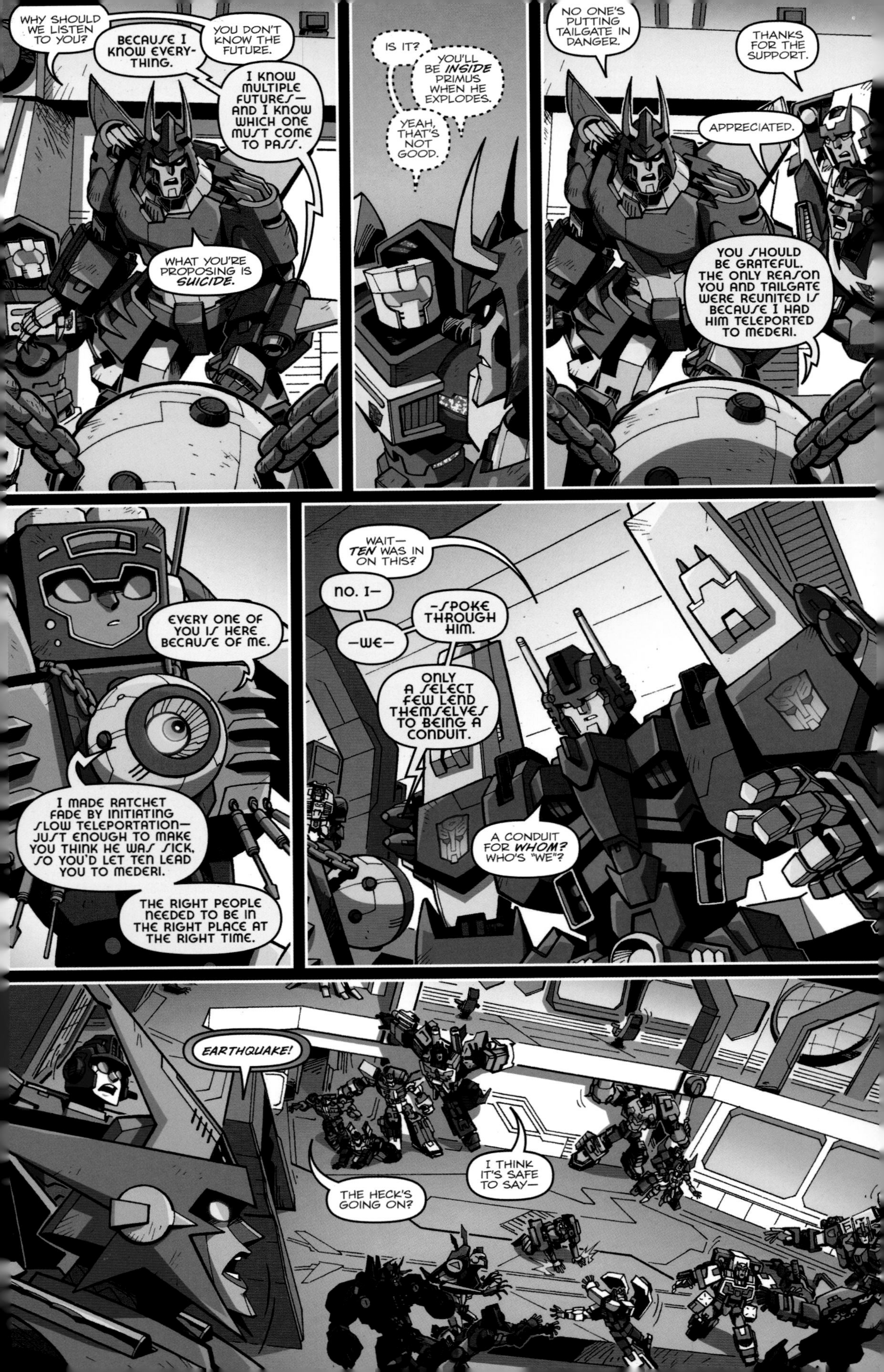
WHY SHOULD WE LISTEN TO YOU?
BECAUSE I KNOW EVERY-THING.
YOU DON'T KNOW THE FUTURE.
I KNOW MULTIPLE FUTURES— AND I KNOW WHICH ONE MUST COME TO PASS.
WHAT YOU'RE PROPOSING IS SUICIDE.
IS IT?
YOU'LL BE INSIDE PRIMUS WHEN HE EXPLODES.
YEAH, THAT'S NOT GOOD.
NO ONE'S PUTTING TAILGATE IN DANGER.
THANKS FOR THE SUPPORT.
APPRECIATED.
YOU SHOULD BE GRATEFUL. THE ONLY REASON YOU AND TAILGATE WERE REUNITED IS BECAUSE I HAD HIM TELEPORTED TO MEDERI.
EVERY ONE OF YOU IS HERE BECAUSE OF ME.
I MADE RATCHET FADE BY INITIATING SLOW TELEPORTATION— JUST ENOUGH TO MAKE YOU THINK HE WAS SICK, SO YOU'D LET TEN LEAD YOU TO MEDERI.
THE RIGHT PEOPLE NEEDED TO BE IN THE RIGHT PLACE AT THE RIGHT TIME.
WAIT— TEN WAS IN ON THIS?
NO. I—
—WE—
-SPOKE THROUGH HIM.
ONLY A SELECT FEW LEND THEMSELVES TO BEING A CONDUIT.
A CONDUIT FOR WHOM? WHO'S "WE"?
EARTHQUAKE!
THE HECK'S GOING ON?
I THINK IT'S SAFE TO SAY—

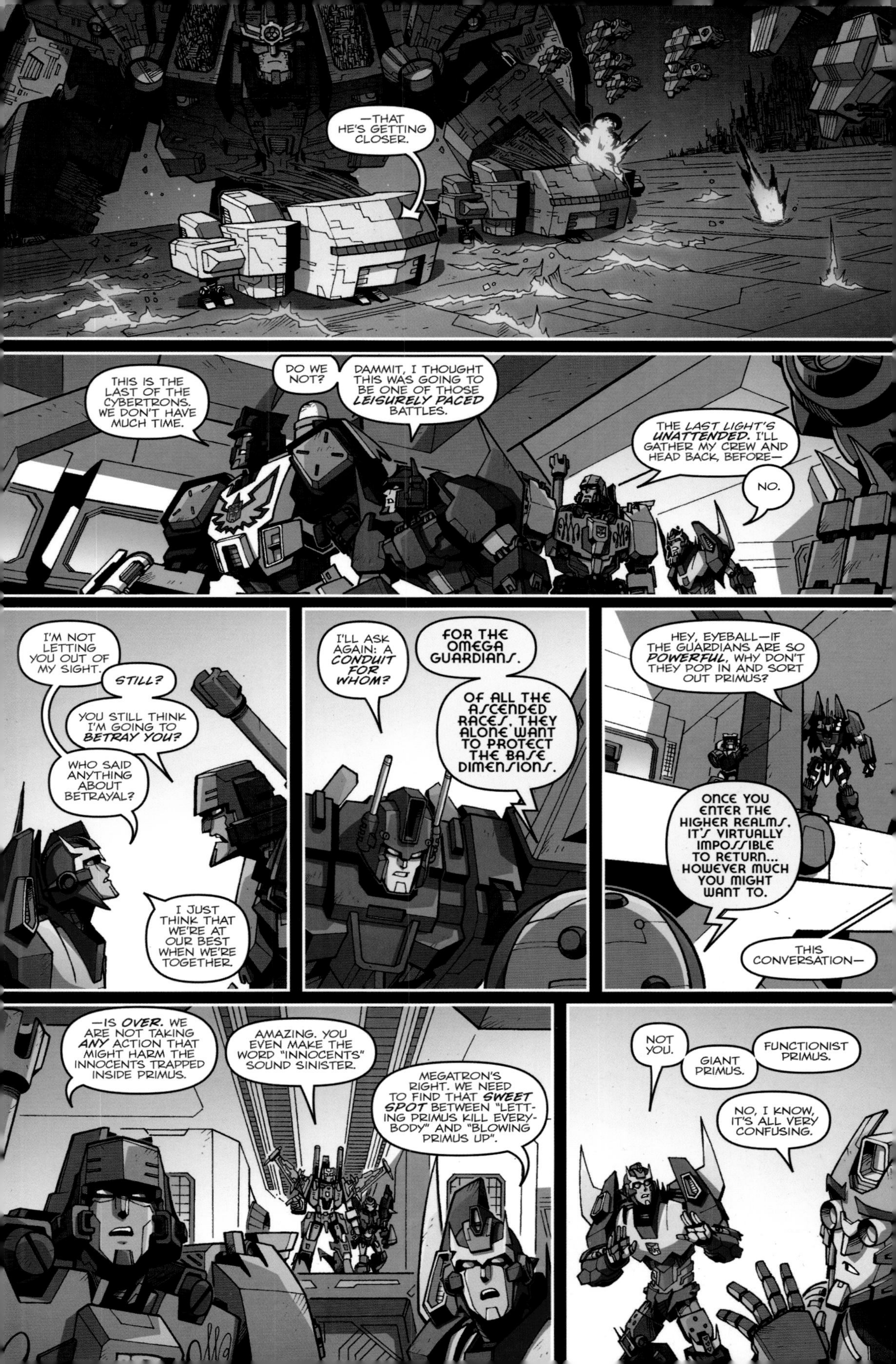
—THAT HE'S GETTING CLOSER.
THIS IS THE LAST OF THE CYBERTRONS. WE DON'T HAVE MUCH TIME.
DO WE NOT?
DAMMIT, I THOUGHT THIS WAS GOING TO BE ONE OF THOSE LEISURELY PACED BATTLES.
THE LAST LIGHT'S UNATTENDED. I'LL GATHER MY CREW AND HEAD BACK, BEFORE—
NO.
I'M NOT LETTING YOU OUT OF MY SIGHT.
STILL?
YOU STILL THINK I'M GOING TO BETRAY YOU?
WHO SAID ANYTHING ABOUT BETRAYAL?
I JUST THINK THAT WE'RE AT OUR BEST WHEN WE'RE TOGETHER.
I'LL ASK AGAIN: A CONDUIT FOR WHOM?
FOR THE OMEGA GUARDIANS.
OF ALL THE ASCENDED RACES, THEY ALONE WANT TO PROTECT THE BASE DIMENSIONS.
HEY, EYEBALL—IF THE GUARDIANS ARE SO POWERFUL, WHY DON'T THEY POP IN AND SORT OUT PRIMUS?
ONCE YOU ENTER THE HIGHER REALMS, IT'S VIRTUALLY IMPOSSIBLE TO RETURN... HOWEVER MUCH YOU MIGHT WANT TO.
THIS CONVERSATION—
—IS OVER. WE ARE NOT TAKING ANY ACTION THAT MIGHT HARM THE INNOCENTS TRAPPED INSIDE PRIMUS.
AMAZING. YOU EVEN MAKE THE WORD "INNOCENTS" SOUND SINISTER.
MEGATRON'S RIGHT. WE NEED TO FIND THAT SWEET SPOT BETWEEN "LETTING PRIMUS KILL EVERYBODY" AND "BLOWING PRIMUS UP".
NOT YOU.
GIANT PRIMUS.
FUNCTIONIST PRIMUS.
NO, I KNOW, IT'S ALL VERY CONFUSING.

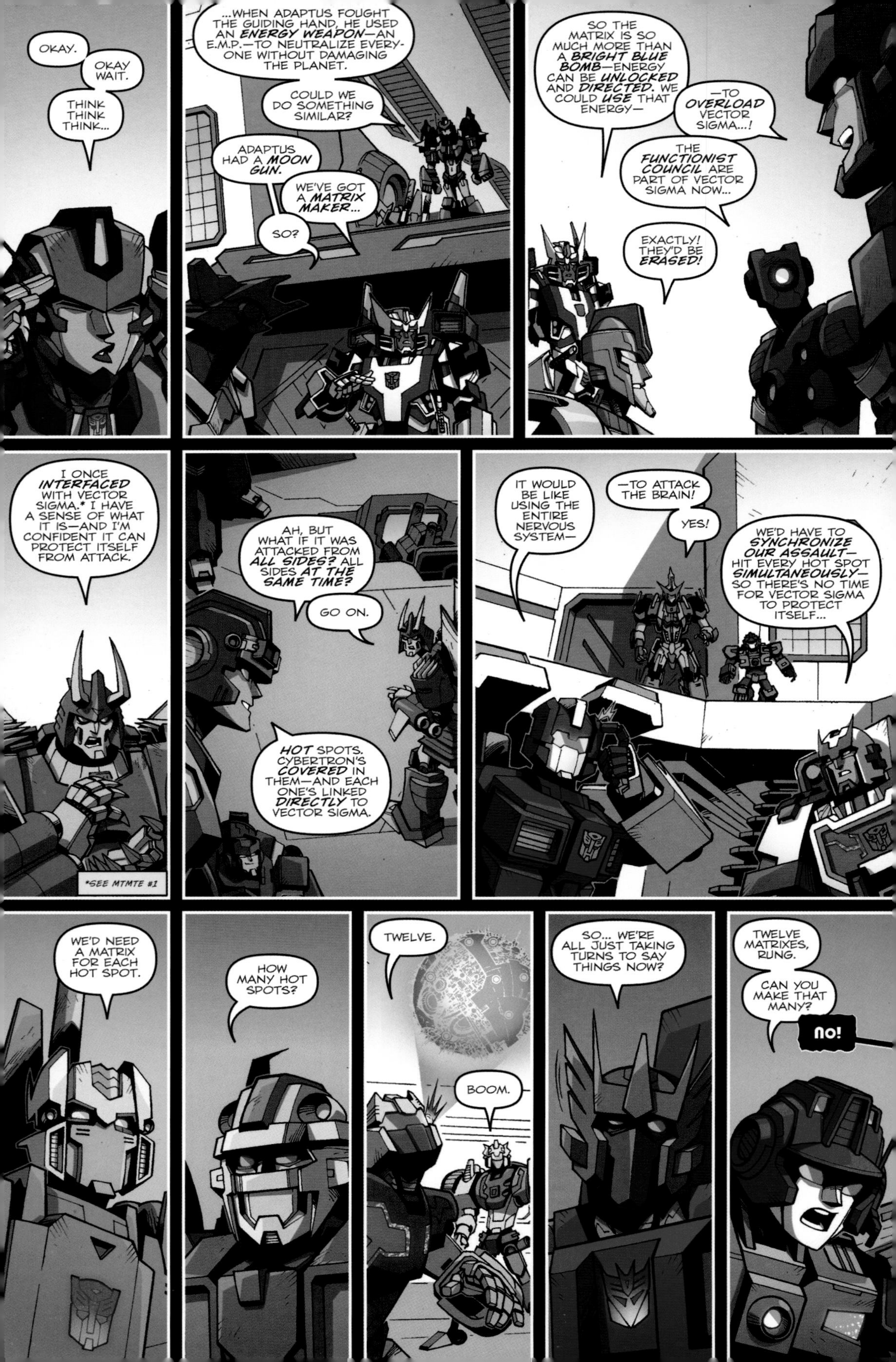
OKAY.
OKAY WAIT.
THINK THINK THINK...
...WHEN ADAPTUS FOUGHT THE GUIDING HAND, HE USED AN ENERGY WEAPON—AN E.M.P.—TO NEUTRALIZE EVERYONE WITHOUT DAMAGING THE PLANET.
COULD WE DO SOMETHING SIMILAR?
ADAPTUS HAD A MOON GUN.
WE'VE GOT A MATRIX MAKER...
SO?
SO THE MATRIX IS SO MUCH MORE THAN A BRIGHT BLUE BOMB—ENERGY CAN BE UNLOCKED AND DIRECTED. WE COULD USE THAT ENERGY—
—TO OVERLOAD VECTOR SIGMA...!
THE FUNCTIONIST COUNCIL ARE PART OF VECTOR SIGMA NOW...
EXACTLY! THEY'D BE ERASED!
I ONCE INTERFACED WITH VECTOR SIGMA.* I HAVE A SENSE OF WHAT IT IS—AND I'M CONFIDENT IT CAN PROTECT ITSELF FROM ATTACK.
*SEE MTMTE #1
AH, BUT WHAT IF IT WAS ATTACKED FROM ALL SIDES? ALL SIDES AT THE SAME TIME?
GO ON.
HOT SPOTS. CYBERTRON'S COVERED IN THEM—AND EACH ONE'S LINKED DIRECTLY TO VECTOR SIGMA.
IT WOULD BE LIKE USING THE ENTIRE NERVOUS SYSTEM—
—TO ATTACK THE BRAIN!
YES!
WE'D HAVE TO SYNCHRONIZE OUR ASSAULT—HIT EVERY HOT SPOT SIMULTANEOUSLY—SO THERE'S NO TIME FOR VECTOR SIGMA TO PROTECT ITSELF...
WE'D NEED A MATRIX FOR EACH HOT SPOT.
HOW MANY HOT SPOTS?
TWELVE.
BOOM.
SO... WE'RE ALL JUST TAKING TURNS TO SAY THINGS NOW?
TWELVE MATRIXES, RUNG.
CAN YOU MAKE THAT MANY?
NO!

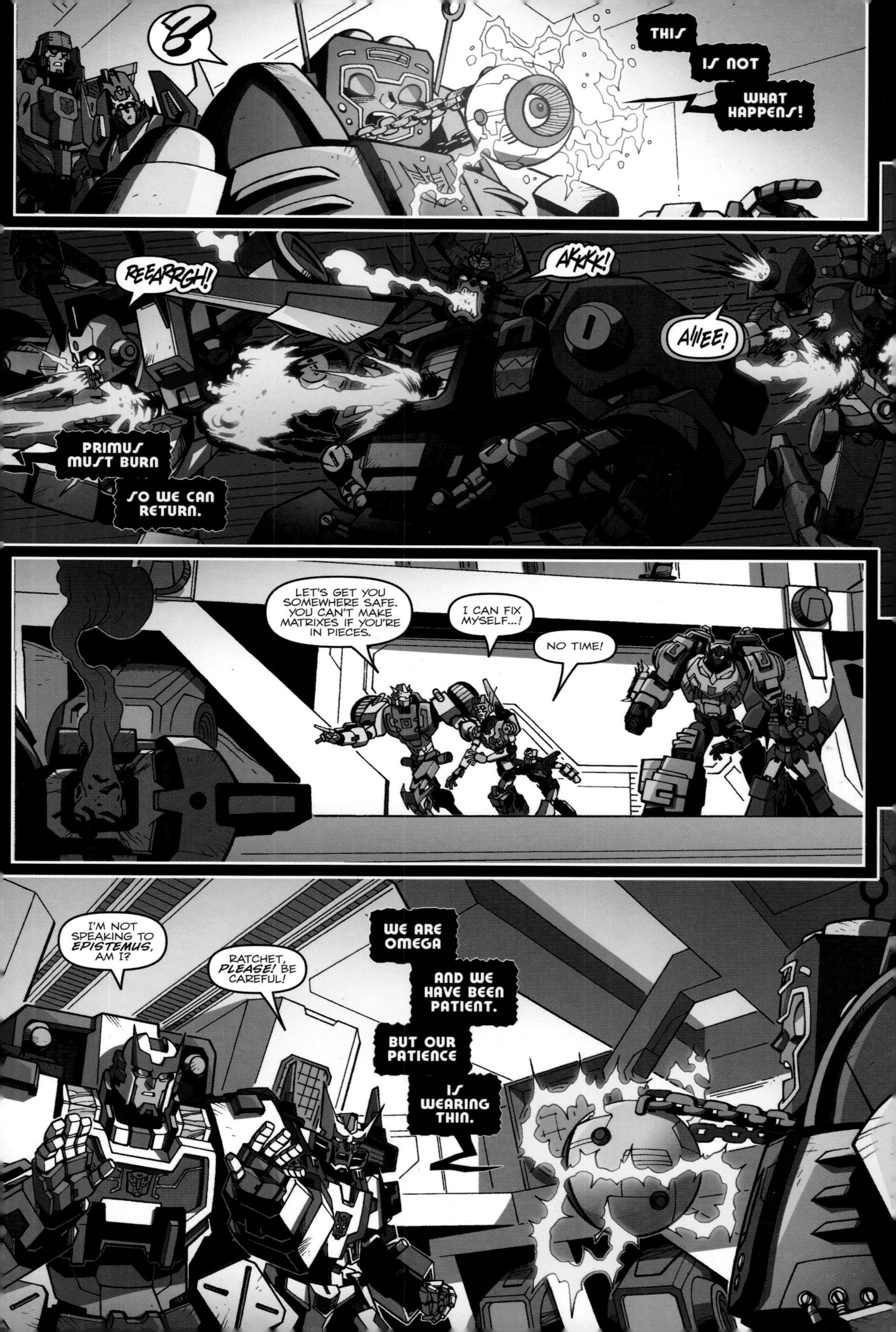
?
THIS
IS NOT
WHAT HAPPENS!
REEARRGH!
AKKKK!
AIIEE!
PRIMUS MUST BURN
SO WE CAN RETURN.
LET'S GET YOU SOMEWHERE SAFE. YOU CAN'T MAKE MATRIXES IF YOU'RE IN PIECES.
I CAN FIX MYSELF...!
NO TIME!
I'M NOT SPEAKING TO EPISTEMUS, AM I?
RATCHET, PLEASE! BE CAREFUL!
WE ARE OMEGA
AND WE HAVE BEEN PATIENT.
BUT OUR PATIENCE
IS WEARING THIN.

YOU'RE SPEAKING TO US FROM WHERE—FROM THE *HIGHER REALMS?* HOW IS THAT POSSIBLE?

THERE IS A FAULT

BETWEEN YOUR WORLD AND OURS.

A FAULT?

A WEAKNESS.

A WHISPER.

A WAY IN.

THE LAST TIME ONE OF US TRIED

TO CROSS OVER

THE TRAUMA KILLED THEM.

WHAT WE CALL THEIR CORPSE

YOU CALL THE WARREN.

KROOM **KROOM** **KROOM**

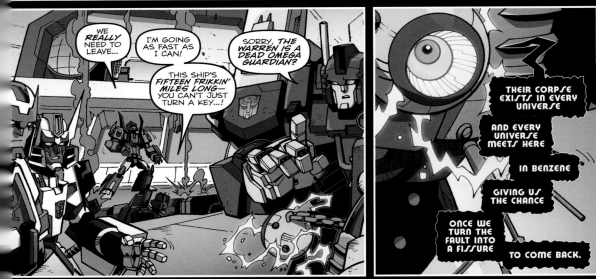

WE *REALLY* NEED TO LEAVE...

I'M GOING AS FAST AS I CAN!

THIS SHIP'S *FIFTEEN FRIKKIN' MILES LONG*—YOU CAN'T JUST TURN A KEY...!

SORRY, *THE WARREN* IS A DEAD OMEGA GUARDIAN?

THEIR CORPSE EXISTS IN EVERY UNIVERSE

AND EVERY UNIVERSE MEETS HERE

IN BENZENE

GIVING US THE CHANCE

ONCE WE TURN THE FAULT INTO A FISSURE

TO COME BACK.

BUT ONLY IF PRIMUS BURNS, RIGHT?

YOU NEED A *PLANET-SIZED EXPLOSION* TO FORCE OPEN THE FISSURE AND GIVE YOU *FULL ACCESS* TO THIS UNIVERSE.

AND THEN WHAT?

THEN WE EAT

EVERYTHING!

NO. BECAUSE WE'RE GOING TO STOP YOU.

STOP US?

YOU CANNOT BEGIN TO IMAGINE WHAT WE ARE.

WE ARE EXPANSIVE.

WE ARE MANIFOLD.

WE EXTEND IN EVERY DIRECTION.

WE EXIST BEYOND THE PERIPHERY OF WHAT YOU TELL YOURSELF IS REAL.

SO WHEN YOU SAY YOU WILL STOP US

EXACTLY

HOW

DO YOU PROPOSE TO DO THAT?

SCRUNCH

THEY DIDN'T SEE *THAT* COMING.

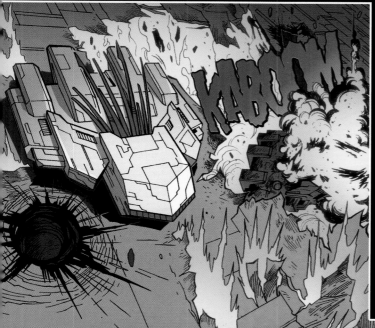

KABOOM

THE *LAST LIGHT'S* TOTALED! I GIVE IT TEN SECONDS BEFORE THE ENTIRE *PLANET* GOES POP!

CRANKCASE— NOT TO LABOR THE POINT—BUT WE REALLY NEED TO BE *ANYWHERE BUT HERE!*

YEAH, THAT *ESCAPE* YOU ORDERED...

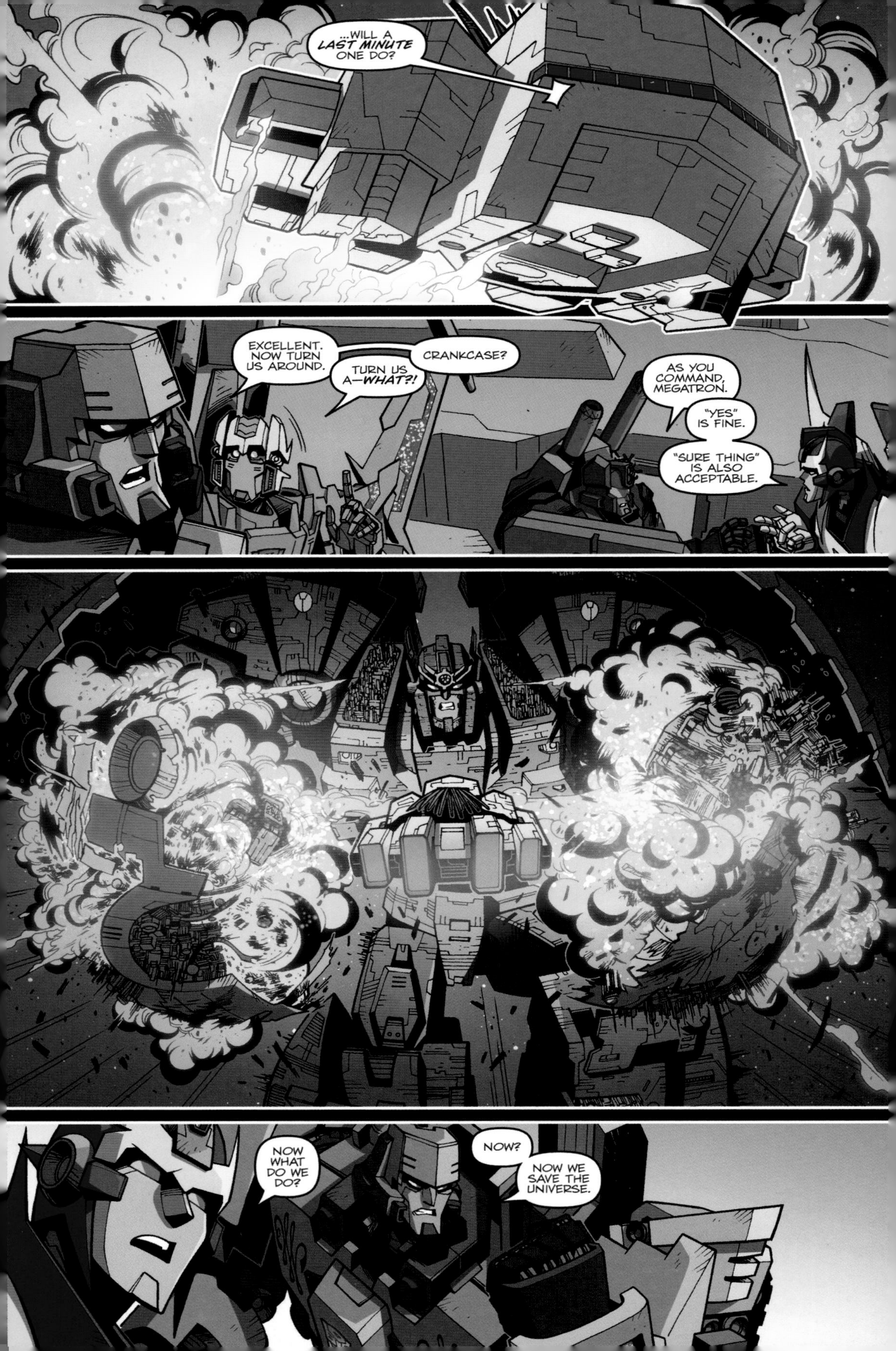
...WILL A LAST MINUTE ONE DO?
EXCELLENT. NOW TURN US AROUND.
CRANKCASE?
TURN US A—WHAT?!
AS YOU COMMAND, MEGATRON.
"YES" IS FINE.
"SURE THING" IS ALSO ACCEPTABLE.
NOW WHAT DO WE DO?
NOW?
NOW WE SAVE THE UNIVERSE.

ART BY **GEOFF SENIOR**
COLORS BY **JOSH BURCHAM**

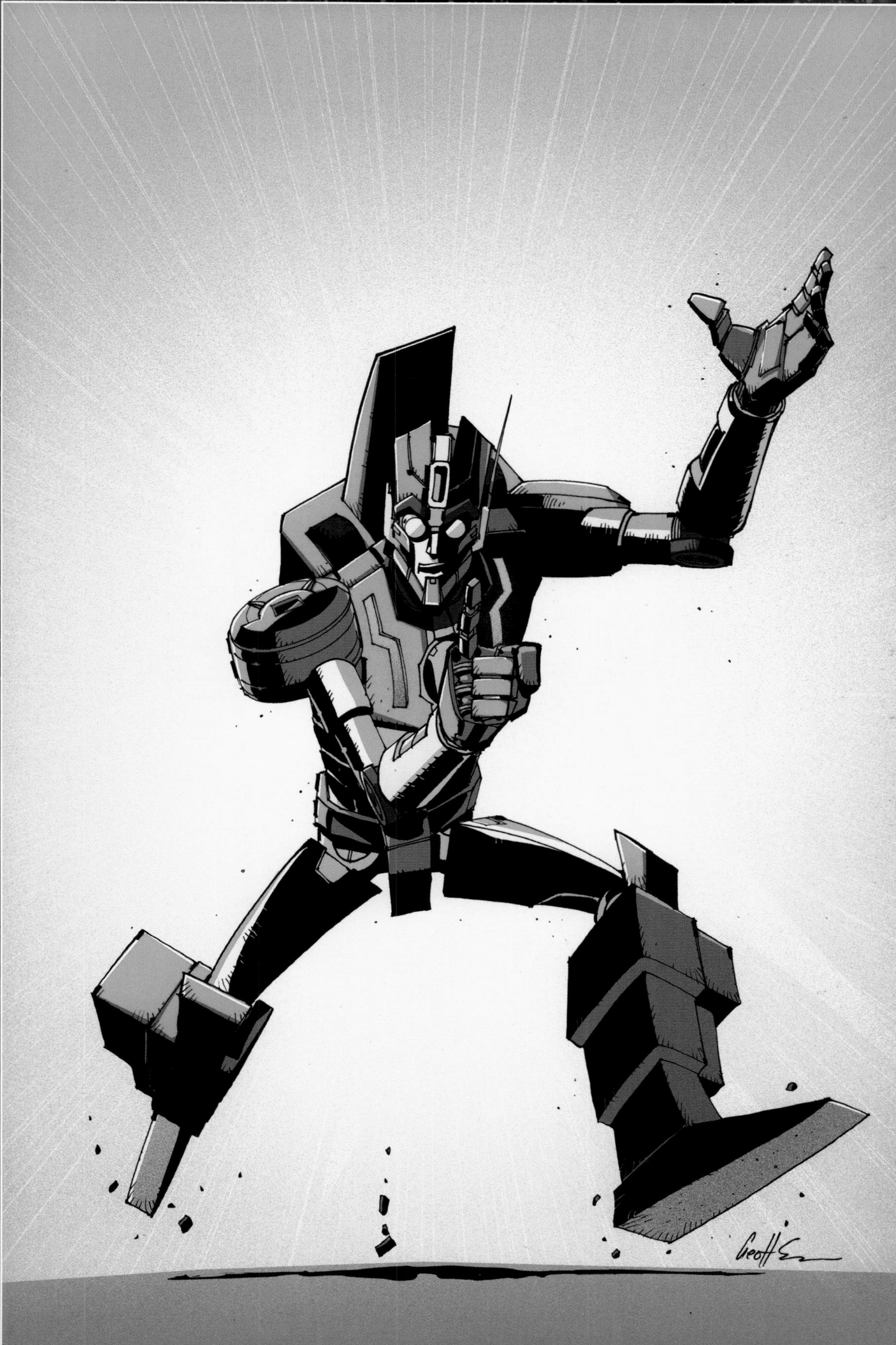

Z4 ART BY NICK ROCHE
COLORS BY JOSH BURCHAM

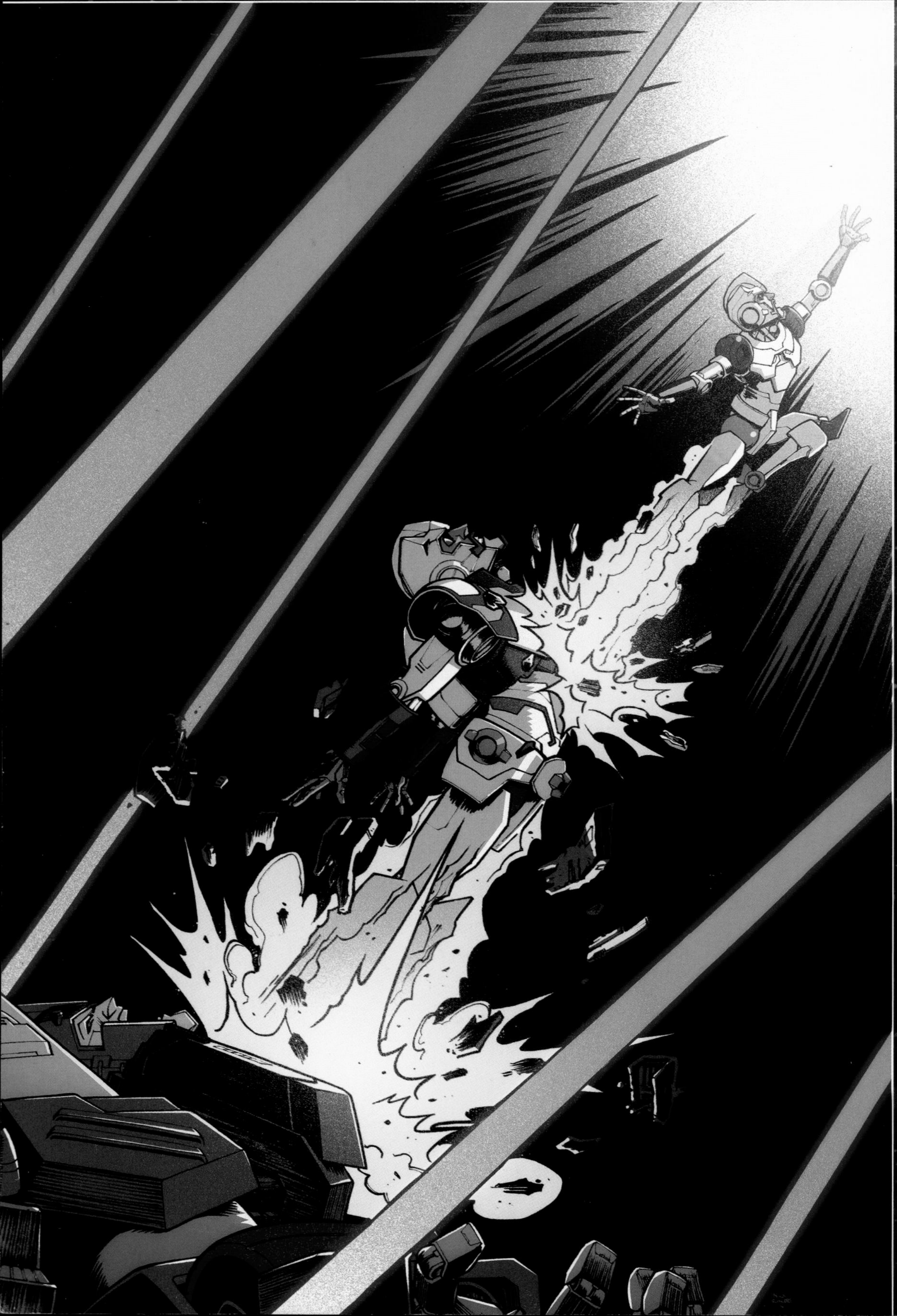

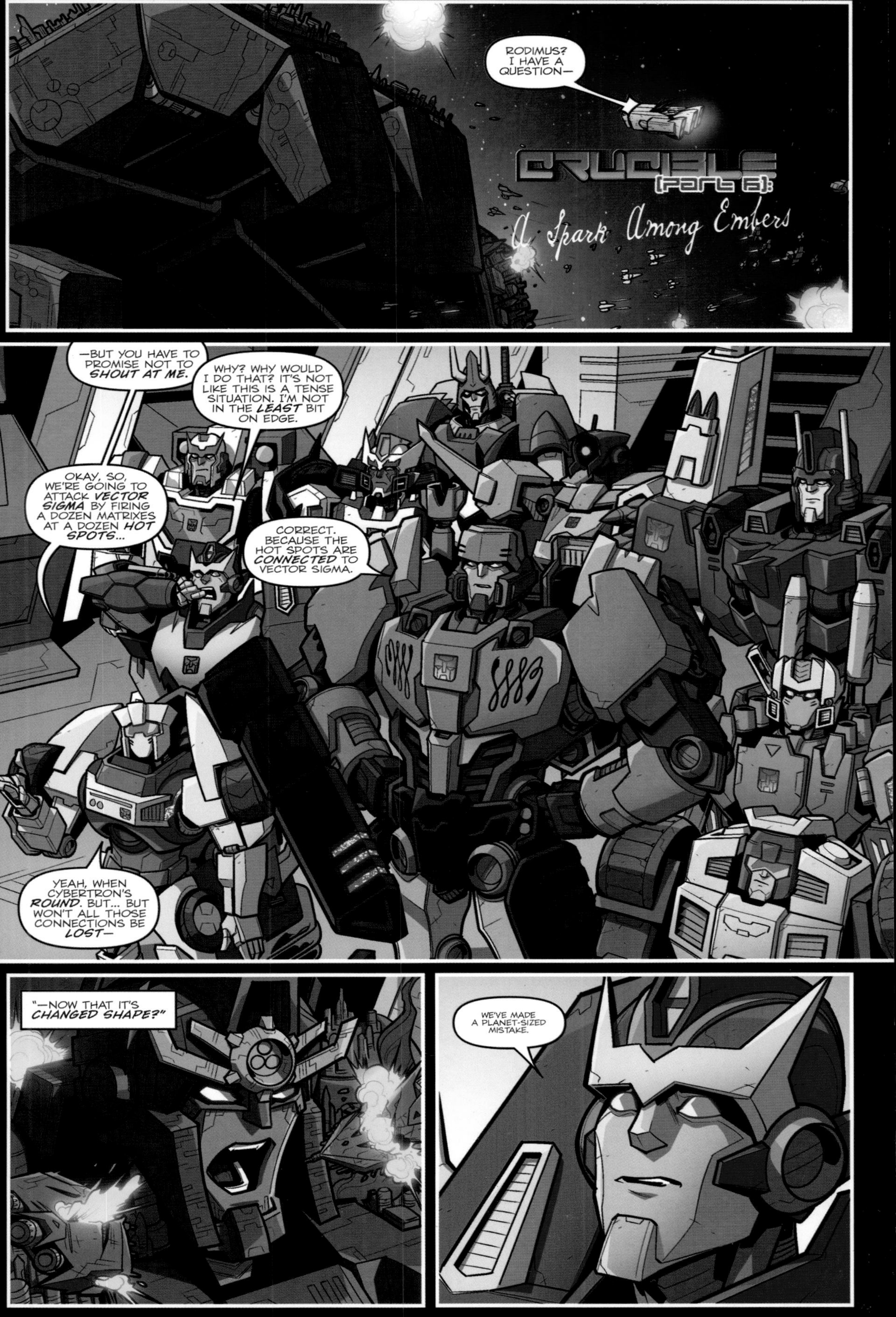
RODIMUS? I HAVE A QUESTION—
CRUCIBLE (PART 6):
A Spark Among Embers
—BUT YOU HAVE TO PROMISE NOT TO SHOUT AT ME.
WHY? WHY WOULD I DO THAT? IT'S NOT LIKE THIS IS A TENSE SITUATION. I'M NOT IN THE LEAST BIT ON EDGE.
OKAY, SO, WE'RE GOING TO ATTACK VECTOR SIGMA BY FIRING A DOZEN MATRIXES AT A DOZEN HOT SPOTS...
CORRECT. BECAUSE THE HOT SPOTS ARE CONNECTED TO VECTOR SIGMA.
YEAH, WHEN CYBERTRON'S ROUND. BUT... BUT WON'T ALL THOSE CONNECTIONS BE LOST—
"—NOW THAT IT'S CHANGED SHAPE?"
WE'VE MADE A PLANET-SIZED MISTAKE.

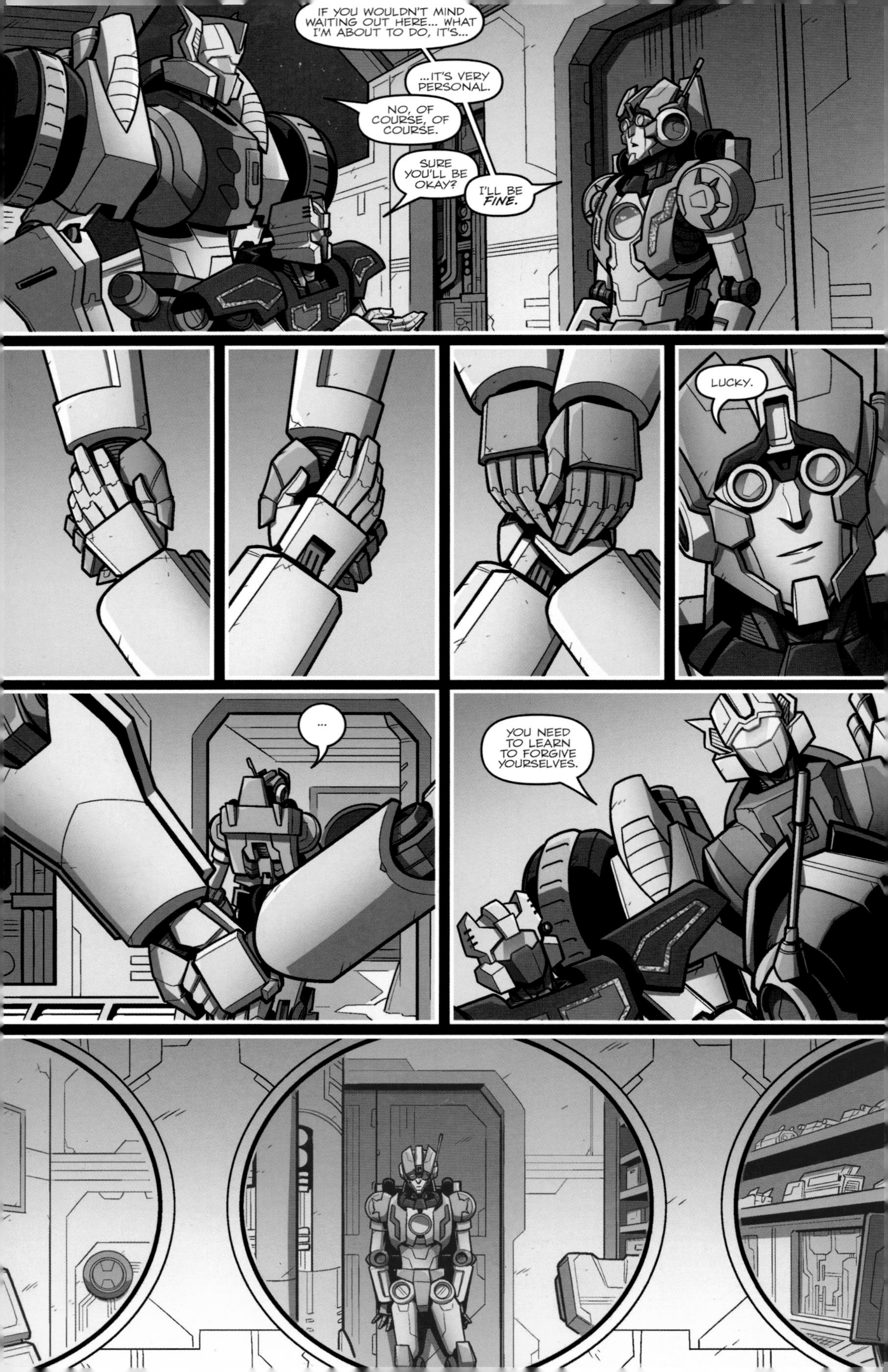
IF YOU WOULDN'T MIND WAITING OUT HERE... WHAT I'M ABOUT TO DO, IT'S...
...IT'S VERY PERSONAL.
NO, OF COURSE, OF COURSE.
SURE YOU'LL BE OKAY?
I'LL BE *FINE.*
LUCKY.
...
YOU NEED TO LEARN TO FORGIVE YOURSELVES.

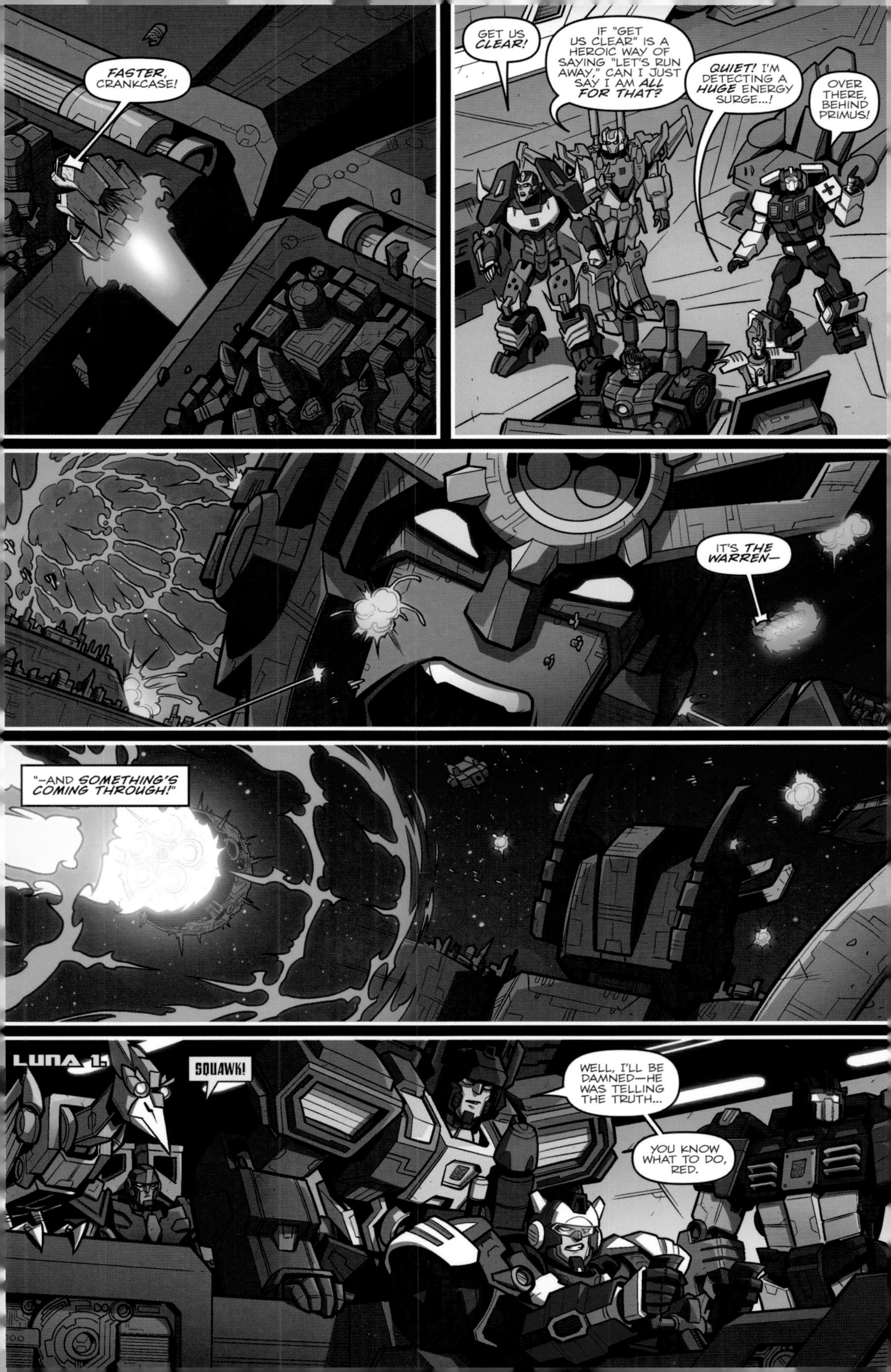
FASTER, CRANKCASE!
GET US CLEAR!
IF "GET US CLEAR" IS A HEROIC WAY OF SAYING "LET'S RUN AWAY," CAN I JUST SAY I AM ALL FOR THAT?
QUIET! I'M DETECTING A HUGE ENERGY SURGE...!
OVER THERE, BEHIND PRIMUS!
IT'S THE WARREN—
"—AND SOMETHING'S COMING THROUGH!"
LUNA-1
SQUAWK!
WELL, I'LL BE DAMNED—HE WAS TELLING THE TRUTH...
YOU KNOW WHAT TO DO, RED.

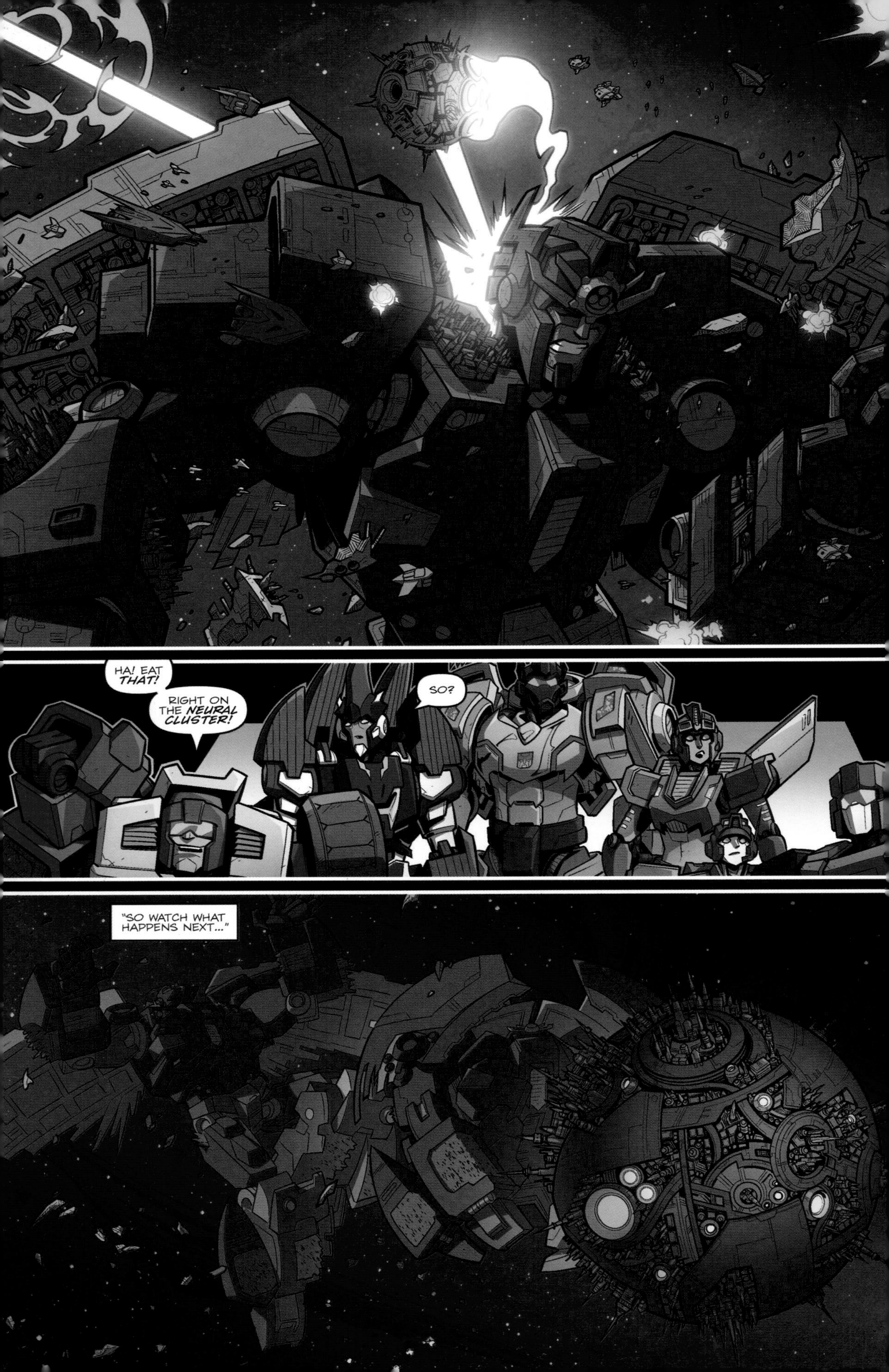

HA! EAT THAT!
RIGHT ON THE NEURAL CLUSTER!
SO?
"SO WATCH WHAT HAPPENS NEXT..."

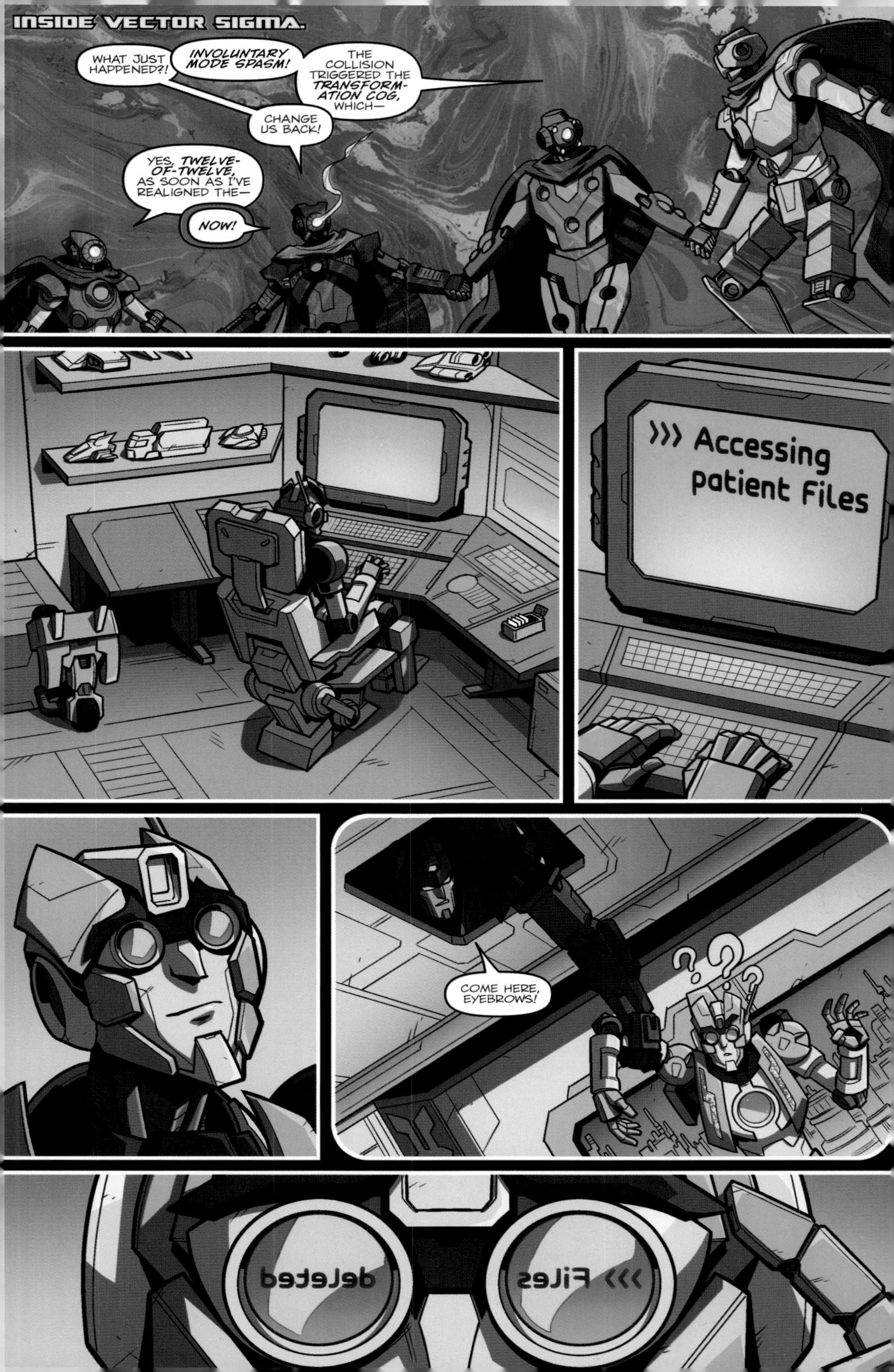
INSIDE VECTOR SIGMA.
WHAT JUST HAPPENED?!
INVOLUNTARY MODE SPASM!
THE COLLISION TRIGGERED THE TRANSFORM-ATION COG, WHICH—
CHANGE US BACK!
YES, TWELVE-OF-TWELVE, AS SOON AS I'VE REALIGNED THE—
NOW!
>>> Accessing patient Files
COME HERE, EYEBROWS!
>>> Files deleted

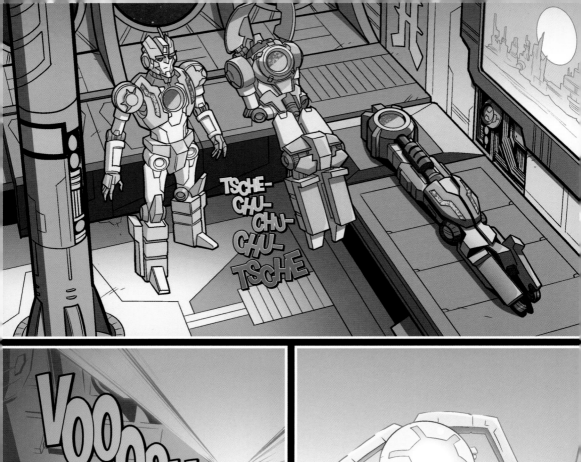

TSCHE-
CHU-
CHU-
CHU-
TSCHE

VOOOSH

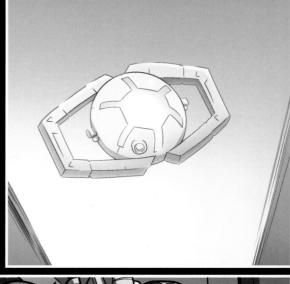

WHERE IS HE? WHERE'S RUNG?

IS HE DONE? HAS HE DONE IT?

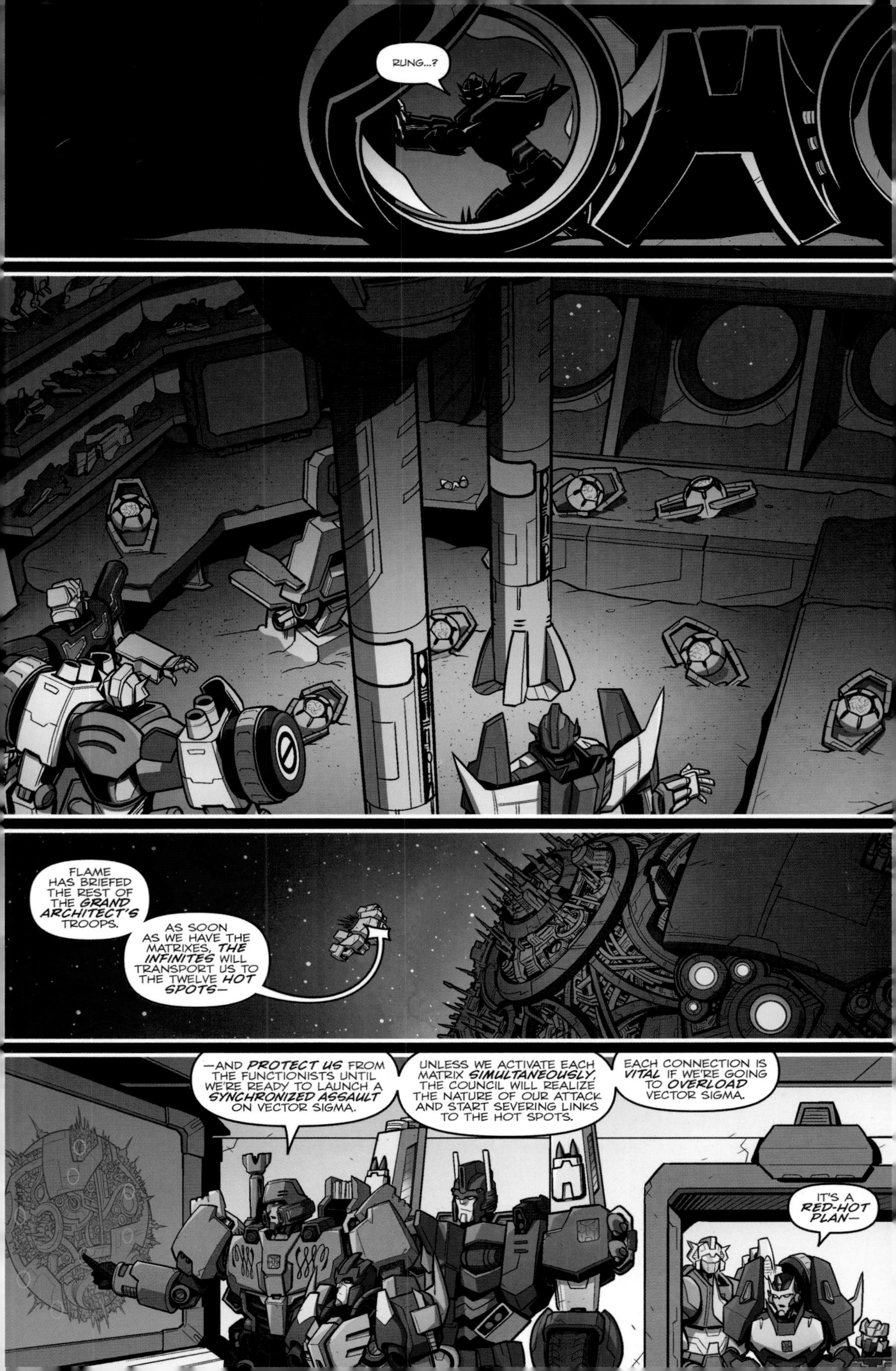
RUNG...?
FLAME HAS BRIEFED THE REST OF THE GRAND ARCHITECT'S TROOPS.
AS SOON AS WE HAVE THE MATRIXES, THE INFINITES WILL TRANSPORT US TO THE TWELVE HOT SPOTS—
—AND PROTECT US FROM THE FUNCTIONISTS UNTIL WE'RE READY TO LAUNCH A SYNCHRONIZED ASSAULT ON VECTOR SIGMA.
UNLESS WE ACTIVATE EACH MATRIX SIMULTANEOUSLY, THE COUNCIL WILL REALIZE THE NATURE OF OUR ATTACK AND START SEVERING LINKS TO THE HOT SPOTS.
EACH CONNECTION IS VITAL IF WE'RE GOING TO OVERLOAD VECTOR SIGMA.
IT'S A RED-HOT PLAN—

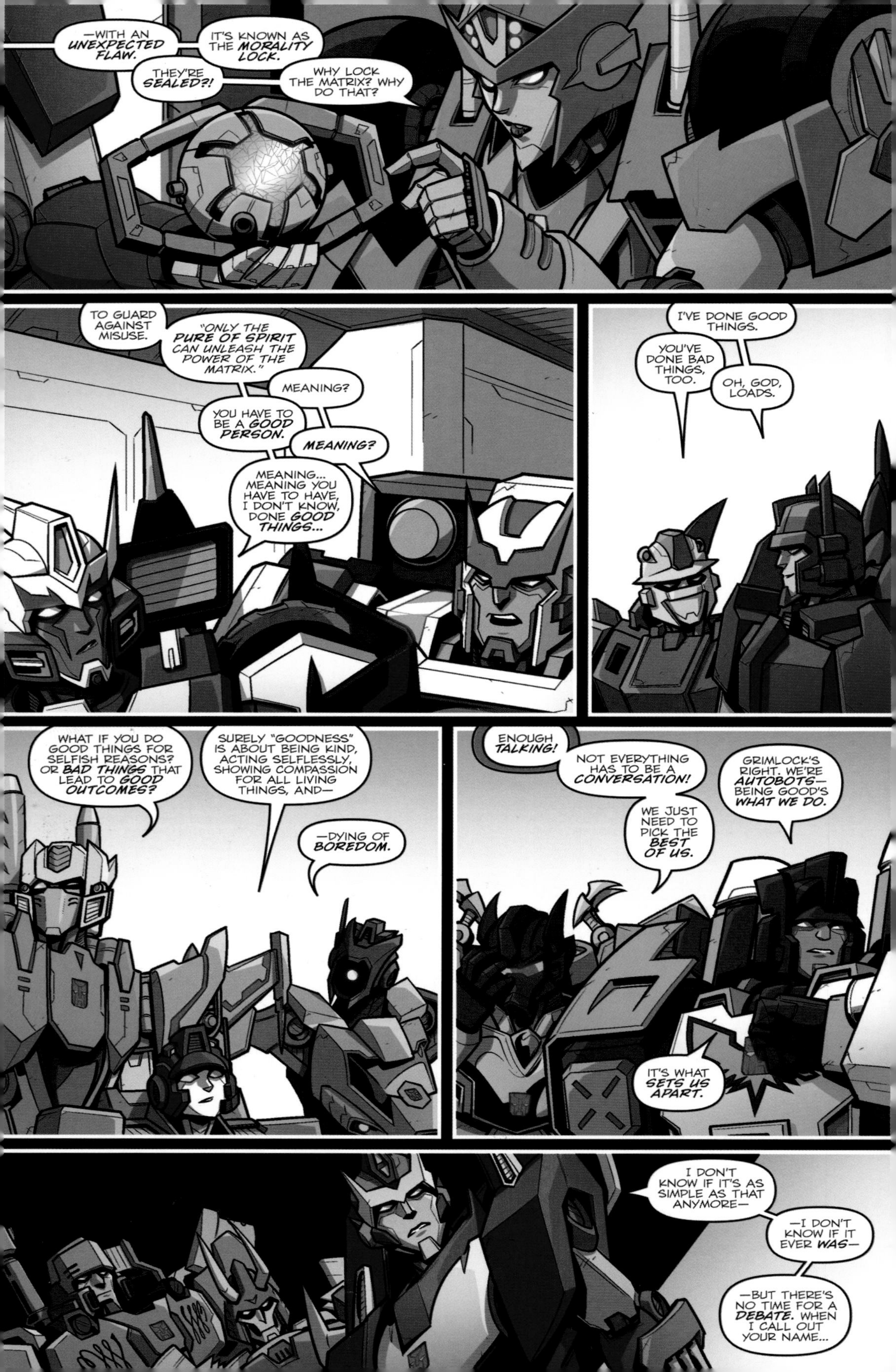
—WITH AN UNEXPECTED FLAW.
IT'S KNOWN AS THE MORALITY LOCK.
THEY'RE SEALED?!
WHY LOCK THE MATRIX? WHY DO THAT?
TO GUARD AGAINST MISUSE.
"ONLY THE PURE OF SPIRIT CAN UNLEASH THE POWER OF THE MATRIX."
MEANING?
YOU HAVE TO BE A GOOD PERSON.
MEANING?
MEANING... MEANING YOU HAVE TO HAVE, I DON'T KNOW, DONE GOOD THINGS...
I'VE DONE GOOD THINGS.
YOU'VE DONE BAD THINGS, TOO.
OH, GOD, LOADS.
WHAT IF YOU DO GOOD THINGS FOR SELFISH REASONS? OR BAD THINGS THAT LEAD TO GOOD OUTCOMES?
SURELY "GOODNESS" IS ABOUT BEING KIND, ACTING SELFLESSLY, SHOWING COMPASSION FOR ALL LIVING THINGS, AND—
—DYING OF BOREDOM.
ENOUGH TALKING!
NOT EVERYTHING HAS TO BE A CONVERSATION!
WE JUST NEED TO PICK THE BEST OF US.
GRIMLOCK'S RIGHT. WE'RE AUTOBOTS— BEING GOOD'S WHAT WE DO.
IT'S WHAT SETS US APART.
I DON'T KNOW IF IT'S AS SIMPLE AS THAT ANYMORE—
—I DON'T KNOW IF IT EVER WAS—
—BUT THERE'S NO TIME FOR A DEBATE. WHEN I CALL OUT YOUR NAME...

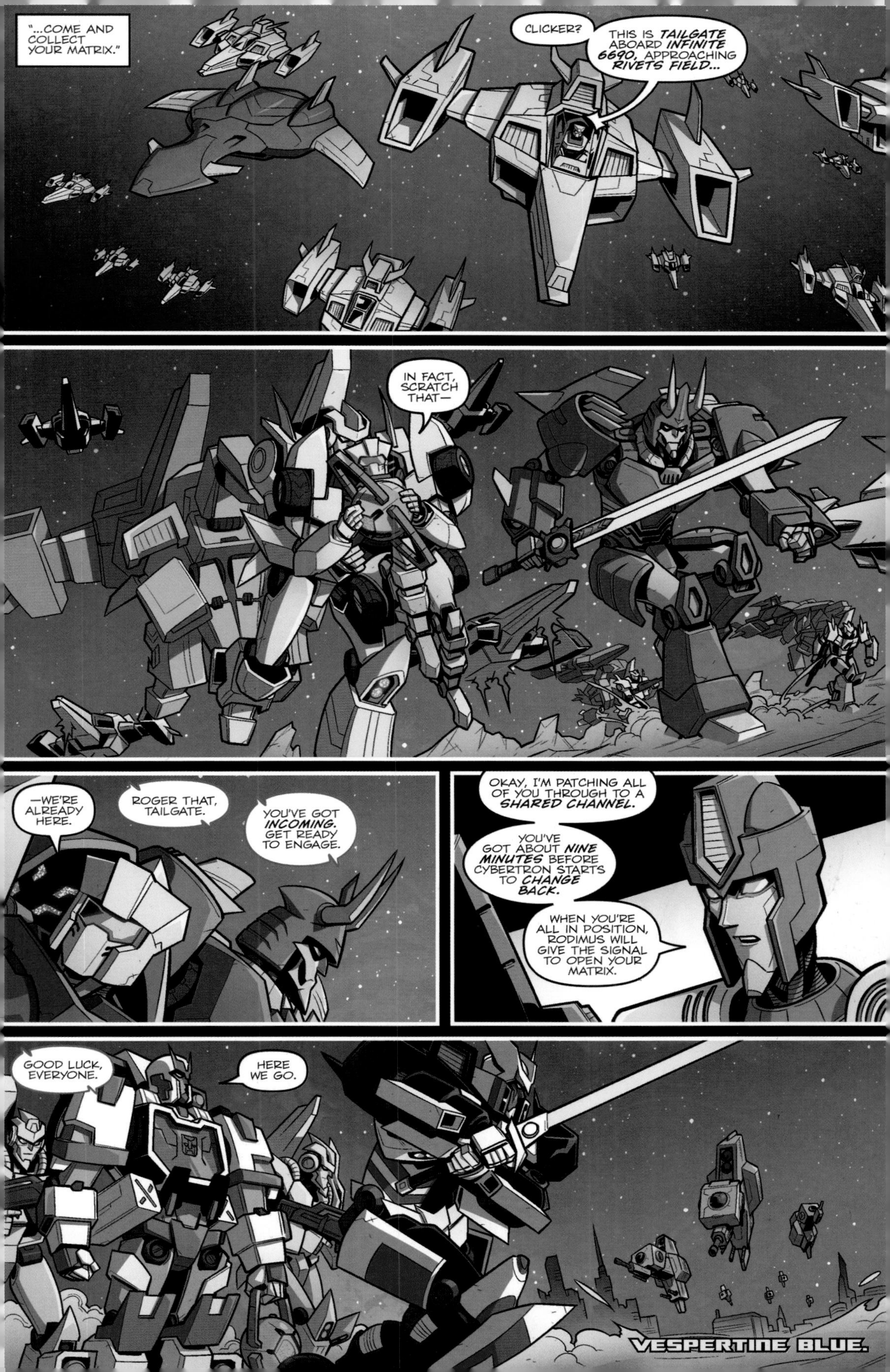
"...COME AND COLLECT YOUR MATRIX."
CLICKER?
THIS IS TAILGATE ABOARD INFINITE 6690, APPROACHING RIVETS FIELD...
IN FACT, SCRATCH THAT—
—WE'RE ALREADY HERE.
ROGER THAT, TAILGATE.
YOU'VE GOT INCOMING. GET READY TO ENGAGE.
OKAY, I'M PATCHING ALL OF YOU THROUGH TO A SHARED CHANNEL.
YOU'VE GOT ABOUT NINE MINUTES BEFORE CYBERTRON STARTS TO CHANGE BACK.
WHEN YOU'RE ALL IN POSITION, RODIMUS WILL GIVE THE SIGNAL TO OPEN YOUR MATRIX.
GOOD LUCK, EVERYONE.
HERE WE GO.
VESPERTINE BLUE.

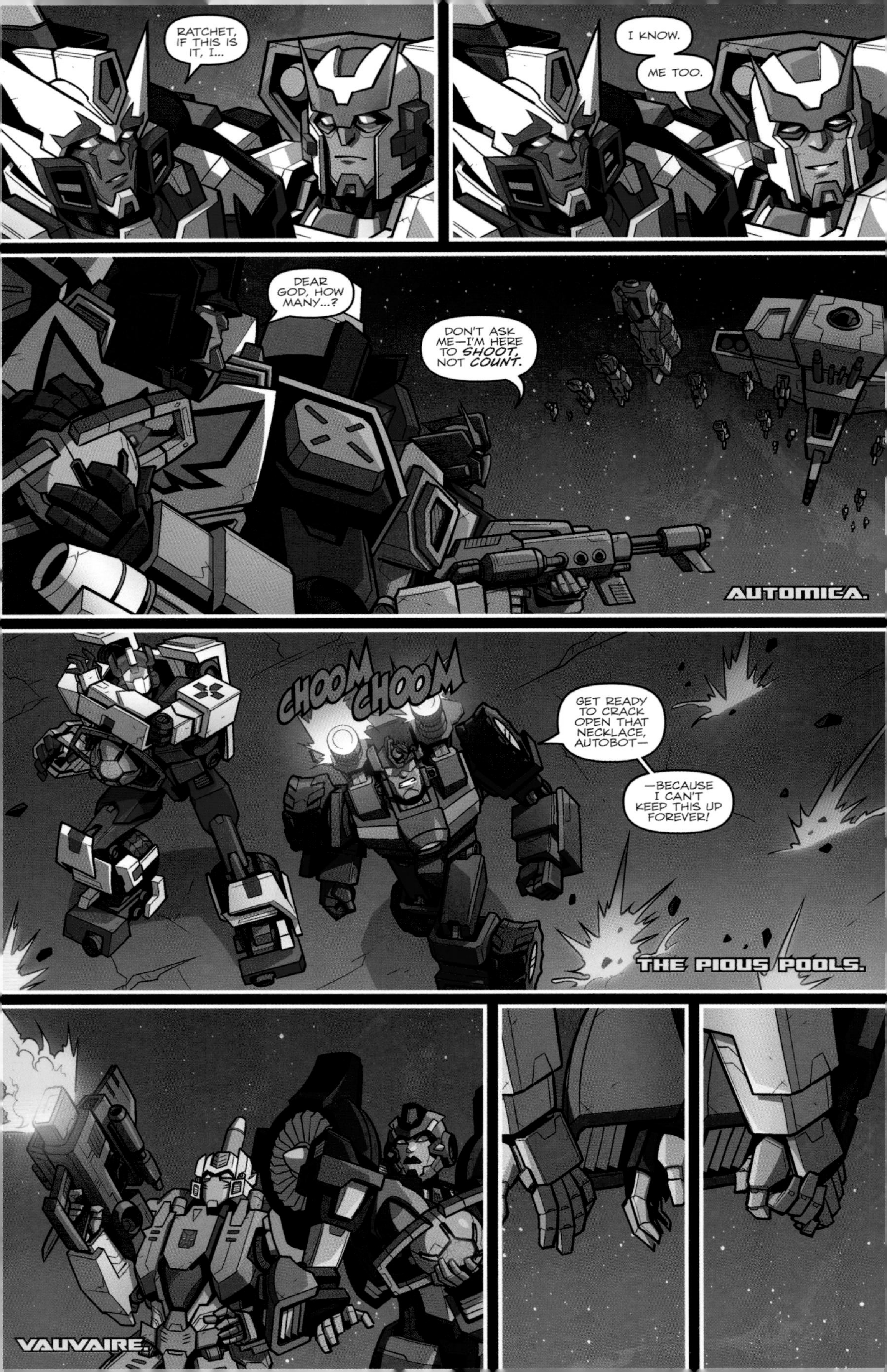
RATCHET, IF THIS IS IT, I...
I KNOW.
ME TOO.
DEAR GOD, HOW MANY...?
DON'T ASK ME—I'M HERE TO SHOOT, NOT COUNT.
AUTOMICA.
CHOOM CHOOM
GET READY TO CRACK OPEN THAT NECKLACE, AUTOBOT—
—BECAUSE I CAN'T KEEP THIS UP FOREVER!
THE PIOUS POOLS.
VAUVAIRE.

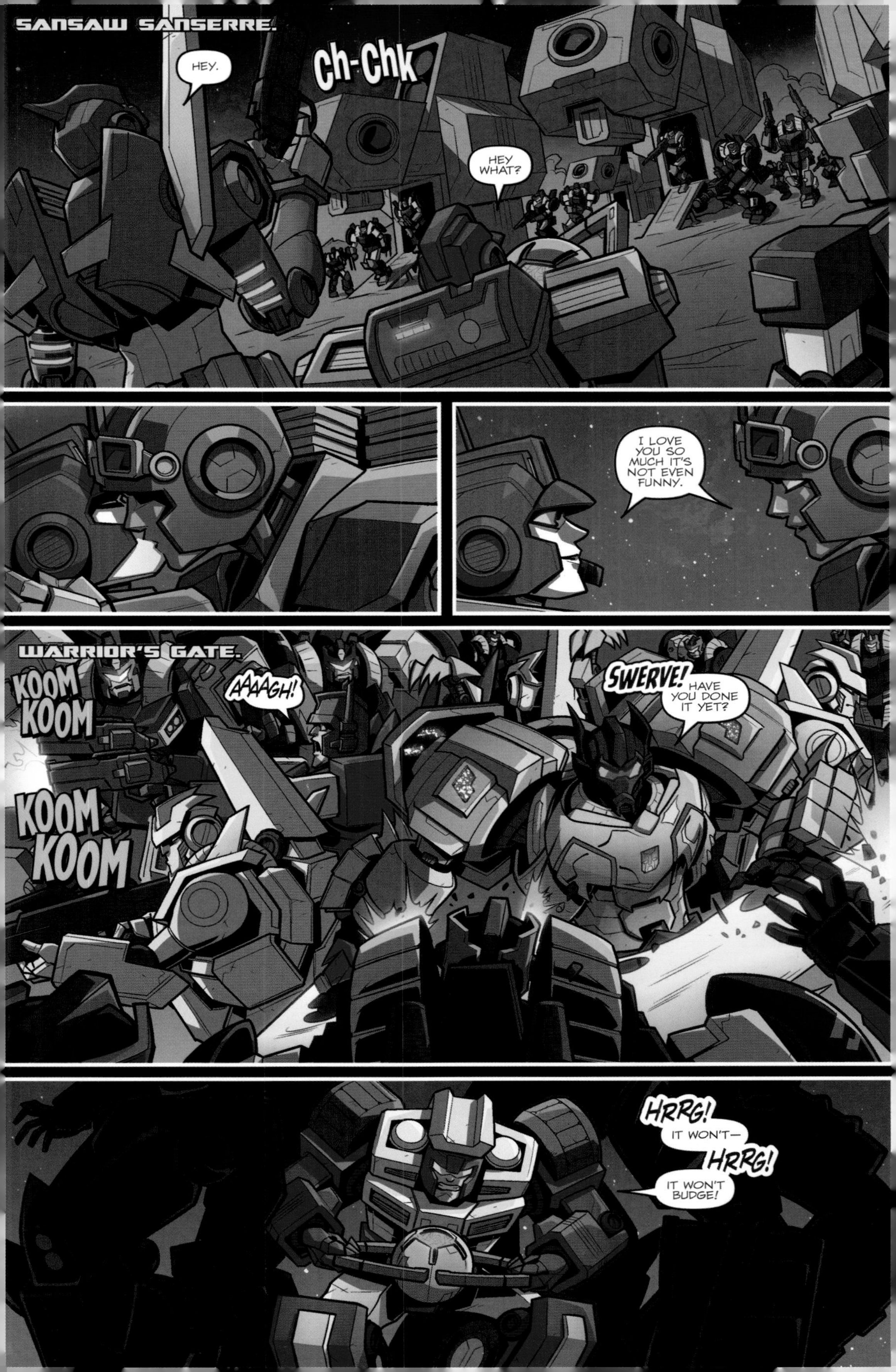
SANSAW SANSERRE.
HEY.
Ch-Chk
HEY WHAT?
I LOVE YOU SO MUCH IT'S NOT EVEN FUNNY.
WARRIOR'S GATE.
KOOM KOOM
AAAAGH!
SWERVE!
HAVE YOU DONE IT YET?
KOOM KOOM
HRRG!
IT WON'T—
HRRG!
IT WON'T BUDGE!

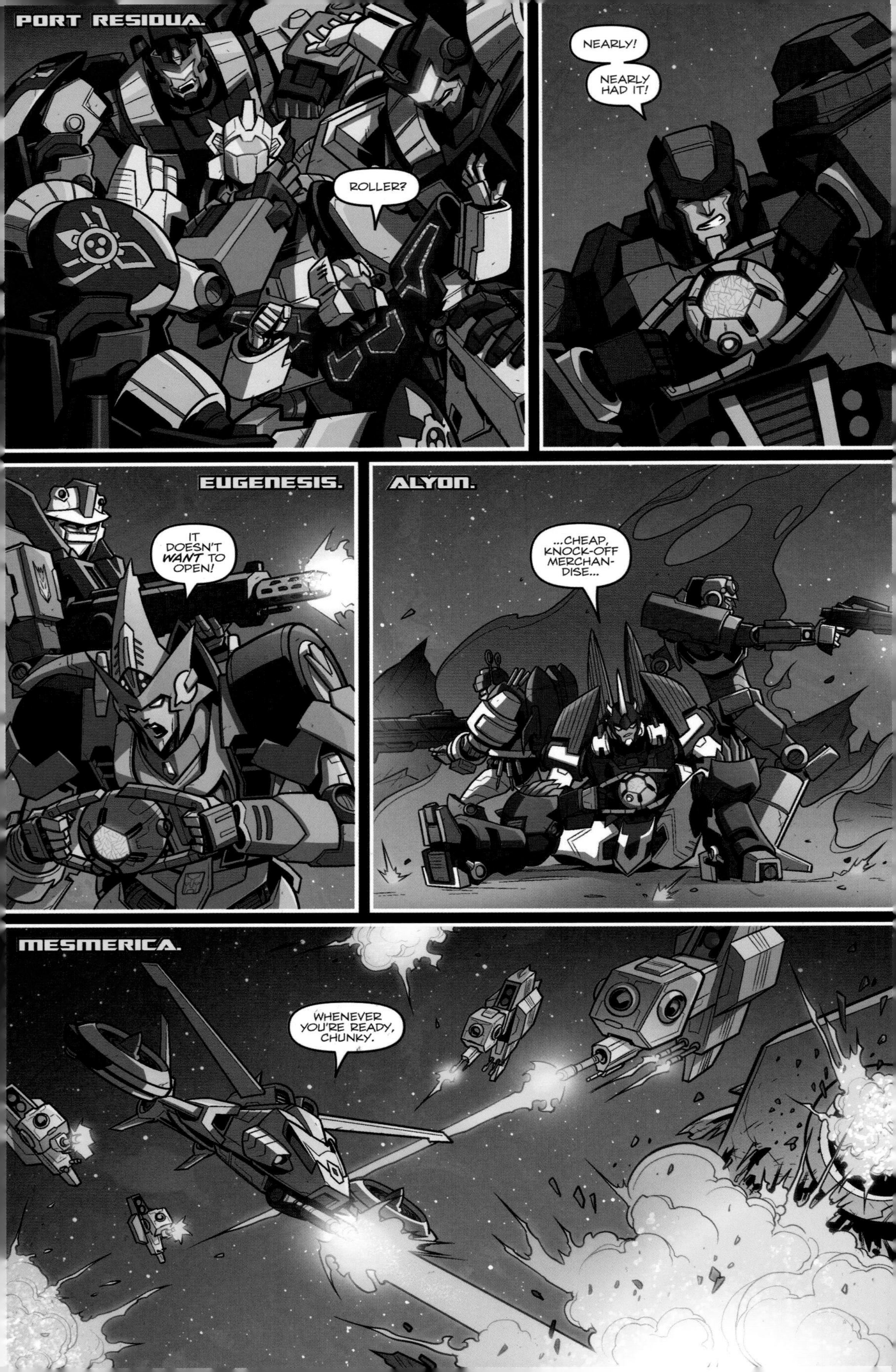
PORT RESIDUA.
ROLLER?
NEARLY!
NEARLY HAD IT!
EUGENESIS.
IT DOESN'T *WANT* TO OPEN!
ALYON.
...CHEAP, KNOCK-OFF MERCHAN-DISE...
MESMERICA.
WHENEVER YOU'RE READY, CHUNKY.

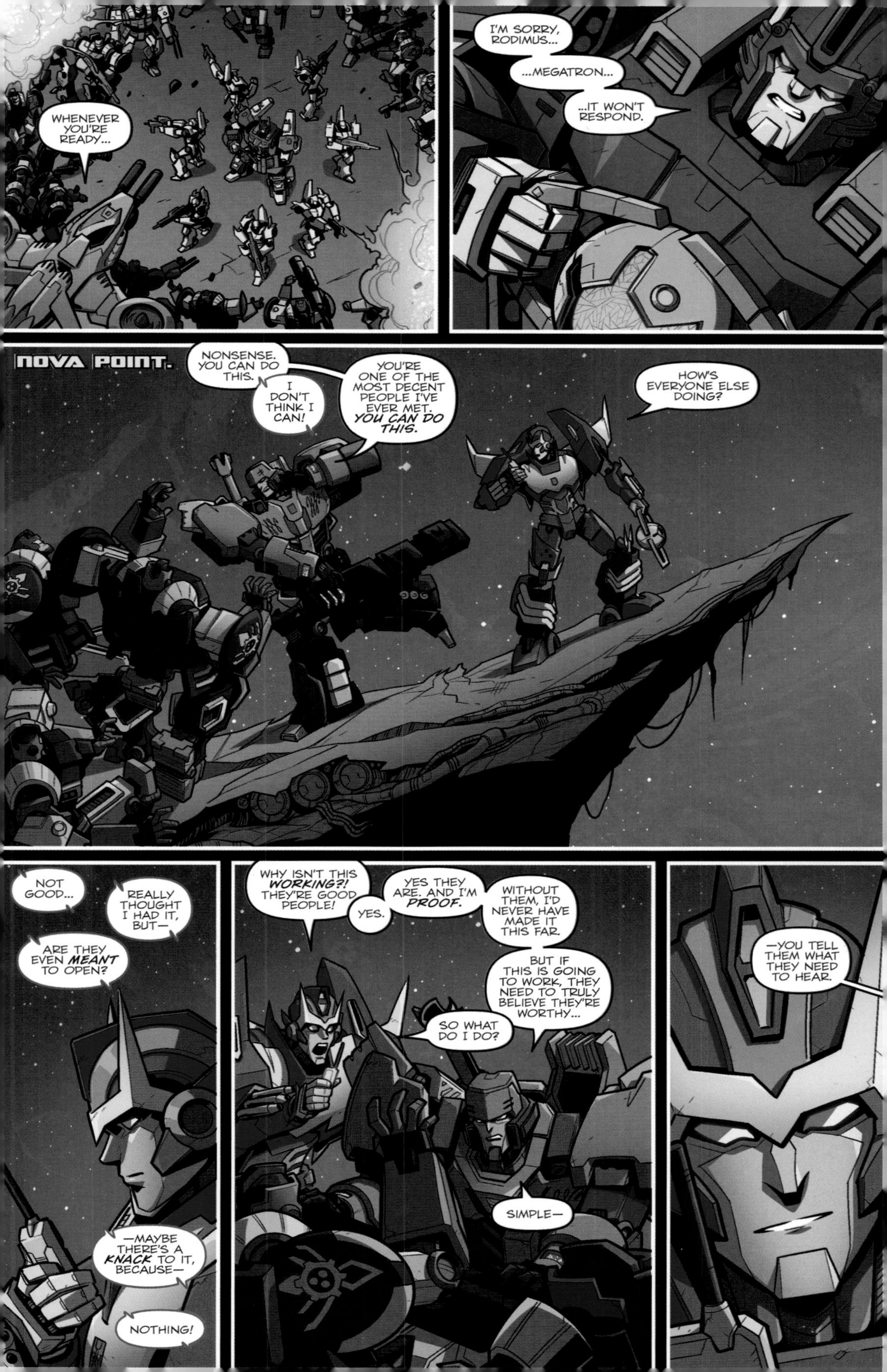
WHENEVER YOU'RE READY...
I'M SORRY, RODIMUS...
...MEGATRON...
...IT WON'T RESPOND.
NOVA POINT.
NONSENSE. YOU CAN DO THIS.
I DON'T THINK I CAN!
YOU'RE ONE OF THE MOST DECENT PEOPLE I'VE EVER MET. YOU CAN DO THIS.
HOW'S EVERYONE ELSE DOING?
NOT GOOD...
REALLY THOUGHT I HAD IT, BUT—
ARE THEY EVEN MEANT TO OPEN?
—MAYBE THERE'S A KNACK TO IT, BECAUSE—
NOTHING!
WHY ISN'T THIS WORKING?! THEY'RE GOOD PEOPLE!
YES.
YES THEY ARE. AND I'M PROOF.
WITHOUT THEM, I'D NEVER HAVE MADE IT THIS FAR.
BUT IF THIS IS GOING TO WORK, THEY NEED TO TRULY BELIEVE THEY'RE WORTHY...
SO WHAT DO I DO?
SIMPLE—
—YOU TELL THEM WHAT THEY NEED TO HEAR.

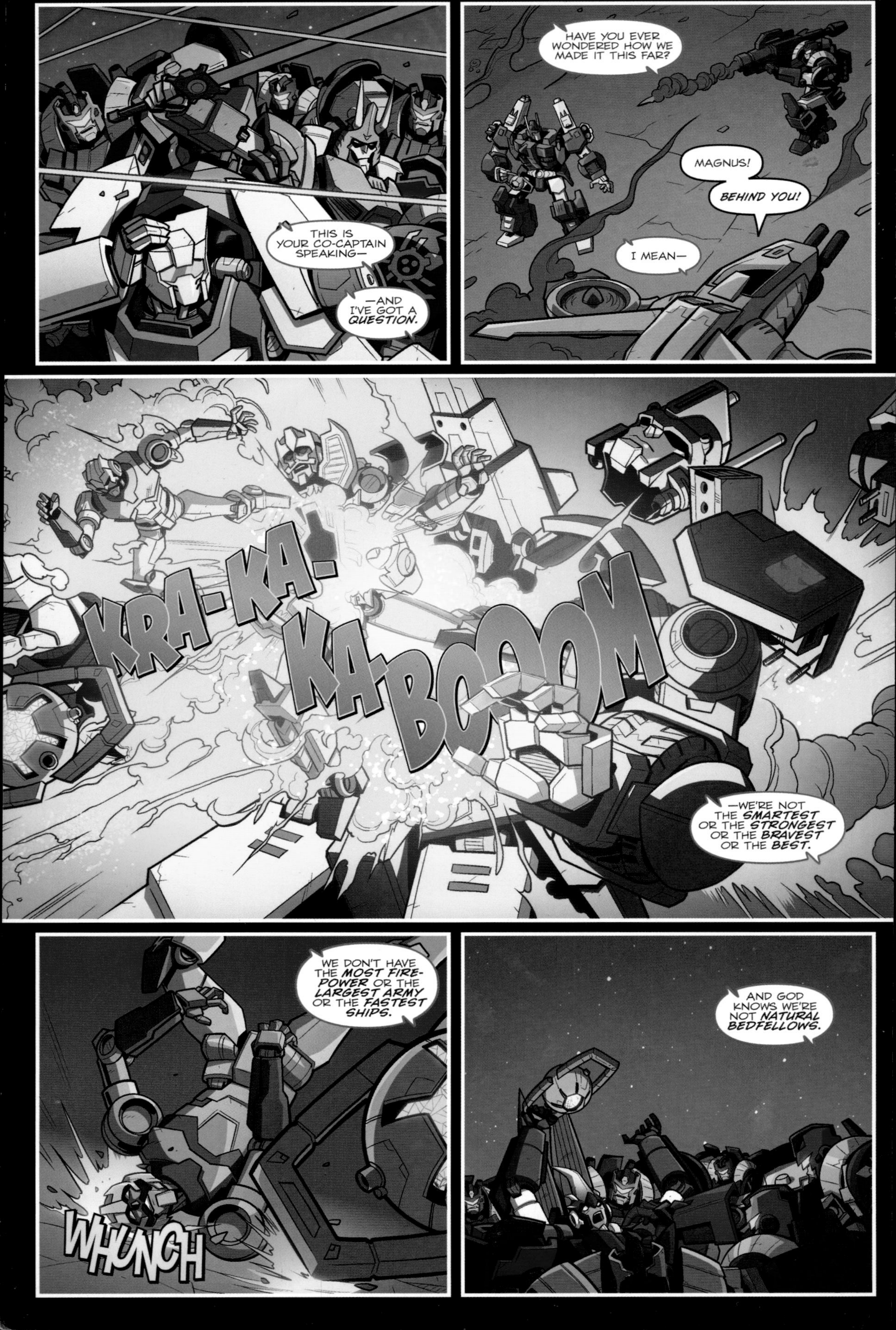
THIS IS YOUR CO-CAPTAIN SPEAKING—
—AND I'VE GOT A QUESTION.
HAVE YOU EVER WONDERED HOW WE MADE IT THIS FAR?
MAGNUS!
BEHIND YOU!
I MEAN—
KRA-KA-KA-BOOOM
—WE'RE NOT THE SMARTEST OR THE STRONGEST OR THE BRAVEST OR THE BEST.
WE DON'T HAVE THE MOST FIRE-POWER OR THE LARGEST ARMY OR THE FASTEST SHIPS.
WHUNCH
AND GOD KNOWS WE'RE NOT NATURAL BEDFELLOWS.

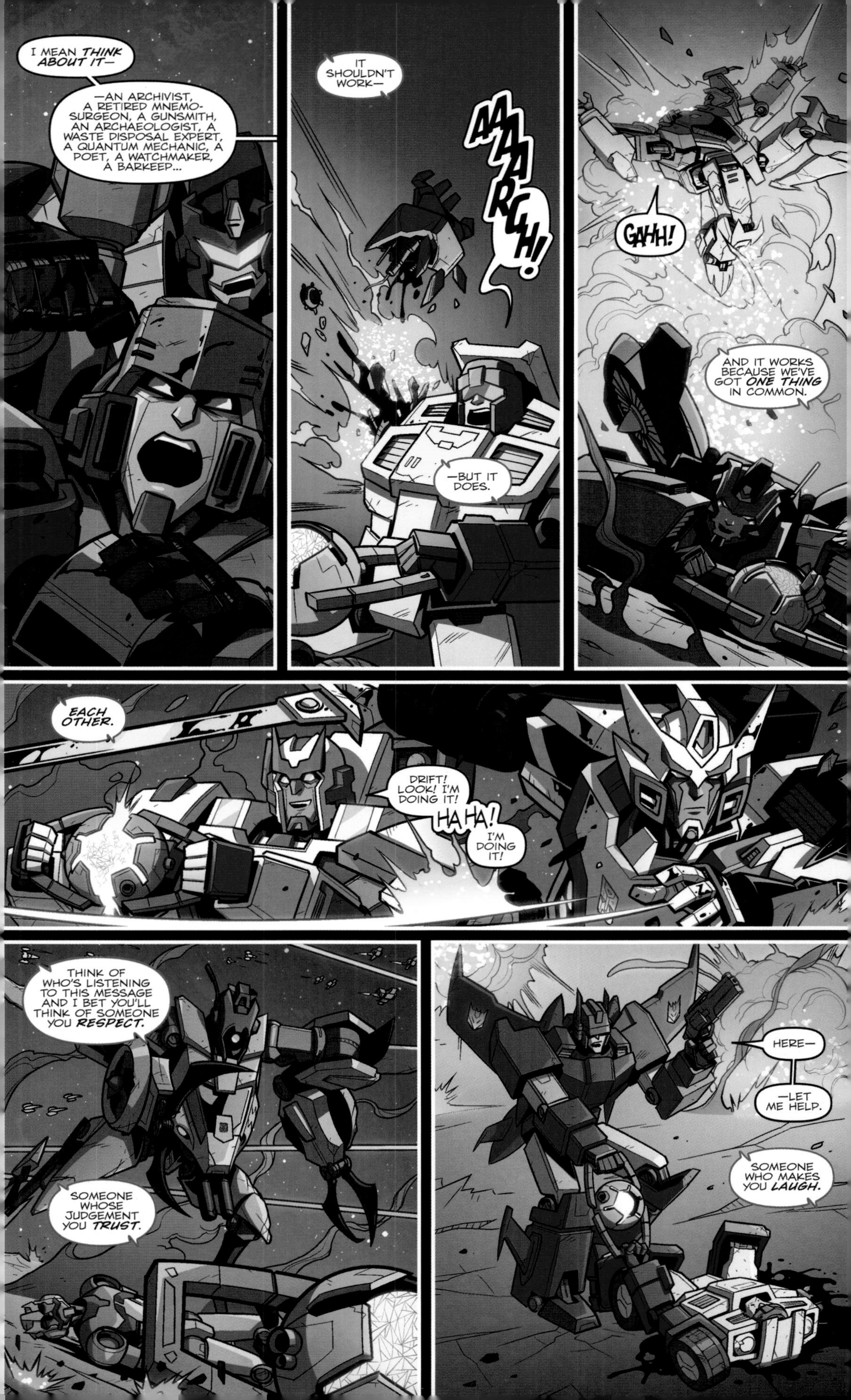
I MEAN THINK ABOUT IT—
—AN ARCHIVIST, A RETIRED MNEMO-SURGEON, A GUNSMITH, AN ARCHAEOLOGIST, A WASTE DISPOSAL EXPERT, A QUANTUM MECHANIC, A POET, A WATCHMAKER, A BARKEEP...
IT SHOULDN'T WORK—
AAAARGH!
—BUT IT DOES.
GAHH!
AND IT WORKS BECAUSE WE'VE GOT ONE THING IN COMMON.
EACH OTHER.
DRIFT! LOOK! I'M DOING IT!
HAHA!
I'M DOING IT!
THINK OF WHO'S LISTENING TO THIS MESSAGE AND I BET YOU'LL THINK OF SOMEONE YOU RESPECT.
SOMEONE WHOSE JUDGEMENT YOU TRUST.
HERE—
—LET ME HELP.
SOMEONE WHO MAKES YOU LAUGH.

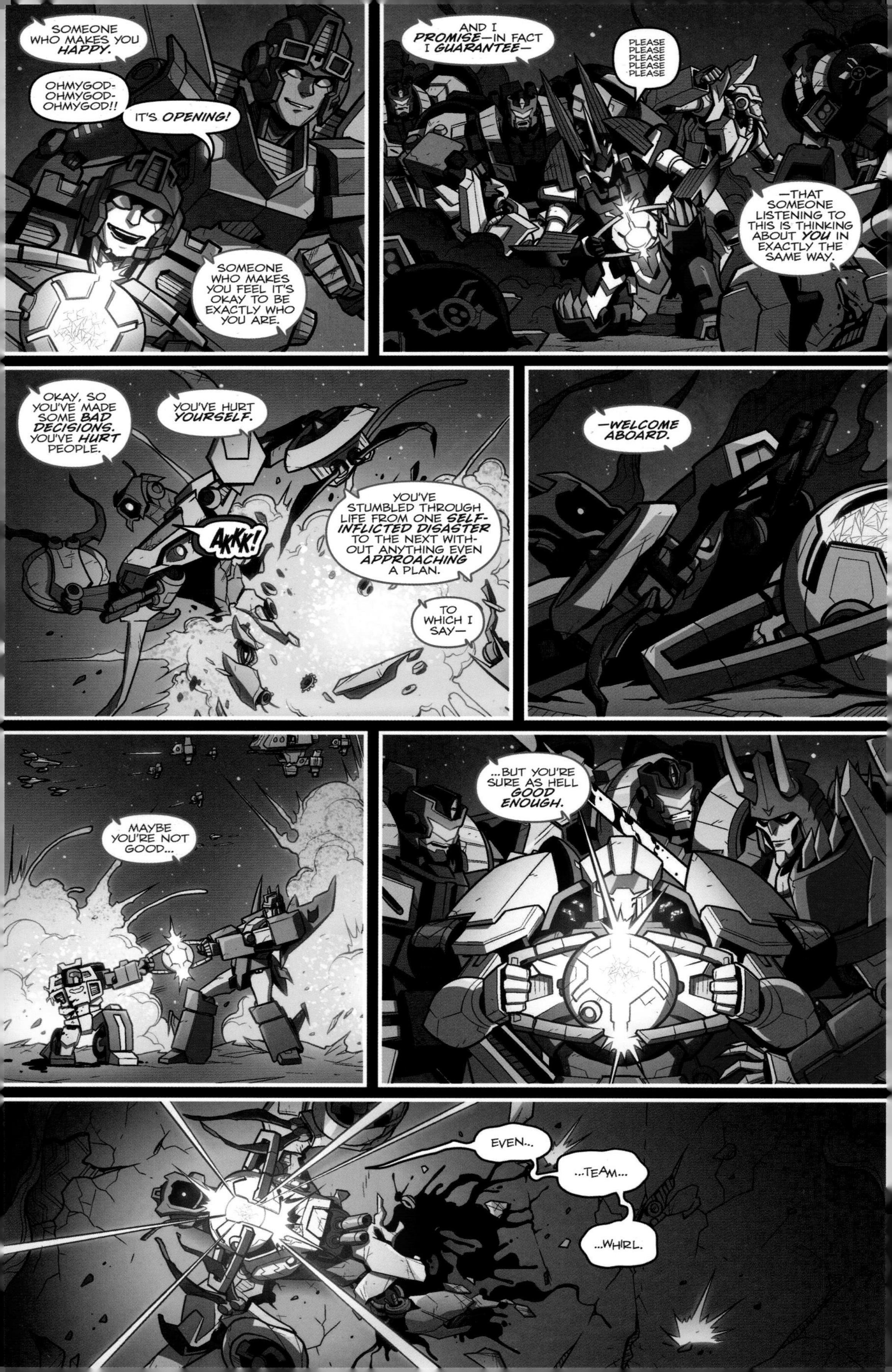
SOMEONE WHO MAKES YOU HAPPY.
OHMYGOD-OHMYGOD-OHMYGOD!!
IT'S OPENING!
SOMEONE WHO MAKES YOU FEEL IT'S OKAY TO BE EXACTLY WHO YOU ARE.
AND I PROMISE—IN FACT I GUARANTEE—
PLEASE PLEASE PLEASE PLEASE PLEASE
—THAT SOMEONE LISTENING TO THIS IS THINKING ABOUT YOU IN EXACTLY THE SAME WAY.
OKAY, SO YOU'VE MADE SOME BAD DECISIONS. YOU'VE HURT PEOPLE.
YOU'VE HURT YOURSELF.
AKKK!
YOU'VE STUMBLED THROUGH LIFE FROM ONE SELF-INFLICTED DISASTER TO THE NEXT WITHOUT ANYTHING EVEN APPROACHING A PLAN.
TO WHICH I SAY—
—WELCOME ABOARD.
MAYBE YOU'RE NOT GOOD...
...BUT YOU'RE SURE AS HELL GOOD ENOUGH.
EVEN...
...TEAM...
...WHIRL.

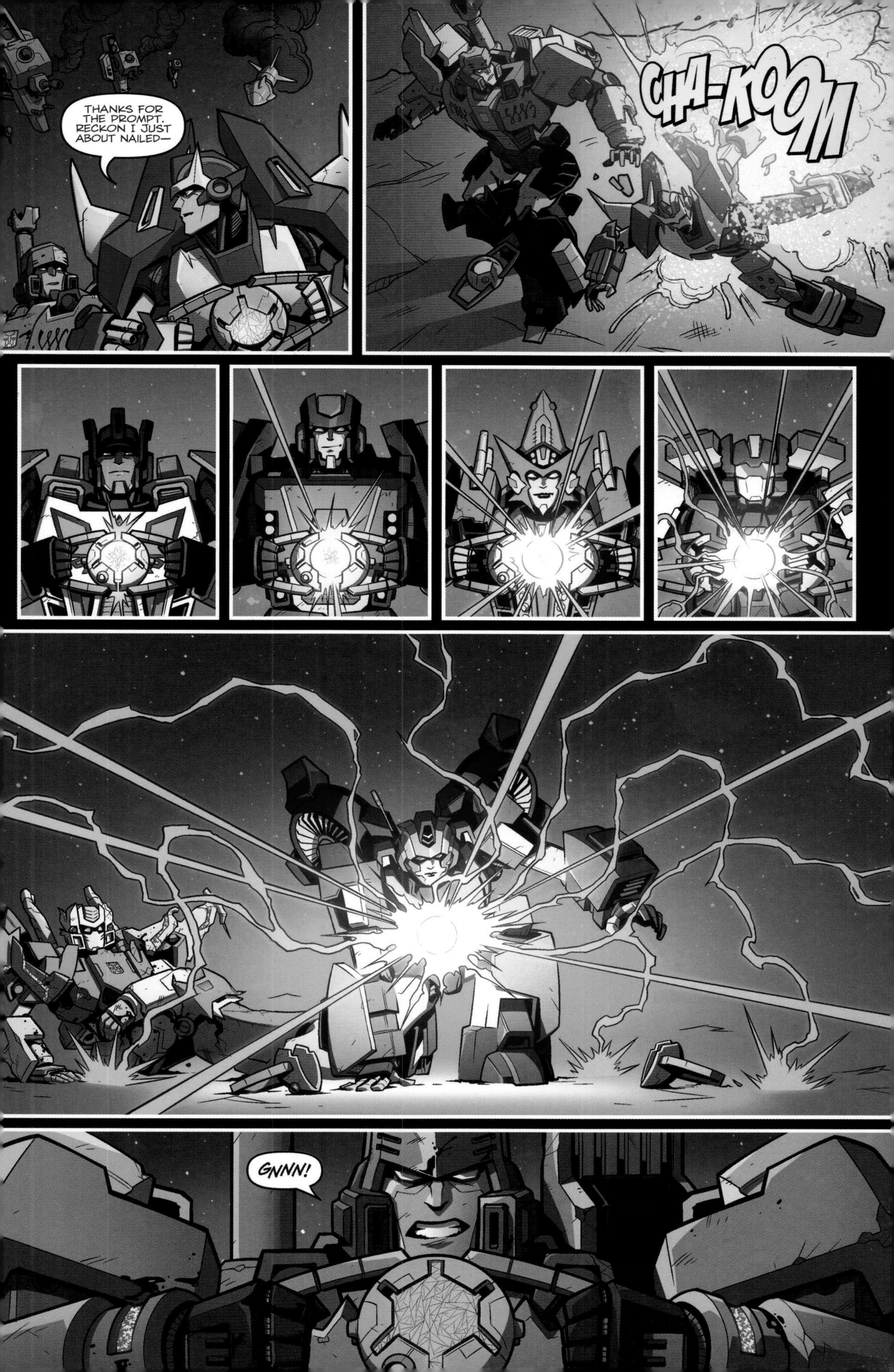
THANKS FOR THE PROMPT. RECKON I JUST ABOUT NAILED—
CHA-KOOM
GNNN!

M-MEGATRON...
I CAN'T DO IT.
IT WON'T LET ME.
G-GIVE IT... HERE...
HNNNNNG!

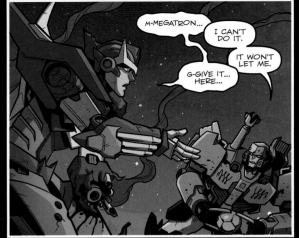

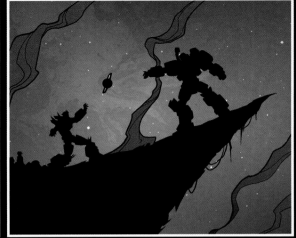

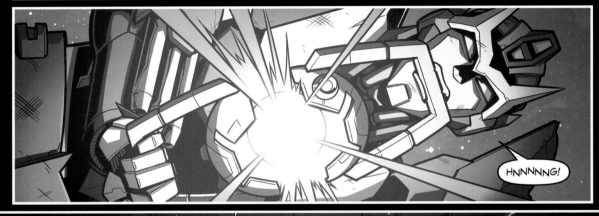

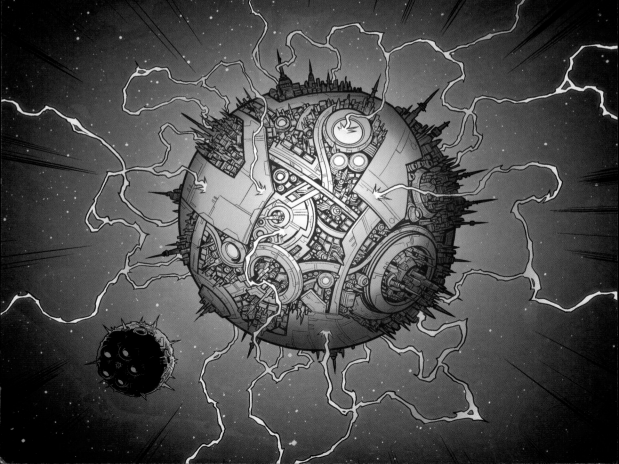

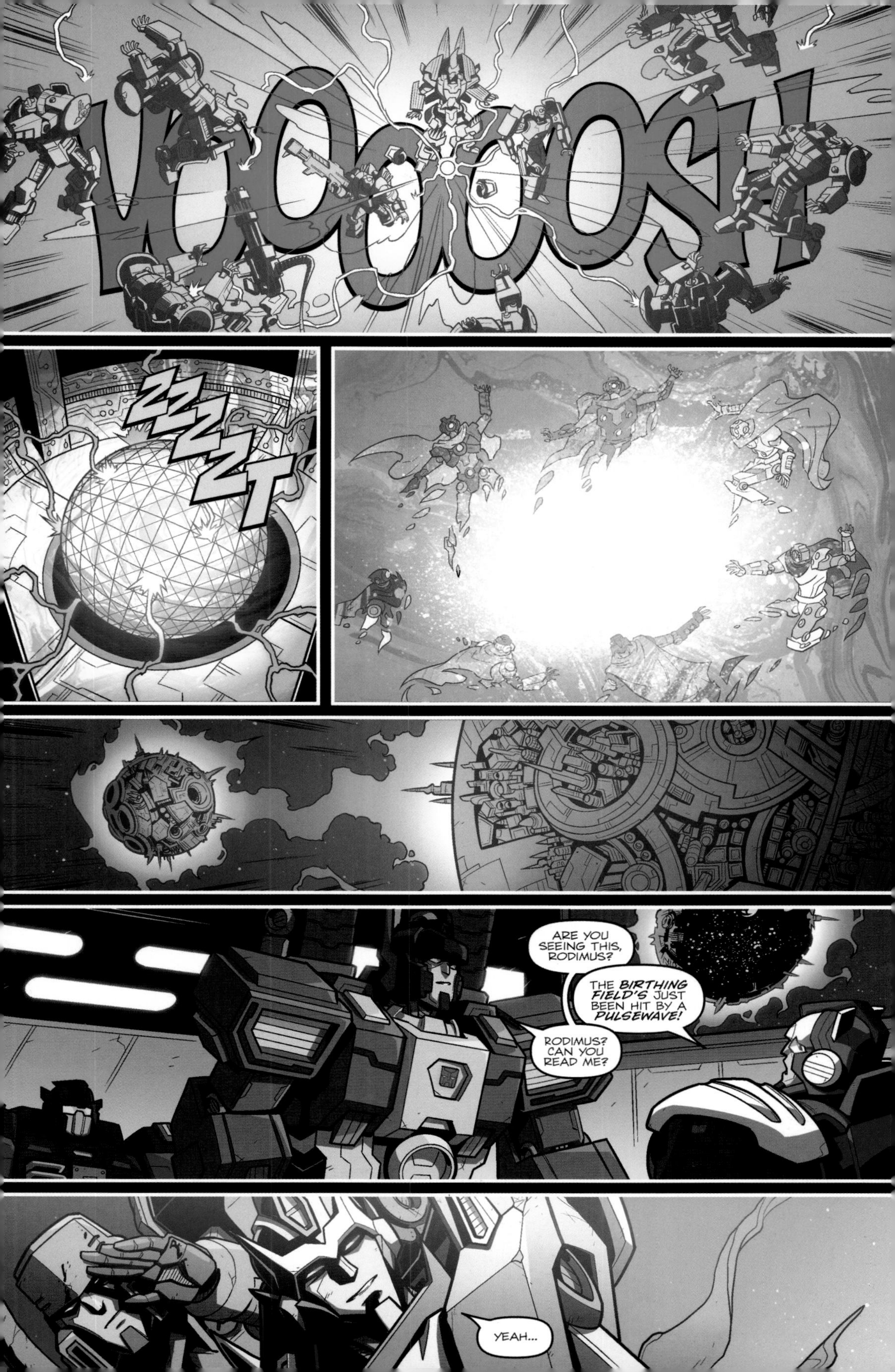
VOOOOSH
ZZZZT
ARE YOU SEEING THIS, RODIMUS?
THE BIRTHING FIELD'S JUST BEEN HIT BY A PULSEWAVE!
RODIMUS? CAN YOU READ ME?
YEAH...

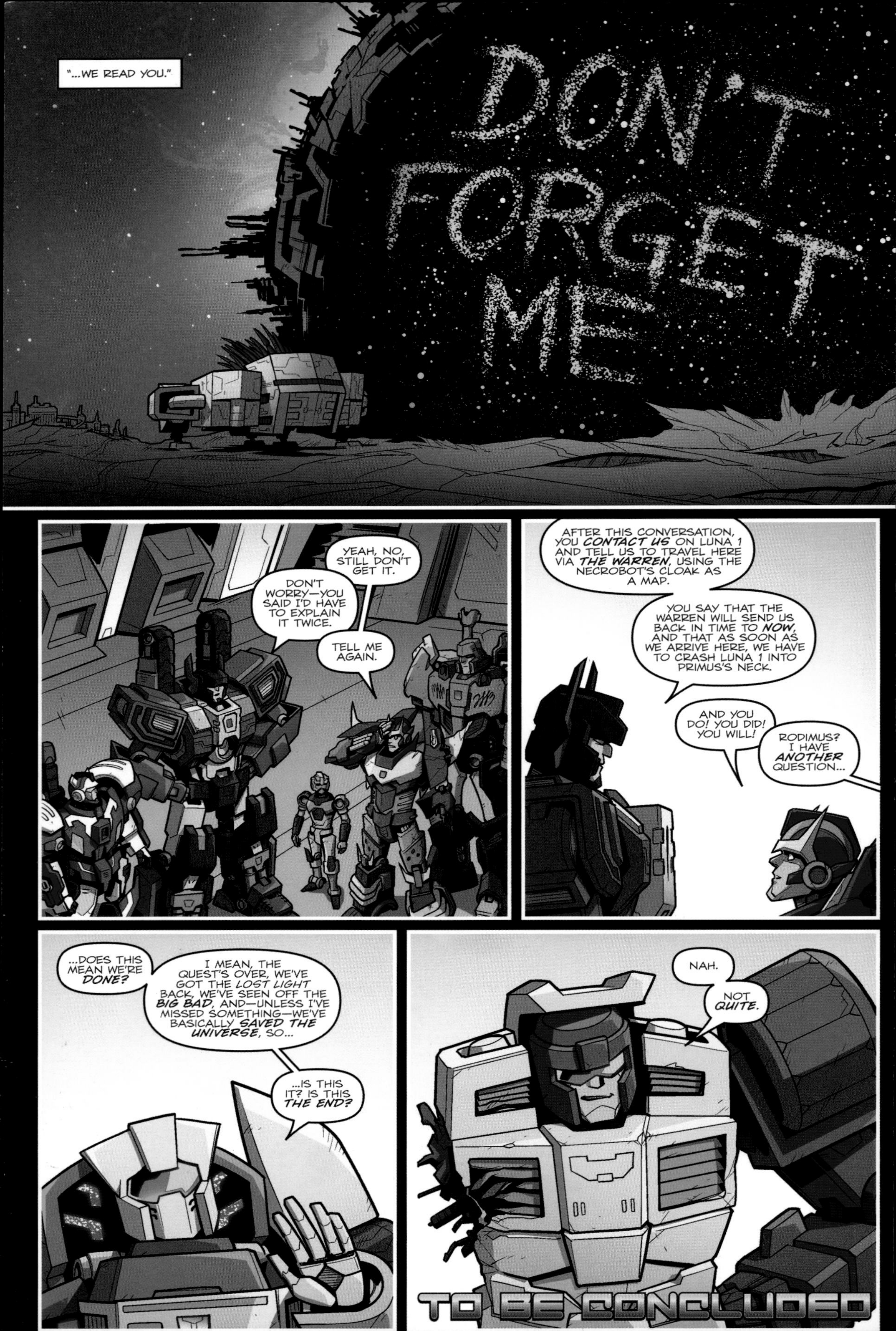
"...WE READ YOU."
DON'T FORGET ME
YEAH, NO, STILL DON'T GET IT.
DON'T WORRY—YOU SAID I'D HAVE TO EXPLAIN IT TWICE.
TELL ME AGAIN.
AFTER THIS CONVERSATION, YOU CONTACT US ON LUNA 1 AND TELL US TO TRAVEL HERE VIA THE WARREN, USING THE NECROBOT'S CLOAK AS A MAP.
YOU SAY THAT THE WARREN WILL SEND US BACK IN TIME TO NOW, AND THAT AS SOON AS WE ARRIVE HERE, WE HAVE TO CRASH LUNA 1 INTO PRIMUS'S NECK.
AND YOU DO! YOU DID! YOU WILL!
RODIMUS? I HAVE ANOTHER QUESTION...
...DOES THIS MEAN WE'RE DONE?
I MEAN, THE QUEST'S OVER, WE'VE GOT THE LOST LIGHT BACK, WE'VE SEEN OFF THE BIG BAD, AND—UNLESS I'VE MISSED SOMETHING—WE'VE BASICALLY SAVED THE UNIVERSE, SO...
...IS THIS IT? IS THIS THE END?
NAH.
NOT QUITE.
TO BE CONCLUDED

ART BY **NICK ROCHE**
COLORS BY **JOSH BURCHAM**

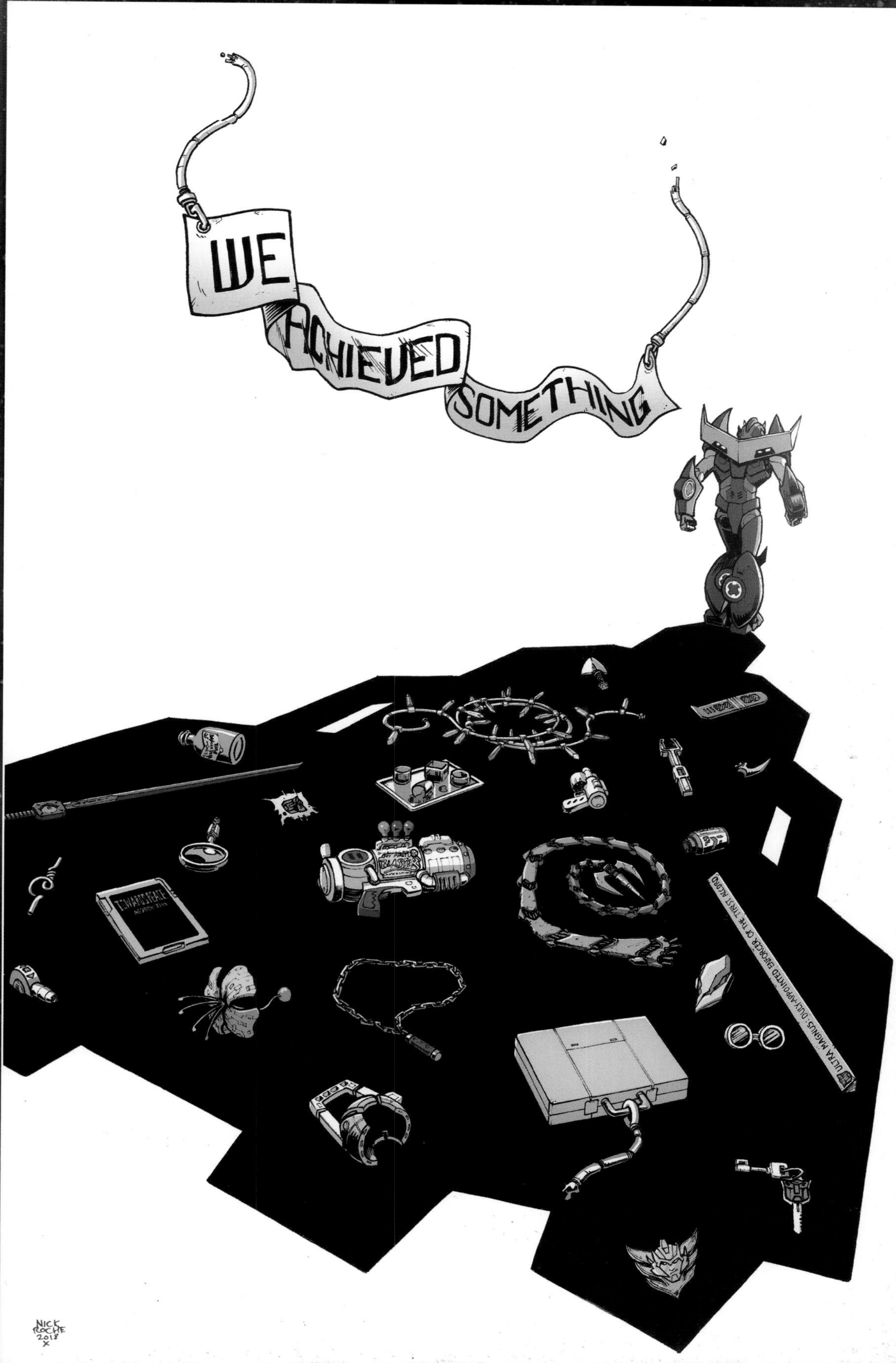
WE
ACHIEVED
SOMETHING
BLASTER
ULTRA MAGNUS, DULY-APPOINTED ENFORCER OF THE TYRST ACCORD
NICK ROCHE 2018

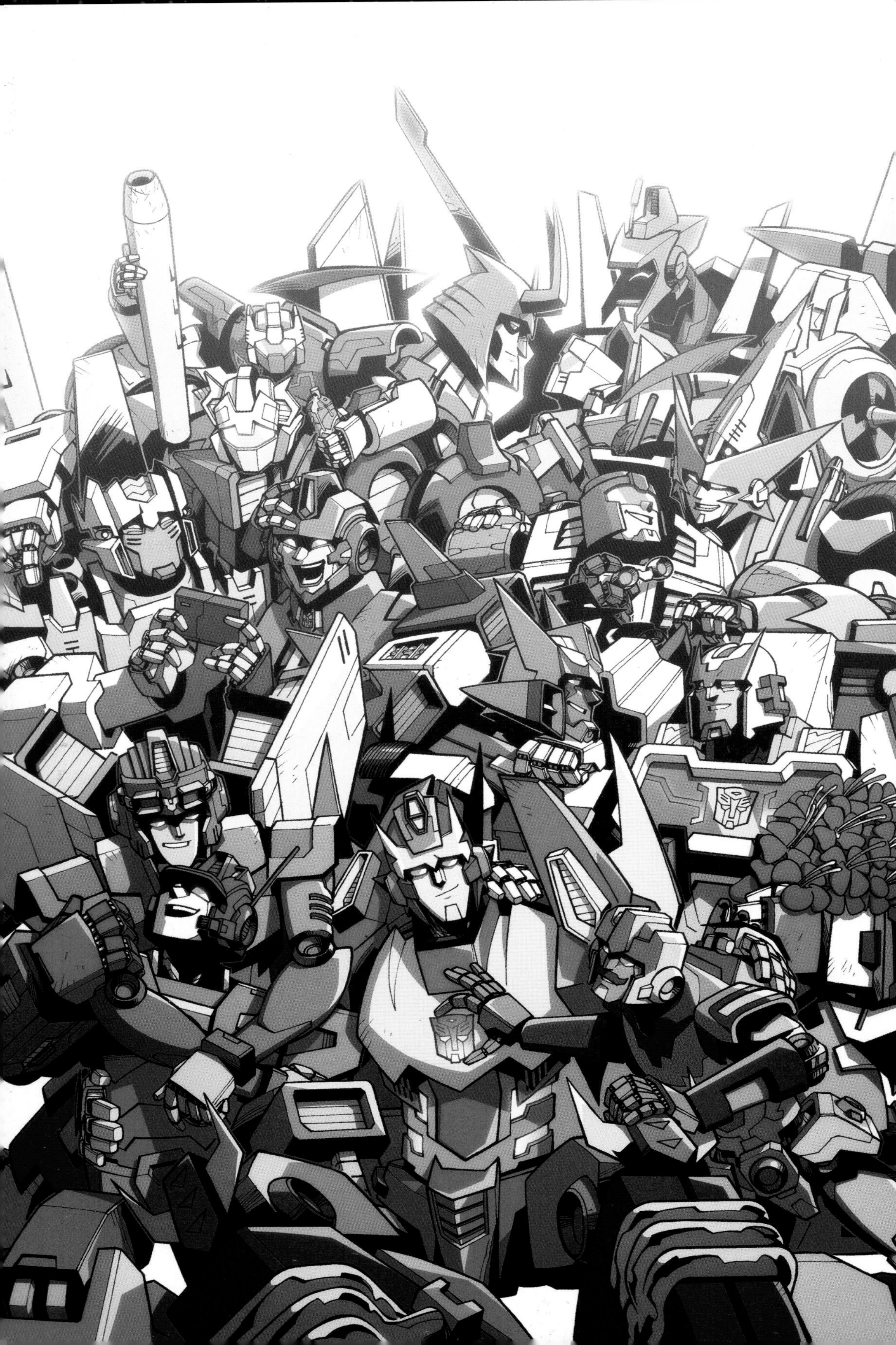

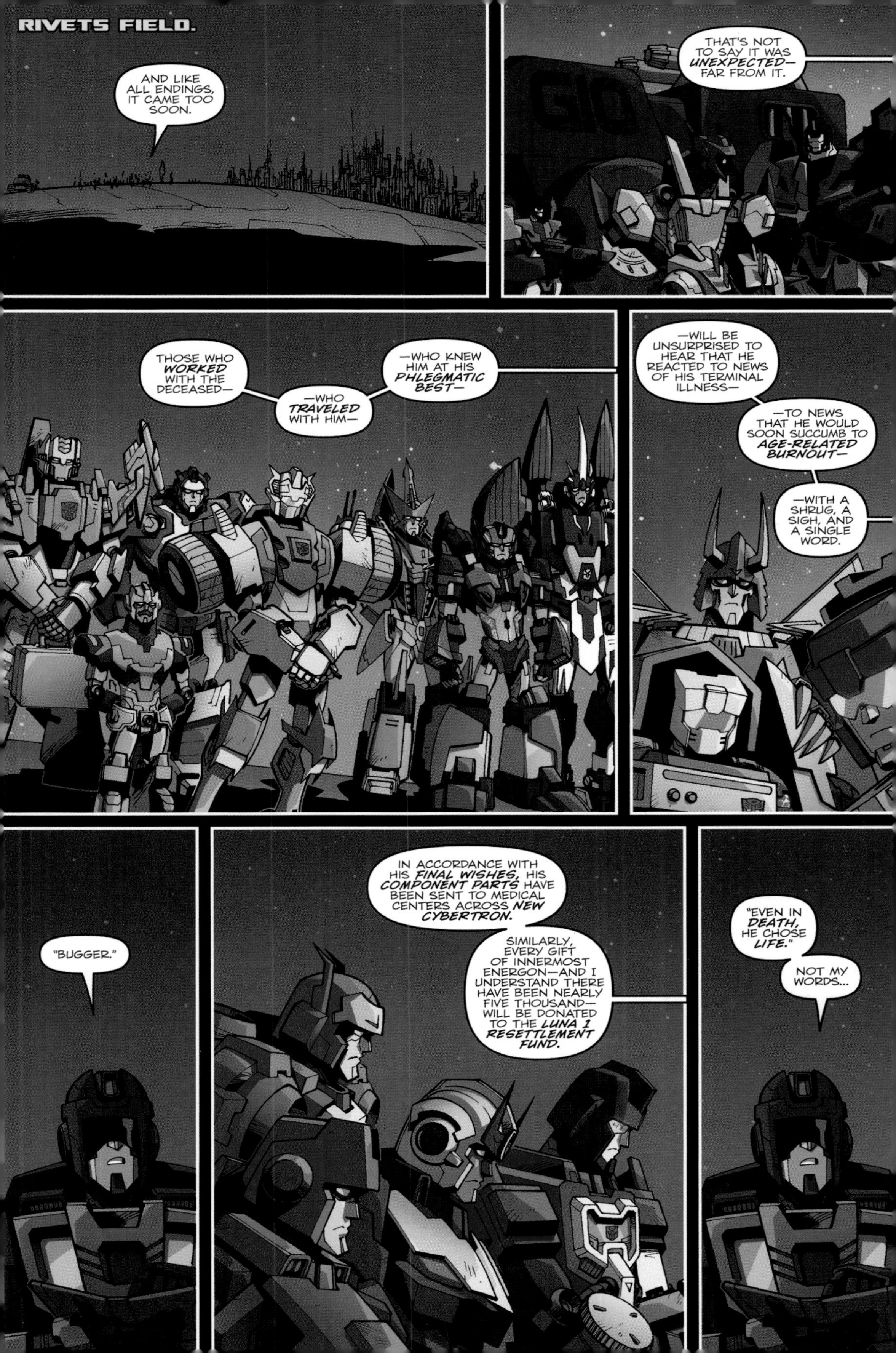
RIVETS FIELD.
AND LIKE ALL ENDINGS, IT CAME TOO SOON.
THAT'S NOT TO SAY IT WAS UNEXPECTED—FAR FROM IT.
THOSE WHO WORKED WITH THE DECEASED—
—WHO TRAVELED WITH HIM—
—WHO KNEW HIM AT HIS PHLEGMATIC BEST—
—WILL BE UNSURPRISED TO HEAR THAT HE REACTED TO NEWS OF HIS TERMINAL ILLNESS—
—TO NEWS THAT HE WOULD SOON SUCCUMB TO AGE-RELATED BURNOUT—
—WITH A SHRUG, A SIGH, AND A SINGLE WORD.
"BUGGER."
IN ACCORDANCE WITH HIS FINAL WISHES, HIS COMPONENT PARTS HAVE BEEN SENT TO MEDICAL CENTERS ACROSS NEW CYBERTRON.
SIMILARLY, EVERY GIFT OF INNERMOST ENERGON—AND I UNDERSTAND THERE HAVE BEEN NEARLY FIVE THOUSAND—WILL BE DONATED TO THE LUNA 1 RESETTLEMENT FUND.
"EVEN IN DEATH, HE CHOSE LIFE."
NOT MY WORDS...

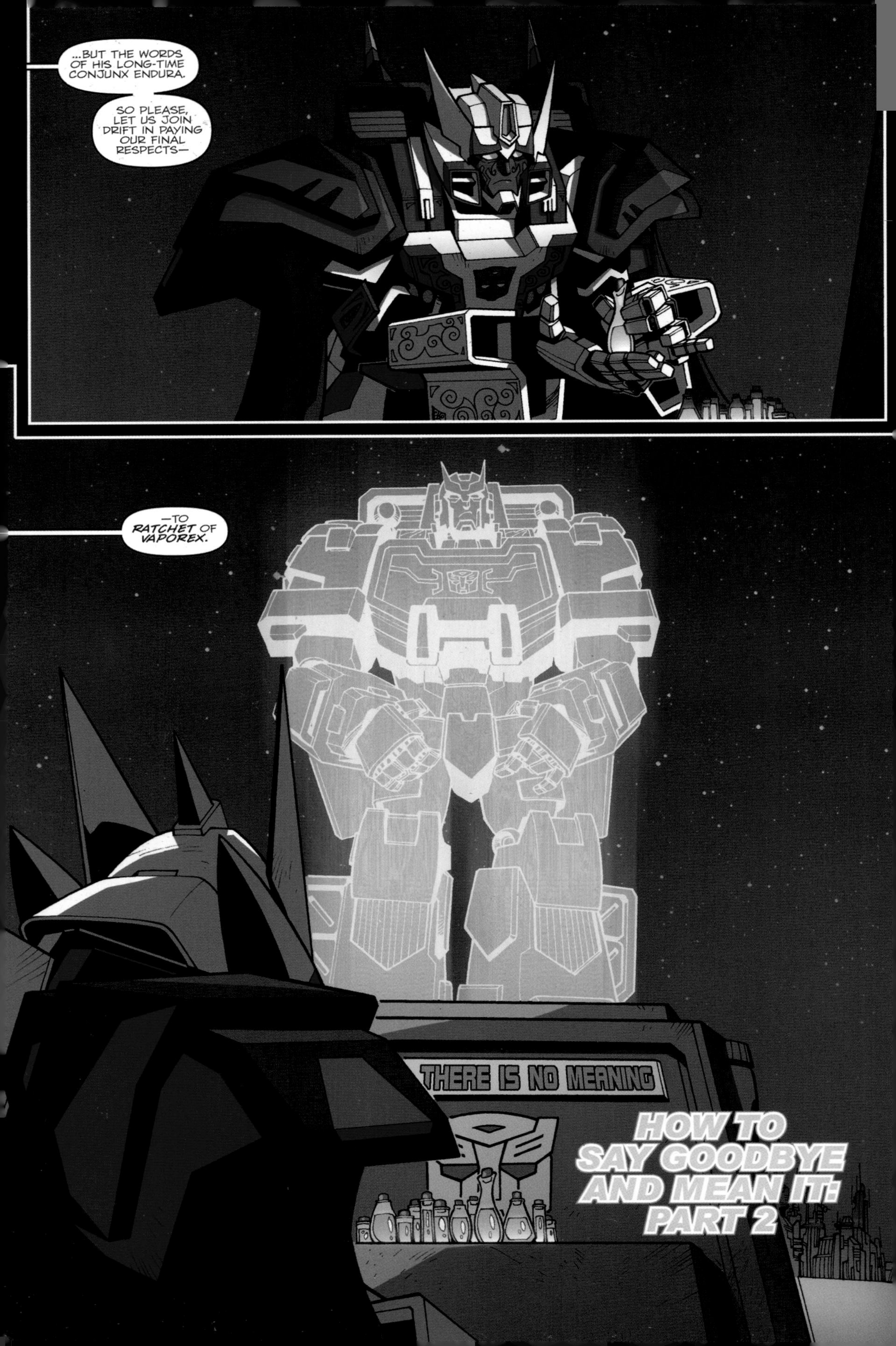
...BUT THE WORDS OF HIS LONG-TIME CONJUNX ENDURA.
SO PLEASE, LET US JOIN DRIFT IN PAYING OUR FINAL RESPECTS—
—TO RATCHET OF VAPOREX.
THERE IS NO MEANING
HOW TO SAY GOODBYE AND MEAN IT: PART 2

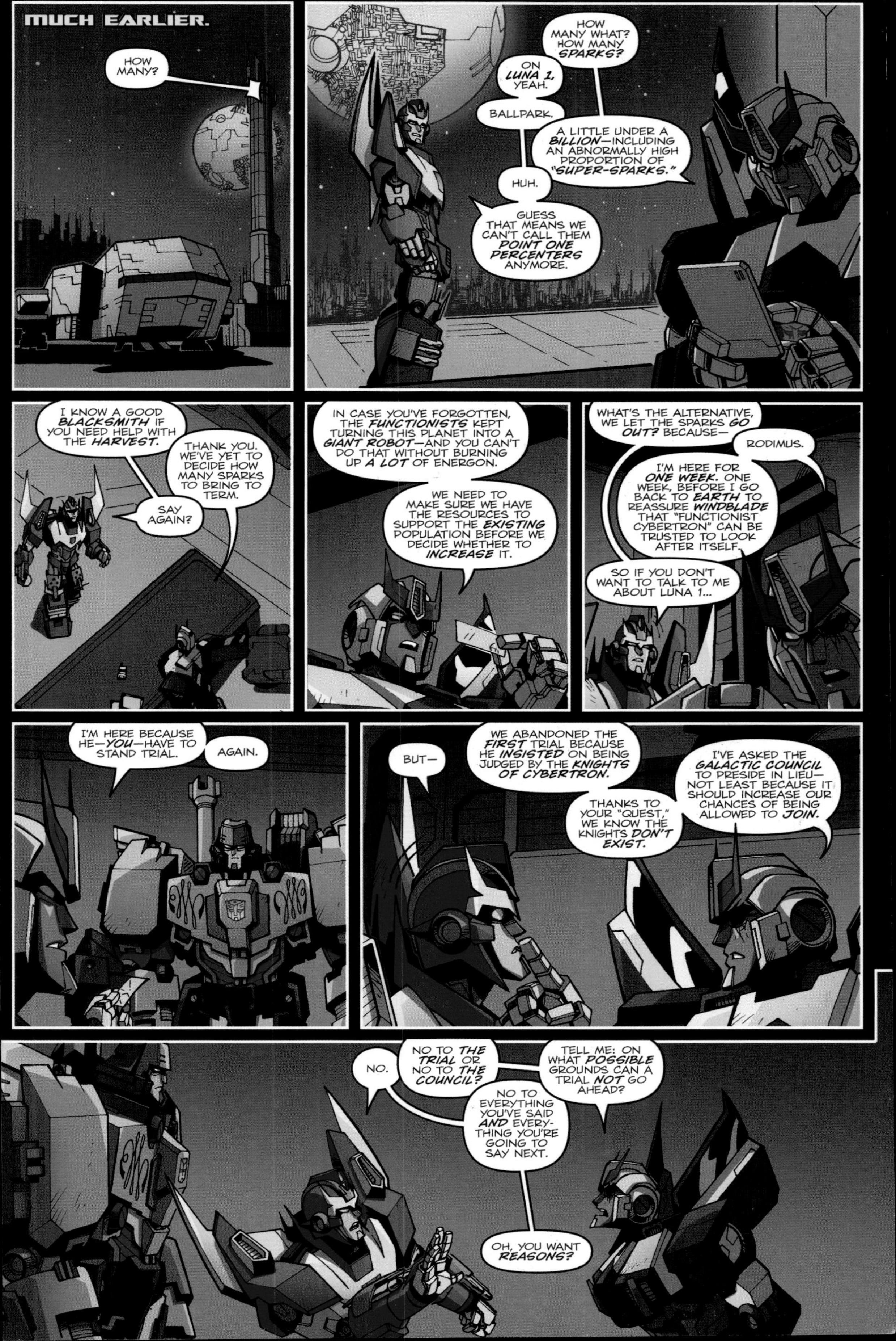
MUCH EARLIER.
HOW MANY?
HOW MANY WHAT? HOW MANY SPARKS?
ON LUNA 1, YEAH.
BALLPARK.
A LITTLE UNDER A BILLION—INCLUDING AN ABNORMALLY HIGH PROPORTION OF "SUPER-SPARKS."
HUH.
GUESS THAT MEANS WE CAN'T CALL THEM POINT ONE PERCENTERS ANYMORE.
I KNOW A GOOD BLACKSMITH IF YOU NEED HELP WITH THE HARVEST.
THANK YOU. WE'VE YET TO DECIDE HOW MANY SPARKS TO BRING TO TERM.
SAY AGAIN?
IN CASE YOU'VE FORGOTTEN, THE FUNCTIONISTS KEPT TURNING THIS PLANET INTO A GIANT ROBOT—AND YOU CAN'T DO THAT WITHOUT BURNING UP A LOT OF ENERGON.
WE NEED TO MAKE SURE WE HAVE THE RESOURCES TO SUPPORT THE EXISTING POPULATION BEFORE WE DECIDE WHETHER TO INCREASE IT.
WHAT'S THE ALTERNATIVE, WE LET THE SPARKS GO OUT? BECAUSE—
RODIMUS.
I'M HERE FOR ONE WEEK. ONE WEEK, BEFORE I GO BACK TO EARTH TO REASSURE WINDBLADE THAT "FUNCTIONIST CYBERTRON" CAN BE TRUSTED TO LOOK AFTER ITSELF.
SO IF YOU DON'T WANT TO TALK TO ME ABOUT LUNA 1...
I'M HERE BECAUSE HE—YOU—HAVE TO STAND TRIAL.
AGAIN.
BUT—
WE ABANDONED THE FIRST TRIAL BECAUSE HE INSISTED ON BEING JUDGED BY THE KNIGHTS OF CYBERTRON.
THANKS TO YOUR "QUEST," WE KNOW THE KNIGHTS DON'T EXIST.
I'VE ASKED THE GALACTIC COUNCIL TO PRESIDE IN LIEU—NOT LEAST BECAUSE IT SHOULD INCREASE OUR CHANCES OF BEING ALLOWED TO JOIN.
NO.
NO TO THE TRIAL OR NO TO THE COUNCIL?
NO TO EVERYTHING YOU'VE SAID AND EVERYTHING YOU'RE GOING TO SAY NEXT.
TELL ME: ON WHAT POSSIBLE GROUNDS CAN A TRIAL NOT GO AHEAD?
OH, YOU WANT REASONS?

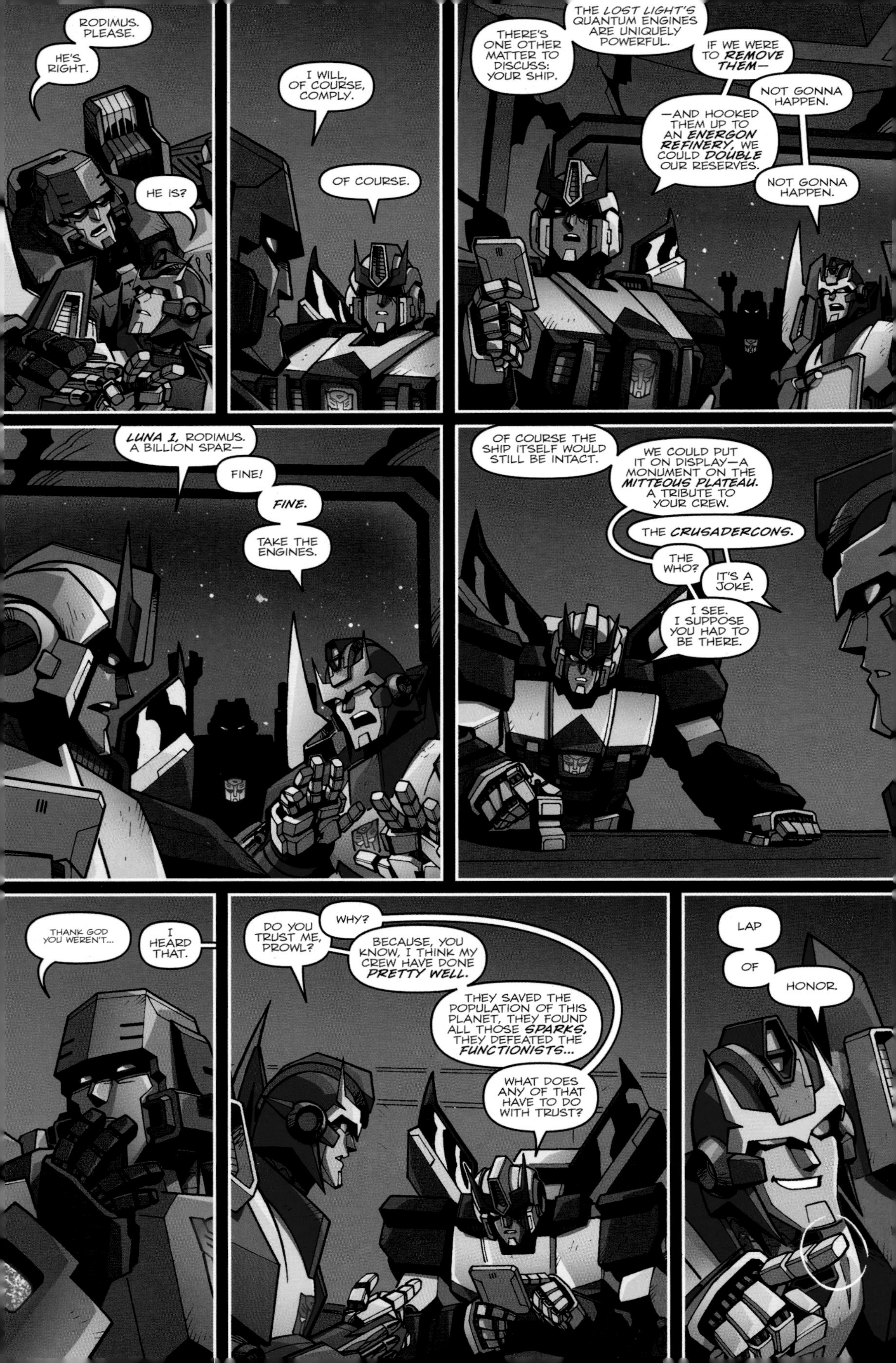
RODIMUS. PLEASE.
HE'S RIGHT.
HE IS?
I WILL, OF COURSE, COMPLY.
OF COURSE.
THERE'S ONE OTHER MATTER TO DISCUSS: YOUR SHIP.
THE LOST LIGHT'S QUANTUM ENGINES ARE UNIQUELY POWERFUL.
IF WE WERE TO REMOVE THEM—
NOT GONNA HAPPEN.
—AND HOOKED THEM UP TO AN ENERGON REFINERY, WE COULD DOUBLE OUR RESERVES.
NOT GONNA HAPPEN.
LUNA 1, RODIMUS. A BILLION SPAR—
FINE!
FINE.
TAKE THE ENGINES.
OF COURSE THE SHIP ITSELF WOULD STILL BE INTACT.
WE COULD PUT IT ON DISPLAY—A MONUMENT ON THE MITTEOUS PLATEAU. A TRIBUTE TO YOUR CREW.
THE CRUSADERCONS.
THE WHO?
IT'S A JOKE.
I SEE. I SUPPOSE YOU HAD TO BE THERE.
THANK GOD YOU WEREN'T...
I HEARD THAT.
DO YOU TRUST ME, PROWL?
WHY?
BECAUSE, YOU KNOW, I THINK MY CREW HAVE DONE PRETTY WELL.
THEY SAVED THE POPULATION OF THIS PLANET, THEY FOUND ALL THOSE SPARKS, THEY DEFEATED THE FUNCTIONISTS...
WHAT DOES ANY OF THAT HAVE TO DO WITH TRUST?
LAP
OF
HONOR.

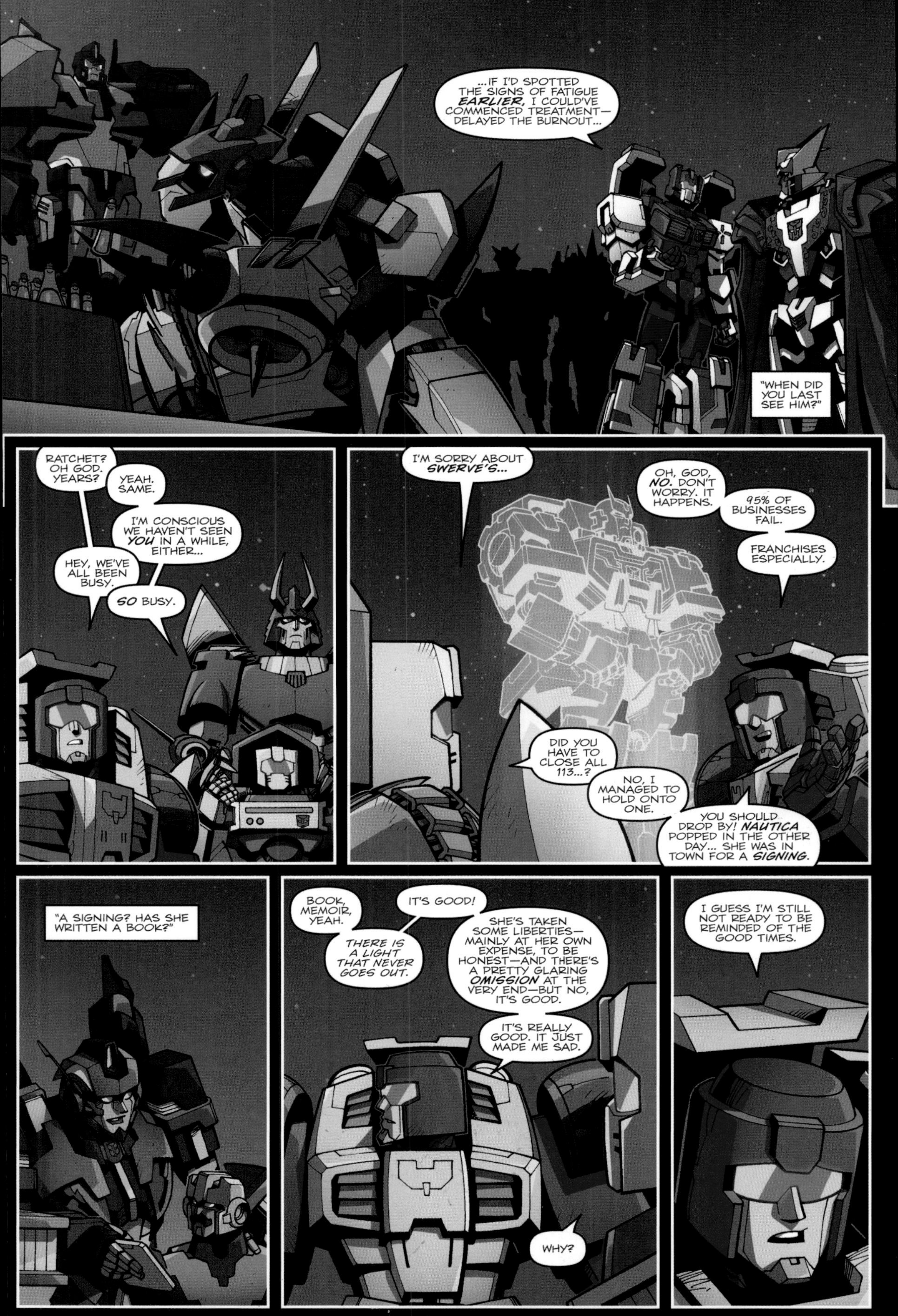
...IF I'D SPOTTED THE SIGNS OF FATIGUE EARLIER, I COULD'VE COMMENCED TREATMENT—DELAYED THE BURNOUT...
"WHEN DID YOU LAST SEE HIM?"
RATCHET? OH GOD. YEARS?
YEAH. SAME.
I'M CONSCIOUS WE HAVEN'T SEEN YOU IN A WHILE, EITHER...
HEY, WE'VE ALL BEEN BUSY.
SO BUSY.
I'M SORRY ABOUT SWERVE'S...
OH, GOD, NO. DON'T WORRY. IT HAPPENS.
95% OF BUSINESSES FAIL.
FRANCHISES ESPECIALLY.
DID YOU HAVE TO CLOSE ALL 113...?
NO, I MANAGED TO HOLD ONTO ONE.
YOU SHOULD DROP BY! NAUTICA POPPED IN THE OTHER DAY... SHE WAS IN TOWN FOR A SIGNING.
"A SIGNING? HAS SHE WRITTEN A BOOK?"
BOOK, MEMOIR, YEAH.
IT'S GOOD!
THERE IS A LIGHT THAT NEVER GOES OUT.
SHE'S TAKEN SOME LIBERTIES—MAINLY AT HER OWN EXPENSE, TO BE HONEST—AND THERE'S A PRETTY GLARING OMISSION AT THE VERY END—BUT NO, IT'S GOOD.
IT'S REALLY GOOD. IT JUST MADE ME SAD.
WHY?
I GUESS I'M STILL NOT READY TO BE REMINDED OF THE GOOD TIMES.

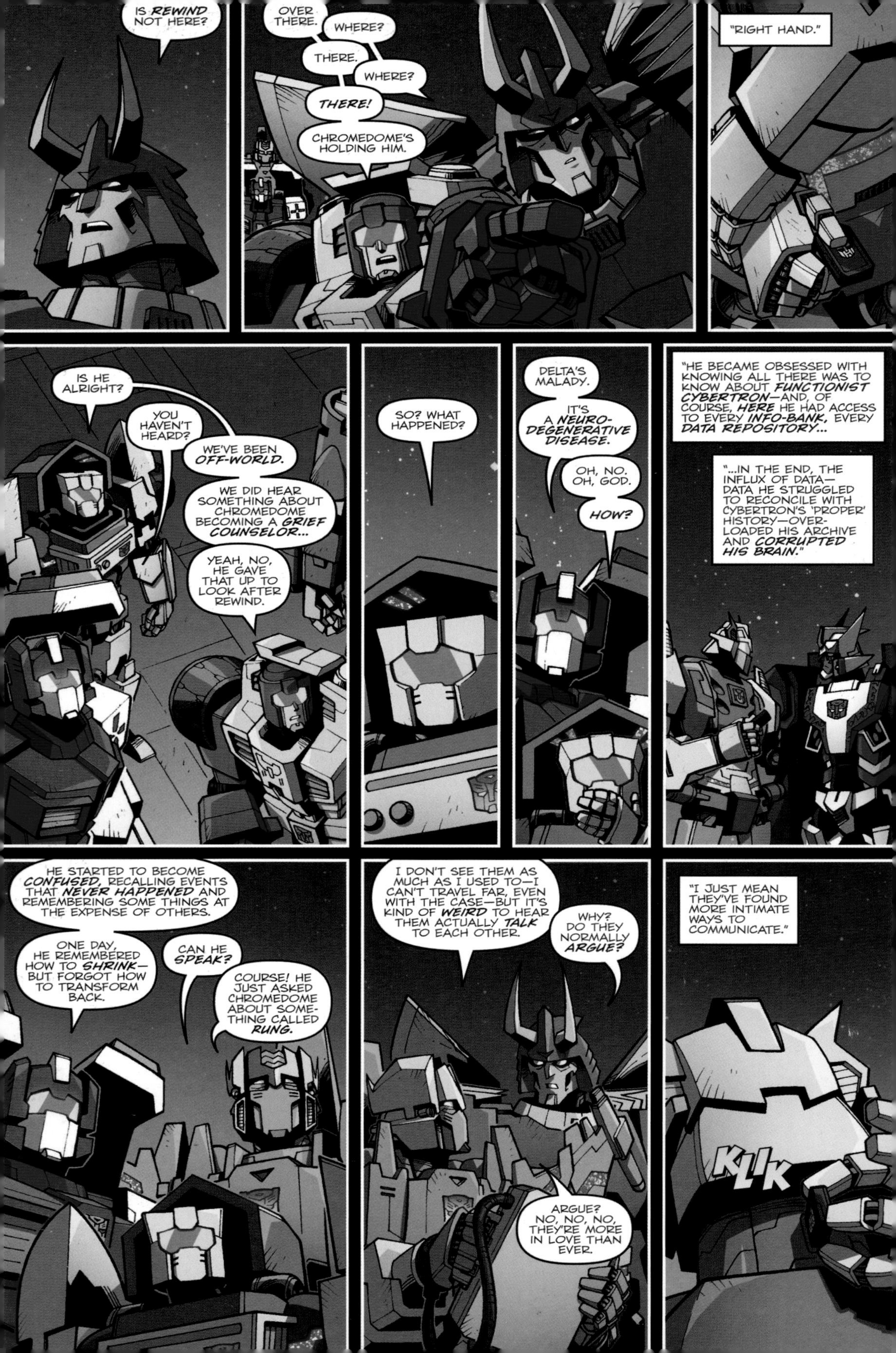
IS REWIND NOT HERE?
OVER THERE.
WHERE?
THERE.
WHERE?
THERE!
CHROMEDOME'S HOLDING HIM.
"RIGHT HAND."
IS HE ALRIGHT?
YOU HAVEN'T HEARD?
WE'VE BEEN OFF-WORLD.
WE DID HEAR SOMETHING ABOUT CHROMEDOME BECOMING A GRIEF COUNSELOR...
YEAH, NO, HE GAVE THAT UP TO LOOK AFTER REWIND.
SO? WHAT HAPPENED?
DELTA'S MALADY.
IT'S A NEURO-DEGENERATIVE DISEASE.
OH, NO. OH, GOD.
HOW?
"HE BECAME OBSESSED WITH KNOWING ALL THERE WAS TO KNOW ABOUT FUNCTIONIST CYBERTRON—AND, OF COURSE, HERE HE HAD ACCESS TO EVERY INFO-BANK, EVERY DATA REPOSITORY...
"...IN THE END, THE INFLUX OF DATA—DATA HE STRUGGLED TO RECONCILE WITH CYBERTRON'S 'PROPER' HISTORY—OVERLOADED HIS ARCHIVE AND CORRUPTED HIS BRAIN."
HE STARTED TO BECOME CONFUSED, RECALLING EVENTS THAT NEVER HAPPENED AND REMEMBERING SOME THINGS AT THE EXPENSE OF OTHERS.
ONE DAY, HE REMEMBERED HOW TO SHRINK—BUT FORGOT HOW TO TRANSFORM BACK.
CAN HE SPEAK?
COURSE! HE JUST ASKED CHROMEDOME ABOUT SOMETHING CALLED RUNG.
I DON'T SEE THEM AS MUCH AS I USED TO—I CAN'T TRAVEL FAR, EVEN WITH THE CASE—BUT IT'S KIND OF WEIRD TO HEAR THEM ACTUALLY TALK TO EACH OTHER.
WHY? DO THEY NORMALLY ARGUE?
ARGUE? NO, NO, NO, THEY'RE MORE IN LOVE THAN EVER.
"I JUST MEAN THEY'VE FOUND MORE INTIMATE WAYS TO COMMUNICATE."
KLIK

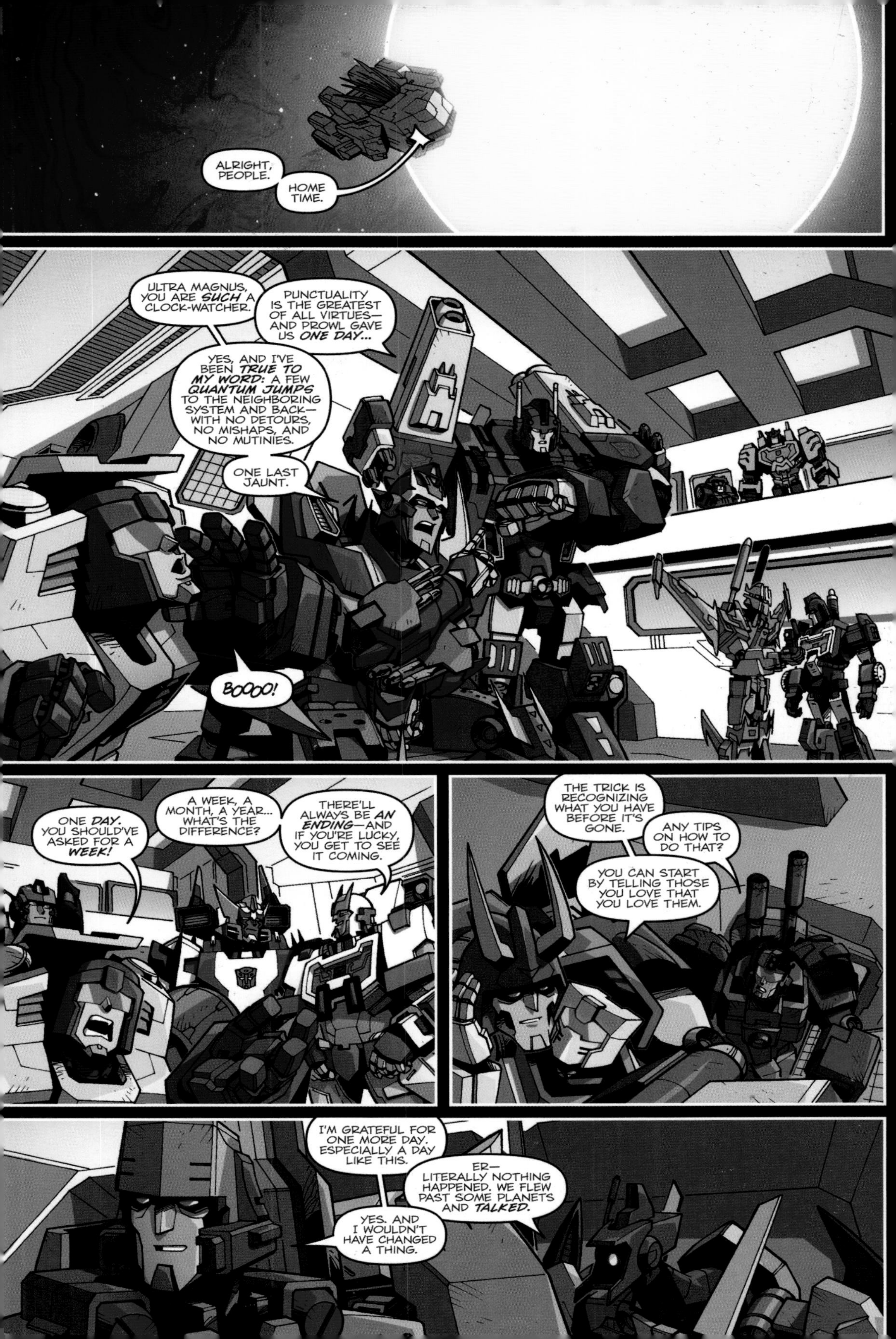

ALRIGHT, PEOPLE.
HOME TIME.
ULTRA MAGNUS, YOU ARE *SUCH* A CLOCK-WATCHER.
PUNCTUALITY IS THE GREATEST OF ALL VIRTUES— AND PROWL GAVE US *ONE DAY*...
YES, AND I'VE BEEN *TRUE TO MY WORD*: A FEW *QUANTUM JUMPS* TO THE NEIGHBORING SYSTEM AND BACK— WITH NO DETOURS, NO MISHAPS, AND NO MUTINIES.
ONE LAST JAUNT.
BOOOO!
ONE *DAY*. YOU SHOULD'VE ASKED FOR A *WEEK!*
A WEEK, A MONTH, A YEAR... WHAT'S THE DIFFERENCE?
THERE'LL ALWAYS BE *AN ENDING*—AND IF YOU'RE LUCKY, YOU GET TO SEE IT COMING.
THE TRICK IS RECOGNIZING WHAT YOU HAVE BEFORE IT'S GONE.
ANY TIPS ON HOW TO DO THAT?
YOU CAN START BY TELLING THOSE YOU LOVE THAT YOU LOVE THEM.
I'M GRATEFUL FOR ONE MORE DAY. ESPECIALLY A DAY LIKE THIS.
ER— LITERALLY NOTHING HAPPENED. WE FLEW PAST SOME PLANETS AND *TALKED*.
YES. AND I WOULDN'T HAVE CHANGED A THING.

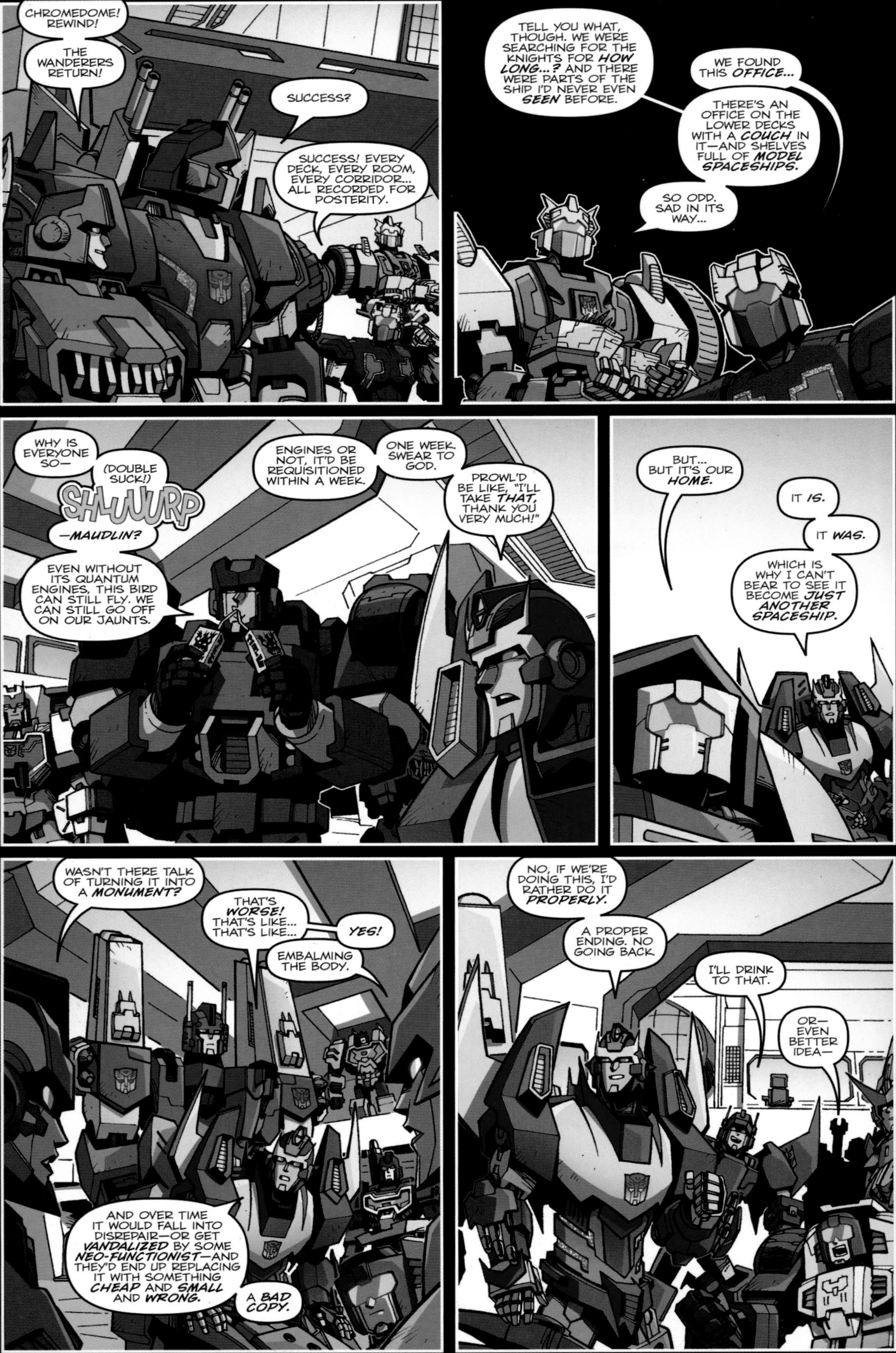
CHROMEDOME! REWIND!
THE WANDERERS RETURN!
SUCCESS?
SUCCESS! EVERY DECK, EVERY ROOM, EVERY CORRIDOR... ALL RECORDED FOR POSTERITY.
TELL YOU WHAT, THOUGH. WE WERE SEARCHING FOR THE KNIGHTS FOR HOW LONG...? AND THERE WERE PARTS OF THE SHIP I'D NEVER EVEN SEEN BEFORE.
WE FOUND THIS OFFICE...
THERE'S AN OFFICE ON THE LOWER DECKS WITH A COUCH IN IT—AND SHELVES FULL OF MODEL SPACESHIPS.
SO ODD. SAD IN ITS WAY...
WHY IS EVERYONE SO—
(DOUBLE SUCK!)
SHLUUURP
—MAUDLIN?
EVEN WITHOUT ITS QUANTUM ENGINES, THIS BIRD CAN STILL FLY. WE CAN STILL GO OFF ON OUR JAUNTS.
ENGINES OR NOT, IT'D BE REQUISITIONED WITHIN A WEEK.
ONE WEEK. SWEAR TO GOD.
PROWL'D BE LIKE, "I'LL TAKE THAT, THANK YOU VERY MUCH!"
BUT... BUT IT'S OUR HOME.
IT IS.
IT WAS.
WHICH IS WHY I CAN'T BEAR TO SEE IT BECOME JUST ANOTHER SPACESHIP.
WASN'T THERE TALK OF TURNING IT INTO A MONUMENT?
THAT'S WORSE! THAT'S LIKE... THAT'S LIKE...
YES!
EMBALMING THE BODY.
AND OVER TIME IT WOULD FALL INTO DISREPAIR—OR GET VANDALIZED BY SOME NEO-FUNCTIONIST—AND THEY'D END UP REPLACING IT WITH SOMETHING CHEAP AND SMALL AND WRONG.
A BAD COPY.
NO, IF WE'RE DOING THIS, I'D RATHER DO IT PROPERLY.
A PROPER ENDING. NO GOING BACK.
I'LL DRINK TO THAT.
OR— EVEN BETTER IDEA—

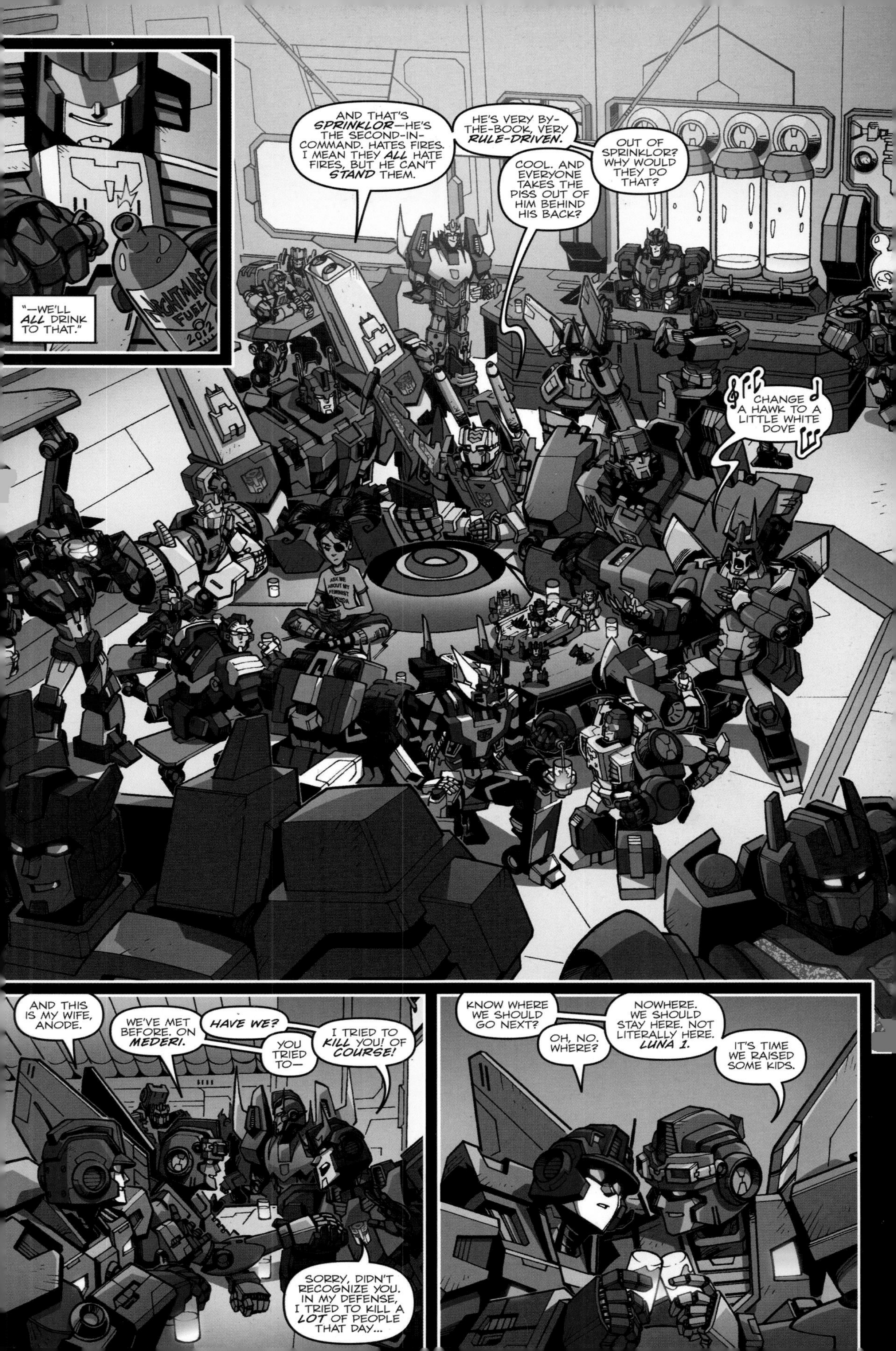
"—WE'LL ALL DRINK TO THAT."
NIGHTMARE FUEL 2012
AND THAT'S SPRINKLOR—HE'S THE SECOND-IN-COMMAND. HATES FIRES. I MEAN THEY ALL HATE FIRES, BUT HE CAN'T STAND THEM.
HE'S VERY BY-THE-BOOK, VERY RULE-DRIVEN.
COOL. AND EVERYONE TAKES THE PISS OUT OF HIM BEHIND HIS BACK?
OUT OF SPRINKLOR? WHY WOULD THEY DO THAT?
CHANGE A HAWK TO A LITTLE WHITE DOVE
AND THIS IS MY WIFE, ANODE.
WE'VE MET BEFORE. ON MEDERI.
HAVE WE?
YOU TRIED TO—
I TRIED TO KILL YOU! OF COURSE!
SORRY, DIDN'T RECOGNIZE YOU. IN MY DEFENSE, I TRIED TO KILL A LOT OF PEOPLE THAT DAY...
KNOW WHERE WE SHOULD GO NEXT?
OH, NO. WHERE?
NOWHERE. WE SHOULD STAY HERE. NOT LITERALLY HERE. LUNA 1.
IT'S TIME WE RAISED SOME KIDS.

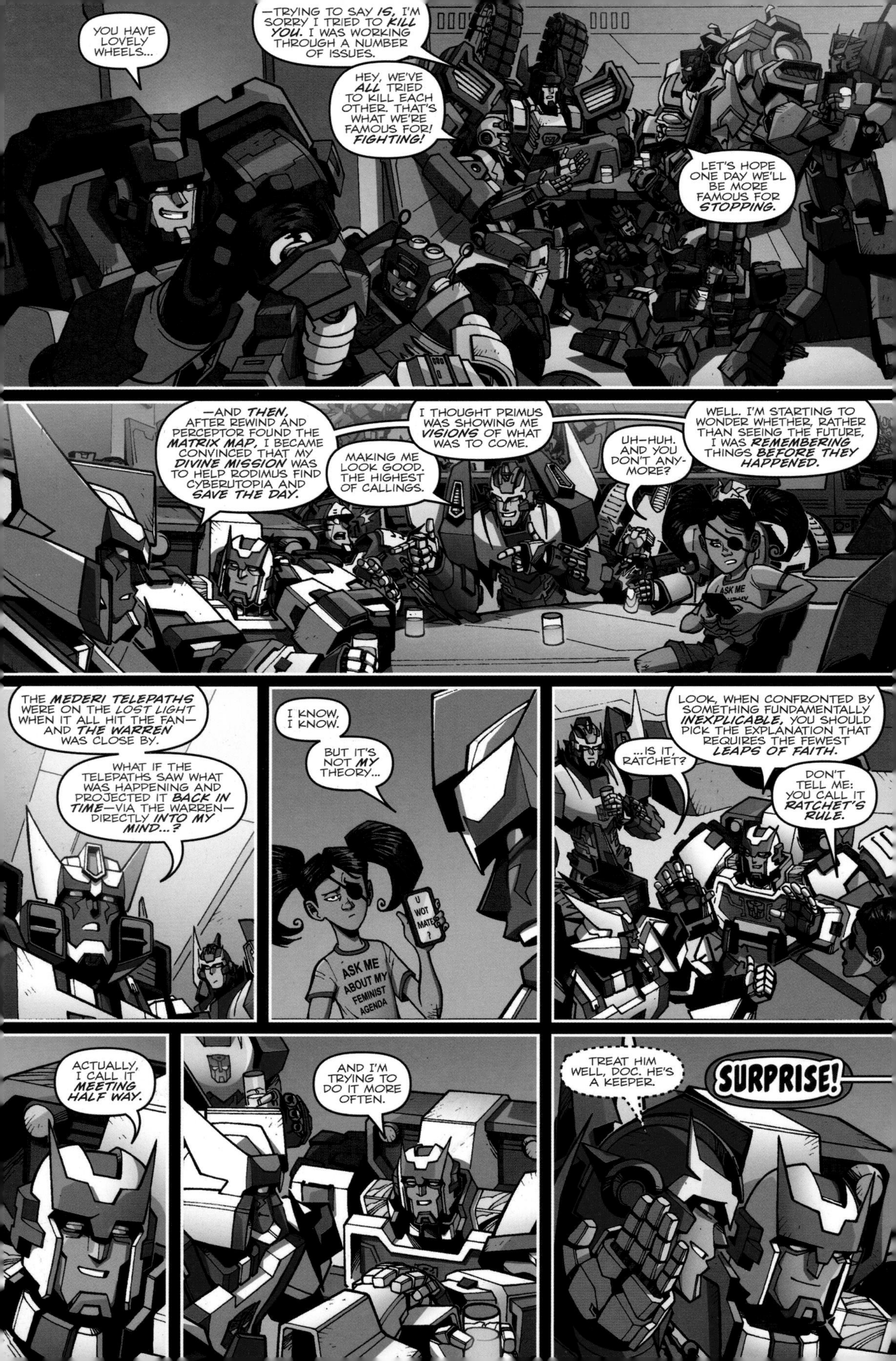
YOU HAVE LOVELY WHEELS...
—TRYING TO SAY IS, I'M SORRY I TRIED TO KILL YOU. I WAS WORKING THROUGH A NUMBER OF ISSUES.
HEY, WE'VE ALL TRIED TO KILL EACH OTHER. THAT'S WHAT WE'RE FAMOUS FOR! FIGHTING!
LET'S HOPE ONE DAY WE'LL BE MORE FAMOUS FOR STOPPING.
—AND THEN, AFTER REWIND AND PERCEPTOR FOUND THE MATRIX MAP, I BECAME CONVINCED THAT MY DIVINE MISSION WAS TO HELP RODIMUS FIND CYBERUTOPIA AND SAVE THE DAY.
MAKING ME LOOK GOOD. THE HIGHEST OF CALLINGS.
I THOUGHT PRIMUS WAS SHOWING ME VISIONS OF WHAT WAS TO COME.
UH-HUH. AND YOU DON'T ANY-MORE?
WELL. I'M STARTING TO WONDER WHETHER, RATHER THAN SEEING THE FUTURE, I WAS REMEMBERING THINGS BEFORE THEY HAPPENED.
THE MEDERI TELEPATHS WERE ON THE LOST LIGHT WHEN IT ALL HIT THE FAN— AND THE WARREN WAS CLOSE BY.
WHAT IF THE TELEPATHS SAW WHAT WAS HAPPENING AND PROJECTED IT BACK IN TIME—VIA THE WARREN—DIRECTLY INTO MY MIND...?
I KNOW, I KNOW.
BUT IT'S NOT MY THEORY...
U WOT MATE ?
ASK ME ABOUT MY FEMINIST AGENDA
LOOK, WHEN CONFRONTED BY SOMETHING FUNDAMENTALLY INEXPLICABLE, YOU SHOULD PICK THE EXPLANATION THAT REQUIRES THE FEWEST LEAPS OF FAITH.
...IS IT, RATCHET?
DON'T TELL ME: YOU CALL IT RATCHET'S RULE.
ACTUALLY, I CALL IT MEETING HALF WAY.
AND I'M TRYING TO DO IT MORE OFTEN.
TREAT HIM WELL, DOC. HE'S A KEEPER.
SURPRISE!

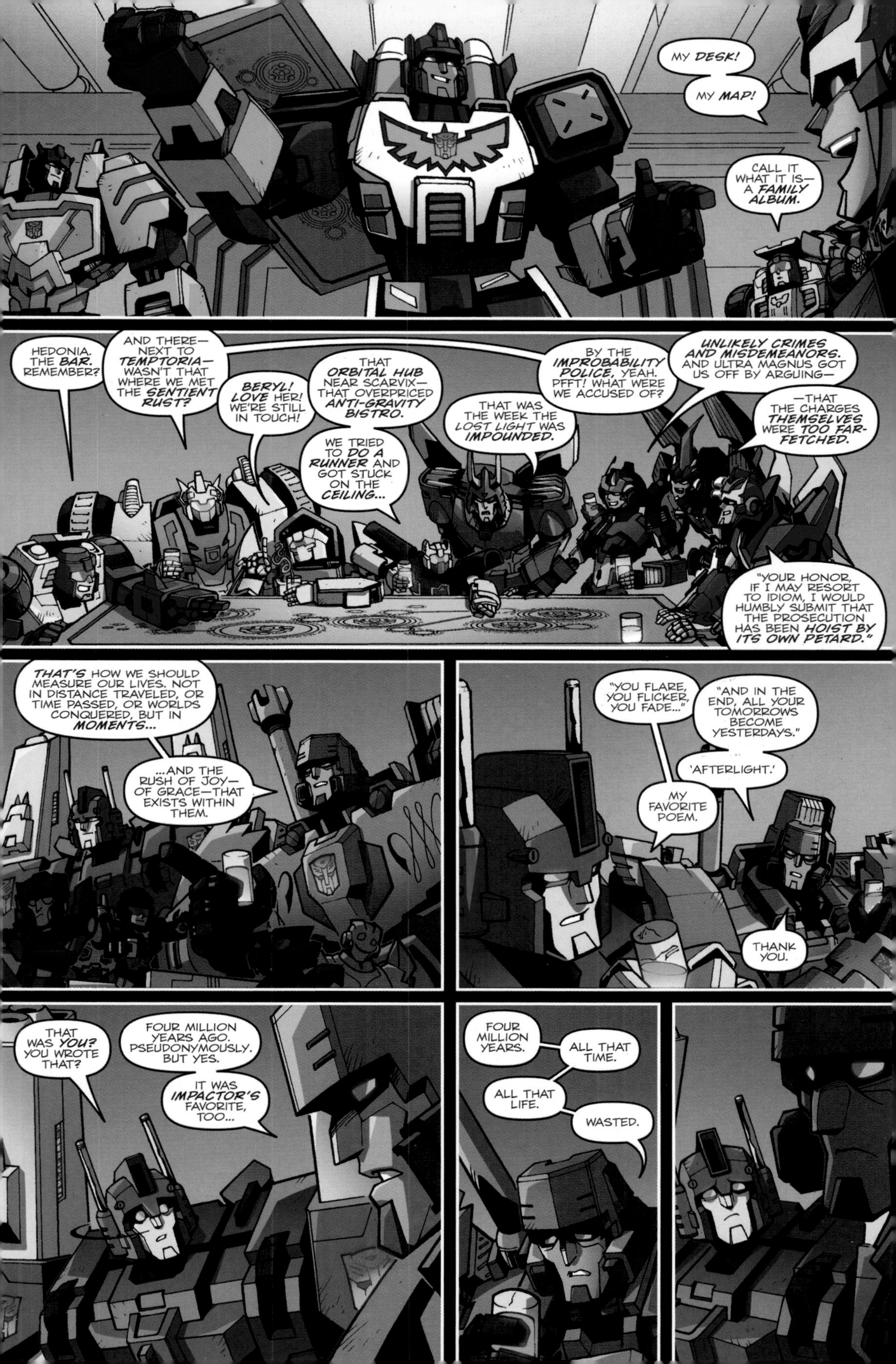
MY DESK!
MY MAP!
CALL IT WHAT IT IS— A FAMILY ALBUM.
HEDONIA. THE BAR. REMEMBER?
AND THERE— NEXT TO TEMPTORIA— WASN'T THAT WHERE WE MET THE SENTIENT RUST?
BERYL! LOVE HER! WE'RE STILL IN TOUCH!
THAT ORBITAL HUB NEAR SCARVIX— THAT OVERPRICED ANTI-GRAVITY BISTRO.
WE TRIED TO DO A RUNNER AND GOT STUCK ON THE CEILING...
THAT WAS THE WEEK THE LOST LIGHT WAS IMPOUNDED.
BY THE IMPROBABILITY POLICE, YEAH. PFFT! WHAT WERE WE ACCUSED OF?
UNLIKELY CRIMES AND MISDEMEANORS. AND ULTRA MAGNUS GOT US OFF BY ARGUING—
—THAT THE CHARGES THEMSELVES WERE TOO FAR-FETCHED.
"YOUR HONOR, IF I MAY RESORT TO IDIOM, I WOULD HUMBLY SUBMIT THAT THE PROSECUTION HAS BEEN HOIST BY ITS OWN PETARD."
THAT'S HOW WE SHOULD MEASURE OUR LIVES. NOT IN DISTANCE TRAVELED, OR TIME PASSED, OR WORLDS CONQUERED, BUT IN MOMENTS...
...AND THE RUSH OF JOY— OF GRACE—THAT EXISTS WITHIN THEM.
"YOU FLARE, YOU FLICKER, YOU FADE..."
"AND IN THE END, ALL YOUR TOMORROWS BECOME YESTERDAYS."
'AFTERLIGHT.'
MY FAVORITE POEM.
THANK YOU.
THAT WAS YOU? YOU WROTE THAT?
FOUR MILLION YEARS AGO. PSEUDONYMOUSLY. BUT YES.
IT WAS IMPACTOR'S FAVORITE, TOO...
FOUR MILLION YEARS.
ALL THAT TIME.
ALL THAT LIFE.
WASTED.

I'D LIKE TO SAY A FEW WORDS.

CLINK CLINK

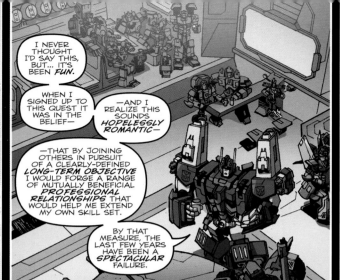

I NEVER THOUGHT I'D SAY THIS, BUT... IT'S BEEN *FUN.*

WHEN I SIGNED UP TO THIS QUEST IT WAS IN THE BELIEF—

—AND I REALIZE THIS SOUNDS *HOPELESSLY ROMANTIC*—

—THAT BY JOINING OTHERS IN PURSUIT OF A CLEARLY-DEFINED *LONG-TERM OBJECTIVE* I WOULD FORGE A RANGE OF MUTUALLY BENEFICIAL *PROFESSIONAL RELATIONSHIPS* THAT WOULD HELP ME EXTEND MY OWN SKILL SET.

BY THAT MEASURE, THE LAST FEW YEARS HAVE BEEN A *SPECTACULAR* FAILURE.

GOOD.

I THOUGHT I WANTED COLLEAGUES... BUT WHAT I ACTUALLY *NEEDED* WAS COMPANIONS.

I STAND BEFORE YOU TODAY AND I AM HONORED AND—AND—AND *HUMBLED* TO COUNT YOU AS MY *FRIENDS.*

ALL OF YOU.

A *TOAST.*

TO ALL OF YOU. TO ALL OF US.

TO THE *LOST LIGHT.*

TO WHAT WE HAD—AND TO WHAT COMES NEXT.

RIGHT! THAT DOES IT!

THAT FLIPPIN' DOES IT!

LOCK IN!

HAHA!

I'M *SERIOUS!* WE'VE GOT ENOUGH ENGEX FOR *AT LEAST* SIX MONTHS!

THIS CAN'T BE IT, *LOTTY!*

WHY NOT?

I KNOW, BUT... THERE'LL BE OTHER QUESTS...

BECAUSE *WE'RE NOT DONE!*

NOT LIKE THIS ONE!

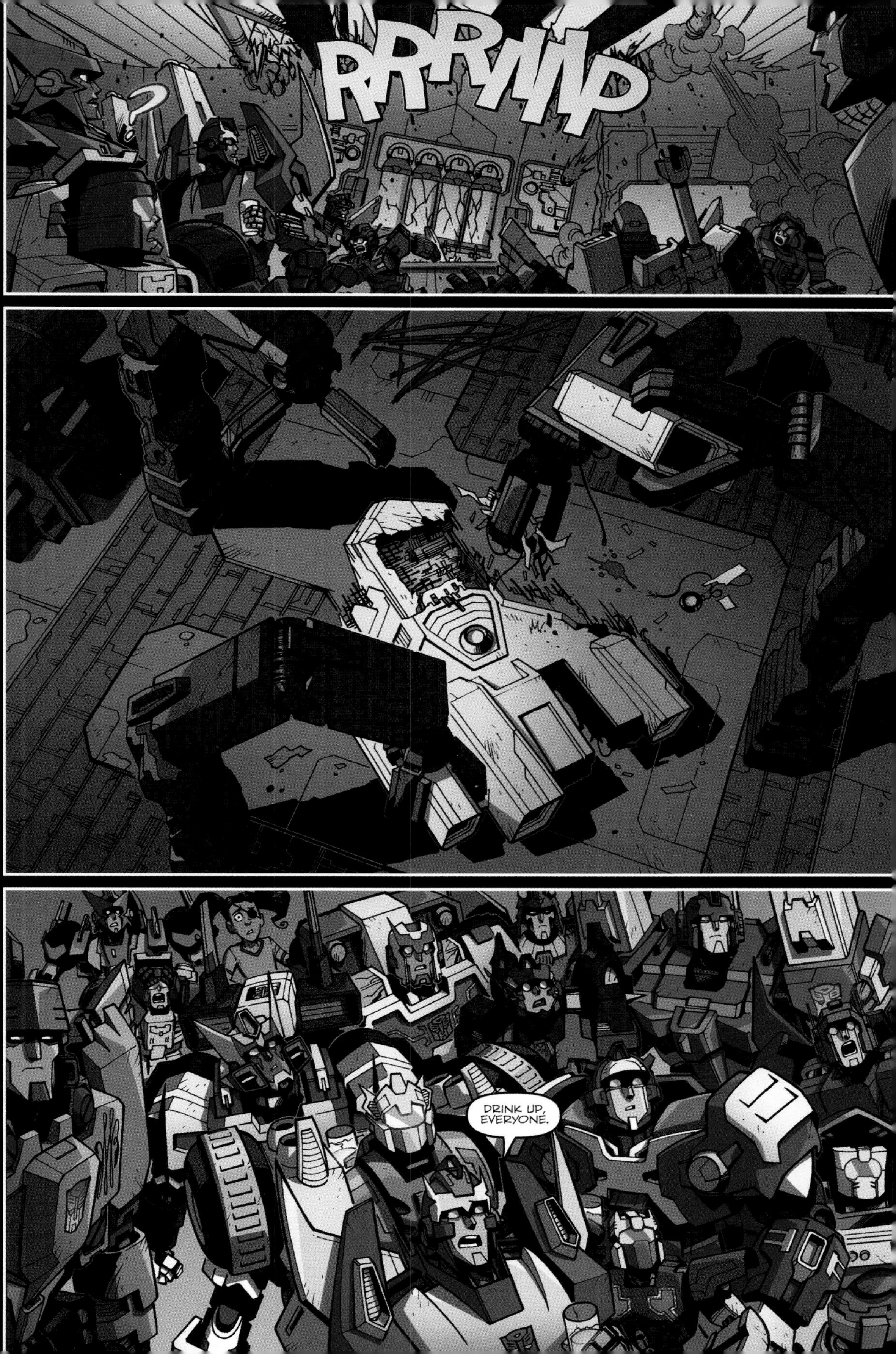
RRRYNNP
DRINK UP, EVERYONE.

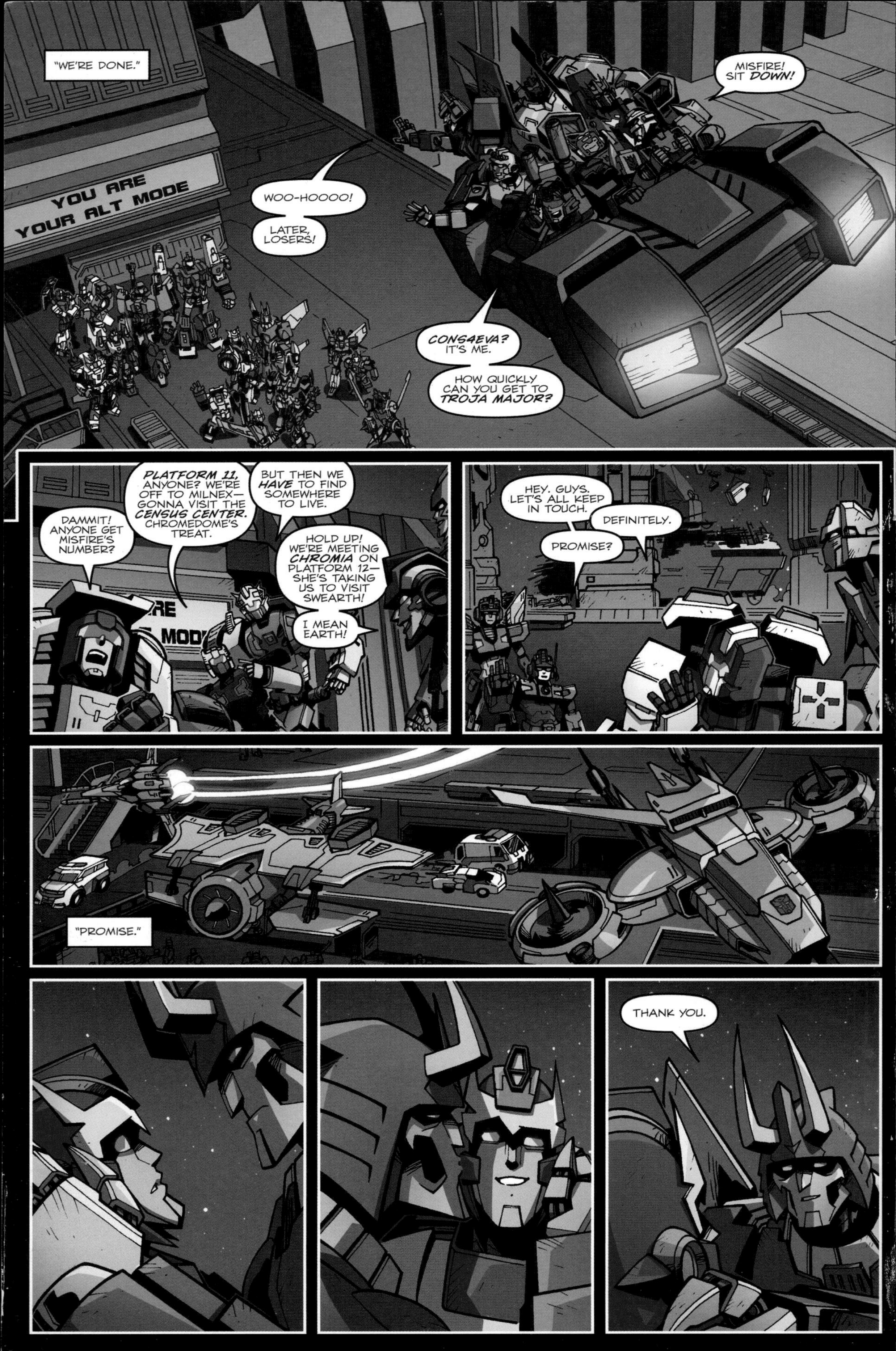
"WE'RE DONE."
YOU ARE YOUR ALT MODE
MISFIRE! SIT DOWN!
WOO-HOOOO!
LATER, LOSERS!
CONS4EVA? IT'S ME.
HOW QUICKLY CAN YOU GET TO TROJA MAJOR?
DAMMIT! ANYONE GET MISFIRE'S NUMBER?
PLATFORM 11, ANYONE? WE'RE OFF TO MILNEX— GONNA VISIT THE CENSUS CENTER. CHROMEDOME'S TREAT.
BUT THEN WE HAVE TO FIND SOMEWHERE TO LIVE.
HOLD UP! WE'RE MEETING CHROMIA ON PLATFORM 12— SHE'S TAKING US TO VISIT SWEARTH!
I MEAN EARTH!
HEY. GUYS. LET'S ALL KEEP IN TOUCH.
DEFINITELY.
PROMISE?
"PROMISE."
THANK YOU.

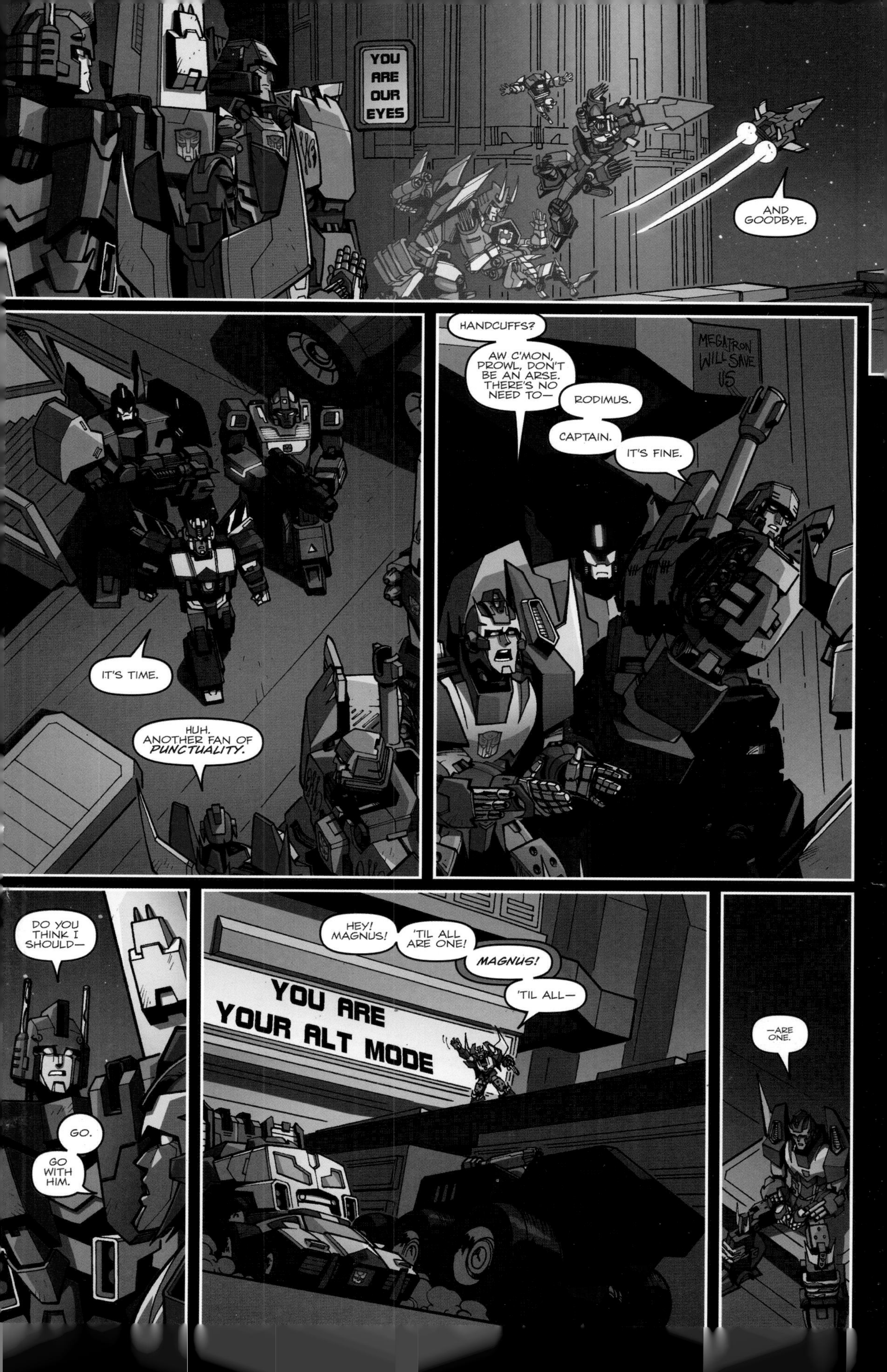
YOU ARE OUR EYES
AND GOODBYE.
MEGATRON WILL SAVE US
IT'S TIME.
HUH. ANOTHER FAN OF *PUNCTUALITY*.
HANDCUFFS?
AW C'MON, PROWL, DON'T BE AN ARSE. THERE'S NO NEED TO—
RODIMUS.
CAPTAIN.
IT'S FINE.
DO YOU THINK I SHOULD—
GO.
GO WITH HIM.
YOU ARE YOUR ALT MODE
HEY! MAGNUS!
'TIL ALL ARE ONE!
MAGNUS!
'TIL ALL—
—ARE ONE.

HONESTLY, NAUTICA, I WON'T HAVE TIME TO READ IT. LUNA 1 IS *ALL-CONSUMING.*

IT'S BEEN YEARS SINCE I EVEN *LOOKED* AT *TERMS OF PEACE.*

MINIMUS. PLEASE. IT'S A GIFT.

SPEAKING OF LUNA 1, HOW GOES THE *BRONZE HARVEST?*

WE PASSED THE HALFWAY MARK LAST MONTH.

500 MILLION SPARKS BROUGHT TO TERM. 500 MILLION *LUNARIANS* GIVEN SOMEWHERE TO LIVE AND HELPED INTO JOBS OF THEIR CHOOSING.

I KNOW PEOPLE WERE WORRIED ABOUT THEM *INTEGRATING,* BUT—

NO, NO, IT'S HOW WELL THEY'VE *BLENDED IN.* IF ANYTHING, I WISH THEY'D MAKE THEIR PRESENCE FELT A BIT *MORE...*

"...SOMETIMES YOU HARDLY NOTICE THEY'RE HERE."

WHIRL. DO YOU HAVE A MOMENT?

BE QUICK— IF YOU'RE *LATE GETTING BACK,* THEY GIVE YOUR *CELL* TO SOME-ONE ELSE.

I'M JOKING. THANKS FOR ARRANGING THE *DAY RELEASE.*

IT WASN'T DIFFICULT. THEY SAID YOU'RE *LOW RISK.*

THEY DIDN'T, DID THEY?

OH, GOD, THE *SHAME* OF IT!

ANYWAY, HERE YOU GO.

A PRESENT FROM RATTY.

SORRY— FROM *RATCHET.*

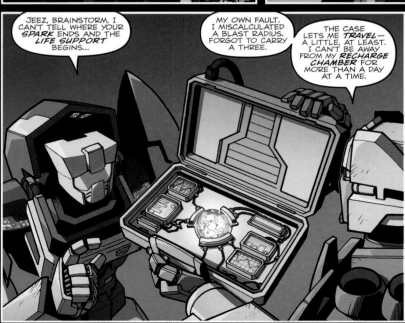

JEEZ, BRAINSTORM, I CAN'T TELL WHERE YOUR *SPARK* ENDS AND THE *LIFE SUPPORT* BEGINS...

MY OWN FAULT. I MISCALCULATED A BLAST RADIUS. FORGOT TO CARRY A THREE.

THE CASE LETS ME *TRAVEL—* A LITTLE, AT LEAST. I CAN'T BE AWAY FROM MY *RECHARGE CHAMBER* FOR MORE THAN A DAY AT A TIME.

IT'S EVEN GOT A LITTLE CLOCK...!

WHIRL MADE IT FOR ME WHEN HE WAS IN G-10.

G-10? GARRUS 10?

THE *PRISON?*

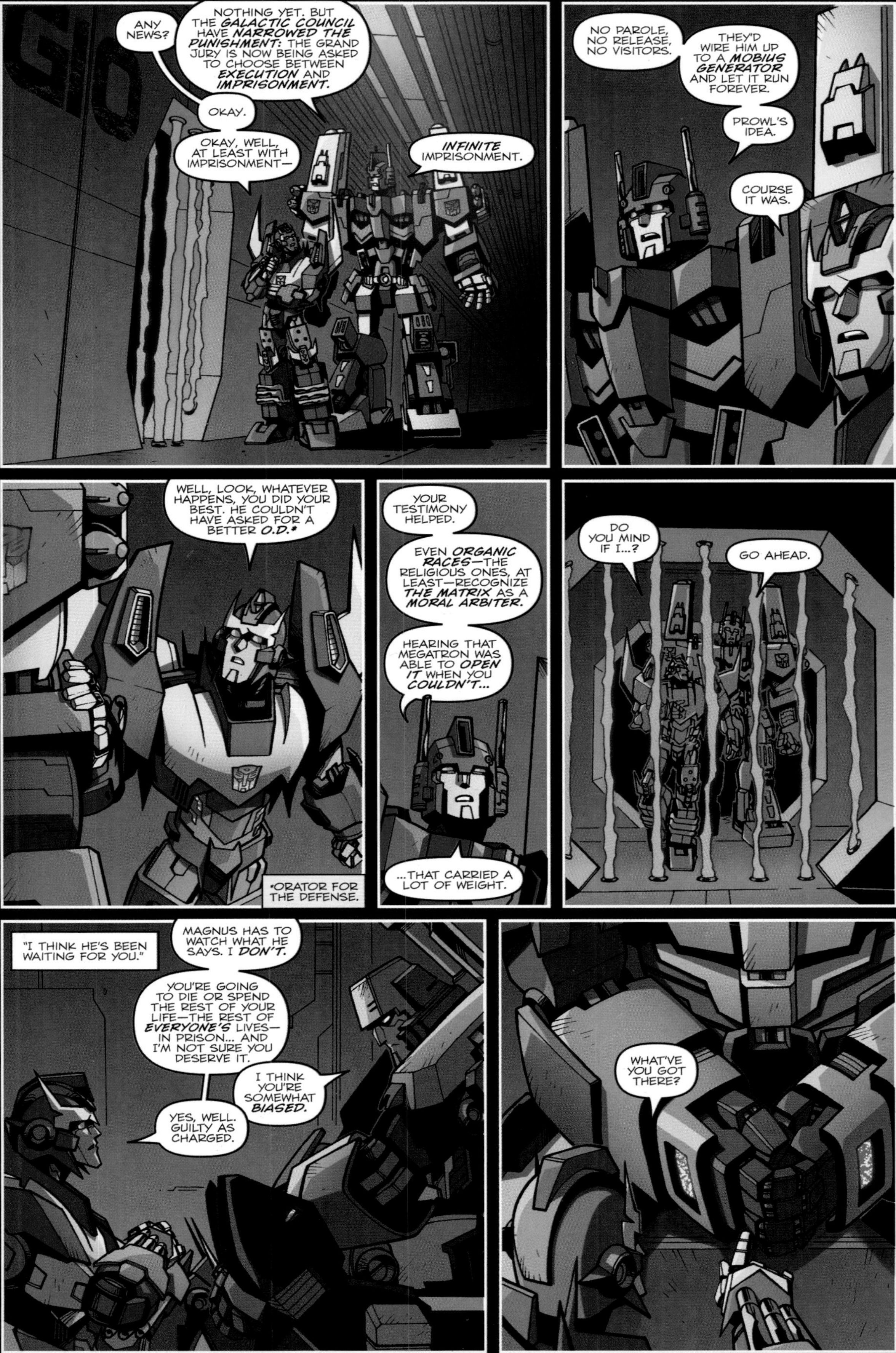
ANY NEWS?
NOTHING YET. BUT THE GALACTIC COUNCIL HAVE NARROWED THE PUNISHMENT: THE GRAND JURY IS NOW BEING ASKED TO CHOOSE BETWEEN EXECUTION AND IMPRISONMENT.
OKAY.
OKAY, WELL, AT LEAST WITH IMPRISONMENT—
INFINITE IMPRISONMENT.
NO PAROLE, NO RELEASE, NO VISITORS.
THEY'D WIRE HIM UP TO A MOBIUS GENERATOR AND LET IT RUN FOREVER.
PROWL'S IDEA.
COURSE IT WAS.
WELL, LOOK, WHATEVER HAPPENS, YOU DID YOUR BEST. HE COULDN'T HAVE ASKED FOR A BETTER O.D.*
*ORATOR FOR THE DEFENSE.
YOUR TESTIMONY HELPED.
EVEN ORGANIC RACES—THE RELIGIOUS ONES, AT LEAST—RECOGNIZE THE MATRIX AS A MORAL ARBITER.
HEARING THAT MEGATRON WAS ABLE TO OPEN IT WHEN YOU COULDN'T...
...THAT CARRIED A LOT OF WEIGHT.
DO YOU MIND IF I...?
GO AHEAD.
"I THINK HE'S BEEN WAITING FOR YOU."
MAGNUS HAS TO WATCH WHAT HE SAYS. I DON'T.
YOU'RE GOING TO DIE OR SPEND THE REST OF YOUR LIFE—THE REST OF EVERYONE'S LIVES—IN PRISON... AND I'M NOT SURE YOU DESERVE IT.
I THINK YOU'RE SOMEWHAT BIASED.
YES, WELL. GUILTY AS CHARGED.
WHAT'VE YOU GOT THERE?

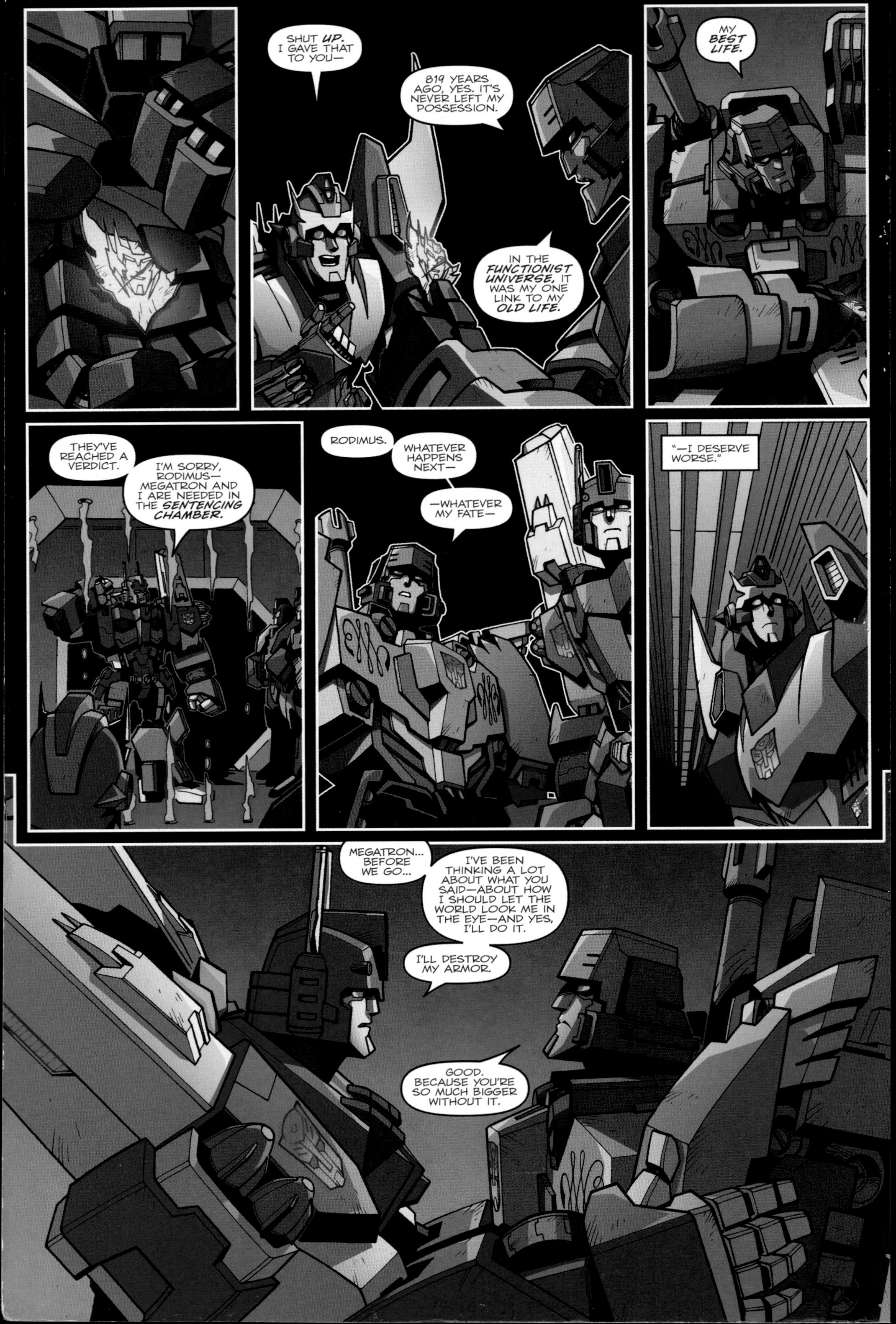
SHUT UP. I GAVE THAT TO YOU—
819 YEARS AGO, YES. IT'S NEVER LEFT MY POSSESSION.
IN THE FUNCTIONIST UNIVERSE, IT WAS MY ONE LINK TO MY OLD LIFE.
MY BEST LIFE.
THEY'VE REACHED A VERDICT.
I'M SORRY, RODIMUS—MEGATRON AND I ARE NEEDED IN THE SENTENCING CHAMBER.
RODIMUS.
WHATEVER HAPPENS NEXT—
—WHATEVER MY FATE—
"—I DESERVE WORSE."
MEGATRON... BEFORE WE GO...
I'VE BEEN THINKING A LOT ABOUT WHAT YOU SAID—ABOUT HOW I SHOULD LET THE WORLD LOOK ME IN THE EYE—AND YES, I'LL DO IT.
I'LL DESTROY MY ARMOR.
GOOD. BECAUSE YOU'RE SO MUCH BIGGER WITHOUT IT.

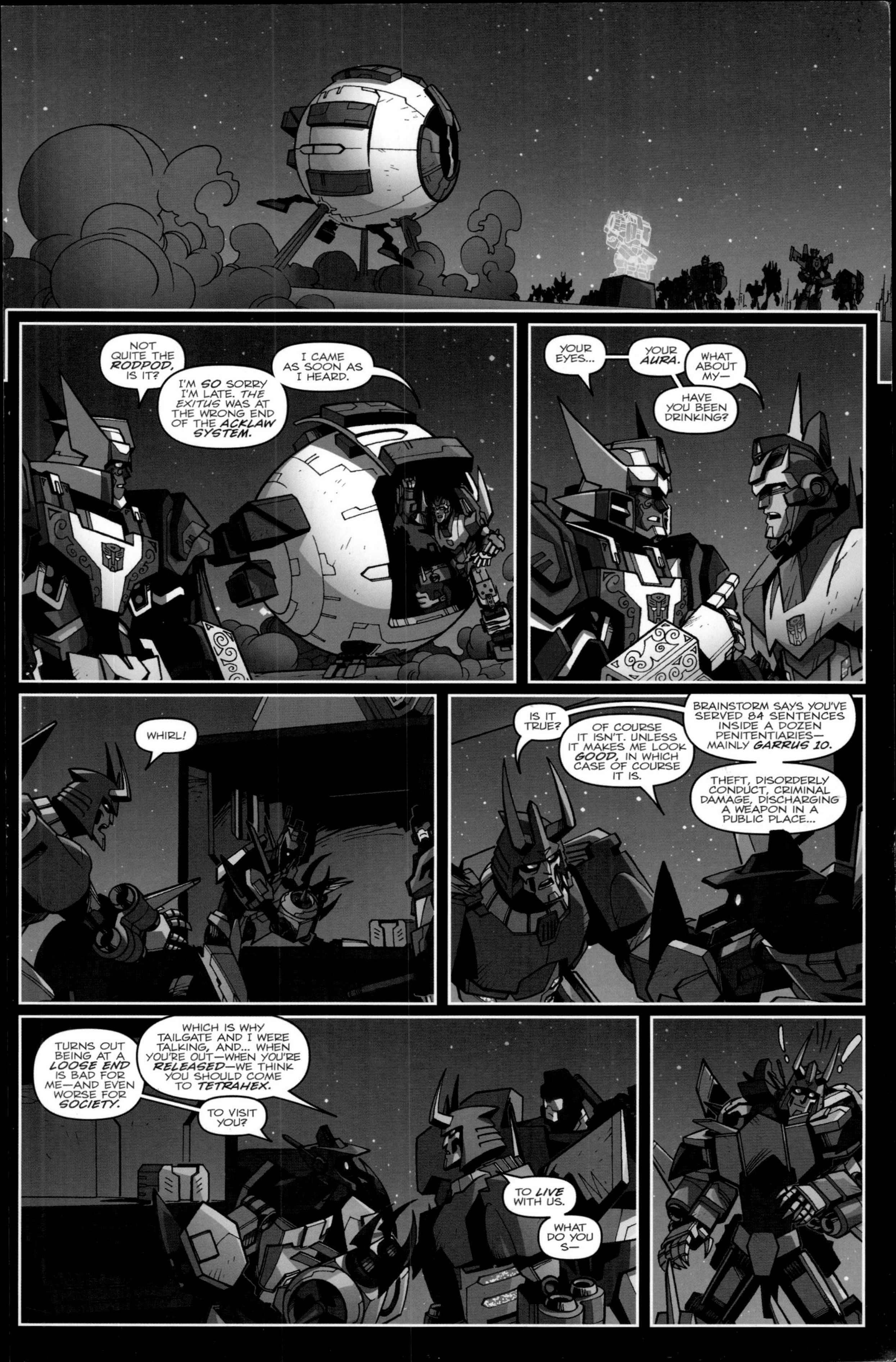
NOT QUITE THE RODPOD, IS IT?
I'M SO SORRY I'M LATE. THE EXITUS WAS AT THE WRONG END OF THE ACKLAW SYSTEM.
I CAME AS SOON AS I HEARD.
YOUR EYES...
YOUR AURA.
WHAT ABOUT MY—
HAVE YOU BEEN DRINKING?
WHIRL!
IS IT TRUE?
BRAINSTORM SAYS YOU'VE SERVED 84 SENTENCES INSIDE A DOZEN PENITENTIARIES— MAINLY GARRUS 10.
THEFT, DISORDERLY CONDUCT, CRIMINAL DAMAGE, DISCHARGING A WEAPON IN A PUBLIC PLACE...
OF COURSE IT ISN'T. UNLESS IT MAKES ME LOOK GOOD, IN WHICH CASE OF COURSE IT IS.
TURNS OUT BEING AT A LOOSE END IS BAD FOR ME—AND EVEN WORSE FOR SOCIETY.
WHICH IS WHY TAILGATE AND I WERE TALKING, AND... WHEN YOU'RE OUT—WHEN YOU'RE RELEASED—WE THINK YOU SHOULD COME TO TETRAHEX.
TO VISIT YOU?
TO LIVE WITH US.
WHAT DO YOU S—

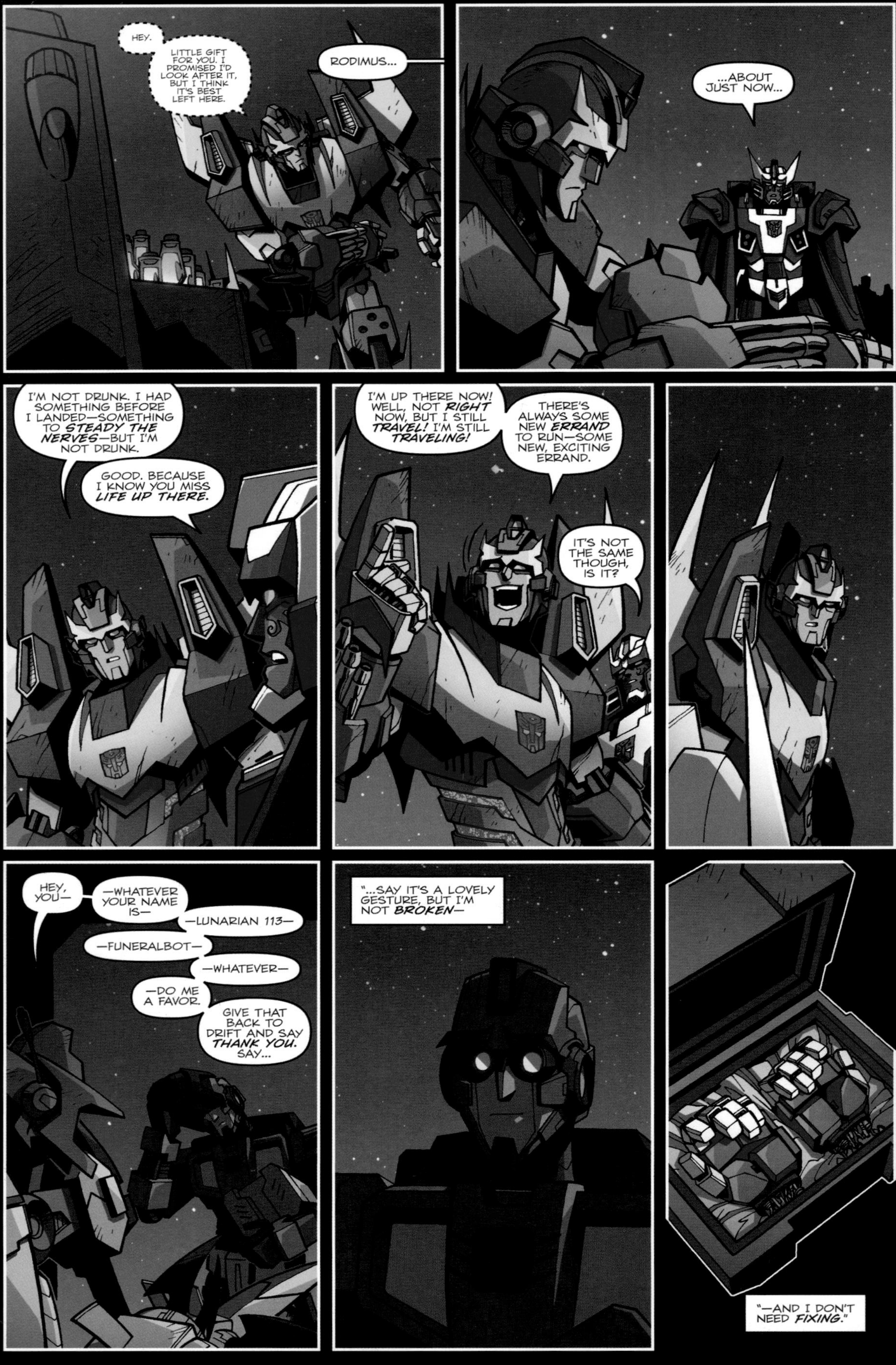
HEY.
LITTLE GIFT FOR YOU. I PROMISED I'D LOOK AFTER IT, BUT I THINK IT'S BEST LEFT HERE.
RODIMUS...
...ABOUT JUST NOW...
I'M NOT DRUNK. I HAD SOMETHING BEFORE I LANDED—SOMETHING TO STEADY THE NERVES—BUT I'M NOT DRUNK.
GOOD. BECAUSE I KNOW YOU MISS LIFE UP THERE.
I'M UP THERE NOW! WELL, NOT RIGHT NOW, BUT I STILL TRAVEL! I'M STILL TRAVELING!
THERE'S ALWAYS SOME NEW ERRAND TO RUN—SOME NEW, EXCITING ERRAND.
IT'S NOT THE SAME THOUGH, IS IT?
HEY, YOU—
—WHATEVER YOUR NAME IS—
—LUNARIAN 113—
—FUNERALBOT—
—WHATEVER—
—DO ME A FAVOR.
GIVE THAT BACK TO DRIFT AND SAY THANK YOU. SAY...
"...SAY IT'S A LOVELY GESTURE, BUT I'M NOT BROKEN—
"—AND I DON'T NEED FIXING."

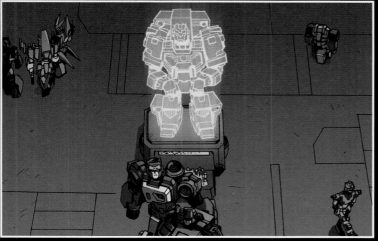

RODIMUS—
BEFORE
YOU GO...

...DO YOU
THINK IT
WORKED?

I KNOW IT WAS *YEARS*
AGO, AND I KNOW NAUTICA
SAID IT WAS A *LONG SHOT*,
BUT... I'VE BEEN THINKING
ABOUT IT A *LOT* NOW
THAT RATTY'S GONE.

WE AGREED
NEVER TO TALK
ABOUT IT.

PLEASE.
FOR ME.

...

I DUNNO,
DRIFT. I DUNNO IF
IT WORKED OR NOT.
I DON'T THINK WE'LL
EVER KNOW.

AND... I
THINK THAT'S
GOOD.

'BECAUSE
IT MEANS WE
CAN KEEP
TELLING
OURSELVES
IT *DID*.

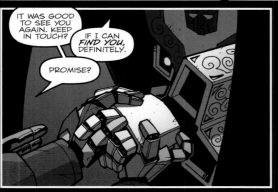

IT WAS GOOD
TO SEE YOU
AGAIN. KEEP
IN TOUCH?

IF I CAN
FIND YOU,
DEFINITELY.

PROMISE?

"PROMISE."

BACK TO
THE EXITUS,
PLEASE.

OF COURSE.
I'LL TELL *CAPTAIN
THUNDERCLASH*
WE'RE ON OUR WAY.

WITHOUT LOVE THERE IS NO MEANING

"A PROPER ENDING...
NO GOING BACK."

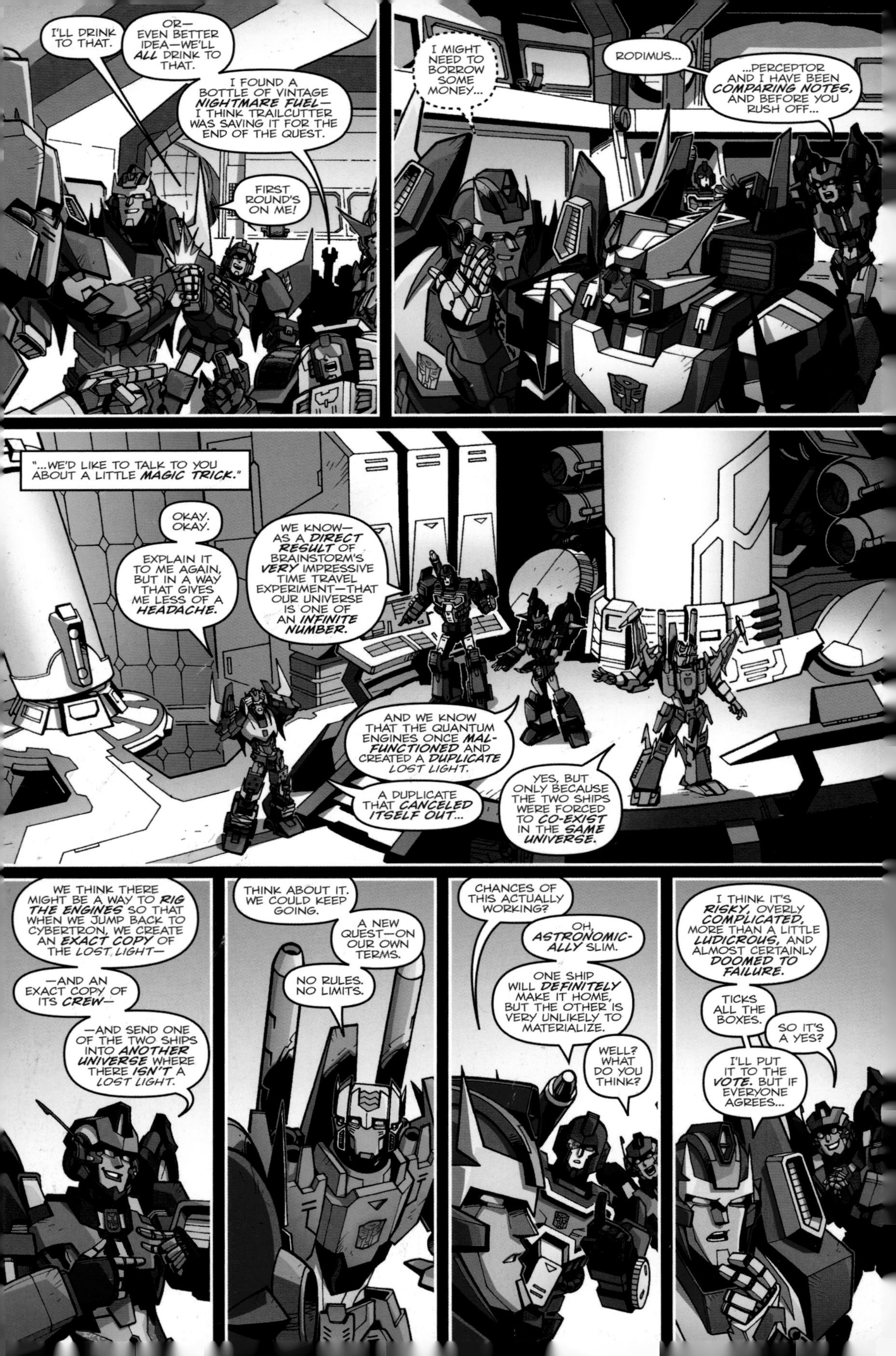
I'LL DRINK TO THAT.
OR— EVEN BETTER IDEA—WE'LL ALL DRINK TO THAT.
I FOUND A BOTTLE OF VINTAGE NIGHTMARE FUEL— I THINK TRAILCUTTER WAS SAVING IT FOR THE END OF THE QUEST.
FIRST ROUND'S ON ME!
I MIGHT NEED TO BORROW SOME MONEY...
RODIMUS...
...PERCEPTOR AND I HAVE BEEN COMPARING NOTES, AND BEFORE YOU RUSH OFF...
"...WE'D LIKE TO TALK TO YOU ABOUT A LITTLE MAGIC TRICK."
OKAY. OKAY.
EXPLAIN IT TO ME AGAIN, BUT IN A WAY THAT GIVES ME LESS OF A HEADACHE.
WE KNOW— AS A DIRECT RESULT OF BRAINSTORM'S VERY IMPRESSIVE TIME TRAVEL EXPERIMENT—THAT OUR UNIVERSE IS ONE OF AN INFINITE NUMBER.
AND WE KNOW THAT THE QUANTUM ENGINES ONCE MALFUNCTIONED AND CREATED A DUPLICATE LOST LIGHT.
A DUPLICATE THAT CANCELED ITSELF OUT...
YES, BUT ONLY BECAUSE THE TWO SHIPS WERE FORCED TO CO-EXIST IN THE SAME UNIVERSE.
WE THINK THERE MIGHT BE A WAY TO RIG THE ENGINES SO THAT WHEN WE JUMP BACK TO CYBERTRON, WE CREATE AN EXACT COPY OF THE LOST LIGHT—
—AND AN EXACT COPY OF ITS CREW—
—AND SEND ONE OF THE TWO SHIPS INTO ANOTHER UNIVERSE WHERE THERE ISN'T A LOST LIGHT.
THINK ABOUT IT. WE COULD KEEP GOING.
A NEW QUEST—ON OUR OWN TERMS.
NO RULES. NO LIMITS.
CHANCES OF THIS ACTUALLY WORKING?
OH, ASTRONOMICALLY SLIM.
ONE SHIP WILL DEFINITELY MAKE IT HOME, BUT THE OTHER IS VERY UNLIKELY TO MATERIALIZE.
WELL? WHAT DO YOU THINK?
I THINK IT'S RISKY, OVERLY COMPLICATED, MORE THAN A LITTLE LUDICROUS, AND ALMOST CERTAINLY DOOMED TO FAILURE.
TICKS ALL THE BOXES.
SO IT'S A YES?
I'LL PUT IT TO THE VOTE. BUT IF EVERYONE AGREES...

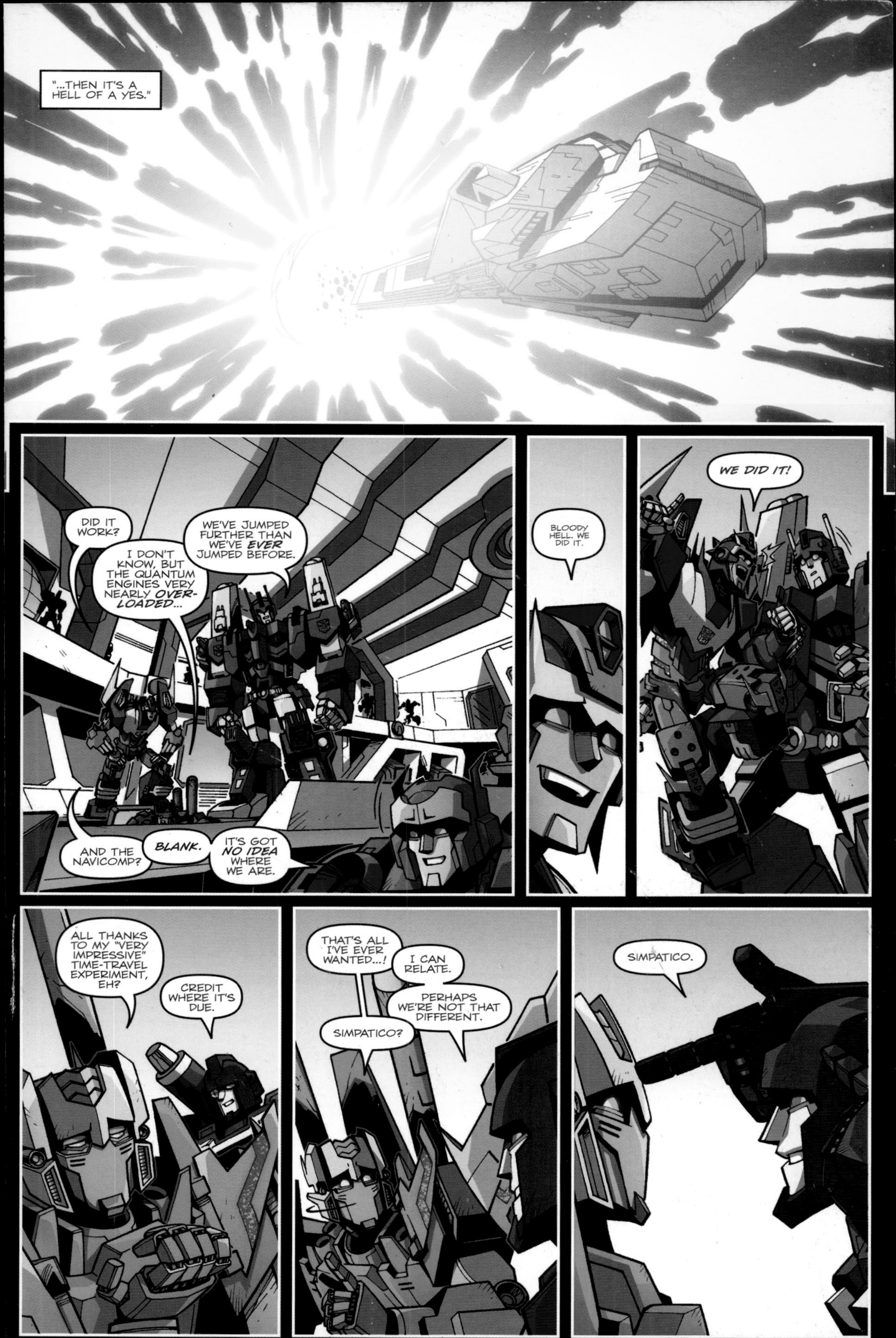
"...THEN IT'S A HELL OF A YES."
DID IT WORK?
I DON'T KNOW, BUT THE QUANTUM ENGINES VERY NEARLY OVER-LOADED...
WE'VE JUMPED FURTHER THAN WE'VE EVER JUMPED BEFORE.
AND THE NAVICOMP?
BLANK.
IT'S GOT NO IDEA WHERE WE ARE.
BLOODY HELL. WE DID IT.
WE DID IT!
ALL THANKS TO MY "VERY IMPRESSIVE" TIME-TRAVEL EXPERIMENT, EH?
CREDIT WHERE IT'S DUE.
THAT'S ALL I'VE EVER WANTED...!
I CAN RELATE.
PERHAPS WE'RE NOT THAT DIFFERENT.
SIMPATICO?
SIMPATICO.

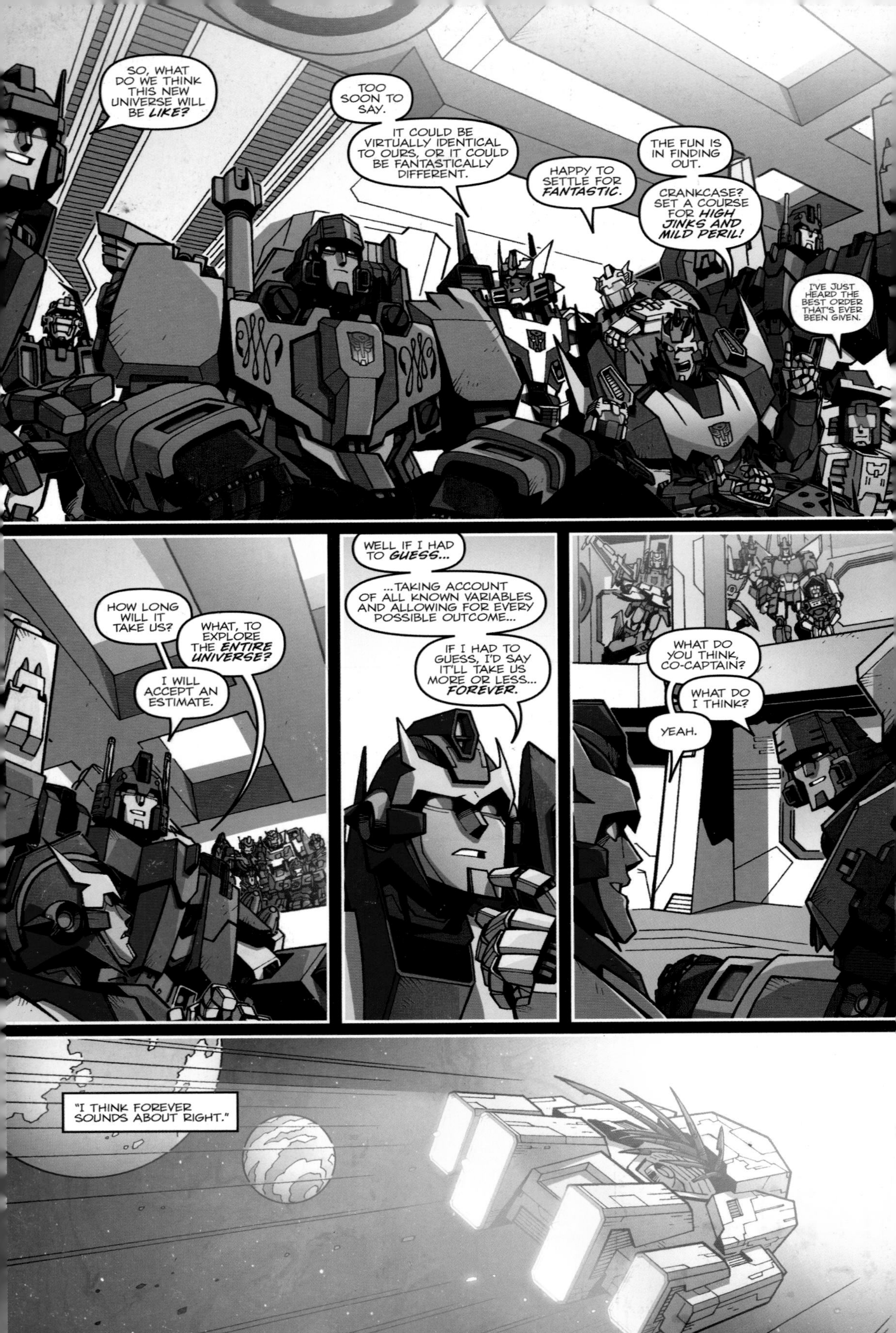
SO, WHAT DO WE THINK THIS NEW UNIVERSE WILL BE LIKE?
TOO SOON TO SAY.
IT COULD BE VIRTUALLY IDENTICAL TO OURS, OR IT COULD BE FANTASTICALLY DIFFERENT.
HAPPY TO SETTLE FOR FANTASTIC.
THE FUN IS IN FINDING OUT.
CRANKCASE? SET A COURSE FOR HIGH JINKS AND MILD PERIL!
I'VE JUST HEARD THE BEST ORDER THAT'S EVER BEEN GIVEN.
HOW LONG WILL IT TAKE US?
WHAT, TO EXPLORE THE ENTIRE UNIVERSE?
I WILL ACCEPT AN ESTIMATE.
WELL IF I HAD TO GUESS...
...TAKING ACCOUNT OF ALL KNOWN VARIABLES AND ALLOWING FOR EVERY POSSIBLE OUTCOME...
IF I HAD TO GUESS, I'D SAY IT'LL TAKE US MORE OR LESS... FOREVER.
WHAT DO YOU THINK, CO-CAPTAIN?
WHAT DO I THINK?
YEAH.
"I THINK FOREVER SOUNDS ABOUT RIGHT."
The End